America Now

Short Readings from Recent Periodicals

ELEVENTH EDITION

EDITED BY

Robert Atwan

Series Editor, *The Best American Essays*

EXERCISES PREPARED WITH THE ASSISTANCE OF

Valerie Duff-Strautmann

Gregory Atwan

Bedford/St. Martin's   Boston • New York

For Bedford/St. Martin's

Vice President, Editorial, Macmillan Higher Education Humanities: Edwin Hill
Editorial Director for English and Music: Karen S. Henry
Publisher for Composition, Business and Technical Writing and Developmental Writing: Leasa Burton
Executive Editor: John Sullivan III
Developmental Editor: Christina Gerogiannis
Production Editor: Annette Pagliaro Sweeney
Production Manager: Joe Ford
Senior Marketing Manager: Jane Helms
Project Management: Cassie Carey, Graphic World, Inc.
Director of Rights and Permissions: Hilary Newman
Text Permissions Researcher: Arthur Johnson
Photo Researcher: Sheri Blaney
Cover Design: William Boardman
Cover Art: Newsstand lit up at night. © Glow Images, Inc. / Getty Images
Composition: Graphic World, Inc.
Printing and Binding: RR Donnelley and Sons

2   3   4   5   6   19   18   17   16   15

For information, write: Bedford/St. Martin's, 75 Arlington Street, Boston, MA 02116   (617-399-4000)

ISBN 978-1-4576-8742-6 (College Edition)
ISBN 978-1-4576-8746-4 (High School Edition)

Acknowledgments

Ajmani, Tim, "Compensation for College Athletes?" The Corsair, Pensacola State College, April 25, 2012. Reprinted by permission of the author.

Aubry, Timothy, "Married Life," excerpted from "A Matter of Life and Death," *The Point*, Issue 7 (Fall 2013). Copyright © 2013. Reprinted by permission of the author.

Beato, Greg, "The Myth of Economic Immobility," *Reason* (May 2014). Copyright © 2014 by *Reason* magazine. All rights reserved. Reprinted by permission.

Berenson, Anna, "Politics for the Rest of Us," *Bates Student*, October 9, 2013. Copyright © 2013. Reprinted by permission of the author.

Bloomberg, Michael, "On the Repression of Free Expression," excerpted from commencement speech, Harvard University, Cambridge, MA, May 29, 2014. Copyright © 2014 Michael R. Bloomberg. All rights reserved. Reprinted with permission.

Brady, Judy, "I Want a Wife," *Ms.* magazine, 1972. Copyright © 1970 by Judy Syfers. Reprinted by permission of the author.

Text acknowledgments and copyrights are continued at the back of the book on pages 371–373, which constitute an extension of the copyright page. Art acknowledgments and copyrights appear on the same page as the art selections they cover. It is a violation of the law to reproduce these selections by any means whatsoever without the written permission of the copyright holder.

About the Editor

Robert Atwan is the series editor of the annual *Best American Essays*, which he founded in 1985. His essays, reviews, and critical articles have appeared in the *New York Times*, the *Los Angeles Times*, the *Atlantic, Iowa Review, Denver Quarterly, Kenyon Review, River Teeth,* and many other publications. For Bedford/St. Martin's, he has also edited *Ten on Ten: Major Essayists on Recurring Themes* (1992), *Our Times,* Fifth Edition (1998), and *Convergences,* Third Edition (2009). He has coedited (with Jon Roberts) *Left, Right, and Center: Voices from Across the Political Spectrum* (1996), and is coeditor with Donald McQuade of *The Writer's Presence,* Eighth Edition (2015). He lives in New York City.

Preface for Instructors

People write for many reasons, but one of the most compelling is to express their views on matters of current public interest. Browse any Web site, newsstand, or library magazine rack, and you'll find an abundance of articles and opinion pieces responding to current issues and events. Too frequently, students see the writing they do in a composition class as having little connection with real-world problems and issues. *America Now*, with its provocative professional and student writing—all very current opinion essays drawn from a range of periodicals—shows students that by writing on the important issues of today, they can influence campus and public discourse and truly make a difference.

The eleventh edition of *America Now* offers a generous sampling of timely and provocative material. *America Now* is designed to immerse introductory writing students in the give-and-take of public dialogue and to stimulate thinking, discussion, and composition. Its overriding instructional principle—which guides everything from the choice of readings and topics to the design of questions—is that participation in informed discussion will help generate and enrich student writing.

America Now encourages its users to view reading, thinking, discussion, and writing as closely interrelated activities. It assumes that (1) attentive reading and reflection will lead to informed discussion; (2) participation in open and informed discussion will result in a broadening of viewpoints; (3) an awareness of different viewpoints will stimulate further reflection and renewed discussion; and (4) this process in turn will lead to thoughtful papers.

The book's general introduction, "The Persuasive Writer: Expressing Opinions with Clarity, Confidence, and Civility," takes the student through these interrelated processes and offers some useful guidelines for engaging in productive discussion that will lead to effective essays. Two annotated student essays serve as models of persuasive writing. Instructors may also find helpful my essay "Writing and the Art of Discussion," which can be found in the instructor's manual.

New to This Edition

Following is a brief overview of the eleventh edition of *America Now*. For a more in-depth description of the book, see "Using *America Now*" beginning on page ix of this preface.

Thirty-five readings—all new and *very* current. Drawn from more than 30 recent periodicals, each current professional reading not only is new to this edition but also has appeared within a year or two of the book's publication. With over half of its selections published in 2014, *America Now* is the most current short essay reader available. Some of the readings you will find in the eleventh edition are by former New York City mayor Michael Bloomberg on the necessity of free expression, critic Heather Havrilesky on a common way in which successful women are portrayed on television, and essayist Christine Granados on her family's attempts to fit in as immigrants.

Twelve classic selections by canonical authors. To help place current issues in a historical context, the book's popular "America Then" component now features both visuals and—new to this edition— memorable short selections by prominent authors, including Langston Hughes, Judy Brady, Henry David Thoreau, and Rachel Carson. Here, these twelve readings—making their first appearance in *America Now* but all longtime classroom favorites—serve as interesting pairings with the book's readings from today.

Relevant, compelling student essays. Of the sixteen student essays in the book, fourteen are new to this edition, and all are recent works by real student writers from across the nation. Highlights in the eleventh edition include Louisiana State University student Jana King's well-considered piece on race in America today, Binghamton University student Macon Fessenden's examination of the facts behind hydrofracking, and University of California, Santa Barbara student Emily Potter's look at the significance of the #YesAllWomen hashtag.

Thirteen unique visual texts cover issues of importance on campuses everywhere—including privacy, financial stability, immigration, and college sports.

New issues of current interest. Eleven of the twelve thematic chapters have been updated to reflect the changing interests of students over the past two years. Sure to spark lively discussion and writing, these topics include freedom of speech, our current political climate, college sports, gender, and the American dream. In a new chapter on love, we ask the question: What makes an American family?

A thoroughly revised introduction. New material on various types of the visual expression of opinion—including timely new editorial cartoons—as well as a fresh example of student writing and a brief overview of America's sometimes-perplexing political spectrum now offers students more help than ever with writing at the college level.

Using *America Now*

Professional and Student Writing from a Wide Variety of Sources

The book's selections by professional writers are drawn from recent periodicals, ranging from specialized journals, such as the *American Scholar*, to influential general magazines, such as *Elle* and the *New Yorker*. As would be expected in a collection that focuses heavily on social trends and current events, *America Now* features several newspapers and news-oriented magazines, including *USA Today*, the *New York Times*, and the *Wall Street Journal*. With its additional emphasis on public discourse, this collection also draws on some of America's leading political magazines, including *The Nation*, *The Weekly Standard*, and *The Progressive*. Also represented are magazines that appeal primarily to specialized audiences, such as *Texas Monthly*, *Wired*, and *Orion*. In general, the selections illustrate the variety of personal, informative, and persuasive writing encountered daily by millions of Americans. The readings are kept short (many under three pages, and some no longer than a page) to hold student interest and to serve as models for the student's own writing. To introduce a more in-depth approach to various topics, the book includes a few longer essays.

America Now also features sixteen published student selections from print and online college newspapers. These recent works reveal student writers confronting in a public forum the same topics and issues that challenge some of our leading social critics and commentators, and they show how student writers can enter into and influence public discussion. In this way, the student selections in *America Now*—complemented by Student Writer at Work interviews—encourage students to see writing as a form of personal and public empowerment. This edition includes nine brief, inspiring interviews in which student authors in the book explain how—and why—they express their opinions in writing. In addition, the book contains two examples of student writing for a classroom assignment.

To highlight models of persuasive writing, each chapter contains an annotated section of a student paper labeled "Looking Closely." The comments point out some of the most effective strategies of the student writers in the book and offer advice for stating a main point, shaping arguments, presenting examples and evidence, using quotations, recommending a course of action, and more.

Timely Topics for Discussion and Debate

Student essays not only make up a large percentage of the readings in this book, but also shape the volume's contents. As we monitored the broad spectrum of online college newspapers—and reviewed several hundred student essays—we gradually found the most commonly discussed campus issues and topics. Issues such as those mentioned on page ix of this preface have provoked so much recent student response that they could have resulted in several single-topic collections. Many college papers do not restrict themselves to news items and editorial opinion but make room for personal essays as well. Some popular student topics are sports, technology, ethnic and racial identity, and the economy, all of which are reflected in the book's table of contents.

To facilitate group discussion and in-class work, *America Now* features twelve bite-sized units. These focused chapters permit instructors to cover a broad range of themes and issues in a single semester. Each can be conveniently handled in one or two class periods. In general, the chapters move from accessible, personal topics (for example, language and social media) to more public and controversial issues (the Second Amendment, politics, and the economy), thus accommodating instructors who prefer to start with personal writing and gradually progress to exposition, analysis, and argument.

Since composition courses naturally emphasize issues revolving around language and the construction of meaning, *America Now* also includes a number of selections designed to encourage students to examine the powerful influence of words and symbols.

The Visual Expression of Opinion

Reflecting the growing presence of advertising in public discussion, among the book's images are opinion advertisements (or "op-ads"). These pieces, which focus on financial responsibility, encourage students to uncover the visual and verbal strategies of an advocacy group trying to influence the consciousness and ideology of a large audience.

Because we live in an increasingly visual culture, the book's introduction offers a section on expressing opinions visually—with striking examples from photojournalism, cartoons, and opinion advertisements.

The Instructional Apparatus: Before, During, and After Reading

To help promote reflection and discussion, the book includes a prereading assignment for each main selection. The questions in "Before You Read" provide students with the opportunity to explore a few of the avenues that lead to fruitful discussion and interesting papers. A full description of the advantages gained by linking reading, writing, and classroom discussion can be found in my introduction to the instructor's manual.

The apparatus of *America Now* supports both discussion-based instruction and more individualized approaches to reading and writing. Taking into account the increasing diversity of students (especially the growing number of speakers for whom English is not their first language) in today's writing programs, the apparatus offers extensive help with college-level vocabulary and features a "Words to Learn" list preceding each selection. This vocabulary list with brief definitions will allow students to spot ahead of time some of the words they may find difficult; encountering the word later in context will help lock it in memory. It's unrealistic, however, to think students will acquire a fluent knowledge of new words by memorizing a list. Therefore, the apparatus following each selection includes additional exercises under the headings "Vocabulary/Using a Dictionary" and "Responding to Words in Context." These sets of questions introduce students to prefixes, suffixes, connotations, denotations, tone, and etymology.

Along with the discussion of vocabulary, other incrementally structured questions follow individual selections. "Discussing Main Point and Meaning" and "Examining Sentences, Paragraphs, and Organization" questions help guide students step-by-step through the reading process, culminating in the set of "Thinking Critically" questions. As instructors well know, beginning students can sometimes be too trusting of what they see in print, especially in textbooks. Therefore, the "Thinking Critically" questions invite students to take a more skeptical attitude toward their reading and to form the habit of challenging a selection from both analytical and experiential points of view. The selection apparatus concludes with "Writing Activities," which emphasize freewriting exercises and collaborative projects.

In addition to the selection apparatus, *America Now* contains end-of-chapter questions designed to stimulate further discussion and writing. The chapter apparatus approaches the reading material from topical and thematic angles, with an emphasis on group discussion. The introductory comments to each chapter highlight the main discussion points and the way selections are linked together. These points and linkages are then reintroduced at the end of the chapter through three sets of interlocking study questions and tasks: (1) a suggested topic for discussion, (2) questions and ideas to help students prepare for class discussion, and (3) several writing assignments that ask students to move from discussion to composition—that is, to develop papers out of the ideas and opinions expressed in class discussion and debate. Instructors with highly diverse writing classes may find "Topics for Cross-Cultural Discussion" a convenient way to encourage an exchange of perspectives and experiences that could also generate ideas for writing.

Acknowledgments

While putting together the eleventh edition of *America Now*, I was fortunate to receive the assistance of many talented individuals. I am enormously grateful to Valerie Duff-Strautmann and Gregory Atwan, who contributed to the book's instructional apparatus and instructor's manual. Liz deBeer of Rutgers University contributed a helpful essay in the instructor's manual on designing student panels ("Forming Forums"), along with advice on using the book's apparatus in both developmental and mainstream composition classes.

To revise a text is to entertain numerous questions: What kind of selections work best in class? What types of questions are most helpful? How can reading, writing, and discussion be most effectively intertwined? This edition profited immensely from the following instructors who generously took the time to respond to the tenth edition: Curtis Allen, Ashland University; Ingrid Bowman, University of California, Santa Barbara; Andrew DiNicola, South Georgia State College; Christy Farnsworth, West Liberty University; April L. Ford, State University of New York at Oneonta; Grant Goldstein, Colonel Zadok Magruder High School; Liz Laurer, Owens Community College; Wanda Moody, Cisco College; Cecilia Ornelas, California State University, Fullerton; Brian Patterson, Yakima Valley Community College; Charles Shackett, Diablo Valley College; and Stephen Swanson, McLennan Community College.

I'd also like to acknowledge instructors who have reviewed previous editions, and whose ideas and suggestions continue to inform the book: Kim M. Baker, Roger Williams University; Kevin Ball, Youngstown State

University; Deborah Biorn, St. Cloud State University; Joan Blankmann, Northern Virginia Community College; Diane Bosco, Suffolk County Community College; Melanie N. Burdick, University of Missouri–Kansas City; Mikel Cole, University of Houston–Downtown; Danielle Davis, Pasadena City College; Darren DeFrain, Wichita State University; Kaye Falconer, Bakersfield College; Steven Florzcyk, the State University of New York–New Paltz; Nancy Freiman, Milwaukee Area Technical College; Andrea Germanos, Saint Augustine College; Jay L. Gordon, Youngstown State University; Kim Halpern, Pulaski Technical College; Jessica Harvey, Alexandria Technical College; Chris Hayes, University of Georgia; Sharon Jaffee, Santa Monica College; Patricia W. Julius, Michigan State University; Jessica Heather Lourey, Alexandria Technical College; Brian Ludlow, Alfred University; Sherry Manis, Foothill College; Terry Meier, Bakersfield College; Melody Nightingale, Santa Monica College; Kimme Nuckles, Baker College; Michael Orlando, Bergen Community College; Thomas W. Pittman, Youngstown State University; Marty Price, Mississippi State University; David Pryor, University of the Incarnate Word; Hubert C. Pulley, Georgia Southern University; Sherry Robertson, Pulaski Technical College; Lynn Sabas, Saint Augustine College; Vicki Lynn Samson, Western Kentucky University and Bowling Green Community College; Jennifer Satterlee, Parkland College; Wendy Scott, Buffalo State College; Andrea D. Shanklin, Howard Community College; Ann Spurlock, Mississippi State University; Linda Weiner, the University of Akron; Frances Whitney, Bakersfield College; Richard A. Williams, Youngstown State University; and Martha Anne Yeager-Tobar, Cerritos College.

Other people helped in various ways. I'm indebted to Barbara Gross of Rutgers University, Newark, for her excellent work in helping to design the instructor's manual for the first edition. Two good friends, Charles O'Neill and the late Jack Roberts, both of St. Thomas Aquinas College, went over my early plans for the book and offered many useful suggestions.

As always, it was a pleasure to work with the superb staff at Bedford/St. Martin's. Jane Helms and Ellen Thibault, my editors on earlier editions, shaped the book in lasting ways. I also am indebted to my developmental editor, Christina Gerogiannis. As usual, Christina provided excellent guidance and numerous suggestions, while doing her utmost best to keep a book that depends on so many moving parts and timely material on its remarkably tight schedule. Christina is also responsible for the student interviews that are such an important feature of this edition. Brenna Cleeland and Cara Kaufman, editorial assistants, skillfully took care of many crucial details. Kalina Ingham and Martha Friedman managed text and art permissions under a tight schedule. Annette Pagliaro Sweeney guided the book through production with patience and care, staying on top of many details, and Sue Brown and Elise Kaiser managed the production process with great attentiveness. I was fortunate to receive the careful copyediting of the staff at Graphic World.

I am grateful to Charles H. Christensen, the retired president of Bedford/St. Martin's, for his generous help and thoughtful suggestions throughout the life of this book. Finally, I especially want to thank cofounder of Bedford/St. Martin's Joan E. Feinberg, who conceived the idea for *America Now*, for her deep and abiding interest in college composition. It has been a great pleasure and privilege to work with her.

Robert Atwan

Get the Most out of Your Course with *America Now*

Bedford/St. Martin's offers resources and format choices that help you and your students get even more out of your book and course. To learn more about or to order any of the following products, contact your Bedford/St. Martin's sales representative, e-mail sales support (**sales_support@ bfwpub.com**), or visit the Web site at **macmillanhighered.com /americanow/catalog.**

Choose from Alternative Formats of America Now

Bedford/St. Martin's offers a range of affordable formats, allowing students to choose the one that works best for them. For details, visit **macmillanhighered.com/americanow/catalog.**

- *Bedford e-Book to Go*
  A portable, downloadable e-book is available at about half the price of the print book. To order the *Bedford e-Book to Go*, use **ISBN 978-1-3190-2179-5**.
- *Other popular e-book formats*
  For details, visit **macmillanhighered.com/ebooks.**

Package with Another Bedford/St. Martin's Title and Save

Get the most value for your students by packaging *America Now* with a Bedford/St. Martin's handbook or any other Bedford/St. Martin's title for a significant discount. To order, please request a package ISBN from your sales representative or e-mail sales support (**sales_support@ bfwpub.com**).

Select Value Packages

Add value to your text by packaging one of the following resources with *America Now*. To learn more about package options for any of the following products, contact your Bedford/St. Martin's sales representative or visit **macmillanhighered.com/americanow/catalog**.

LaunchPad Solo for Readers and Writers provides engaging content and new ways to get the most out of your course. Our newest set of online materials provides all the skill-specific content that you need to teach your class. *LaunchPad Solo for Readers and Writers* includes multimedia content and assessments, including LearningCurve adaptive quizzing, organized into prebuilt, curated units for easy assigning and monitoring of student progress. Get all our great resources and activities in one fully customizable space online; then assign and mix our resources with yours. Student access is free when packaged with *America Now*. Order **ISBN 978-1-4576-8742-6** to ensure your students can take full advantage. Students who rent a book or buy a used book can purchase access to online materials at **macmillanhighered.com/americanow/catalog**.

i-series is a popular series that presents multimedia tutorials in a flexible format—because there are things you can't do in a book.

- *ix visualizing composition 2.0* helps students put into practice key rhetorical and visual concepts. To order *ix visualizing composition* packaged with the print book, contact your sales representative for a package ISBN.
- *i-claim: visualizing argument* offers a new way to see argument— with six multimedia tutorials, an illustrated glossary, and a wide array of multimedia arguments. To order *i-claim: visualizing argument* packaged with the print book, contact your sales representative for a package ISBN.

Portfolio Keeping: A Guide for Students, **Third Edition, by Nedra Reynolds and Elizabeth Davis** provides all the information students need to use the portfolio method successfully in a writing course. *Portfolio Teaching*, a companion guide for instructors, provides the practical information instructors and writing program administrators need to use the portfolio method successfully in a writing course. To order *Portfolio Keeping* packaged with the print book, contact your sales representative for a package ISBN.

Make Learning Fun with Re:Writing 3

macmillanhighered.com/rewriting

New open online resources with videos and interactive elements engage students in new ways of writing. You'll find tutorials about using common digital writing tools, an interactive peer review game, Extreme Paragraph Makeover, and more—all for free and for fun. Visit **macmillanhighered .com/rewriting**.

Instructor Resources

macmillanhighered.com/americanow/catalog

You have a lot to do in your course. Bedford/St. Martin's wants to make it easy for you to find the support you need—and to get it quickly.

From Discussion to Writing: Instructional Resources for Teaching America Now is available in print and as a PDF that can be downloaded from the Bedford/St. Martin's online catalog at the URL above. In addition to chapter overviews and answers to the questions in the book, the instructor's manual includes an introduction by author Robert Atwan titled "Writing and the Art of Discussion," a useful section on forming classroom forums, sample syllabi, and correlations to the Council of Writing Program Administrators' Outcomes Statement.

Teaching Central offers the entire list of Bedford/St. Martin's print and online professional resources in one place. You'll find landmark reference works, sourcebooks on pedagogical issues, award-winning collections, and practical advice for the classroom—all free for instructors. Visit **macmillanhighered.com/teachingcentral**.

Bits collects creative ideas for teaching a range of composition topics in an easily searchable blog format. A community of teachers—leading scholars, authors, and editors—discuss revision, research, grammar and style, technology, peer review, and much more. Take, use, adapt, and pass the ideas around. Then, come back to the site to comment or share your own suggestion. Visit **bedfordbits.com**.

Brief Contents

Contents

1

Social Media: What Do We Gain? What Do We Lose?   43

Are social networks like Facebook adding to our lives and conversations, or just muddying them with information overload? An essayist links unnecessary status updates to our deepest psyches . . . A California State University student says technology can be positive if we don't "rely on it to do things we've known how to do for years" . . . Research indicates that parents, not teens, may be to blame for social networking addictions . . . A great American writer and thinker wonders whether the technology of communication is outpacing what we have to say to one another.

Language: Do Words Matter?   61

Do the words we use matter? Does it make a difference whether we say *girl* or *woman*, *handicapped* or *disabled*? Can words do individual and social harm? A noted linguist and best-selling author thinks it's a serious mistake to call women bossy . . . *Smithsonian* magazine reports research on what may be the world's most common word . . . A series of "sound bites" offers a range of opinion on the controversial name of the Washington football team . . . A University of Maryland student says the "Redskins" name isn't "cool, interesting, relevant, or competitive" . . . "How we name things matters," argues a prominent essayist who goes on to show how our consumer culture corrupts our language, society, and politics . . . "What is wrong with *black*?" asks one of the nation's greatest African American writers.

3

Free Speech: Is It Endangered on Campus?   89

Should a university be a hotbed for robust, unflinching dialogue on social issues? What about when some of the material injures students, especially those with traumas in their pasts? A journalist outlines a new academic movement for "trigger warnings" and cautions that some course material may be upsetting . . . A student defends these warnings as important safeguards for students with post-traumatic stress disorder (PTSD) and other conditions . . . A fellow student argues that they threaten freedom of speech . . . Students must keep debate going on campus, warns a leading political figure . . . A prominent advocate of free speech reminds us that the debate over the debate has been going on in American schools for years.

4

Diversity: How Is the Face of America Changing? 115

What does diversity mean for Americans today? Is the country becoming more diverse or more homogenous? In what direction should we steer it? A journalist surveys the changing complexion of America . . . In Texas, an essayist recalls her mother's attempts (and sometimes failures) to fit in as an immigrant . . . Can positive stereotypes also do harm, asks an Asian American student who denounces the assumption that she's smart . . . A writer and world traveler shares what he's learned from other languages . . . A 100-year-old editorial argues for a more culturally unified union.

5

Race: Does It Still Matter? 141

What are the issues facing minorities today? Is America a racially just country, or have we still not mended the wounds of past oppression? A philosopher digs into hidden forms of racism . . . A student agrees that we must act to balance the scales of privilege . . . Is our attention to race misplaced, asks a controversial columnist and neurosurgeon . . . A noted author explores his own heritage and warns against oversimplified ethnic categories . . . One of America's greatest writers and orators outlines the agenda for decades of discussion.

6

Guns: Can the Second Amendment Survive?   171

Should Americans still have the right to own guns? Or does our public safety demand that we curb it? A lyrical essayist reminds us of what's at stake behind the gun battle . . . A columnist argues for private responsibility instead of public regulation . . . One student argues that guns can make us safer . . . Another insists they do the opposite . . . A cartoonist mocks the way both sides discuss gun violence . . . An Oklahoma poet explores her own fear of guns . . . A literary critic dissects the wording of the constitutional right to "keep and bear Arms."

7

College Sports: Should Student Athletes Be Paid?   199

Some colleges and the National Collegiate Athletic Association (NCAA) make big money from college sports. So should athletes on their teams get a cut? A political sportswriter says free play in college sports is nothing more than exploitation . . . A cartoonist raises the extreme implications of cutting a check to student athletes . . . A student opines that compensation would improve players' academic performance . . . Following a classic joke, a legendary journalist exposes the sorry state of education for athletes.

8

Marriage: What Does It Mean Today?   221

Can "traditional" marriage be saved? Should it? A columnist makes a plea for what couples have always gotten right . . . A cultural critic thinks same-sex marriage threatens American traditions — and that's a good thing . . . A student celebrates the diversity of her relationship and explores what it means for the changing face of partnership . . . In "what other situation do you promise to do something for the rest of your life?" an essayist asks about marriage . . . A classic radical author brands American marriage "a failure."

9

The Environment: Is the Crisis Overblown?   245

Is our natural environment in crisis? Are we making the world too hot for us to handle? One conservative argues that the facts aren't clear enough to say either way . . . An activist responds to a popular accusation from the right . . . One of the leading climate-change scientists lays out the problem and a possible solution . . . Research explores some of the reasons people deny there's a problem . . . A student responds to half-informed environmental outrage on campus . . . The mother of the modern conservation movement imagines what might be at stake.

10

American Politics: Must We Be Partisan?   273

Why is America so bitterly divided between left and right, blue and red, and Democrat and Republican? Is there anything we can — or should — do? A pair of political scientists dissect the geographic origin of our political sentiments . . . Evolutionary biology has something to say about how we form opinions, maintains the author of a book on the roots of political orientation . . . One student essayist reminds us to speak up even when we don't fit into neat categories . . . A writer wonders why politicians aren't required to pass examinations as are so many other professionals . . . The man said to have "invented" America had some second thoughts about its founding document.

A Rhetorical Table of Contents

America Now includes numerous examples of rhetorical strategies that aid us in expressing ourselves clearly, cogently, and convincingly. Listed below are eight of the most common rhetorical categories with a brief account of how they are generally used in both verbal and visual texts. Nearly every selection in the book relies on more than one category, so you will find that several selections appear multiple times. The selections listed are those that most effectively demonstrate—either in whole or in their various segments—a particular strategy.

R.A.

1 *NARRATION* Some uses: telling a story; reporting or summarizing a sequence of events; constructing a historical chronology; recounting a biography or autobiography; detailing how something is done or comes about; breaking down a process into a sequence of events.

5 *CLASSIFICATION* Some uses: dividing a subject into several key parts; organizing material into categories; making distinctions; constructing outlines; arranging ideas in the most appropriate order; viewing an issue from its various sides.

6 *COMPARISON AND CONTRAST* Some uses: finding similarities among different things or ideas; finding differences among similar things or ideas; organizing material through point-by-point resemblance or disparity; forming analogies; expressing a preference for one thing or position over another.

7 *CAUSE AND EFFECT* Some uses: identifying the cause of an event or trend; examining how one thing has influenced another; looking at the consequences of an action or idea; assigning credit, blame, or responsibility.

8 *ARGUMENT AND PERSUASION* Some uses: convincing someone that an opinion is correct; defending or refuting a position; gaining support for a course of action; making proposals; resolving conflicts to reach consent or consensus. (At the end of the following list, you will find a collection of the Debates in *America Now*.)

DEBATES

America Now

Short Readings from Recent Periodicals

The Persuasive Writer
Expressing Opinions with Clarity, Confidence, and Civility

It is not possible to extricate yourself from the questions in which your age is involved.

— Ralph Waldo Emerson, "The Fortune of the Republic" (1878)

What Is *America Now*?

America Now collects very recent essays and articles that have been carefully selected to encourage reading, provoke discussion, and stimulate writing. The philosophy behind the book is that interesting, effective writing originates in public dialogue. The book's primary purpose is to help students proceed from class discussions of reading assignments to the production of complete essays that reflect an engaged participation in those discussions.

The selections in *America Now* come from two main sources — from popular, mainstream periodicals and from college newspapers available on the Internet. Written by journalists and columnists, public figures and activists, as well as by professors and students from all over the country, the selections illustrate the types of material read by millions of Americans every day. In addition to magazine and newspaper writing, the book features a number of recent opinion advertisements (what I call "op-ads" for short). These familiar forms of "social marketing" are often sponsored by corporations or nonprofit organizations and advocacy groups to promote policies, programs, and ideas such as gun control, family planning, literacy, civil rights, or conservation. Such advertising texts allow the reader to pinpoint and discuss specific techniques of verbal and visual persuasion that are critical in the formation of public opinion.

I have gathered the selections into twelve units that cover today's most widely discussed issues and topics: social media, racial identity, college sports, environmentalism, and so on. As you respond to the readings in your discussion and writing, you will be actively taking part in some of the major controversies of our time. Although I have tried in this new edition of *America Now* to represent as many viewpoints as possible on a variety of controversial topics, it's not possible in a collection of this scope to include under each topic either a full spectrum of opinion or a universally satisfying balance of opposing opinions. For some featured topics, an entire book would be required to represent the full range of opinion; for others, a rigid pro-con, either-or format could distort the issue and perhaps overly polarize students' responses to it. Selections within a unit usually illustrate the most commonly held opinions on a topic so that readers will get a reasonably good sense of how the issue has been framed and the public discourse and debate it has generated. But if a single opinion isn't immediately or explicitly balanced by an opposite opinion, or if a view seems unusually idiosyncratic, that in no way implies that it is somehow editorially favored or endorsed. Be assured that questions following *every* selection will encourage you to analyze and critically challenge whatever opinion or perspective is expressed in that selection.

Participation is the key to this collection. I encourage you to view reading and writing as a form of participation. I hope you will read the selections attentively, think about them carefully, be willing to discuss them in class, and use what you've learned from your reading and discussion as the basis for your papers. If you do these things, you will develop three skills necessary for successful work in college and beyond: the ability to read critically, to discuss topics intelligently, and to write persuasively. These skills are also sorely needed in our daily lives as citizens. A vital democracy depends on them. The reason democracy is hard, said the Czech author and statesman Václav Havel, is that it requires the participation of everyone.

America Now invites you to see reading, discussion, and writing as closely related activities. As you read a selection, imagine that you have entered into a discussion with the author. Take notes as you read. Question the selection. Challenge its point of view or its evidence. Compare your experience with the author's. Consider how different economic classes or other groups are likely to respond. Remember, just because something appears in a newspaper or book doesn't make it true or accurate.

Form the habit of challenging what you read. Don't be persuaded by an opinion simply because it appears in print or because you believe you should accept it. Trust your own observations and experiences. Though logicians never say so, personal experiences and keen observations often form the basis of our most convincing arguments.

Participating in Class Discussion: Six Basic Rules

Discussion is a learned activity. It requires a variety of essential skills: speaking, listening, thinking, and preparing. The following six basic rules are vital to healthy and productive discussion.

1. **Take an active speaking role.** Good discussion demands that everyone participates, not (as so often happens) just a vocal few. Many students remain detached from discussion because they are afraid to speak in a group. This fear is quite common — psychological surveys show that speaking in front of a group is one of our worst fears. It helps to remember that most people will be more interested in *what* you say than in how you say it. Once you get over the initial fear of speaking in public, your confidence will improve with practice.

2. **Listen attentively.** No one who doesn't listen attentively can participate in group discussion. Just think of how many senseless arguments you've had because either you or the person with whom you were talking completely misunderstood what was said. A good listener not only hears what someone is saying but also understands *why* he or she is saying it. Listening carefully also leads to good questions, and when interesting questions begin to emerge, you know good discussion has truly begun.

3. **Examine all sides of an issue.** Good discussion requires that we be patient with complexity. Difficult problems rarely have obvious and simple solutions, nor can they be easily summarized in popular slogans. Complex issues demand to be turned over in our minds so that we can see them from a variety of angles. Group discussion broadens our perspective and deepens our insight into difficult issues and ideas.

4. **Suspend judgment.** To fully explore ideas and issues, you need to be open-minded and tolerant of other opinions, even when they contradict your own. Remember, a discussion is not a debate. Its primary purpose is communication, not competition. The goal of group discussion should be to open up a topic so that everyone is exposed to a spectrum of attitudes. Suspending judgment does not mean you shouldn't hold a strong belief or opinion about an issue; it means that you should be receptive to rival beliefs or opinions. An opinion formed without an awareness of other points of view — one that has

continued

not been tested against contrary ideas — is not a strong opinion but merely a stubborn one.

5. **Avoid abusive or insulting language.** Free and open discussion occurs only when we respect the beliefs and opinions of others. If we speak in ways that fail to show respect for differing viewpoints — if we resort to name-calling or use demeaning and malicious expressions, for example — not only do we embarrass ourselves, but we also close off the possibility for an intelligent and productive exchange of ideas. Some popular radio and television talk shows are poor models of discussion: Shouting insults and engaging in hate speech are usually the last resort of those who have little to say.

6. **Be prepared.** Discussion is not merely random conversation. It demands a certain degree of preparation and focus. To participate in class discussion, you must consider assigned topics beforehand and read whatever is required. Develop the habit of reading with pen in hand, underlining key points, and jotting down questions, impressions, and ideas in your notebook. The notes you bring to class will be an invaluable aid.

When your class discusses a selection, be especially attentive to what others think of it. It's always surprising how two people can read the same article and reach two entirely different interpretations. Observe the range of opinion. Try to understand why and how people arrive at different conclusions. Do some seem to miss the point? Do some distort the author's ideas? Have someone's comments forced you to rethink the selection? Keep a record of the discussion in your notebook. Then, when you begin to draft your paper, consider your essay as an extension of both your imaginary conversation with the author and the actual class discussion. If you've taken detailed notes of your own and the class's opinions about the selection, you should have more than enough information to get started.

What Are Opinions?

One of the primary aims of *America Now* is to help you learn through models and instructional material how to express your opinions in a persuasive, reasonable, civil, and productive fashion. But before we look at effective ways of expressing opinion, let's first consider opinions in general: What are they? Where do they come from?

When we say we have an opinion about something, we usually mean that we have come to a conclusion that something appears true or seems to be valid. But when we express an opinion about something, we are not claiming we are 100 percent certain that something is so. Opinion does not imply certainty and, in fact, is accompanied by some degree of doubt and skepticism. As a result, opinions are most likely to be found in those areas of thought and discussion where our judgments are uncertain. Because human beings know so few things for certain, much of what we believe, or discuss and debate, falls into various realms of probability or possibility. These we call opinions.

Journalists often make a distinction between fact and opinion. Facts can be confirmed and verified and therefore do not involve opinions. We ordinarily don't have opinions about facts, but we can and often do have opinions about the interpretation of facts. For example, it makes no sense to argue whether Washington, D.C., is the capital of the United States since it's an undisputed fact that it is. It's a matter of record and can be established with certainty. Thus, we don't say we have an opinion that Washington, D.C., is the nation's capital; we know for a fact that it is. But it would be legitimate to form an opinion about whether that city is the best location for the U.S. capital and whether it should permanently remain the capital. In other words:

- *Washington, D.C., is the capital of the United States of America* is a statement of fact.
- *Washington, D.C., is too poorly located to be the capital of a vast nation* is a statement of opinion.

Further, simply not knowing whether something is a fact does not necessarily make it a matter of opinion. For example, if we don't know the capital of Brazil, that doesn't mean we are then free to form an opinion about what Brazilian city it might be. The capital of Brazil is a verifiable fact and can be identified with absolute certainty. There is no conflicting public opinion about which city is Brazil's capital. The answer is not up for grabs. These examples, however, present relatively simple, readily agreed-upon facts. In real-life disputes, a fact is not always so readily distinguished from an opinion; people argue all the time about whether something is a fact. It's therefore a good idea at the outset of any discussion or argument to try to arrive at a mutual agreement of the facts that are known or knowable and those that could be called into question. Debates over abortion, for example, often hinge on biological facts about embryonic development that are themselves disputed by medical experts.

An opinion almost always exists in the climate of other, conflicting opinions. In discourse, we refer to this overall context of competing opinions as public controversy. Every age has its controversies. At any given time, the public is divided on a great number of topics about which it holds a variety of different opinions. Often the controversy is reduced to two opposing positions; for example, we are asked whether we are pro-life or pro-choice; for or against government health care; in favor of or opposed to same-sex marriage; and so on. This book includes many such controversies and covers multiple opinions. One sure way of knowing that something is a matter of opinion is that the public is divided on the topic. We often experience these divisions firsthand as we mature and increasingly come into contact with those who disagree with our opinions.

Some opinions are deeply held — so deeply, in fact, that those who hold them refuse to see them as opinions. For some people on certain issues there can be no difference of opinion; they possess the Truth, and all who differ hold erroneous opinions. This frequently happens in some controversies, where one side in a dispute is so confident of the truth of its position that it cannot see its own point of view as one of several possible points of view. For example, someone may feel so certain that marriage can exist only between a man and a woman that he or she cannot acknowledge the possibility of another position. If one side cannot recognize the existence of a different opinion, cannot entertain or tolerate it, argues not with the correctness of another's perspective but denies the possibility that there can legitimately be another perspective, then discussion and debate become all but impossible.

To be open and productive, public discussion depends on the capacity of all involved to view their own positions, no matter how cherished, as opinions that can be subject to opposition. There is nothing wrong with possessing a strong conviction, nor with believing our position is the better one, nor with attempting to convince others of our point of view. What is argumentatively wrong and what prevents or restricts free and open discussion is twofold: (1) the failure to recognize our own belief or position as an opinion that could be mistaken; and (2) the refusal to acknowledge the possibility that another's opinion could be correct.

Is one person's opinion as good as another's? Of course not. Although we may believe that everyone has a right to an opinion, we certainly wouldn't ask our mail carrier to diagnose the cause of persistent heartburn or determine whether a swollen gland could be a serious medical problem. In such instances, we respect the opinion of a trained physician. And even when we consult a physician, in serious matters we often seek second and even third opinions just to be sure. An auto mechanic is in a better position to evaluate a used car than someone who's never repaired a car; a lawyer's opinion on whether a contract is valid is more reliable than that belonging to someone who doesn't understand the legal nature of contracts. If an airline manufacturer wants to test a new cockpit instrument design, it solicits opinions from experienced pilots, not passengers. This seems obvious, and yet people continually are persuaded by those who can claim little expert knowledge on a subject or issue: For example, how valuable or trustworthy is the opinion of a celebrity who is paid to endorse a product?

When expressing or evaluating an opinion, we need to consider the extent of our or another person's knowledge about a particular subject. Will anyone take our opinion seriously? On what authority do we base our position? Why do we take someone else's opinion as valuable or trustworthy? What is the source of the opinion? How reliable is it? How biased? One of the first Americans to study the effects of public opinion, Walter Lippmann, wrote in 1925, "It is often very illuminating, therefore, to ask yourself how you get at the facts on which you base your opinion. Who actually saw, heard, felt, counted, named the thing, about which you have an opinion?" Is your opinion, he went on to ask, based on something you heard from someone who heard it from someone else, who in turn heard it from someone else?

How Do We Form Opinions?

How can we possibly have reasonable opinions on all the issues of the day? One of the strains of living in a democracy that encourages a diversity of perspectives is that every responsible citizen is expected to have informed opinions on practically every public question. What do you think about the death penalty? About dependency on foreign oil? About the way the media cover the news? About the extent of racial discrimination? Certainly no one person possesses inside information or access to reliable data on every topic that becomes part of public controversy. Still, many people, by the time they are able to vote, have formed numerous opinions. Where do these opinions come from?

Although social scientists and psychologists have been studying opinion formation for decades, the sources of opinion are multiple and constantly shifting, and individuals differ so widely in experience, cultural background, and temperament that efforts to identify and classify the various ways opinion is formed are bound to be tentative and incomplete. What follows is a brief, though realistic, attempt to list some of the practical ways that Americans come by the opinions they hold.

1. *Inherited opinions.* These are opinions we derive from earliest childhood — transmitted via family, culture, traditions, customs, regions, social institutions, or religion. For example, young people may identify themselves as either Democrats or Republicans because of their family affiliations. Although these opinions may change as we mature, they are often ingrained. The more traditional the culture or society, the more likely the opinions that grow out of early childhood will be retained and passed on to the next generation.

2. *Involuntary opinions.* These are opinions that we have not culturally and socially inherited or consciously adopted but that come to us through direct or indirect forms of indoctrination. They could be the customs of a cult or the propaganda of an ideology. Brainwashing is an extreme example of how one acquires opinions involuntarily. A more familiar example is the constant reiteration of advertising messages: We come to possess a favorable opinion of a product not because we have ever used it or know anything about it but because we have been "bombarded" by marketing to think positively about it.

3. *Adaptive opinions.* Many opinions grow out of our willingness — or even eagerness — to adapt to the prevailing views of particular groups, subgroups, or institutions to which we belong or desire to belong. As many learn, it's easier to follow the path of least resistance than to run counter to it. Moreover, acting out of self-interest, people often adapt their opinions to conform to the views of bosses or authority figures, or they prefer to succumb to peer pressure rather than oppose it. An employee finds himself accepting or agreeing with an opinion because a job or career depends on it; a student may adapt her opinions to suit those of a professor in the hope of receiving a better grade; a professor may tailor his opinions in conformity with the prevailing beliefs of colleagues. Adaptive opinions are often weakly held and readily changed, depending on circumstances. But over time they can become habitual and turn into convictions.

4. *Concealed opinions.* In some groups in which particular opinions dominate, certain individuals may not share the prevailing attitudes, but rather than adapt or "rock the boat," they keep their opinions to themselves. They may do this merely to avoid conflict or out of much more serious concerns — such as a fear of ostracism, ridicule, retaliation, or job loss. A common example is seen in the person who by day quietly goes along with the opinions of a group of colleagues but at night freely exchanges "honest" opinions with a group of friends. Some individuals find diaries and journals to be an effective way to express concealed opinions, and many today find online chat rooms a space where they can anonymously "be themselves."

5. *Linked opinions.* Many opinions are closely linked to other opinions. Unlike adaptive opinions, which are usually stimulated by convenience and an incentive to conform, these are opinions we derive from an enthusiastic and dedicated affiliation with certain groups, institutions, or parties. For example, it's not uncommon for someone to agree with every position his or her political party endorses — this phenomenon is usually called "following a party line." Linked opinions may not be well thought out on every narrow issue: Someone may decide to be a Republican or a Democrat or a Green or a Libertarian for a few specific reasons — a position on war, cultural values, the environment, civil liberties, and so forth — and then go along with, even to the point of strenuously defending, all of the other positions the party espouses because they are all part of its political platform or system of beliefs. In other words, once we accept opinions A and B, we are more likely to accept C and D, and so on down the chain. As Ralph Waldo Emerson succinctly put it, "If I know your sect, I anticipate your argument."

6. Considered opinions. These are opinions we have formed as a result of firsthand experience, reading, discussion and debate, or independent thinking and reasoning. These opinions are formed from direct knowledge and often from exposure and consideration of other opinions. Wide reading on a subject and exposure to diverse views help ensure that our opinions are based on solid information and tested against competing opinions. One simple way to judge whether your opinion is carefully thought out is to list your reasons for holding it. Some people who express opinions on a topic are not able to offer a single reason for why they have those opinions. Of course, reasons don't necessarily make an opinion correct, but people who can support their opinions with one or more reasons are more persuasive than those who cannot provide any reasons for their beliefs (see "How to Support Opinions").

This list is not exhaustive. Nor are the sources and types above mutually exclusive; the opinions of any individual may derive from all six sources or represent a mixture of several. As you learn to express your opinions effectively, you will find it useful to question yourself about the origins and development of those opinions. By tracing the process that led to the formation of our present opinions, we can better understand ourselves — our convictions, our inconsistencies, our biases, and our blind spots.

From Discussion to Writing

As this book amply demonstrates, we live in a world of conflicting opinions. Each of us over time has inherited, adopted, and gradually formed many opinions on a variety of topics. Of course, there are also a good number of public issues or questions about which we have not formed opinions or have undecided attitudes. In many public debates, members have unequal shares at stake. Eighteen-year-olds, for example, are much more likely to become impassioned over the government reviving a military draft or a state raising the legal age for driving than they would over Medicare cuts or Social Security issues. Some public questions personally affect us more than others.

Thus, not all the issues covered in this book will at first make an equal impact on everyone. But whether you take a particular interest in a given topic or not, this book invites you to share in the spirit of public controversy. Many students, once introduced to the opposing sides of a debate or the multiple positions taken toward a public issue, will begin to take a closer look at the merits of different opinions. Once we start evaluating these opinions, once we begin stepping into the shoes of others and learning what's at stake in certain positions, we often find ourselves becoming involved with the issue and may even come to see ourselves as participants. After all, we are all part of the public, and to a certain extent all questions affect us: Ask the eighteen-year-old if he or she will be equipped to deal with the medical and financial needs of elderly parents, and an issue that appears to affect only those near retirement will seem much closer to home.

As mentioned earlier, *America Now* is designed to stimulate discussion and writing grounded in response to a variety of public issues. A key to using this book is to think about discussion and writing not as separate activities but as interrelated processes. In discussion, we hear other opinions and formulate our own; in writing, we express our opinions in the context of other opinions. Both discussion and writing require articulation and deliberation. Both require an aptitude for listening carefully to others. Discussion stimulates writing, and writing in turn stimulates further discussion.

Group discussion stimulates and enhances your writing in several important ways. First, it supplies you with ideas. Let's say that you are participating in a discussion on the importance of ethnic identity (see selections in Chapter 4). One of your classmates mentions some of the problems a mixed ethnic background can cause. But suppose you also come from a mixed background, and when you think about it, you believe that your mixed heritage has given you more advantages than disadvantages. Hearing her viewpoint may inspire you to express your differing perspective on the issue. Your perspective could lead to an interesting personal essay.

Suppose you now start writing that essay. You don't need to start from scratch and stare at a blank piece of paper or computer screen for hours. Discussion has already given you a few good leads. First, you have your classmate's opinions and attitudes to quote or summarize. You can begin your paper by explaining that some people view a divided ethnic identity as a psychological burden. You might expand on your classmate's opinion by bringing in additional information from other student comments or from your reading to show how people often focus on only the negative side of mixed identities. You can then explain your own perspective on this topic. Of course, you will need to give several examples showing *why* a mixed background has been an advantage for you. The end result can be a first-rate essay, one that takes other opinions into account and demonstrates a clearly established point of view. It is personal, and yet it takes a position that goes beyond one individual's experiences.

Whatever the topic, your writing will benefit from reading and discussion, activities that will give your essays a clear purpose or goal. In that way, your papers will resemble the selections found in this book: They will be a *response* to the opinions, attitudes, experiences, issues, ideas, and proposals that inform current public discourse. This is why most writers write; this is what most newspapers and magazines publish; this is what most people read. *America Now* consists entirely of such writing. I hope you will read the selections with enjoyment, discuss the issues with an open mind, and write about the topics with purpose and enthusiasm.

The Practice of Writing

Suppose you wanted to learn to play the guitar. What would you do first? Would you run to the library and read a lot of books on music? Would you then read some instructional books on guitar playing? Might you try to memorize all the chord positions? Then would you get sheet music for songs you liked and memorize them? After all that, if someone handed you an electric guitar, would you immediately be able to play like Jimi Hendrix or Eric Clapton?

I don't think you would begin that way. You probably would start out by strumming the guitar, getting the feel of it, trying to pick out something familiar. You probably would want to take lessons from someone who knows how to play. And you would practice, practice, practice. Every now and then your instruction book would come in handy. It would give you basic information on frets, notes, and chord positions, for example. You might need to refer to that information constantly in the beginning. But knowing the chords is not the same as knowing how to manipulate your fingers correctly to produce the right sounds. You need to be able to *play* the chords, not just know them.

Learning to read and write well is not that much different. Even though instructional books can give you a great deal of advice and information, the only way anyone really learns to read and write is through constant practice. The only problem, of course, is that nobody likes practice. If we did, we would all be good at just about everything. Most of us, however, want to acquire a skill quickly and easily. We don't want to take lesson after lesson. We want to pick up the instrument and sound like a professional in ten minutes.

Wouldn't it be a wonderful world if that could happen? Wouldn't it be great to be born with a gigantic vocabulary so that we instantly knew the meaning of every word we saw or heard? We would never have to go through the slow process of consulting a dictionary whenever we stumbled across an unfamiliar word. But, unfortunately, life is not so easy. To succeed at anything worthwhile requires patience and dedication. Watch a young figure skater trying to perfect her skills and you will see patience and dedication at work; or watch an accident victim learning how to maneuver a wheelchair so that he can begin again an independent existence; or observe a new American struggling to learn English. None of these skills are quickly or easily acquired. Like building a vocabulary, they all take time and effort. They all require practice. And they require something even more important: the willingness to make mistakes. Can someone learn to skate without taking a spill? Or learn a new language without mispronouncing a word?

What Is "Correct English"?

One part of the writing process may seem more difficult than others — correct English. Yes, nearly all of what you read will be written in relatively correct English. Or it's probably more accurate to say "corrected" English, because most published writing is revised or "corrected" several times before it appears in print. Even skilled professional writers make mistakes that require correction.

Most native speakers don't actually *talk* in "correct" English. There are numerous regional patterns and dialects. As the Chinese American novelist Amy Tan says, there are "many Englishes." What we usually consider correct English is a set of guidelines developed over time to help standardize written expression. This standardization — like any agreed-upon standards such as weights and measures — is a matter of use and convenience. Suppose you went to a vegetable stand and asked for a pound of peppers and the storekeeper gave you a half pound but charged you for a full one. When you complained, he said, "But that's what *I* call a pound." Life would be very frustrating if everyone had a different set of standards: Imagine what would happen if some states used a red light to signal "go" and a green one for "stop." Languages are not that different. In all cultures, languages — especially written languages — have gradually developed certain general rules and principles to make communication as clear and efficient as possible.

You probably already have a guidebook or handbook that systematically sets out certain rules of English grammar, punctuation, and spelling. Like our guitar instruction book, these handbooks serve a very practical purpose. Most writers — even experienced authors — need to consult them periodically. Beginning writers may need to rely on them far more regularly. But just as we don't learn how to play chords by merely memorizing finger positions, we don't learn how to write by memorizing the rules of grammar or punctuation.

Writing is an activity, a process. Learning how to do it — like learning to ride a bike or prepare a tasty stew — requires *doing* it. Correct English is not something that comes first. We don't need to know the rules perfectly before we can begin to write. As in any activity, corrections are part of the learning process. You fall off the bike and get on again, trying to "correct" your balance this time. You sample the stew and "correct" the seasoning. You draft a paper about the neighborhood you live in, and as you (or a classmate or instructor) read it over, you notice that certain words and expressions could stand some improvement. And step by step, sentence by sentence, you begin to write better.

Writing as a Public Activity

Many people have the wrong idea about writing. They view writing as a very private act. They picture the writer sitting all alone and staring into space waiting for ideas to come. They think that ideas come from "deep" within and reach expression only after they have been fully articulated inside the writer's head.

These images are part of a myth about creative writing and, like most myths, are sometimes true. A few poets, novelists, and essayists do write in total isolation and search deep inside themselves for thoughts and stories. But most writers have far more contact with public life. This is especially true of people who write regularly for magazines, newspapers, and professional journals. These writers work within a lively social atmosphere in which issues and ideas are often intensely discussed and debated. Nearly all the selections in this book illustrate this type of writing.

As you work on your own papers, remember that writing is very much a public activity. It is rarely performed alone in an "ivory tower." Writers don't always have the time, the desire, the opportunity, or the luxury to be all alone. They may be writing in a newsroom with clacking keyboards and noise all around them; they may be writing at a kitchen table, trying to feed several children at the same time; they may be texting on subways or buses. The great English novelist D. H. Lawrence (1885–1930) grew up in a small impoverished coal miner's cottage with no place for privacy. It proved to be an enabling experience. Throughout his life, he could write wherever he happened to be; it didn't matter how many people or how much commotion surrounded him.

There are more important ways in which writing is a public activity. Writing is often a response to public events. Most of the articles you encounter every day in newspapers and magazines respond directly to timely or important issues and ideas, topics that people are currently talking about. Writers report on these topics, supply information about them, and discuss and debate the differing viewpoints. The units in this book all represent topics now regularly discussed on college campuses and in the national media. In fact, all of the topics were chosen because they emerged so frequently in college newspapers.

When a columnist decides to write on a topic like the impact of today's economy on young people, she willingly enters an ongoing public discussion about the issue. She hasn't just made up the topic. She knows that it is a serious issue, and she is aware that a wide variety of opinions have been expressed about it. She has not read everything on the subject but usually knows enough about the different arguments to state her own position or attitude persuasively. In fact, what helps make her writing persuasive is that she takes into account the opinions of others. Her own essay, then, becomes a part of the continuing debate and discussion, one that you in turn may want to join.

Such issues are not only matters for formal and impersonal debate. They also invite us to share our *personal* experiences. Many of the selections in this book show how writers participate in the discussion of issues by drawing on their experiences. For example, the essay by Christine Granados, "True Colors," is based largely on the author's personal observations and experience, though the topic — assimilation into American culture — is one widely discussed and debated by countless Americans. You will find that nearly every unit of *America Now* contains a selection that illustrates how you can use your personal experiences to discuss and debate a public issue.

Writing is public in yet another way. Practically all published writing is reviewed, edited, and re-edited by different people before it goes to press. The author of a magazine article has most likely discussed the topic at length with colleagues and publishing professionals and may have asked friends or experts in the field to look over his or her piece. By the time you see the article in a magazine, it has gone through numerous readings and probably quite a few revisions. Although the article is credited to a particular author, it was no doubt read and worked on by others who helped with suggestions and improvements. As a beginning writer, you need to remember that most of what you read in newspapers, magazines, and books has gone through a writing process that involves the collective efforts of several people besides the author. Students usually don't have that advantage and should not feel discouraged when their own writing doesn't measure up to the professionally edited materials they are reading for a course.

How to Support Opinions

In everyday life, we express many opinions, ranging from (as the chapters in this collection indicate) weighty issues such as race relations or the environment to personal matters such as our Facebook profile. In conversation, we often express our opinions as assertions. An assertion is merely an opinionated claim — usually of our likes or dislikes, agreements or disagreements — that is not supported by evidence or reasons. For example, *"Amnesty for illegal immigrants is a poor idea"* is merely an assertion about public policy — it states an opinion, but it offers no reason or reasons why anyone should accept it.

When entering public discussion and debate, we have an obligation to support our opinions. Simple assertions — *"Men are better at math than women"* — may be provocative and stimulate heated debate, but the discussion will go nowhere unless reasons and evidence are offered to support the claim. The following methods are among the most common ways you can support your opinions.

1. **Experts and authority.** You support your claim that the earth is growing warmer by citing one of the world's leading climatologists; you support your opinion that a regular diet of certain vegetables can drastically reduce the risk of colon cancer by citing medical authorities.

2. **Statistics.** You support the view that your state needs tougher drunk driving laws by citing statistics that show that fatalities from drunk driving have increased 20 percent in the past two years; you support the claim that Americans now prefer smaller, more fuel-efficient cars by citing surveys that reveal a 30 percent drop in SUV and truck sales over the past six months.

3. **Examples.** You support your opinion that magazine advertising is becoming increasingly pornographic by describing several recent instances from different periodicals; you defend your claim that women can be top-ranked chess players by identifying several women who are. Note that when using examples to prove your point, you will almost always require several; one example will seldom convince anyone.

4. **Personal experience.** Although you may not be an expert or authority in any area, your personal experience can count as evidence in support of an opinion. Suppose you claim that the campus parking

continued

facilities are inadequate for commuting students, and, a commuter yourself, you document the difficulties you have every day with parking. Such personal knowledge, assuming it is not false or exaggerated, would plausibly support your position. Many reporters back up their coverage with their eyewitness testimony.

5. **Possible consequences.** You defend an opinion that space exploration is necessary by arguing that it could lead to the discovery of much-needed new energy resources; you support an opinion that expanding the rights of gun ownership is a mistake by arguing that it will result in more crime and gun-related deaths.

These are only a few of the ways opinions can be supported, but they are among the most significant. Note that providing support for an opinion does not automatically make it true or valid; someone will invariably counter your expert with an opposing expert, discover conflicting statistical data, produce counterexamples, or offer personal testimony that contradicts your own. Still, once you've offered legitimate reasons for what you think, you have made a big leap from "mere opinion" to "informed opinion."

The American Political Spectrum: A Brief Survey

It's almost impossible to engage in public discourse today without immediately encountering terms like *liberal* and *conservative, right wing* and *left wing, libertarian* and *progressive.* Our discussion on public issues is largely framed by these affiliations, as well as by the big political parties (Republicans and Democrats) and the smaller ones (Tea Party, Green, and others) that are formed to advance the causes of those affiliations in government.

These terms don't necessarily account for how complex the spectrum of public opinion actually is. But for the most part, the distinctions revolve around two key questions: *What role should government play in regulating our behavior?* and *What role should government play in controlling the economy and our economic lives?* Most Americans agree on having a representative government that is elected (and can be removed) and is responsible to the people. Commentators and op-ed columnists on all stretches of the spectrum more or less take this for granted. We also pretty much agree that the government should intervene in our lives at times, and should be restrained at other times. Our debates are nearly always about exactly how much the state should intervene *socially* and *economically.*

In general, American liberals believe the government has a major role in regulating the economy, providing services that are available to everyone, and promoting economic equality among citizens. Conservatives often quote President Ronald Reagan's remark that "government is not the solution to our problem; government is the problem." Most conservatives believe that government mismanages money, that taxes should be lower, and that liberal social programs are wasteful and should be reduced or eliminated. Liberals gravitate towards government as the economic engine, while conservatives believe that engine is the private sector.

Socially, conservatives tend to believe that individuals should be held to a standard of conduct consistent with past tradition. Many mainstream conservatives disapprove of same-sex marriage and abortion, think criminals should be punished harshly, and want religion to be a part of public life to some degree. Liberals mistrust government in the social sphere, and they tend to promote extended liberties, such as legalized same-sex marriage, and consider bans on abortion or severe penalties for drug use an invasion of personal privacy. A liberal is more likely to defend a newspaper's claim to free speech against a conservative claim that speech may be unpatriotic or harmful.

Of course, that's only the beginning of the story. Other points of view hover between these ideological pillars. Libertarians dislike the power of government in both the economic and social spheres. They argue government should stay out of both the bedroom and the boardroom, advocating for much less intervention in the economy but often maintaining traditionally liberal positions on social issues. Many libertarians go further than both mainstream liberals and conservatives, arguing for instance that drugs should be legalized and the government should not deliberately manipulate the money supply. Opposite the libertarians are statists, believers in big government, who are economically liberal but socially conservative — this ideology is rather rare in the recent American political climate and the term is rarely used with positive connotations.

Centrists, on the other hand, are common but difficult to analyze. They either hold to a variety of positions too inconsistent with any one group to affiliate with it, or take positions that fall in between those of liberals and conservatives, or libertarians and statists. For instance, a centrist position on gun control might be that government should be allowed to ban assault and automatic weapons, but individuals should have the right to keep handguns. Many centrists feel that the economy should shift to be more equitable, but very gradually. Centrists are not, of course, lethargic or dispassionate in their beliefs — their beliefs are simply in the middle. Politicians who are called moderate Democrats or moderate Republicans tend to be centrists.

There are quite a few other political positions in addition to these five groups. Progressives, for instance, believe that it's government's task to advance the human condition in a substantial way. Progressives are a great deal like liberals, but focus more on using the levers of government to check the power large institutions like corporations have in the public sphere. They often believe that society should aspire to something like total economic parity between people, a goal of which many liberals feel wary. Recently, progressives have often attacked mainstream liberal positions, and a number of politicians now call themselves progressives instead of liberals.

Populists, meanwhile, believe in the power of the people collectively, and desire the outcome that provides the most benefit to the most people. However, populists are typically antagonistic to government itself, which they believe to be part of a privileged elite.

Despite the many ideologies in the American political landscape, conversation is most often framed by the division between the two major political parties. It is oversimplified to say that Democrats are liberals and Republicans are conservatives, but it is a convenient place to start. You'll often hear references to "conservative Republicans" and "liberal Democrats," who take more extreme stances on some issues. Recently, the Tea Party has made a significant impact with an ideology that focuses on economic libertarianism. Analysts debate whether Tea Party members are just conservative Republicans (most elected Tea Party officials actually run as Republicans) or a libertarian party. Though the Tea Party's focus is on the economy, polls show that most Tea Party members are socially conservative. Some progressives and populists vote for the Green Party, which emphasizes the environment but also advocates for high taxes on the rich and wealth redistribution.

Some issues, however, throw the Republican-conservative-Democratic-liberal equation off entirely. Consider military action, such as America's invasion of Iraq and Afghanistan. Not knowing any better, one might imagine Democrats would approve more of foreign wars, which cost money, create government jobs, and enhance the power of the government. However, those wars have, until recently, found more support from Republicans. Gun control is another issue in which conservatively aligned people tend to take the more socially liberal position: Government shouldn't make laws against guns in the name of maintaining law and order.

In response to these complications, many sociologists have developed a more geographical approach to the origin of American opinion. (For more on this, see Laura Meckler and Dante Chinni's "City vs. Country: How Where We Live Deepens the Nation's Political Divide" in Chapter 10.) They point out that most American conservatives statistically live and vote more in rural and suburban areas. Their conservative opinions, these theorists argue, is a result of the landscape in which they live, where people are more isolated from each other, need and use government services less, and see fewer changes occurring around them. In these areas, religion, gun culture, and the military are traditional forces of social cohesion, perhaps explaining some of the anomalies listed above.

Liberals, on the other hand, are far more heavily concentrated in cities, where they are close to their neighbors, rely more heavily on government services like police and sanitation, and have more contact with people on all parts of the economic ladder. Tea Party member and former Congresswoman Michele Bachmann once lampooned liberal Democrats by saying that their vision was for all Americans to "move to the urban core, live in tenements, [and] take light rail to their government jobs." Her joke contains a truth — many liberal positions seem concordant with urban life. Of course, in an age of unprecedented geographical mobility, it's an open question whether the places liberals and conservatives tend to live are the cause or the *result* of their opinions.

Writing for the Classroom: Two Annotated Student Essays

The following student essays perfectly characterize the kind of writing that *America Now* features and examines. Written by Kati Mather, a student at Wheaton College in Massachusetts, and Erika Gallion, a student at Ashland University in Ohio, the essays will provide you with a convenient and effective model of how to express an opinion on a public issue in a concise and convincing manner.

The essays also embody the principles of productive discussion outlined throughout this introduction. In fact, each essay was especially commissioned to perform a double service: to show a writer clearly expressing opinions on a timely topic that personally matters to her and, at the same time, demonstrate how arguments can be shaped to advance the possibility of further discussion instead of ending it.

The two essays demonstrate two different ways of handling a topic, in this case the values of a college education. The first, Kati Mather's "The Many Paths to Success — With or Without a College Education," provides an example of expressing an opinion based on personal experience alone. The second, Erika Gallion's "What's in a Major?" shows a student expressing an opinion by responding to an opposing opinion. In addition, the second example shows how opinions can be expressed with references to reading and research.

Although there are many other approaches to classroom writing (too many to be fully represented here), these two should provide students with accessible and effective models of the types of writing they will most likely be required to do in connection with the assignments in *America Now*.

Each essay is annotated to help you focus on some of the most effective means of expressing an opinion. First, read through each essay and consider the points the writer is making. Then, return to the essays and analyze more closely the key parts highlighted for examination. This process is designed to help you see how writers construct arguments to support their opinions. It is an analytical process you should begin to put into practice on your own as you read and explore the many issues in this collection. A detailed explanation of the highlighted passages follows each selection.

Expressing an Opinion Based on Personal Experience Alone

The first essay, Kati Mather's "The Many Paths to Success — With or Without a College Education," expresses an opinion that is based almost entirely on personal experience and reflection. In her argument that Americans have grown so predisposed to a college education that they dismiss other forms of education as inferior, Mather shows how this common attitude can lead to unfair stereotypes. Her essay cites no formal evidence or outside sources — no research, studies, quotations, other opinions, or assigned readings. Instead, she relies on her own educational experience and the conclusions she draws from it to support her position.

Kati Mather wrote "The Many Paths to Success — With or Without a College Education" when she was a senior at Wheaton College in Massachusetts, majoring in English and Italian studies.

Kati Mather
The Many Paths to Success — With or Without a College Education

1

Opens with personal perspective

I always knew I would go to college. When I was younger, higher education was not a particular dream of mine, but I understood that it was the expected path. (1) Even as children, many of us are so thoroughly groomed for college that declining the opportunity is unacceptable. Although I speak as someone who could afford such an assumption, even my peers without the same economic

1

advantages went to college. <u>Education is important, but I believe our common expectations — that everyone can and should go to college, and that a college education is necessary to succeed — and the stigmas attached to those who forgo higher education, are false and unfair.</u>

<u>In the past, only certain fortunate people could attain a college education. But over time, America modernized its approach to education, beginning with compulsory high school attendance in most states, and then evolving into a system with numerous options for higher learning.</u> (2) Choices for post-secondary education today are overwhelming, and — with full- and part-time programs offered by community colleges, state universities, and private institutions — accessibility is not the issue it once was. In our frenzy to adhere to the American dream, which means, among other things, that everyone is entitled to an education, the schooling system has become too focused on the social expectations that come with a college education. It is normally considered to be the gateway to higher income and an upwardly mobile career. But we would all be better served if the system were instead focused on learning, and on what learning means to the individual.

<u>It is admirable that we are committed to education in this country, but not everyone should be expected to take the college track. Vocational education, for instance, seems to be increasingly a thing of the past, which is regrettable because careers that do not require a college degree are as vital as those that do. If vocational schooling were more widely presented as an option — and one that everyone should take the time to consider — we would not be so quick to stereotype those who do not attend traditional academic institutions. Specialized labor such as construction, plumbing, and automobile repair are crucial to a healthy, functioning society.</u> (3) While a college education can be a wonderful thing to possess, we need people to aspire to other forms of education, which include both vocational schooling and learning skills on the job. Those careers (and there are many others) are as important as teaching, accounting, and medicine.

Despite the developments in our educational system that make college more accessible, financial constraints exist for many — as do family pressures and expectations, intellectual limitations, and a host of other obstacles. Those obstacles warrant neither individual criticism nor far-reaching stereotypes. For example, a handful of students from my high

2

2
Establishes main point early

3

3
Supports main point

4

school took an extra year or two to graduate, and I sadly assumed that they would not be as successful as those who graduated on time. I did not stop to consider their situations, or that they might simply be on a different path in life than I was. Looking back, it was unfair to stereotype others in this way. Many of them are hard-working and fulfilled individuals today. There is no law that says everyone has to finish high school and go to college to be successful. Many famous actors, musicians, artists, and professional athletes will freely admit that they never finished high school or college, and these are people we admire, who could very well be making more money in a year than an entire graduating class combined. (4) Plus, we applaud their talent and the fact that they chose their own paths. But banking on a paying career in the arts or sports is not a safe bet, which is why it is so important to open all practical avenues to young people and to respect the choices they make.

4
Provides examples of alternatives to college

We should focus on this diversity instead of perpetuating the belief that everyone should pursue a formal college education and that those who do not are somehow inadequate. There are, of course, essential skills learned in college that remain useful throughout life, even for those who do not pursue high-powered careers. As a student myself, I will readily admit that a college education plays an important role in a successful life. The skills we have the opportunity to learn in college are important to "real" life, and some of these can be used no matter what our career path. (5) Among other things, I've learned how to interact with different people, how to live on my own, how to accept rejection, how to articulate what I want to say, and how to write. Writing is one of the most useful skills taught in college because written communication is necessary in so many different aspects of life.

5
Offers balanced view of alternatives

I hope that my college education will lead to success and upward mobility in my career. But I can also allow that, once out of college, most students want to find a job that relates to their studies. In these hard times, however, that may not always be the case. I know from my own experience that other jobs — including those that do not require a college education — can be meaningful to anyone with the will to work and contribute. I'm grateful for the opportunities I've had that led to my college education, and though I do think we have grown too rigid in our thinking about the role of education, I also think we have the chance to change our attitudes and approaches for everyone's benefit.

<u>The widespread belief that everyone must go to college</u>   7
<u>to be a success, and that everyone *can* go to college, is not</u>
<u>wholly true. Of course, many people will benefit greatly from</u>

6
Closes by summa-
rizing position

<u>a quality education, and a quality education is more accessi-</u>
<u>ble today than ever before. But college is not the only option.</u>
(6) Hard-working people who do not take that path can still
be enormously successful, and we should not think otherwise. We can all disprove stereotypes. There are countless
accomplished people who are not formally educated.

This country offers many roads to success, but we must   8
remember that embracing diversity is essential to all of us.
While I will not deny that my education has helped me
along my chosen path, I firmly believe that, had I taken a
different one, it too would have enabled me to make a valuable contribution to our society.

Comments

The following comments correspond to the numbered annotations
that appear in the margins of Kati Mather's essay.

1. Opens with personal perspective. Mather begins her essay with
an effective opening sentence that at once identifies her background and
establishes the personal tone and perspective she will take throughout. The word *always* suggests that she personally had no doubts about
attending college and knew it was expected of her since childhood. Thus,
she is not someone who opted to skip college, and she is writing from
that perspective. As a reader, you may want to consider how this perspective affects your response to arguments against attending college;
for example, would you be more persuaded if the same argument had
been advanced by someone who decided against a college education?

2. Establishes main point early. Mather states the main point of
her essay at the end of paragraph 1. She clearly says that the "common
expectations" that everyone should attend college and that only those
who do so will succeed are "false and unfair." She points out that those
who don't attend college are stigmatized. These general statements
allow her to introduce the issue of stereotyping in the body of her essay.

3. Supports main point. Although Mather does not offer statistical evidence supporting her assumption that a college education
is today considered a necessity, she backs up that belief with a brief
history of how the increasing accessibility of higher education in
the United States has evolved to the point that a college degree now
appears to be a universal entitlement.

4. Provides examples of alternatives to college. In paragraph 3, Mather introduces the subject of vocational education as an alternative to college. She believes that vocational training is not sufficiently presented to students as an option, even though such skills are as "vital" to society as are traditional college degrees. If more students carefully considered vocational schooling, she maintains, we would in general be less inclined to "stereotype" those who decide not to attend college. In paragraph 4, she acknowledges how she personally failed to consider the different situations and options faced by other students from her high school class.

5. Offers balanced view of alternatives. In paragraph 5, Mather shows that she is attempting to take a balanced view of various educational options. She thus avoids a common tendency when forming a comparison — to make one thing either superior or inferior to the other. At this point in the argument, some writers might have decided to put down or criticize a college education, arguing that vocational training is even better than a college degree. By stating how important college can be to those who choose to attend, Mather resists that simplistic tactic and strengthens her contention that we need to assess all of our educational options fairly, without overvaluing some and undervaluing others.

6. Closes by summarizing position. In her concluding paragraphs, Mather summarizes her position, claiming that "college is not the only option" and reminding readers that many successful careers were forged without a college degree. Her essay returns to a personal note: Had she decided not to attend college, she would still be a valuable member of society.

Expressing an Opinion in Response to an Opposing Opinion

As mentioned earlier in this introduction, most of our opinions develop as a response to the opinions of others. It is difficult to imagine having an opinion in a complete vacuum. Much of the writing we encounter takes the form of a response to opinions that currently circulate in the media. In this case, the student essay is a response to a specific opinion piece that the *Washington Post* published in 2012: Michelle Singletary's "Not All College Majors Are Created Equal." The general topic — the value of a college education — has been covered frequently in the news ever since the economic downturn combined with a student loan crisis stimulated a broad discussion about the financial advantages of attending college. Singletary herself was responding to the general issue by arguing that college was worthwhile but only if one selected a major that paid off with high employment and competitive salaries.

We asked Gallion to read Singletary's essay carefully and take notes on her responses, to note points she agreed with and others she didn't, to research other relevant material, and then to shape those responses and additional information into a short essay that presented her considered opinion on the issue. Note that Gallion, an English major, doesn't respond by recounting her own experiences and defending her career choice. Instead, she follows two of the most effective methods of composing an opinion essay: (1) she forms her opinion as a response to an opposing opinion, and (2) she supports her response with additional reading and research that she discovered independently. These represent two common methods of learning to write for the classroom.

Erika Gallion (student essay)
What's in a Major?

1

In January of 2012, columnist Michelle Singletary wrote a piece for the *Washington Post* titled "Not All College Majors Are Created Equal." In it, Singletary discusses the importance of choosing a major that leads to a career after graduation—with the view that job preparation is the greatest benefit of a college education and, without it, the other benefits aren't worth the price. In fact, her essay implies that if a student selects a major that does *not* lead to a well-paying career right away, then attending college may not have been worth it. (1) Although Singletary makes a good case for the importance of career planning, her essay fails to describe fully the meaning of a college education. Colleges exist as more than preparatory schools for the job market and, despite the major students choose, we all generally benefit from attending college. (2)

1
Cites opposing view concisely

2
Establishes main point early

2

Singletary begins her argument by explaining a "game" she plays with college students in which she asks them their majors. She suggests that an English major, for example, without an internship will have no job after graduation, whereas an engineering major with three internships will find a job (Singletary, washingtonpost.com). Her argument that these majors are unequal is weakened because her example proves only that having one or more internships will benefit a student in a job search, regardless of the major. Of course an engineering major with three internships will find a job, but what about an English major who also took advantage of

3
*Challenges oppo-
nent's claim*

internships? Would she also have an equal chance of finding a job? Singletary's scenario privileges engineering majors
because it does not give students in the humanities, arts, and
social sciences equal credentials. (3)

3

4
*Offers an alterna-
tive argument*

Despite Singletary's argument that college is best taken
advantage of by students who enroll in a highly paid major,
there are many students today who simply want to pursue a
certain subject because they love it. (4) Singletary makes it
seem as if students who choose to study the arts, humanities, or social sciences do not consider the worth of their
major. But college is a serious investment, and it's safe to
say that most of these students are completely aware of the
extra schooling or work it will take to succeed in their area

5
*Supports alterna-
tive view with apt
quotations*

of interest. Academic courses are more than simply strategy-
sessions for a future career. As *Reason* editor Nick Gillespie
writes in his article "Humanities Under Siege," "You should
be going to college to have your mind blown by new ideas"
(Gillespie, reason.com). If students feel truly passionate
about their majors their academic experiences will be much
more interesting and desirable. The majors that Singletary
views as unimportant because of the job market "will give
you the tools to figure out who you are and what you want
to be" (Gillespie). (5) Career options represent only one
aspect of a college education. And it's worth considering
that if every prospective student were to major in engineering merely because of a more easily attainable career after
graduation, those jobs would soon be all taken.

6
*Offers another
view with support*

Most importantly, Singletary overlooks how much students learn and grow outside of the academic curriculum.
As a result of a survey, the U.K's *Daily Mail* published a list of
the top fifty lessons students actually learn during their time
in college. The top three results are: budgeting and prioritiz-
ing, living with others, and doing a weekly food shop (Smith,
dailymail.co.uk). Interestingly enough, only ten of these top
fifty lessons have anything to do with academics at all. Most
of these lessons involve cleaning, socializing, and making
time for relaxation. The college years are a prime time for
learning important and practical life lessons. College teaches
more than just academics: in this sense, college majors ARE
created equal. (6)

4

7
*Summarizes her
position*

Although Singletary's concerns are understandable and
make perfect sense in this day and age, her desire for prospective students to major in only those areas that guarantee
an immediate high-paying career is disappointing. College
benefits any student with an academic passion, whether it's

5

English or engineering. As long as a student remains dedicated and determined, a major in any subject can be rewarding and worthwhile. (7)

8
*Demonstrates
sources*

Works Cited (8)

Gillespie, Nick. "Humanities Under Siege." *Reason.* Reason, 19 March 2013. Web. 2 Apr. 2014.

Singletary, Michelle. "Not All College Majors Are Created
Equal." *Washington Post.* Washington Post, 14 Jan. 2012.
Web. 2 Apr. 2014.

Smith, Jennifer. "Making Spaghetti Bolognese, Building
Flat Pack Furniture and Going Three Nights Without
Sleep: What Students REALLY Learn at University."
Mail Online. Daily Mail, 12 Nov. 2013. Web. 2 Apr. 2014.

Comments

The following comments correspond to the numbered annotations
that appear in the margins of Erika Gallion's essay.

1. Cites opposing view concisely. Because her readers may be
unfamiliar with Singletary's position, Gallion needs to offer a brief
summary. With little space for a detailed summary, she provides the
gist of Singletary's argument in two sentences. Gallion's concision
allows her to move straight into her own argument. But note that she
will refer to various other points made by Singletary throughout the
essay. Had she started with a full summary of Singletary's argument,
including long quotations, the reader might feel burdened with too
much extraneous information.

2. Establishes main point early. With little space to waste, Gallion clearly establishes her main point at the end of her first paragraph.
As opposed to Singletary's view, she sees colleges to be "more than
preparatory schools for the job market." One doesn't attend college
simply for the purpose of finding a job. No matter what major students
select, they will "all generally benefit from attending college." These
comments show her dominant point of view, and the body of her essay
will support and reinforce it.

3. Challenges opponent's claim. In crafting an opinion essay that
takes an opposing view of another opinion, the writer should examine weaknesses in the opposing argument. Here, Gallion objects to an
argument Singletary makes to support her point that all majors are not
created equal. She points out that Singletary creates an unfair scenario
in which an engineering major with several internships easily finds a

job and she contrasts this with an English major without internships who finds no job. Gallion argues that this argument is unfair because it "privileges" one major over another.

4. Offers an alternative argument. In effective arguments, it is usually not enough to discredit or refute an opponent's reasoning or claims. The writer ought to offer alternative arguments, other ways of viewing an issue. Note how Gallion accomplishes this by suggesting that many students attend college to study something they "love," and that this is sufficient motivation outside of selecting a major simply because it would make one more employable.

5. Supports alternative view with apt quotations. Gallion enhances her own point that students often select certain majors because they "love" them by citing remarks written by the political writer Nick Gillespie, who offers reasons for attending college that have nothing to do with the job market. Note that such quotations do not "prove" one's point, but they have the important effect of showing readers that other people, sometimes significant writers and experts, agree with your position and disagree with your opponent. It is also important to note that the author she cites did not appear in Singletary's essay but that Gallion found the quotation independently, thus broadening the range of opinion.

6. Offers another view with support. Gallion develops her argument in opposition to Singletary's view by citing another source she found independently. Note that this source offers more objective data in the form of a survey that examined what students actually learn in college. As Gallion reports, these lessons have little to do with academics and more to do with practical skills. This information allows her to directly reverse Singletary's central claim. Since the lessons learned in college have little to do with the classroom and course work, majors are irrelevant. Or as Gallion points out: "in this sense, college majors ARE created equal."

7. Summarizes her position. In her concluding paragraph, Gallion summarizes her position. She concedes Singletary's concern about jobs, especially in today's world, but ends by saying she finds that point of view disappointing. Her final sentences restate the opinion she has expressed throughout her essay: that the benefits of a college education can apply to all majors.

8. Demonstrates sources. Gallion provides a "Works Cited" list to indicate the precise sources of her quotations. This list, arranged in alphabetical order by the authors' last names (not in the order that the citations appeared in the essay), allows readers to find the works she cites.

STUDENT WRITER AT WORK
Erika Gallion

R.A. What inspired you to write this essay?

E.G. Reading Michelle Singletary's "Not All College Majors Are Created Equal" made me think about the true worth of a college education. Singletary's focus on finding a career and making money made me want to respond with something about what the "nonmaking money" majors do. I wanted to stress the importance of learning about something an individual loves and show the positives of majoring in things like the arts or humanities.

R.A. Are your opinions unusual or fairly mainstream given the general climate of discourse on campus?

E.G. I think there are a few who would agree with me, especially since I'm living on a liberal arts campus. But in the world of research, I think there's been much discourse about Singletary's view. More and more parents are stressing career-driven majors instead of valuing the education classes within the humanities (for example). And that worries me.

R.A. Who was your prime audience?

E.G. I wanted to specifically write this for potential students thinking or worrying about what to major in. I think it is important to advocate for things like true education and/or true passion. I also wanted to write to the current students majoring within the majors that Singletary views as unnecessary. I think it is empowering and comforting to see someone advocate for the opinions you have.

R.A. How long did it take for you to write this piece? Did you revise your work? What were your goals as you revised?

E.G. I drafted this about three times. It took me about two-and-a-half weeks to completely finish it. The revision process included my using more action verbs instead of using *is* a lot. I also focused on cutting things out that were unnecessary to the piece as a whole.

R.A. What do you like to read?

E.G. I love reading novels, short stories, essay collections, memoirs, poetry. Anything, really. As far as magazines go, I love reading *Time* and *National Geographic*. There are multiple blogs on tumblr that I frequently read. My heart lies in the literature realm.

R.A. What topics most interest you as a writer?

E.G. Issues surrounding multiculturalism and diversity. I love reading about different cultures and/or religions and the issues that surround them. As a writer,

I like to attempt to tackle these issues because of how important they are in today's connected world.

R.A. Are you pursuing a career in which writing will be a component?

E.G. Yes. I'm going to graduate school for Higher Education Administration and afterwards, I hope to pursue a career at the university level helping with international student services. Being able to write well is essential in any career.

R.A. What advice do you have for other student writers?

E.G. Make time for it! I know how busy being a student is, but in order to develop writing skills, you have to sit down and spend time writing.

The Visual Expression of Opinion

Public opinions are expressed in a variety of ways, not only in familiar verbal forms such as persuasive essays, magazine articles, or newspaper columns. In newspapers and magazines, opinions are often expressed through photography, political cartoons, and paid opinion advertisements (or op-ads). Let's briefly look at these three main sources of visual opinion.

Photography

At first glance, a photograph may not seem to express an opinion. Photography is often considered an "objective" medium: Isn't the photographer simply taking a picture of what is actually there? But on reflection and careful examination, we can see that photographs can express subjective views or editorial opinions in many different ways.

    1. A photograph can be deliberately set up or "staged" to support a position, point of view, or cause. For example, though not exactly staged, the renowned World War II photograph of U.S. combat troops triumphantly raising the American flag at Iwo Jima on the morning of February 23, 1945, was in fact a reenactment. After a first flag raising was photographed, the military command considered the flag too small to be symbolically effective (though other reasons are also cited), so it was replaced with a much larger one and the event reshot. The 2006 Clint Eastwood film *Flags of Our Fathers* depicts the reenactment and the photograph's immediate effect on reviving a war-weary public's patriotism. The picture's meaning was also more symbolic than actual, as the fighting on the island went on for many days after the flag was raised. Three of the six Americans who helped raise the famed sec-

AP Photo/Joe Rosenthal

"Flag Raising at Iwo Jima," taken by combat photographer Joe Rosenthal on February 23, 1945.

ond flag were killed before the fighting ended. The photograph, which was also cropped, is considered the most reproduced image in photographic history.

2. A photographer can deliberately echo or visually refer to a well-known image to produce a political or emotional effect. Observe how the now-famous photograph of firefighters raising a tattered American flag in the wreckage of 9/11 instantly calls to mind the heroism of the Iwo Jima marines.

3. A photographer can shoot a picture at such an angle or from a particular perspective to dramatize a situation, to make someone look less or more important, or to suggest imminent danger. A memorable photograph taken in 2000 of Cuban refugee Elián González, for example, made it appear that the boy, who was actually in no danger whatsoever, was about to be shot. (See photograph on page 33.)

4. A photographer can catch a prominent figure in an unflattering position or embarrassing moment, or in a flattering and lofty fashion. Newspaper or magazine editors can then decide based on their political

© 2001 North Jersey Media Group

"Three Firefighters Raising the Flag," taken by Thomas E. Franklin, staff photographer for *The Record* (Bergen County, NJ), on September 11, 2001.

or cultural attitudes whether to show a political figure in an awkward or a commanding light.

5. A photograph can be cropped, doctored, or digitally altered to show something that did not happen. For example, a photo of a young John Kerry was inserted into a 1972 Jane Fonda rally to show misleadingly Kerry's association with Fonda's anti–Vietnam War activism. Dartmouth College has created a Web site that features a gallery of doctored news photos. (See http://www.fourandsix.com/photo-tampering-history.)

6. A photograph can be taken out of context or captioned in a way that is misleading.

These are only some of the ways the print and online media can use photographs for editorial purposes. Although most reputable news sources go to great lengths to verify the authenticity of photographs, especially those that come from outside sources, and enforce stiff penalties on photographers who manipulate their pictures, some experts in the field maintain that doctoring is far more common in the media than the public believes.

"We can no longer afford to accept news photography as factual data," claims Adrian E. Hanft III, a graphic designer, in an August 2006 photography blog. "If we are realistic," he continues, "we will come to the conclusion that much of the photography in the news is fake — or at least touched up to better tell the story. It is relatively simple to doctor a photo and everybody knows it. The fact that the term 'Photoshop it' is a part of the English vernacular shows just how accustomed to fake photography we have become. The interesting thing is that in the face of the massive amounts of doctored photos, most people still expect photos in the news to be unaltered. I think this has something to do with a human desire for photographs to be true. We know the cover photo of Teri Hatcher (of "Desperate Housewives" fame) is touched-up but we don't question it because we *want* her to look like that. Likewise when we see news stories that confirm our beliefs we want them to be true.

As photo manipulation becomes easier and easier, there is an increase in the demand for photographs that confirm what people want to believe. The market responds by flooding the world with 'fake' photography. Today people can believe almost anything they want and point to photography that 'proves' their beliefs."

Political Cartoons

The art of American political cartoons goes back to the eighteenth century; Benjamin Franklin was allegedly responsible for one of the nation's earliest cartoons. Almost from the start, political cartoonists developed what would become their favored techniques and conventions. Because cartoonists hoped to achieve an immediate intellectual and emotional impact, usually with imagery and a brief written message, they soon realized that exaggeration worked better than subtlety and that readily identified symbols were more quickly comprehended than nuanced or unusual imagery. The political cartoon is rarely ambiguous — it takes a decided position that frequently displays enemies negatively and friends positively. Rarely does a political cartoonist muddy the waters by introducing a mixed message or entertaining an opposing view. A cartoonist, unlike a columnist, cannot construct a detailed argument to support a position, so the strokes applied are often broad and obvious.

The humorous impact of most political cartoons depends on a combination of elements. Let's look at two relatively recent cartoons and examine the role of **context, iconography, exaggeration, irony, caption,** and **symbol**. Please note that the following cartoons are included for illustrative purposes only. They were not selected for their political and social opinions or for their artistic skill but primarily because they conveniently demonstrate the major elements and techniques of the political cartoon. Many other recent cartoons could just as easily have been selected.

First, a note about **context**. Chances are that if you don't know the political situation the cartoonist refers to, you won't "get" the cartoon's intended message. So it's important to remember that the cartoon's meaning depends on previously received information, usually from standard news sources. In other words, most cartoonists expect their audience to know a little something about the news story the cartoon refers to. Unlike the essayist, the cartoonist works in a tightly compressed verbal and visual medium in which it is unusually difficult to summarize the political context or the background the audience requires for full comprehension. This is one reason that cartoonists often work with material from headlining stories that readers are likely to be familiar with. In many cases, the audience needs to supply its own information to grasp the cartoon's full meaning.

Let's examine the context of the cartoon "Government Listens to Its Citizens." The cartoonist expects his audience to be familiar with an ongoing news story: Documents leaked in the summer of 2013 showed that the National Security Administration (NSA) conducts extensive telephonic surveillance of people, including U.S. citizens, to an extent that made many Americans uncomfortable. The cartoon also plays on another, more perennial, complaint about the U.S. government, namely that it is unresponsive to the needs and demands of its public. The cartoonist depicts the Capitol Dome, seat and symbol of the U.S. legislature, literally flipped over to reveal a giant surveillance satellite dish. The message is clear — government *is* in fact listening to you, but maybe not in the ways you'd choose to have it do so. Notice how much the cartoonist expects the audience to bring to his cartoon, however. If you hadn't heard of the NSA spying scandal, the cartoon would be far more confusing. Imagine how you'd interpret the imagery if you didn't know the context of the cartoon.

Note the elements of **iconography**. Iconography is the use of shorthand images that immediately suggest an incident, idea, era, institution, and so on. Such images are intended to reflect immediately and clearly what they stand for. For example, a teenager with a pack of cigarettes rolled up inside the sleeve of his T-shirt is iconographic of the 1950s; a cap and gown indicates an academic; a briefcase represents a businessperson or a public official; a devil is traditionally represented with horns and a pitchfork. In this cartoon, the Capitol Dome immediately suggests not only Washington, but also all that American government is supposed to stand for: democracy, inclusiveness, openness, and justice for everyone. In the cartoon, this symbol of a people's government is turned on its head. On the other side is another icon — the parabolic dish that immediately conjures up thoughts of espionage, secrecy, and invasion of privacy.

Note, too, the cartoon's use of **exaggeration** and unrealistic depiction: We are not meant to think that the Capitol Dome actually conceals a spy satellite, or — what would be equally ridiculous — that the controversial phone monitoring is going on in the Capitol building itself. The image is an extreme, hyperbolic representation of the frustrations its cartoonist wants to express. In expressing it as a cartoon, of course, he takes obvious liberties for the sake of demonstrating how big of a problem he thinks the alleged spying is.

To "get" the cartoon's full meaning is to understand its clever use of **visual irony**. Although it's a large literary subject, irony can be understood

"Government Listens to Its Citizens," by *Roll Call* cartoonist R. J. Matson, published on June 17, 2013.

simply as a contrast between what appears to be expressed and what is actually being expressed. The contrast is often humorous and could be sarcastic, as when someone says after you've done something especially dumb, "Nice work!" What appears to be expressed (verbally) in the cartoon is that the government is finally "listening" to its citizens, something many of those citizens have claimed it has failed to do. What is actually expressed (visually) is that this statement is literally true, because it is "listening" to those citizens in a questionably legal way. Note also that this cartoon's irony is almost entirely dependent on its **caption**—without the apparently ordinary citizen delivering the line, with its telling double meaning of the word *listens*, the cartoon would have far less impact and meaning.

However, cartoons can be equally effective without a caption, and with few or little words to push their messages. Let's look at another cartoon from 2013, Nate Beeler's "Gay Marriage." This cartoon comes on the heels of a decision by the U.S. Supreme Court striking down key aspects of the Defense of Marriage Act (DOMA), a 1996 law that refused gay and lesbian couples federal recognition for their marriages, even when states recognized them. The DOMA decision was seen as a major victory for gay rights. In the cartoon, a gay couple celebrates the decision with a warm embrace, but it's an unexpected couple: Lady Justice, the personification of blind justice familiar from courthouses, and the Statue of Liberty.

"Gay Marriage," by *Columbus Dispatch* cartoonist Nate Beeler, published on June 26, 2013.

Notice how the cartoonist tells a story with only one static image, rich in **symbol**. Justice appears to have dropped her iconic sword and scales as she's rushed into Liberty's arms, though she's still in her traditional blindfold. She carries the DOMA ruling with her, as if it's coming straight from the Supreme Court. Both characters look far more relaxed and joyous than they do in the well-known poses of the statues, signaling that this is a moment of jubilation for both. The image makes a conventional case for gay marriage to those who oppose it: These two women appear to be in love in the sense of the love that marriage exists to acknowledge. It's their symbolism, however, that makes this cartoon complete: The Supreme Court ruling has not only made the path for gay marriage easier, but also is itself a kind of "marriage" between liberty and justice — a pair of words that immediately makes us think "for all."

Opinion Ads

Most of the ads we see and hear daily try to persuade us to buy consumer goods like cars, cosmetics, and cereal. Yet advertising does more than promote consumer products. Every day we also encounter numerous ads that promote not things but opinions. These opinion advertisements (op-ads) may take a variety of forms — political commercials, direct mail from advocacy groups seeking contributions, posters and billboards, or paid newspaper and magazine announcements. Sometimes the ads are released by political parties and affiliated organizations, sometimes by large corporations hoping to influence policy, and sometimes by public advocacy groups such as Amnesty International, the National Association for the Advancement of Colored People, the National Rifle Association, or — as we see on page 39 — the Ad Council, a nonprofit organization that distributes and promotes public service campaigns on a wide variety of important issues.

One of the Ad Council's recent campaigns attempted to promote financial literacy; that is, to advise people on how to think about the ways they waste money and to encourage them to save. These ads were prompted by the economic woes facing the nation over the past several years. Teaming up with the American Institute of Certified Public Accountants (AICPA), the Ad Council began targeting messages to those younger Americans who were feeling the financial pinch most severely. The ads used an image and text to persuade people to pay closer attention to the way they spend and directed them to an interactive site called "Feed the Pig," which offered practical tips on how to develop better spending habits and save money over time.

These three ads, which first appeared in magazines and newspapers, represent only a tiny sample of the hundreds of such print ads readers come across daily. To examine carefully their verbal and visual techniques — whether you agree with the message or not — will help you become better acquainted with the essentials of rhetorical persuasion.

In print advertising, an ad's central argument is known as body copy, body text, or simply copy to distinguish it from the headline, illustrations, and other visuals. Note that all three ads reproduced here consist of three main elements: a visual image, a headline, and a body text in smaller type. This is typical of all kinds of advertising campaigns — whether print or new media — which try for a uniformity of design and message though each particular ad may appear different. Let's look at these three elements — image, headline, and copy — more closely.

1. Image. Each advertisement features an arresting image that reinforces the ad's overall message. The creators of the ads clearly expect that readers will look first at the images, and therefore they want them to be intriguing: a common french fry container stuffed not with fries but with rolled up ten- and twenty-dollar bills visually makes the point that the food you may order for lunch is equivalent to money; familiar take-out containers strikingly packed into a safe like gold bars also visually make the connection between food and money; and a young man searching a beach with a metal detector that is hovering over a buried pirate's chest drives home the notion of unrealistic financial dreams.

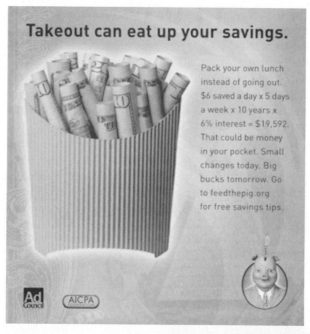

Takeout can eat up your savings.

Pack your own lunch instead of going out. $6 saved a day x 5 days a week x 10 years x 6% interest = $19,592. That could be money in your pocket. Small changes today. Big bucks tomorrow. Go to feedthepig.org for free savings tips.

Until this happens, start a savings plan.

Having money isn't about dumb luck. It's about a smart plan. Brew your own coffee, brown bag it to work, pay down that high-interest credit card. Saving just a few dollars a day can translate to literally thousands a year. And that's a much more reliable pile of gold. Small changes today. Big bucks tomorrow. Go to feedthepig.org for more free savings tips.

feedthepig.org

Would you rather have $46,000 or a whooooole lotta take-out?

Cook your own dinner instead of ordering in. $9 saved a day x 5 days a week x 10 years x 6% interest = $46,694. That could be money in your pocket. Small changes today. Big bucks tomorrow. Go to feedthepig.org for free savings tips.

feedthepig.org

Ads are usually addressed to a particular audience, known in the advertising profession as the "target audience." This audience may be defined by sex, income, age, race, educational level, hobbies, or other characteristics. When an individual or a group is featured in an ad, it often signals that a particular audience is being targeted. Note that the only character that appears in these three ads is someone young. This suggests that the ad's creators are hoping to appeal to those in a younger age bracket, those who are still in a financial planning stage.

2. Headline. An effective headline needs to capture the audience's attention in a few words.

Though brief, headlines can be difficult to write since so much content needs to be compressed and still engage the audience's interest. Each of the headlines reprinted here demonstrates some common feature of an effective headline:

Puns: When appropriate, headline writers like to use puns, such as "Takeout can *eat up* your savings." Puns are words or expressions that have two different meanings in the same context. "Eat up" can mean literally to devour food as well as to rapidly devour any commodity ("SUVs eat up a lot of gas").

Questions: Effective ads often use questions in their headlines. The questions are usually known as "rhetorical questions," meaning that the answer is obvious: "Would you rather have $46,000 or a whooooole lotta take-out?"

Image References: Some headlines like to refer the reader directly to the image. Images can only do so much persuasive work. Imagine how you would respond to the image of the young man with a metal detector if you had no verbal copy whatsoever. You would have no clue of what the image is intended to mean. The headline tells us how to "read" the image: "Until this happens, start a savings plan." Note that the key word in the headline is "this." The ad invites you to verbalize the image. We may all come up with different ways of saying it, but "this" will invariably refer to "luckily finding buried treasure."

3. Copy. Those writing and designing ads usually place the central argument in the body copy, which, as we can see from the financial literacy ads, comprises the main text. Ads differ significantly in the amount of text used. Sometimes the persuasive elements can be simply an image and a headline. But often some verbal argument is employed to support the ad's message. The body copy will usually pick up details from the image and headline but also supply new information. Two of the three ads encourage their audience to save money by packing their own lunch or cooking their own dinner and avoiding expensive take-out. The third ad encourages broader changes in habits.

Do the math: The first two ads argue their point with simple arithmetic. If you pack your own lunch or cook your own dinner five times a week, then over a ten-year period you will be ahead $19,592 in lunches and $46,694 in dinners. Yes, that's an impressive $66,286 total. But where, an attentive reader might ask, are these numbers coming from? If we pack our own lunches and cook our own dinners, won't that cost something as well? We can't make lunch or dinner for nothing. Food may cost less at the supermarket than at a restaurant, but it still costs something. The ads claim that we will save $6 by packing our lunch and $9 by cooking dinner but they don't say (a) how those costs are arrived at or (b) whether those amounts take into account what it costs to buy the food we prepare ourselves.

There's another bit of mystery in the math: Where does 6% interest come from? Most savings and checking accounts today offer interest rates that barely reach 1%. Are the ads suggesting that readers invest the money they are saving in other ways (the stock market?) and that this would be the average gain over ten years? And that there is no risk? This figure also remains unexplained.

Tag lines: In advertising and marketing, a tag line is a memorable phrase closely associated with the brand or message that is repeated often in a campaign. Note that all three ads repeat (in addition to other language) the phrase "Small changes today. Big bucks tomorrow." The pun on "changes" is of course intentional. Small change now can accumulate into big bucks in the future. But in this case the word *changes* suggests not just coins but also a change in one's lifestyle.

Taking action: Most opinion ads often conclude with a call to take some direct action — vote, write, call, redeem a coupon, register a complaint, and so on. The financial literacy ads not only suggest that readers act to change their sloppy and wasteful economic habits, but they also invite them to visit a Web site called "feedthepig.org" for more savings tips. The pig stands for an old-fashioned piggy bank (and "feeding" again reinforces the connection between money and eating). Because of the Internet, an ad today is able to continue and expand its message in ways that could never have been done in earlier times.

Writing as Empowerment

Writing is one of the most powerful means of producing social and political change. Through their four widely disseminated gospels, the first century evangelists helped propagate Christianity throughout the world; the writings of Adam Smith and Karl Marx determined the economic systems of many nations for well over a century; Thomas Jefferson's "Declaration of Independence" became a model for countless colonial liberationists; the carefully crafted speeches of Martin Luther King Jr. and the books and essays of numerous feminists altered twentieth-century consciousness. In the long run, many believe, "The pen is mightier than the sword."

Empowerment does not mean instant success. It does not mean that your opinion or point of view will suddenly prevail. It does mean, however, that you have made your voice heard, that you have given your opinions wider circulation, and that you have made yourself and your position a little more visible. And sometimes you get results: A newspaper prints your letter; a university committee adopts your suggestion; people visit your Web site. Throughout this collection, you will encounter writing specifically intended to inform and influence a wide community.

Such influence is not restricted to professional authors and political experts. This collection features a large number of student writers who are actively involved with the same current topics and issues that engage the attention of professionals — the environment, racial and ethnic identity, gender differences, and so on. The student selections, all of them previously published and written for a variety of reasons, are meant to be an integral part of each unit, to be read in conjunction with the professional essays, and to be criticized and analyzed on an equal footing.

America Now urges you to voice your ideas and opinions — in your notebooks, in your papers, in your classrooms, and, most important, on your campus and in your communities. Reading, discussing, and writing will force you to clarify your observations, attitudes, and values, and as you do, you will discover more about yourself and the world. These are exciting times. Don't sit on the sidelines of controversy. Don't retreat into invisibility and silence. Jump in and confront the ideas and issues currently shaping America.

Social Media: What Do We Gain? What Do We Lose?

In 1995, a *Newsweek* editorial warned readers to "discount the fawning techno-burble about virtual communities. Computers and networks isolate us." For years since, pundits have debated whether online networks are permanent fixtures or just a passing fad — and what effect they might have on our social and professional lives.

The first question seems more and more definitively answered. With billions of dollars in revenue and well over half of American adults with at least one social-networking profile, Web sites like Facebook, Twitter, and Instagram seem to be here to stay. The other question, though, is still open. Do these virtual meeting places enhance our communication, our careers, our studies, and our friendships? Or is constant connectivity coming at the expense of real connection?

Andrew Santella believes that new technology is not driving our oversharing — we are. In "This Is Not About You," Santella maintains that narcissism — the desire to have the world know every detail of your life, even that Instagram of your lunch — has been around long before the wireless card. Technology has simply enabled it. "Social networks depend on the belief that we all have a story to tell, we all have some pictures to show and the world wants to hear from us," he writes. "Sustaining that illusion requires at least a little narcissism."

A perspective from a California State University, Los Angeles, student agrees that our online lives may be interfering with our actual ones, but she makes the case that our lack of activity, not our abundance of it, is the problem. "Going out into the real world is so much less appealing when you can accomplish everything you need to during the day from the comfort of your bed with a few keystrokes," Yzzy Gonzalez writes in "Technology Taking Over?" Gonzalez adds that technology can improve our lives immensely, but warns us to take a break and get outside once in a while.

But to those who claim our digital links are fast corroding human ones — especially among today's youth — Clive Thompson says the numbers beg to differ. Restrictive parenting and tight, college-minded schedules have, according to his Spotlight on Research selection, left teens with "neither the time nor the freedom to hang out." In "The Parent Trap," Thompson argues that parents should blame themselves for their kids' "avid migration to social media," a direct result of these new, offline realities.

Critics of social media should also note that they are the latest in a long line of skeptics armed with similar arguments about the decline of discourse. More than 150 years before *Newsweek* bashed chat rooms and bulletin boards, one of America's greatest essayists, Henry David Thoreau, critiqued the telegraph, the latest way technology was zapping messages across the continent at the time. In this chapter's "America Then," Thoreau laments that though communication was advancing at a breakneck speed even then, the sad truth may be that we have "nothing important to communicate."

Andrew Santella

This Is Not About You

[*Notre Dame* Magazine, Summer 2013]

BEFORE YOU READ

Are we all loud narcissists, thanks to social networking? Is there a value to silence in today's world?

WORDS TO LEARN

pedestrian (para. 1): a walker (noun)

histrionic (para. 1): overly dramatic (adjective)

cosseted (para. 1): coddled (adjective)

ensure (para. 2): to guarantee (verb)

ingratiating (para. 3): agreeable (adjective)

jeremiad (para. 7): a lengthy lamentation or complaint (noun)

critique (para. 7): an evaluation or criticism (noun)

ode (para. 8): a poem written in celebration of something or someone (noun)

monomaniac (para. 8): someone who fixates on one thing (noun)

demise (para. 8): death (noun)

defiant (para. 9): boldly resistant (adjective)

nonconformity (para. 9): refusal to comply with prevailing attitudes or standards (noun)

shallowly (para. 9): superficially (adverb)

gregarious (para. 9): sociable (adjective)

glib (para. 10): facile or superficial (adjective)

My street in Brooklyn is the main pedestrian approach to the ironically misnamed Harmony Playground, a destination for the loudest and most histrionic of the neighborhood's children. On weekends they pass in procession under my window, cosseted in their SUV-like strollers, screaming their heads off. Is everyone's sippy cup just out of reach? Have they all dropped their sock monkeys? I can't be sure. My wife, however, has nicknamed our street Tantrum Alley. 1

Andrew Santella is a writer and editor whose work has appeared in GQ, *the* New York Times Book Review, Slate, Details, *and the* New York Times Magazine, *among others. He has authored around sixty nonfiction books for children and is the managing editor of Elmhurst College's* Prospect Magazine.

In his 1914 essay, "On Narcissism," Sigmund Freud[1] argued that all   2
infants are narcissists, masters at manipulating their parents to get what
they want. What he didn't say is just how much noise they can make in
the process. For Freud, the narcissism of kids was perfectly healthy and
even necessary. Evolutionary biology backs him up. Born unable to care
for themselves — compare human babies with the much more quickly
self-sufficient offspring of other animals — babies learn to treat their parents like servants to ensure their own survival.

This accounts for the scene on Tantrum Alley and for the array of   3
ingratiating qualities — the soul-lifting smile, the adorable babbling, the
irresistible smell of baby head — that babies deploy to ensure our continued devotion. Or servitude, if you prefer.

So why does narcissism of the adult variety bother us so much? We   4
see it everywhere. The shameless bragger. The bullying liar. The relentlessly self-absorbed conversationalist.

Critics of Barack Obama like to call him "Narcissist-in-Chief." Ben   5
Affleck recently called all actors narcissists. Disgraced bicyclist Lance
Armstrong went on *Oprah* to call *himself* a narcissist. As commonly used,
the term is not so much a diagnosis as an all-purpose slap-down for anyone we think has become too full of himself. In fact, the term may have
more currency in popular culture than it does in medicine. The fifth edition of the *Diagnostic and Statistical Manual of Mental Disorders*, from
the American Psychiatric Association, not long ago dropped narcissism
from its menu of personality disorders.

What most of us are talking about when we talk about narcissism is   6
only distantly related to a doctor's diagnostic criteria. It's partly a matter
of fairness.

What bothers us about narcissists is that they demand and claim   7
more than their fair share of attention. In a time of economic anxiety,
like ours, that kind of grasping tends to provoke a backlash. Thirty
years ago, in the wake of another recession, the social critic Christopher
Lasch wrote a best-selling jeremiad called *The Culture of Narcissism*.
Lasch announced that America was populated by coldly calculating
self-aggrandizers angling "for competitive advantage through emotional
manipulation." His critique resonated with readers stung by the hard
times of the mid-1970s and bewildered by an ever more exhibitionist
popular culture. (See the entry on "streaking" in Wikipedia, youngsters.)

---

[1] Sigmund Freud (para. 2): Austrian physician known as the father of psycho-
analysis

A current of rampant individualism has always run through U.S. life and art. Think of Emerson's[2] essay "Self-Reliance," a prose ode to the power of the genius in all of us; or Melville's *Moby-Dick*, a story about how one monomaniac's obsessive quest produces the demise of an entire (shipboard) society. But Lasch and others thought that economic forces had come to shape the American character in disturbing ways. The historian Warren Susman argued that a 19th century Culture of Character focused on duty and manners had given way to a 20th century Culture of Personality focused on charisma and attractiveness.

> A current of rampant individualism has always run through U.S. life and art.

8

"The social role demanded of all in the new Culture of Personality was that of a performer," Susman wrote. "Every American was to become a performing self." The old defiant Emersonian nonconformity had been reduced to a shallowly gregarious patter designed to get us ahead.

9

The best place to see this dynamic at work today is, of course, on such social media sites as Facebook and Twitter and Instagram. The prevailing tone there is as glib, slick and self-promoting as was found in any Jazz Age self-help manual: "Try in every way to have a ready command of the manners which make people think, 'He's a mighty likable fellow.'" Or maybe the comparison is to the little kids on my street screaming for notice in their strollers: *Pay attention! Look at me!*

10

Social networks depend on the belief that we all have a story to tell, we all have some pictures to show and the world wants to hear from us. Sustaining that illusion requires at least a little narcissism. After all, who cares what I had for lunch? Who would possibly want to see a picture of it? But maybe the illusion is easier for some generations to sustain than for others. Here's actress and writer Lena Dunham on her father's view of Twitter: "He's like, 'Why would I want to tell anybody what I had for a snack, it's private?' And I'm like, 'Why would you even have a snack if you didn't tell anybody? Why bother eating?'"

11

This attitude turns digital self-display into an existential act: I tweet, therefore I am. And if I stop, I cease to exist, to at least some segment of my world. Not that this is necessarily evidence of pathological narcissism. The whole digital system of exchange, the digital capitalist economy, demands

12

---

[2] Ralph Waldo Emerson (para. 8): American essayist and poet who led the Transcendentalist movement in the mid-1800s

we keep providing content. It demands that we — and note here the juvenile nature of the imperatives, straight out of the preschool lexicon — keep sharing and poking and liking.

If there is anything narcissistic about all this, it is that it is self-defeating. We think of narcissists as being obsessed with winning, but Narcissus himself could never win. He could never possess the prize he sought — his own image — because every time he stooped to approach it, it vanished in the ripples of the pond. It remained ever out of reach.   13

The digital economy depends on our continual engagement. If we stop providing content, the whole thing shuts down. The too-frequent Tweeter, the Facebook status-updater who needs to share every detail of every workout strikes us as narcissistic. He is playing the game we all play but is playing too intensely, trying too hard.   14

The problem is that trying harder doesn't work, either. The effort cancels itself out. Art, performance, even worship all require silence as well as statement. And the true narcissist has probably discovered that silence, too, can be a source of strength, of power. That's a truth the tantrum-throwing kids on my street have not yet learned, and it's one forgotten in the glib new world of social networking.   15

Susan Sontag called silence "the artist's ultimate other-worldly gesture." It is the ultimate transcendence, which may be why silence is part of so many spiritual traditions.   16

"God is silent," Woody Allen said. "Now if only man would shut up."   17

VOCABULARY/USING A DICTIONARY

1. What are *narcissists* (para. 2) preoccupied with?
2. What part of speech is *rampant* (para. 8)? What is the opposite of *rampant*?
3. What is *charisma* (para. 8)? What is a *charismatic* person like?

RESPONDING TO WORDS IN CONTEXT

1. What part of speech is *slap-down* (para. 5)? What does it mean? Is it being used literally or figuratively?
2. What do you usually think of when you hear the word *currency*? How is *currency* used differently in paragraph 5?
3. How do you understand the phrase *economic anxiety* (para. 7)? Are there other references to *economics* in that paragraph? Where else is economy mentioned in the essay?

DISCUSSING MAIN POINT AND MEANING

1. What bothers us so much about "narcissism of the adult variety" (para. 4)? When do we feel it is expected or natural?

2. In paragraph 12, Santella refers to the "preschool lexicon" used by people on social media — "keep sharing and poking and liking." Why do you think he calls this the "preschool lexicon"?
3. When does Santella talk about silence? What point is he making about silence?

EXAMINING SENTENCES, PARAGRAPHS, AND ORGANIZATION

1. What is the effect of using *self*-words in this essay?
2. Where in the essay does Santella circle back to his opening narrative? Do his returns strengthen or weaken his point? How so?
3. Santella alludes to a classical quote in paragraph 12. Can you identify it? Do you know the actual reference? How has he changed the quotation?

THINKING CRITICALLY

1. In what ways are you narcissistic? Do those ways match up with Santella's descriptions at all?
2. What do you find appealing or off-putting about people who are narcissists? What might be considered their strengths or weaknesses?
3. What are the main differences between a "Culture of Character" and a "Culture of Personality" (para. 8)?

WRITING ACTIVITIES

1. Write a profile of one of the adult narcissists Santella describes: "The shameless bragger. The bullying liar. The relentlessly self-absorbed conversationalist." How do these traits show up on social media? Describe situations in which they might appear, and discuss how social media lends itself to providing a platform for these particular forms of narcissism.
2. Consider the quotations Santella ends with: Susan Sontag's silence is "the artist's ultimate other-worldly gesture" and Woody Allen's "God is silent. Now if only man would shut up." Using these quotations as a prompt, write a brief response to what one or the other speaker is saying about silence.
3. Seek out and read Ralph Waldo Emerson's essay "Self-Reliance." Do you think his essay has led to the narcissism Santella describes in his essay? In what ways?

Yzzy Gonzalez (student essay)

Technology Taking Over?

[*University Times,* California State University,
Los Angeles, February 11, 2013]

BEFORE YOU READ
How technology dependent are you? How many times a day do you use technology in your daily life?

WORDS TO LEARN
dependent (para. 1): reliant on someone or something else (noun)
supreme (para. 2): highest in rank (adjective)
impact (para. 5): influence (noun)
avid (para. 5): enthusiastic (adjective)

portability (para. 6): the quality of being able to be moved or carried easily (noun)
redundant (para. 6): unnecessary or repetitive (adjective)

L et me tell you about my morning routine. I wake up to the sound of Sleep Time, a smartphone app that keeps track of my sleep patterns during the night. Afterwards, I jump in the shower, get dressed for the day (based on what weather.com is telling me to expect), and start making breakfast to the sound of my iPod dock blasting Kate Nash. I eat my breakfast reading theSkimm, Deadline Hollywood, Cupcakes and Cashmere, and many more news sites and blogs, all on my laptop. Finally, when it's time for school or work, I make sure to grab my phone before I leave, because without it, I would have absolutely no means of survival in the real world. Hi, I'm Yzzy Gonzalez and I'm technology dependent.

I wouldn't be surprised if some of you realize that your routine is extremely similar. It's how today's society works: technology reigns supreme. While a lot of the newest technology is made so it's easier for us and our lifestyles, it also makes us extremely dependent on whatever gateways it opens for us. I can't even count the number of times you hear about people driving back

> It's how today's society works: technology reigns supreme.

Yzzy Gonzalez is a student at California State University, Los Angeles.

50

home because they forgot their phone or the number of times someone checks their mobile Instagram feed during one hour. Whatever the reason, today's current generation is technology-obsessed.

There are a few peeves I have about current technology. First, it enables me to do things that I will probably regret at the end of the day. For example, mobile banking that allows you to transfer between your accounts instantly. While its main benefit is to give you money when you need it, it also enables your increasing spending habits. Yes, I could think, "oh I don't have money to buy that cardigan" knowing I could have money in a few minutes, but it would be a lot more reasonable for me to know I can't have money to buy that cardigan unless I drive to the nearest ATM or Bank of America and ask for an account transfer.

3

On that note, technology is killing face-to-face interaction. Going out into the real world is so much less appealing when you can accomplish everything you need to from the comfort of your bed with a few keystrokes. It astounds me that online grocery shopping is currently a thing. You're going to wish that you went to the store and personally picked out your strawberries when the ones you get delivered are half-rotten. (I'm kidding, don't worry.)

4

Meanwhile, technology's impact on the newspaper and book industry is making them obsolete. People buy Kindles and Nooks so they can have ten million books in their hands rather than just one, but because of that, places like Borders and Barnes and Noble are closing stores and going out of business. As an avid fan of paperback books (and paper products in general), this breaks my heart, but that's technology for you. Improving on what already exists.

5

Please don't see me as a technology hater. There is definitely a silver lining to this cloud. Technology constantly succeeds because of its portability and ways of connecting people. It can be redundant when it comes to the mundane everyday things, but when you can talk to your friend in another state because of FaceTime on your iPhone, you really can't deny how amazing that is.

6

Technology will always change, try to make life easier, offer cool new advances, and be important to a growing society, but it's just as important not to become dependent on it and rely on it to do things we've known how to do for years. No one will get hurt if you just take a day away from the phone or computer and enjoy the outdoors, or pick up a newspaper instead of staring at an electronic screen; it might just be the right amount of change in your daily atmosphere.

7

This article was written with a MacBook. A pen and paper were not used during the writing process at all.

8

VOCABULARY/USING A DICTIONARY
1. What is a *cardigan* (para. 3)?
2. What has happened if something is *obsolete* (para. 5)?
3. If something is *mundane* (para. 6), what does that mean?

RESPONDING TO WORDS IN CONTEXT
1. What is a *peeve*, based on what Gonzalez writes in paragraph 3?
2. What is the difference between *everyday* (para. 6) and *every day*?
3. When Gonzalez refers to *technology,* what is she speaking of?

DISCUSSING MAIN POINT AND MEANING
1. Is Gonzalez happy about the use of technology, or does she feel it's too much?
2. What is technology doing to the newspaper and book industry, according to Gonzalez?
3. What can people do to change their habits in this technology-driven world?

EXAMINING SENTENCES, PARAGRAPHS, AND ORGANIZATION
1. In her first paragraph, how does Gonzalez indicate the role technology plays in her life?
2. Gonzalez ends paragraph 4 with a parenthetical. Why do you think she ends with that?
3. What do you think of Gonzalez's use of second person in this essay? What would the essay be like written in third person?

THINKING CRITICALLY
1. What would life be like without Internet and smartphones? What would be different?
2. Do you think you'd be happier without technology in your daily life? What would make you happier if it disappeared?
3. Are there other things you can think of about technology that really matter to you? Gonzalez includes the point about being able to have face time with a friend in another state. Do you have examples like that about technology's plus side?

WRITING ACTIVITIES
1. Gonzalez goes over her entire morning schedule in all its technological detail. In a brief writing exercise, consider your own morning routine and include all the technology you use, just on your way out the door (or choose a different time of day and catalogue the technology used).
2. Consider a life before the technological revolution. Describe what that would be like. Do things happen faster or slower? Do you feel more connected or less connected to the world and people around you?

3. Is technology dependency a real problem? In pairs, talk about what it means to be technology dependent as Gonzalez presents it in this essay. Can you form a list of other potential issues? Discuss your ideas with the class, and write a brief essay about your pair and class discussions.

LOOKING CLOSELY

Beginning with a Specific Instance

Opening an essay can be the hardest part of the process. A writer has to draw the reader in with a compelling and animated introduction — and simultaneously establish credibility and knowledge in the depths of his or her topic. One of the best ways to accomplish these twin goals is to avoid the urge to be general. While you might assume that you want to cover the totality of your topic in an opening paragraph, it is often more effective to start with a concrete example and branch out from there.

Yzzy Gonzalez, a freshman at California State University, Los Angeles, writes about the broad topic of the role of technology, particularly the Internet, in our lives. But notice how she begins with her own day, providing copious examples of the phenomenon she describes from her personal experience. Gonzalez's opening paragraph is particularly effective because her readers will likely share some of those experiences, and shared experiences draw readers closer to authors. The specifics she mentions are also far more engaging than a dry, general discussion of the topic — she saves an overview for later paragraphs, after she has created a connection and confirmed her understanding of the topic.

1 *She offers us a story*	<u>Let me tell you about my morning routine</u> (1). I wake up to the sound of Sleep Time, a smartphone app that keeps track of my sleep patterns during the night. Afterwards, I jump in the shower, get dressed for the day (based on what weather.com is telling me to expect), and start making breakfast to the sound of my iPod dock blasting Kate Nash. <u>I eat my breakfast reading theSkimm, Dead-</u>
2 *Specific sites establish depth*	<u>line Hollywood, Cupcakes and Cashmere</u> (2), and many more news sites and blogs, all on my laptop. Finally, when it's time for school or work, I make sure to grab my phone before I leave, because without it, I would have absolutely no means of survival in the real world. Hi, I'm Yzzy Gonzalez and I'm technology dependent.

STUDENT WRITER AT WORK

Yzzy Gonzalez

R.A. What inspired you to write this essay? And publish it in your campus paper?

Y.G. I wrote this essay based on my real life experiences with using technology while going to college. I published it in the campus paper as part of my weekly column, "Freshman Focus," in which I wrote about topics that I felt like freshmen on the campus could relate to.

R.A. What was your main purpose in writing this piece?

Y.G. I wanted to look deeper into the loss of "old school" traditions due to the convenience of technology.

R.A. Who was your prime audience?

Y.G. My audience was the freshmen students at my university, though my piece could apply to any student, or even anyone living in the digital era.

R.A. What response have you received to this piece?

Y.G. This piece has gotten more favorable reviews than other works of mine, partly because people have said it was extremely relatable. The feedback has just made me realize how everyone is affected by the rise of technology.

R.A. Have you written on this topic since?

Y.G. Not long after I wrote this piece, I wrote a research paper on technology's influence on friendships. I've read a few novels on the interaction between humans and technology, and how it is preferred over real human interaction.

R.A. What topics interest you as a writer?

Y.G. I am interested in human profiles when it comes to news writing, but I also enjoy freestyle creative writing. I usually focus on topics of change, like growing up, and life in designated areas such as the city or the suburbs.

R.A. Do you plan to continue writing for publication?

Y.G. I do!

R.A. What advice do you have for other student writers?

Y.G. Write often and write what you like!

Spotlight on Research

Clive Thompson

The Parent Trap: How Teens Lost the Ability to Socialize

[*Wired*, January 2014]

Clive Thompson is a blogger, journalist, and technology writer. He has been a freelance contributor for The New York Times *Magazine, The* Washington Post, Lingua Franca, Shift, Entertainment Weekly, *and others. He is a columnist at* Wired, *and is a long-time blogger, launching his science-and-technology blog,* "Collision Detection," *in 2002.*

Are teenagers losing their social skills? Parents and pundits seem to think so. Teens spend so much time online, we're told, that they're no longer able to handle the messy, intimate task of hanging out face-to-face. "After school, my son is on Facebook with his friends. If it isn't online, it isn't real to him," one mother recently told me in a panic. "Everything is virtual!" Now, I'm not convinced this trend is real. I've read the evidence about the "narcissism epidemic" and the apparent decline in empathy in young people, and while it's intriguing, it's provisional. Lots of work offers the opposite conclusion, such as Pew surveys finding that kids who text the most also socialize the most in person. But for the sake of argument, let's agree that we have a crisis. Let's agree that kids aren't spending enough time together mastering social skills. Who's responsible? Has crafty Facebook, with its casino-like structure of algorithmic nudging, hypnotized our youth? If kids can't socialize, who should parents blame? Simple: They should blame themselves. This is the argument advanced in *It's Complicated: The Social Lives of Networked Teens,* by Microsoft researcher Danah Boyd. Boyd — full disclosure, a friend of mine — has spent a decade interviewing hundreds of teens about their online lives. What she has found, over and over, is that teenagers would love to socialize face-to-face with their friends. But adult society won't let them. "Teens aren't addicted to social media. They're addicted to each other," Boyd says. "They're not allowed to hang out the way you and I did, so they've moved it online."   1

It's true. As a teenager in the early '80s I could roam pretty widely with my friends, as long as we were back by dark. But over the next three decades, the media began delivering a metronomic diet of horrifying but rare child-abduction stories, and parents shortened the leash on their kids. Politicians warned of incipient waves of youth wilding and superpredators (neither of which emerged). Municipalities crafted anti-loitering laws and curfews to keep young people from congregating alone. New neighborhoods had fewer public spaces. Crime rates plum-   2

continued

meted, but moral panic soared. Meanwhile, increased competition to get into college meant well-off parents began heavily scheduling their kids' after-school lives.

The result, Boyd discovered, is that today's teens have neither the   3 time nor the freedom to hang out. So their avid migration to social media is a rational response to a crazy situation. They'd *rather* socialize F2F, so long as it's unstructured and away from grown-ups. "I don't care where," one told Boyd wistfully, "just not home." Forget the empathy problem — these kids crave seeing friends in person.

In fact, Boyd found that many high school students flock to foot-   4 ball games not because they like football but because they can meet in an unstructured context. They spend the game chatting, ignoring the field and their phones. You don't need Snapchat when your friends are right beside you.

So, parents of America: The problem is you; the solution is you. If   5 you want your kids to learn valuable face-to-face skills, conquer your own irrational fears and give them more freedom. They want the same face-to-face intimacy you grew up with. "Stranger danger" panic is the best gift America ever gave to Facebook.

DRAWING CONCLUSIONS

1. Who or what is the potential problem for teens who have lost the ability to socialize? Who or what is the real problem, in Thompson's opinion?

2. What do you believe is the assumption Thompson makes about parents in this article? Where do you find words that make Thompson's assumptions clear to the reader?

3. What example does Thompson give that indicates teens actually *do* want to socialize? What about this example speaks to the importance of face-to-face time?

Henry David Thoreau

Nothing Important to Communicate?

The first telegraph.

The telegraph, invented simultaneously in Europe and America in the first half of the 19th century, was perhaps the most significant innovation in communication to its date. One of its inventors, Samuel Morse, used the machine in 1838 to transmit a short message by means of coded electric charges across a 3-mile stretch in New Jersey and shocked the world. Within a few years, Morse's famous code was being used to send nearly instantaneous messages across continents and oceans, something people had only dreamt of for centuries. One modern writer, Tom Standage, has called the telegraph "the Victorian Internet," referring to the era in which it debuted, because of the revolution in communication this sudden connection brought about.

57

Like the modern Internet, though, telegraphy had its critics. Was it really such a good thing to be able to speak to someone thousands of miles away without moving a muscle (except perhaps a finger muscle or two), or thinking through a letter someone would have to hand deliver? Henry David Thoreau, an early critic of modernity, and particularly of its comforting but alienating technological advances, wrote of the electric telegraph's pitfalls in his famous wilderness contemplation, Walden. *In the excerpt that follows, Thoreau concentrates on the enthusiasm surrounding the instant international message, and suggests some of it may be misplaced. What, we ask, do we really have to say to each other? And might constant contact with everyone actually dilute it?*

As you read this brief excerpt, consider how Thoreau's arguments might apply to communication today, particularly social networking. What would Thoreau think of Facebook and Twitter? Would you agree with any of those contentions?

AMERICA THEN . . .

Our inventions are wont to be pretty toys, which distract our attention   1
from serious things. They are but improved means to an unimproved end, an end which it was already but too easy to arrive at; as railroads lead to Boston or New York. We are in great haste to construct a magnetic telegraph from Maine to Texas, but Maine and Texas, it may be, have nothing important to communicate. Either is in such a predicament as the man who was earnest to be introduced to a distinguished deaf woman, but when he was presented, and one end of her ear trumpet was put into his hand, had nothing to say. As if the main object were to talk fast and not to talk sensibly. We are eager to tunnel under the Atlantic and bring the Old World some weeks nearer to the new, but perchance the first news that will leak through into the broad, flapping American ear will be that the Princess Adelaide has the whooping cough. After all, the man whose horse trots a mile in a minute does not carry the most important messages.

BACKGROUND AND CONTEXT

1. Paraphrase, in your own words, the example of the man who "had nothing to say" to the distinguished deaf woman. What is Thoreau trying to express with this metaphor? Why is the "ear trumpet" an effective analogy for this predicament?

2. What does Thoreau mean by his example "Princess Adelaide has the whooping cough"? What sort of news is he talking about? What would an example of the modern equivalent be? Do you agree that this is the "first news" new communication technology is likely to carry us? Why or why not?

STRATEGY, STRUCTURE, AND STYLE

1. Characterize the way Thoreau makes his point. Does he proceed by logical argument or by illustrative example? Do you consider his means of advancing his argument effective? Why or why not?

2. What is the tone of the paragraph? Is it despairing, playful, comedic, or somewhere in between? Does Thoreau sound like he thinks technology will be the ruin of his society, or is he simply poking fun at it? What cues in this short excerpt let you in on Thoreau's complex state of mind about his subject?

COMPARISONS AND CONNECTIONS

1. Compare the way Thoreau offers examples of contemporary technology with the way Yzzy Gonzalez lists the technologies in her life (p. 50). Which one provides a more effective critique of the goods and ills expanded communication brings into our worlds?

2. Rewrite Thoreau's paragraph, sentence by sentence, for today's world. Whether or not you agree with his critique, try to apply it to your world. Provide fresh examples and analogies for the digital media age.

Discussing the Unit

SUGGESTED TOPIC FOR DISCUSSION

Social media and other forms of electronic communication allow us to connect with far more people — more frequently — than was possible in the past. Do texts, e-mails, and social media exchanges offer the potential of strengthening social bonds, or do electronic connections run more wide than deep? What is lost when e-exchanges replace phone or face-to-face conversations? Conversely, does communicating electronically offer any unique advantages?

PREPARING FOR CLASS DISCUSSION

1. In certain text-messaging and social media exchanges, people present edited versions of themselves — versions that while perhaps less flawed than the senders or posters really are also lack complexity and truth. In what situations might such discrepancies between a text or post and reality be especially problematic? Why?

2. The essays in this chapter focus on the impact of social networking on our schedules and our images of ourselves, but don't touch on one of the other major concerns critics have about social networks — their lack of privacy. Are you worried that you have less control over your privacy than you did before the advent of social networks? If so, why? If not, explain the concerns some people have about their privacy online and whether you think those concerns are overblown.

FROM DISCUSSION TO WRITING

1. Imagine a world without social networking: Twitter, Facebook, Snapchat, Instagram, and all the rest suddenly disappear tomorrow. What would happen? How would it affect your day-to-day life? Write a short description of what you think would happen — in your own life, and in the world at large.

2. Consider carefully Henry David Thoreau's attitude towards the telegraph. Why do you think he doesn't hail it as a triumph of technology? What does he appear concerned about? In a short essay, discuss how applicable his comments about this old technology are to today's social media?

TOPICS FOR CROSS-CULTURAL DISCUSSION

1. Many students today came of age with social media as a way of life; students of previous generations did not. Based on the essays from this chapter and on your own experiences and observations, how would you characterize this generation? How might you distinguish it from Americans older than forty, who grew up forming connections through face-to-face interactions, phone calls, and letters?

2. Beginning in 2010, crowd-sourced videos, Twitter feeds, and other social media kept the world up-to-date about the uprisings spreading through the Middle East and North Africa — and continue to do so today in conflicts and events throughout the world. As this development shows, social media allows people not only to build and maintain social connections but also to get the word out about important news developments, especially when traditional media can't, or won't, do so. Compared with traditional news coverage, what might be the benefits and drawbacks of news reports coming from "citizen journalists" using social media? Does social media have the potential to be a lasting and popular news source, not only overseas but also in the United States? Why or why not?

Language: Do Words Matter?

How do the words we use in everyday conversation matter? Does it make any difference if we say *girl* instead of *woman* or *colored people* instead of *people of color*? Do some words indicate a hostile attitude? Do some words inflict harm? In "'Bossy' Is More Than a Word to Women," the noted linguist and best-selling author Deborah Tannen examines a commonly used word often applied to women and defends a campaign being waged against the word by various organizations. Tannen points out that *bossy* "is not just a word but a frame of mind" and that it sends "girls and women the message that they'll be disliked — or worse — if they exercise authority."

Some words we use all the time can help defuse controversy and aid clarification. A "Spotlight on Research" feature by Arika Okrent takes a close look at a word that might not seem to be a word: *huh?* Recent linguistic studies have concluded that *huh* is not only a genuine word but also a "universal word," found in nearly every culture and language. As Okrent says, *huh?* also "has the added virtue of being nonthreatening." When words appear to be threatening, however, they can arouse intense controversy. Take the word *redskin*, which many American Indians (along with many Americans in general, President Obama among them) find hostile, insulting, and racist. That's why for decades there have been so many demands for the owners of the Washington Redskins to change the name of their football team. Recently, in an open letter published in the *Washington Post*, the team's current owner, Dan Snyder, defended the name of his franchise. Snyder had also told reporters in May 2013 that "We'll never change the name. It's that simple, NEVER—you can use caps." But as pressure continues to mount and many influential sports writers and commentators protest the name, it will be interesting to see if Snyder can maintain his position. This chapter's "In Brief" covers a range of "sound bites" on the controversy, as many noted sportswriters, Native Americans, athletes, and even the President have all expressed strong opinions. Weighing in on the issue a few years before it became overheated, Greg Nasif, then a University of Maryland history major, relies on humor to make some serious points about racist stereotypes. In "Washington, Yea! Redskins, Boo!" he examines many other team names and writes that *Redskins* isn't "cool, interesting, relevant, or competitive."

"How we name things matters," says the prominent essayist Scott Russell Sanders. In "Language Versus Lies," he reminds us of the powerful influence words exert on our lives, especially the words employed in advertising and politics: "Commerce appropriates and corrupts the language for everything we value, from adventure to zest, and it leads us to expect that all public uses of language will be dishonest and manipulative."

In "America Then," we look at another word with racist overtones: *black*. In his short classic dialogue essay, "That Word *Black*," the distinguished African American writer and poet Langston Hughes ponders the word *black* (an insulting term at a time when *Negro* was the preferred designation) and shows how it can be rescued from centuries of negative connotations.

Deborah Tannen

"Bossy" Is More Than a Word to Women

[*USA Today,* March 11, 2014]

BEFORE YOU READ

Do authority figures act differently based on their gender? How do you respond to women in authority? Would you respond differently if the same authority figure were a man?

WORDS TO LEARN

innumerable (para. 1): countless (adjective)

associated (para. 14): (past tense, uses *with*): connected (verb)

confidence (para. 14): belief in oneself (noun)

competence (para. 14): ability (noun)

aggressive (para. 14): forceful, often to the point of being hostile (adjective)

W hat do Sonia Sotomayor, Hillary Clinton and Sheryl Sand-   1
berg share with innumerable other prominent women? They've all been called bossy. And why, with all the important issues women deal with, should anyone pick a fight over a word, as Sandberg's *Lean In* team, together with the Girl Scouts[1], have just done?

The campaign, called "Ban Bossy" claims that the word holds women   2
back.

How can a word — especially a weak one like "bossy" — do that? It   3
isn't even as virulent as that other word that starts with "b," which is also hurled at women.

---

[1] Girl Scouts (para. 1): Founded in the early twentieth century, the Girl Scouts is an organization that endeavors to train girls to become leaders and upstanding citizens.

Deborah Tannen is a professor of linguistics at Georgetown University. She is the author of You Just Don't Understand: Women and Men in Conversation, *which was a number one* New York Times *best seller for eight months. She has written many books and articles on the subject of language and was a fellow at the Center for Advanced Study in the Behavioral Sciences following a term in residence at the Institute for Advanced Study in Princeton, New Jersey.*

WHAT'S IN A WORD?

Sotomayor and Clinton are Exhibit A for why the word matters: that others had called them bossy was used to argue they were ill-suited for the public offices they sought.   4

But the way this word can work against women in public life has roots that go deep — way back to the family and the playground.   5

When I wrote *You Just Don't Understand: Women and Men in Conversation*, I was struck that girls and women are so often called "bossy." Don't men tell others what to do just as often, if not more often? I encountered the same question when I wrote a book about sisters, *You Were Always Mom's Favorite!* Again and again, women told me that their oldest sister was bossy.   6

SANDBERG AN OLDEST SISTER

So I wasn't surprised to read in Sandberg's book — right up front — that she is an oldest sister. This family dynamic throws into relief the injustice of the label: Oldest sisters are put in the position of boss in relation to younger siblings, but when they behave as that position requires, they're resented for it — and called bossy.   7

Why does this happen to sisters more than brothers, and to prominent women but not prominent men?   8

Research on children at play holds a clue. Children tend to play with others of the same sex and learn to play, and talk, differently. Girls tend to use language to maintain and negotiate closeness — who's in, who's out? — by telling secrets and reassuring each other that they're the same, that no one thinks she's better than the others.   9

Boys tend to use language to negotiate their status in the group — who's up, who's down? — by taking center stage or by talking about who's best at what. If a boy tells other boys what to do and they listen, he's the leader. That's why boys are free to — no, they're expected to — say things such as "Gimme that!"   10

> A girl who tells other girls what to do is not liked, and girls who aren't liked are often locked out.

A girl who tells other girls what to do is not liked, and girls who aren't liked are often locked out. If boys aren't liked, they might be mistreated but are still allowed to play.   11

DIFFERENCE IN LANGUAGE

Given this risk of being locked out, girls have to find other ways to get their way, such as making suggestions starting with "let's." When girls and boys become women and men, those same ways of talking carry over into the workplace.   12

I once had high-ranking women and men record everything they 13
said for a week, then shadowed them and interviewed them and their
co-workers. I found that women in authority, more often than men in
similar positions, used language in ways that sounded a lot like what
researchers observed among girls at play. Instead of "do this," women
managers would say "let's . . ." or "what you could do," or soften the
impact by making their statements sound like questions.

In short, women at work are in a double bind: If they talk in these 14
ways, which are associated with and expected of women, they seem to
lack confidence, or even competence. But if they talk in ways expected of
someone in authority, they are seen as too aggressive.

That's why "bossy" is not just a word but a frame of mind. Let's 15
agree to stop sending girls and women the message that they'll be
disliked — or worse — if they exercise authority.

Wait. I'll put that differently: Think twice before calling a woman at 16
work, a girl on the playground — or your oldest sister — bossy.

VOCABULARY/USING A DICTIONARY

1. Does the word *virulent* (para. 3) have a positive or negative connotation?
   What does it mean? How might you guess its meaning from similar words?
2. What part of speech is the word *prominent* (para. 8), and what does it mean?
3. How does one *negotiate* (para. 9) something? What part of speech is the
   word negotiate?

RESPONDING TO WORDS IN CONTEXT

1. "To throw something into *relief*" (para. 7) is an idiom. What do you think the
   idiom means, based on context? What are the other definitions of the word
   relief?
2. You may have heard the word *status* (para. 10) used before — as a noun
   meaning "condition," as in "a Facebook status." Here it is used differently:
   "Boys tend to use language to negotiate their *status* in the group." How does
   Tannen use the word *status*?
3. Have you ever heard the phrase *double bind* (para. 14)? Do you know what it
   means? What clues are given in this context?

DISCUSSING MAIN POINT AND MEANING

1. According to Tannen, where do women and men start learning the "rules"
   about how they should or should not behave with others? Are the "rules" the
   same for men and women?
2. What problem does Tannen identify about women and how they conduct
   themselves as authority figures?
3. How does Tannen show that "'bossy' is not just a word but a frame of
   mind"?

EXAMINING SENTENCES, PARAGRAPHS, AND ORGANIZATION

1. Tannen opens with the sentences: "What do Sonia Sotomayor, Hillary Clinton and Sheryl Sandberg share with innumerable other prominent women? They've all been called bossy." How does this opening hint at Tannen's concerns in this essay?

2. Consider the sentence "That's why boys are free to — no, they're expected to — say things such as 'Gimme that!'" (para. 10). What does she accomplish with the structure of this sentence?

3. How does Tannen's conclusion both reflect the point of her essay and state her position on how women in authority should act?

THINKING CRITICALLY

1. If someone is "bossy," how does he or she act? What are the positives and negatives associated with being "bossy"?

2. Why might boys and girls receive different messages in childhood about what's okay and what's not in terms of their behavior with others? Do you think these perceptions are inherent to boys and girls, or are they learned attitudes?

3. How does Tannen establish herself in the body of the essay as a woman "in authority"? Is establishing that fact important to the essay?

WRITING ACTIVITIES

1. Have you ever been called bossy? Have you ever been called a leader? Write a short personal essay that describes the situation and explores your feelings about what you were called. Introduce ideas about how your gender might have influenced how others perceived you (you are welcome to refer to the Tannen essay in your paper).

2. Research Sonia Sotomayor, Hillary Clinton, and Sheryl Sandberg. What are their accomplishments? In a brief essay, summarize their achievements. Based on what you've read, write about how they interacted with others in their careers or personal lives. Do they appear to be strong authority figures? Did they ever present themselves in ways that would make them seem less bossy, or did they embrace the idea of being seen as domineering?

3. In a freewriting exercise, choose a public figure or celebrity you admire, male or female. What traits do you like about this person? What is his or her personality like? How does he or she interact with others? Write as much as you possibly can; then, go back and chart the information you've gathered into a "positive" or "negative" column. For every positive or negative attribute, consider how that attribute might be interpreted in a different light.

Spotlight on Research

Arika Okrent

Everybody in Almost Every Language Says "Huh"? HUH?!

[*Smithsonian Magazine*, March 2014]

Arika Okrent is a linguist with a PhD in psycholinguistics from the University of Chicago. She has written several books on the topic, including In the Land of Invented Languages: Esperanto Rock Stars, Klingon Poets, Loglan Lovers, and the Mad Dreamers Who Tried to Build a Perfect Language. *Okrent was featured in the 2011 documentary* The Universal Language.

Listen to one end of a phone conversation, and you'll probably hear a rattle   1
of *ah's, um's* and *mm-hm's*. Our speech is brimming with these fillers, yet linguistic researchers haven't paid much attention to them until now. New research by Mark Dingemanse and colleagues at the Max Planck Institute for Psycholinguistics, in Nijmegen, the Netherlands, has uncovered a surprisingly important role for an interjection long dismissed as one of language's second-class citizens: the humble *huh?*, a sort of voiced question mark slipped in when you don't understand something. In fact, they've found, *huh?* is a "universal word," the first studied by modern linguists.

Dingemanse's team analyzed recordings of people speaking ten differ-   2
ent languages, including Spanish, Chinese and Icelandic, as well as indigenous languages from Ecuador, Australia and Ghana. Not only did all of the languages have a word intended to initiate a quick clarification, but its form always resembled *huh?* The utterance, they argue, isn't a mere grunt of stupefaction but a remarkable linguistic invention.

In each of the languages investigated, the vowel is produced with a rela-   3
tively relaxed tongue (never a vowel that requires you to lift your tongue, like "ee," or pull the tongue back, like "oo"). And if any sound comes before the vowel, it is either an "h" sound or what's called a glottal stop, a consonant sound formed by a complete closure of the glottis, the thin space between the vocal folds. (You use a glottal stop between the two parts of "uh oh" or the two syllables of "better," if you say it with an extreme cockney accent.)

It's not unusual, of course, for languages to have words or sounds in com-   4
mon: The English "number" and Spanish *numero*, for instance, share a Latin ancestor. And languages may adopt words from other languages (which is how words such as the slang OK spread widely). But it's a basic linguistic principle that when there is no shared origin or word swapping, the word for a given thing will be arbitrarily different in different languages: So there's "house" in English, *maison* (French), *fángzi* (Chinese) and *huan* (Lao).

Huh? appears to be anything but arbitrary. Dingemanse's team has   5
already confirmed the similarities with speech transcripts from 21 additional

continued

languages, many of them unrelated. Are the researchers sure that *huh?* will turn up in every language in the world? "No," Dingemanse says. "But we are ready to place bets."

What makes *huh* a word — and not, alternatively, the equivalent of a yelp? A laugh, cry or growl, however meaningful, isn't considered language; even a dog communicates sadness with a whimper. A true word is learned, and follows certain linguistic rules, depending on the language spoken. *Huh?* fits this definition: For one thing, *huh* has no counterpart in the animal kingdom; for another, unlike innate vocalizations, children don't use it until they start speaking. Moreover, in Russian, which doesn't have an "h" sound, *huh?* sounds more like *ah?* In languages using a falling intonation for questions, like Icelandic, *huh?* also falls. All in all, Dingemanse concludes that *huh?* is a bona fide word with a specific purpose "crucial to our everyday language."   6

But why would *huh?* sound similar in every language? To explain that, Dingemanse draws on evolutionary theory, saying the word is the result of "selective pressures in its conversational environment." In a sense, *huh?* is such a highly efficient utterance for serving its particular narrow function that it has emerged in different languages independently again and again — what's known as convergent evolution, or the appearance of a feature in different, often unrelated organisms presumably because it works so well. Sharks and dolphins, Dingemanse says, "arrived at the same body plan not because they share certain genes, but because they share an environment."   7

The dynamic, often fraught environment of human conversation, in which grave misunderstanding or a hurt feeling or an embarrassing gaffe is never more than a syllable away, calls for a word that instantly signals a need for clarification, is as brief as possible and is easy to produce, without complicated tongue coordination or lip movement. Without much planning — no searching one's memory for the "right" word — a listener can interject a sleek, streamlined, wonderfully unambiguous word to keep the dialogue going. *Huh?*   8

Other interjections probably play a similar role, greasing the wheels of conversation, and they too may turn out to be universal. We won't know for sure until linguists take a listen.   9

What we do know is that *huh?* has a rightful place in dialogue. And it has the added virtue of being nonthreatening. In that sense it definitely beats *what?*   10

DRAWING CONCLUSIONS

1. How are interjections different from other parts of speech? Why might they lend themselves to being more universal?

2. In what ways do different sounds/words "grease the wheels" of conversation? Why is such "grease" needed?

3. How is the evolution of *huh?* similar to the evolution of certain features of sharks and dolphins? Does such a theory make sense to you?

Sound Bites: What's in a Name?

Native American images and logos have long been a part of the cultural history of the United States: a profile of an American Indian began appearing on the U.S. penny in 1859 and tobacco stores often featured a carved wooden statue of what became known as a "cigar store Indian" to attract customers. In 1912 the Boston baseball team named themselves the "Braves" (now in Atlanta) and three years later the Cleveland team began calling themselves the "Indians." The current Washington football team which dates back to 1932 was soon after its founding renamed the "Boston Redskins."

The controversy over the name is not new but has been alive for decades and every now and then is re-ignited by a comment, demonstration, or newsworthy event. Sparking the current heated controversy was mainly the Washington team owner's categorical statement that he would never change the name. This prompted many media outlets to weigh in and that led to a national debate on whether the word "Redskins" was a racial slur or an innocent label. A great deal of the debate was fueled by leading sports personalities. In October 2013, during a nationally televised game between the Redskins and Dallas Cowboys (one of the biggest rivalries in sports as their names indicate), NBC commentator Bob Costas called the word "an insult, a slur, no matter how benign the present day intent." On the other side of the issue, former player, coach and now ESPN commentator Mike Ditka a few months earlier defended the name, calling the debate over it "so stupid it's appalling." His position was backed up by former vice-presidential candidate and news personality, Sarah Palin.

As you'll see below in our assorted "sound bites," a number of people — despite what the team's owner declares — think the change of name is inevitable, that eventually enough political, economic, and social pressure will be put on the franchise so that a new name will be found. A large number of media outlets have stated that they will no longer use the word in print and on their broadcasts. The team also faces legal pressure from the government's trademark office which decided the word was "disparaging" to Native Americans and therefore no longer eligible for trademark registration and protection. As you read the comments below, consider your position: do you think the name should be changed? If not, why not? And if you do, what name would you change it to?

"The owners of professional sports franchises like the Cleveland Indians, the Atlanta Braves and the Washington Redskins continue to disrespect the heritage of Native American people with mascots and logos that insultingly portray aspects of our culture as a cheap cartoon — and nothing more."

— Ray Halbritter, Oneida Nation Representative
(*Daily News*, February 22, 2013)

"If Halbritter has a problem with the Redskins, he's got more problems than that in D.C. Among this city's great monuments is the memorial to Jefferson whose Declaration of Independence speaks of those 'merciless Indian Savages, whose known rule of warfare, is an undistinguished destruction, of all ages, sexes and conditions.'"

— Pat Buchanan
(*WND*, October 21, 2013)

"If I were the owner of the team and I knew that there was a name of my team — even if it had a storied history — that was offending a sizeable group of people, I'd think about changing it."

— President Barack Obama
(in an interview published by the
Associated Press, October 5, 2013)

"We'll never change the name. It's that simple. NEVER — you can use caps."

— Dan Snyder, owner of the Washington football
team since 1999, to reporters in May 2013
(*USA Today*, May 10, 2013)

"Cool down, Dan. It is not that big a deal as long as you find a good name to replace the old one. I'd even prefer that you keep the Native American reference since this area of the country was home to several tribes. So here are my suggestions for new names: 'Tribe'; 'Nation'; 'Rebels'; 'Potomacs' and 'Native Americans.'"

— Author and news commentator Juan Williams
(*FoxNews.com*, October 13, 2013)

"The Redskins name will change sooner than you think — two or three years, tops."

— Sports columnist Chris Chase
(*USA Today*, October 8, 2013)

"Off in the distance the wheels of change are grinding. You may not be able to hear them yet. But it's only a matter of time until 'Redskins' is gone."

— Sports columnist Tony Kornheiser,
(*The Washington Post*, March 5, 1992)

"Non-Natives may never quite understand how deep the term 'red-skins' cuts into ancient wounds that have never quite healed, and maybe it's not reasonable to expect them to. But every time Dan Snyder refuses to change his NFL team's name, even with tribes paying for powerful ads in opposition. . . Snyder plunges a long, twisted blade into our hearts."

— Baxter Holmes
(*Esquire.com,* June 17, 2014)

"This page has for many years urged the local football team to change its name. . . . But the matter seems clearer to us now than ever, and while we wait for the National Football League to catch up with thoughtful opinion and common decency, we have decided that, except when it is essential for clarity or effect, we will no longer use the slur ourselves. That's the standard we apply to all offensive vocabulary. . . ."

— *The Washington Post* Editorial Board
(May 22, 2014)

"No one picks a team name as a means of disparagement. San Francisco didn't choose the name '49ers' because it wanted to mock the foolish desperation of people panning for gold in the mid-19th century. . . . Team nicknames and logos invariably denote fierceness and strength, which in the context of the NFL are very good things."

— Rich Lowry
(*National Review Online,* October 8, 2013)

"It's been the name of the team since the beginning of football. It has nothing to do with something that happened lately, or something that somebody dreamed up. This was the name, period. Leave it alone. These people are silly — asinine, actually, in my opinion."
— Former football star, coach and ESPN commentator, Mike Ditka
(in an interview cited in the *Washington Post,* August 19, 2014)

"When you hear a Native American say that 'Redskins' is degrading, it's almost like the N-word for a black person. . . . If they feel that way, then it's not right. They are part of this country. It's degrading to a certain race. Does it make sense to have the name?'"

— Champ Bailey, retired football star
and former Washington Redskins player
(*USA Today Sports,* June 11, 2014)

Greg Nasif (student essay)

Washington, Yea! Redskins, Boo!

[*The Diamondback*, the University of Maryland, October 13, 2011]

BEFORE YOU READ

Have you thought about the racial implications behind sports team names like the Redskins, Indians, or Chiefs? What do you think these names are trying to convey? Do you think they are appropriate for professional sports teams? Why or why not?

WORDS TO LEARN

monikers (para. 2): names (noun)

T o all of my friends among the Washington Redskins faithful, I   1
wish to convey my congratulations that your team is not God-
awful this year. But I'm going to ruin your day by asking: Seriously, what the hell is a Redskin?

Sports nicknames generally convey certain qualities — creativity, rel-   2
evance, competitiveness, ferocity, mystique — and many other things that
don't describe a Redskin. That name isn't
remotely relevant, there's no mystique, and

> The ferocity is based on an ancient stereotype.

the ferocity is based on an ancient stereotype. Society has moved on from promoting teams with racist monikers (81 percent
of Native Americans are unoffended by
their patronage in sports). But the Redskins
have found innovative ways to be profoundly racist. They refused to inte-
grate their team until buckling to federal pressure to do so in 1962.

Meanwhile, other teams that use Native American mascots tend to   3
narrow their identification. The Atlanta Braves (the Redskins' original
nickname until they presumably determined it wasn't racist enough)
use the term for a Native American warrior, which also happens to be
a synonym for courage. The Florida State Seminoles represent a specific cultural aspect of Florida's history. The Kansas City Chiefs repre-

---

Greg Nasif graduated in 2012 from the University of Maryland, where he majored in U.S. history, with a minor in astronomy.

sent leadership, and are also a nod to a former mayor who helped spread awareness of Native American culture in the Boy Scouts. There's your example of mystique.

Let's look at some other teams with outstanding names, beginning   4
with my hometown favorite, the New England Patriots. Our nation's fight for independence began in Massachusetts; the term "patriot" is synonymous with the region, and it's easy to rally behind. If you disagree, you can go live in Russia. And who can forget the Patriots winning their first Super Bowl just months after the September 11 attacks, when Patriots' owner Robert Kraft held the Lombardi Trophy high and said, "We are all Patriots, and tonight, the Patriots are world champions!" Perfect.

What else is out there? The Dallas Cowboys have a good image going.   5
Cowboys are associated with fearlessness, boldness, and adventure. They are also historically linked to Texas. Well done. The name "Forty-niners" is a reference to the Gold Rush of 1849. It's an interesting choice, but I give more credit to the Pittsburgh Steelers, a nod to the industry that built their city. Steel also implies toughness, endurance . . . do I need to continue? It's steel.

As for the San Diego Chargers . . . charge up, bro! It's a weird pick,   6
but it works for the surfer bros. The Baltimore Ravens are named for Edgar Allan Poe's poem "The Raven," as Poe lived in Baltimore for some time and is buried there. So that nickname is relevant, and the raven is a fierce creature. I also appreciate how they've incorporated the Maryland flag into their symbol. Still, they named a football team after a poem.

I'm generally not much a fan of using ferocious animals as mascots.   7
When St. Louis fans call their team the Rams, I remind them they are, in fact, humans. However, I give credit to Chicago for matching two of their teams (Bears and Cubs).

As a Super Bowl XLII attendant, I will always resent the Giants for   8
robbing my Patriots of a perfect 19–0 season. But I respect their name choice, a reference to a city that's larger than life. (Go to hell, Giants fans.)

A lot goes into naming a football team, and most of the sports teams   9
I've mentioned did a pretty good job picking their mascots. But Redskins, your team didn't. It's not cool, interesting, relevant, or competitive. Washington is our nation's capital, named for a man who led an unorganized military to victory over a much more powerful enemy, a general who could bloodlessly have become George I of the Kingdom of America, but chose instead to relinquish his power to the people.

I could write thirty of these columns about George Washington's   10
epic awesomeness. Our nation's capital is named for the man even King George III of England begrudgingly acknowledged as "the greatest man

who ever lived." Yet all the city's proud football team reminds us is that our nation was built upon stolen land and broken promises.

Good luck with the remainder of the season, Redskins fans. Just 11 know that for every generation its finest hour comes from breaking the cherished traditions of the past.

VOCABULARY/USING A DICTIONARY

1. Define the word *mystique* (para. 2).
2. What does the word *patriot* (para. 4) mean and what are the origins of the word?
3. Define *forty-niner* (para. 5).

RESPONDING TO WORDS IN CONTEXT

1. In the sentence, "It's a weird pick, but it works for the surfer bros" (para. 6), what kinds of connotations does the word *bros* have?
2. Nasif writes, "Our nation's capital is named for the man even King George III of England begrudgingly acknowledged as 'the greatest man who ever lived'" (para. 10). What does *begrudgingly* mean here?
3. When Nasif says, "The Dallas Cowboys have a good image going" in paragraph 5, what does he mean by *image*?

DISCUSSING MAIN POINT AND MEANING

1. What is Nasif's overall argument in this essay? Is his point clear? Why or why not?
2. What are Nasif's reasons for believing team names like Braves, Seminoles, and Chiefs are acceptable, but Redskins is not?
3. What are the author's thoughts on the Baltimore Ravens' team name?

EXAMINING SENTENCES, PARAGRAPHS, AND ORGANIZATION

1. What is the purpose of introducing George Washington and the history of Washington, D.C., in the second-to-last paragraph?
2. How are the essay's paragraphs arranged and formed? What would you say is the organizing principle? Do you think the organization is clear and focused?
3. Describe the tone of this essay. Is it appropriate to the subject matter? Why or why not?

THINKING CRITICALLY

1. In paragraph 10, Nasif states, "Yet all the city's proud football team reminds us is that our nation was built upon stolen land and broken promises." Do you believe this is what the Redskins' name represents? Why or why not? How does this statement compare to the statements Nasif made earlier regarding Washington's choice of name?

2. What bias does Nasif admit to in the essay, and how might that affect his analysis of team names? Do you think this bias is appropriate or acceptable in this essay? Why or why not?
3. Look back at the teams that Nasif determines have "outstanding names." Do you agree with his assessment of the team names? Explain why or why not.

WRITING ACTIVITIES

1. Consider Nasif's tone and use of humor in this essay. In your opinion, do they help or hurt his argument? Can a lighthearted tone ever successfully explain a serious topic? Why or why not?
2. Using Nasif's essay as a guide, write an essay that is in the form of an open letter to a group of people and makes an argument you think that group needs to hear. Use specific examples to support your argument.
3. In a short essay, take the opposite position of Nasif, and defend the use of the name Redskins. Even if you don't believe in it, think of ways to counter Nasif's claims and support the opposite argument.

LOOKING CLOSELY

Using Examples

In any discussion or debate, nothing is more persuasive than well-chosen examples. We often use examples to back up a generalization with concrete instances or to support a claim. The examples *show* what we mean. We can easily see the effective use of appropriate examples in "Washington, Yea! Redskins, Boo!" an essay by University of Maryland student Greg Nasif. Arguing that the name "Redskins" is stereotypical and inappropriate, Nasif assembles numerous examples of other sports teams to establish his point. Note that he isn't critical of all team names but cites those he feels are relevant to the team's image in one way or another.

1
A football team name that is relevant

Let's look at some other teams with outstanding names, beginning with my hometown favorite, the New England Patriots. Our nation's fight for independence began in Massachusetts; the term "patriot" is synonymous with the region, and it's easy to rally behind. (1) If you disagree, you can go live in Russia. And who can forget the Patriots winning their first Super Bowl just months after the September 11 attacks, when Patriots' owner Robert Kraft

held the Lombardi Trophy high and said, "We are all Patriots, and tonight, the Patriots are world champions!" Perfect.

What else is out there? The Dallas Cowboys have a good image going. Cowboys are associated with fearlessness, boldness, and adventure. They are also historically linked to Texas. Well done. The name "Forty-niners" is a reference to the Gold Rush of 1849. It's an interesting choice, but I give more credit to the Pittsburgh Steelers, a nod to the industry that built their city. Steel also implies toughness, endurance . . . do I need to continue? It's steel. (2)

2
Strengthens his point by adding three more examples of relevant names

STUDENT WRITER AT WORK

Greg Nasif

Courtesy of Greg Nasif

R.A. What inspired you to write this essay? And publish it in your campus paper?

G.N. I love football, and many of my friends are Redskins fans. I enjoy stirring the pot, but I don't always enjoy being too serious about it; I saw this as an opportunity to combine humor, wit, and a dash of politics. The common evaluation of all the team names was the cream of the crop. To me, it was the kind of thing that would undoubtedly hook a reader in and keep them coming back. It's also something I think about frequently. How does a city take pride in itself? How does it manifest itself? Sports are a major part of that, perhaps the purest way a city identifies itself relative to other American cities, and I wanted to explore that.

R.A. What response have you received to this piece? Has the feedback you have received affected your views on the topic you wrote about?

G.N. Many of my friends didn't talk to me about it, which amused me. The comments appeared mixed; many people attacked me, many attacked my points, a few seemed to agree but express indifference, some even suggested their own new team names. The only thing you could say about the response was that it was voluminous: I started a conversation, and I'm very satisfied with that.

R.A. How long did it take for you to write this piece? Did you revise your work? What were your goals as you revised?

G.N. I was planning this column longer than most any other I had ever written — for over 6 months. I thought of it last spring but never thought of a time to print it. I finally saw my opportunity with the Redskins' early success last season. Initially I drafted the major points and comparisons, I cut many of them, and finally wrote the actual column in the two weeks before it ran. I generally brainstorm, outline, write, rewrite, edit with the ruthlessness of Attila the Hun, submit, request to change my submission, then remark to myself how shamefully little I edited.

R.A. Do you generally show your writing to friends before submitting it? Do you collaborate or bounce your ideas off others?

G.N. This is one topic I spoke about with many people, mostly friends. I had many discussions like the main comparisons in this piece, where I evaluated mascots and team names from each city. In terms of my writing, I generally find other people just want to tell me how to write in their own way and I don't often seek their discretion. However, I do have my dad review my articles, and I would say I take 20 percent of his suggestions.

R.A. What advice do you have for other student writers?

G.N. Write. Write even if no one will read it. Keep a journal. Write down every-thing that makes you laugh or cry. Realize that 90 percent of what you write might never be read by anyone but you. But it only takes one reader for it to matter, even if it is only you.

Also, brainstorm and outline. You'd be surprised how much better your writing is if you stack like phrases together and morph them into one stron-ger point. Think of your points like rain clouds: They are much stronger with a much richer center if they are bunched up as opposed to if they are scattered about. Better than making a light drizzle on a thousand people is just making it pour on twenty people. I'm talking buckets. Just make it rain and don't stop.

Scott Russell Sanders

Language Versus Lies

[*The Progressive*, December 2012/January 2013]

BEFORE YOU READ

Do you ever stop to consider the words spoken by politicians, the media, and advertisers? Do they speak and write honestly? Is it possible to speak and write honestly all the time?

WORDS TO LEARN

merchandising (para. 3): the preparation to sell items through advertising (noun)

disposable (para. 3): able to be thrown away (adjective)

imply (para. 3): to indicate or suggest (verb)

nuisance (para. 3): something or someone annoying (noun)

frenzied (para. 4): wild or frantic (adjective)

exaggerate (para. 4): to overstate (verb)

logo (para. 4): a graphic representation of a brand

onslaught (para. 4): onset or violent attack (noun)

drone (para. 4): hum (verb)

Scott Russell Sanders is an essayist and the author of twenty fiction and nonfic-tion books. He is a contributing editor to Audubon *magazine and won the John Burroughs Nature Essay Award in 2000. He has been awarded the Lannan Literary Award, the Mark Twain Award, and the Cecil Woods Award for Nonfiction, among others. He received his PhD from Cambridge University in 1971.*

barrage (para. 5): an overwhelming quantity (noun)

monopolize (para. 5): to keep entirely to oneself (verb)

appropriate (para. 5): to take possession of (verb)

manipulative (para. 5): controlling and using to one's advantage (adjective)

cynical (para. 6): distrusting or disparaging (adjective)

cataclysmic (para. 7): pertaining to violent upheaval (adjective)

sordid (para. 9): dirty (adjective)

chicanery (para. 9): trickery (noun)

flimflam (para. 9): deception (noun)

concisely (para. 10): succinctly (adverb)

candid (para. 10): sincere (adjective)

slovenly (para. 10): untidy (adjective)

obliteration (para. 11): the act of total destruction (noun)

inure (para. 14): to become accustomed or habituated to (verb)

immersion (para. 14): absorption (noun)

candor (para. 15): state of openness (noun)

elimination (para. 17): removal of (noun)

gargantuan (para. 19): enormous (adjective)

advocate (para. 20): to support (verb)

charlatan (para. 21): a quack (noun)

O n a trip to the grocery store with my mother soon after I learned to read, I noticed bottles of dishwashing soap called Joy. The name evoked the feeling I had when romping with a puppy or rolling down a grassy hill. I did not see how that feeling could be put in a bottle, as if it were orange juice or milk. When I asked my mother why the soap was named Joy, she replied, "To make you want to buy it, dear." 1

This may have been the first time I grasped that words can be used to deceive as well as to convey something true about the world. Since then, merchants and advertisers have reinforced the lesson for me time and again, right up to this morning, when I bicycled past a billboard that showed a frosty bottle of Coca-Cola alongside the slogan "Open Happiness." 2

We all know that merchandizing is designed to seduce us by linking something we value (joy, sex, health, adventure, power, status, comfort, family) with something for sale (soap, soda, cars, cell phones, insurance, medicine, video games, credit cards). The links may be verbal, visual, or both. Disposable diapers are marketed as Luv. Coal is promoted as green energy. Agricultural poisons hide behind trade names such as Harmony, Liberty, Prosper, and Prestige. Bloated SUVs, bearing names such as Expedition and Yukon, are presented in ads against a backdrop of mountains, even though most of their miles (typically fifteen per gallon) will be spent hauling kids, commuters, and groceries around town. The names and photos imply that by cruising in a three-ton automobile you can be Lewis, Clark, or Sacajawea[1], without the nuisance of mosquitoes, grizzly bears, or sweat. 3

These tricks are childishly simple, of course, yet they fool enough people enough of the time to drive our frenzied consumerism, thereby justifying the billions of dollars spent annually on advertising. It is difficult to exaggerate the pervasiveness of sales pitches. We are assaulted by ads through television, radio, websites, catalogs, billboards, spam, product placement in films, brand names on the garments of passersby, motel card keys, signs on the roofs of taxis and the sides of buses, loudspeakers at gas pumps, and virtually every other visible, audible, or legible medium. Recently, merchants have begun paying people to wear logos on their foreheads as temporary tattoos. On the beach of an island where I was building a sandcastle with my granddaughters last summer — safely distant, I imagined, from the commercial onslaught — we were forced to listen hour upon hour to the drone of airplanes dragging banners overhead hawking movies and liquor.   4

The barrage of ads aims to stir in us a constant craving, and to persuade us that we can satisfy our craving by spending money. So much is obvious. But ubiquitous merchandising affects more than our buying habits. It monopolizes our attention. It trains us to think of ourselves as consumers, defined by our purchases and possessions, rather than as citizens, defined by our membership in communities. It distracts us from genuine sources of happiness, many of which are not for sale, such as nature, storytelling, evening strolls, and service to our neighbors. Worst of all, commerce appropriates and corrupts the language for everything we value, from adventure to zest, and it leads us to expect that all public uses of language will be dishonest and manipulative.   5

> The barrage of ads aims to stir in us a constant craving

Made cynical by the lies of merchants, we are more likely to shrug at the lies of politicians, generals, pundits, televangelists, and propagandists.   6

The link between the deceptions of advertising and those of public life first became evident to me in the 1950s, when the cataclysmic power that destroyed Hiroshima and Nagasaki[2] was touted as the "peaceful atom," and when racial segregation in the South was defended in the name of "states' rights."   7

---

[1] Lewis, Clark, Sacajawea (para. 3): Sacajawea was the Native American woman who led the Lewis and Clark expedition through the western United States after the Louisiana Purchase

[2] Hiroshima and Nagasaki (para. 7): Two Japanese cities on which the United States used atomic weapons in the final stages of World War II

Covering up ugly realities with pretty words is a practice as old, I   8
suspect, as human speech. The ancient Greeks had a name for it, *euphe-*
mismos, which has come into English as *euphemism*, meaning a word of
good omen, a word that masks the stark truth.

There is a long, sordid history of such verbal chicanery in America: 9
Slavery was justified as an effort to "civilize savages"; the uprooting and
massacre of indigenous people was declared to be the work of "Manifest
Destiny"; Jim Crow[3] laws pretended to guarantee "separate but equal"
status for African Americans. From the beginnings of union organizing in
the nineteenth century, workers agitating for a living wage and safer conditions have been denounced as communists, socialists, or anarchists;
the prisons holding Japanese Americans during World War II were called
"Relocation Centers" or "Citizen Isolation Centers"; during the Vietnam
War, the slaughter of civilians under U.S. bombs was described as "col-
lateral damage," a bit of flimflam still in use today by military apologists.

George Orwell warned of such distortions, most famously in *1984*   10
with its lexicon of "Newspeak," and more concisely in "Politics and the
English Language," an essay published in the immediate aftermath of
World War II. The essay opens by arguing that "the slovenliness of our
language makes it easier for us to have foolish thoughts," and that the
careful, candid use of language "is a necessary first step towards political regeneration." More troubling than slovenly language, the essay
goes on to say, is language cleverly "designed to make lies sound truthful and murder respectable, and to give an appearance of solidity to
pure wind."

In Orwell's day, genocide was disguised as "the final solution," as it   11
has been disguised as "ethnic cleansing" in our day. The deliberate burning of Dresden[4] and other cities through concentrated aerial attacks was
labeled "area bombing" by the British and "precision bombing" by the
Americans. The latter phrase, implying that the obliteration of human
works and human beings is a technological achievement, continues to be
favored by Pentagon spokesmen and TV anchors.

How we name things matters, as merchants and manufacturers rec-   12
ognize. It matters all the more in politics, where labels and slogans often
have life or death consequences.

The second Bush Administration initially referred to 9/11 as a   13
crime, which would have made it a matter for the police and FBI. But

---

[3] Jim Crow (para. 9): Refers to laws of racial segregation put into place in the
    American South following the Civil War

[4] Dresden (para. 11): German city bombed in 1945 by Allied Forces

soon the script changed, and officials were calling it an act of war, which made it a matter for the Pentagon. The 2001 invasion of Afghanistan, code-named "Operation Enduring Freedom," and the 2003 invasion of Iraq, code-named "Operation Iraqi Freedom," duly followed. Soon torture became "enhanced interrogation." The handing over of prisoners to thuggish regimes became "extraordinary rendition." Suspects targeted by the U.S. for assassination, without criminal charges or trial, became "unlawful combatants," a ruse designed to exclude them from protection under the Geneva Conventions[5]. The mental ravaging suffered by soldiers — bluntly called "shell shock" during World War I — became "post-traumatic stress disorder," a bland term often further reduced to an acronym, PTSD, which obscures the origins of these wounds.

War, torture, and assassination have been sold to the American   14
people with the same methods used in marketing any new product, and with as little regard for the truth. It may seem a stretch to compare the deceptive naming of torture with the deceptive naming of herbicide, or to compare the claim that war will bring freedom with the claim that a soft drink will bring happiness. While the stakes may be different in politics and commerce, however, the rhetorical moves are the same, and the dishonesty of one inures us to the dishonesty of the other. Instead of making us more resistant to such manipulation, our immersion in advertising has made us numb to it.

Since there appears to be no limit to the spread of commerce, and   15
no likelihood that apologists for immoral acts will suddenly be seized by candor, what can we do? We can examine every slogan and label critically, those we use ourselves as well as those we encounter in the public arena. We can challenge euphemisms. We can insist that torture is torture, murder is murder, poison is poison. We can expose verbal tricks. We can defend the names of things we value from those who would corrupt them.

We can maintain, for example, that corporations are legal constructs,   16
not persons, and therefore not entitled to the rights of human beings, regardless of what a slender majority on the Supreme Court might argue.

We can explain that "outsourcing" means the elimination of jobs in   17
one place by moving them to another place, usually abroad, where labor is cheaper and safeguards for workers and nature are weaker.

---

[5] The Geneva Conventions (para. 13): Treatises that establish international law for the humanitarian treatment of armed forces, medical personnel, prisoners, and civilians during a time of war

We can show that what the coal industry calls "mountaintop removal 18 mining" is really mountain devastation mining, because the forests, animals, topsoil, and stone blasted from the peaks and dumped into waterways are not simply "removed," as a hat or the lid of a pot might be, but are permanently shattered, fouling streams, destroying habitats, and erasing beauty.

We can explain that "death taxes" are not levied on the dead, who 19 have passed beyond reach of the IRS, but on the heirs, who did nothing to earn the money; and they are levied, moreover, only on a tiny fraction of estates, the gargantuan ones, which typically accumulate tax-free in shelters available only to the superrich.

We can observe that abortion opponents who advocate the "right to 20 life" of fetuses rarely show equal concern for the needs of the resulting children, let alone for the fate of the millions of species that are being driven to extinction by the relentless growth of human population.

There is no shortage of "pure wind" blowing through legislatures, 21 courtrooms, the studios of talk shows, or the briefing rooms of corporate and military apologists. But we need not give in to lies. We need not surrender language, the greatest of all our common creations, to charlatans. We can defend the things we love, and language itself, by striving to speak and write clearly, accurately, and honestly.

VOCABULARY/USING A DICTIONARY

1. What does *reinforced* (para. 2) mean? What can you tell about it if you break it down into its various parts?
2. What is a *slogan* (para. 2)? What *slogan* can you point to in this essay?
3. If people are *agitating* (para. 9) for something, what are they doing?

RESPONDING TO WORDS IN CONTEXT

1. Sanders writes, "This may have been the first time I grasped that words can be used to *deceive* as well as to *convey* something . . ." (para. 2). What do these words mean? Are they opposites?
2. What does Sanders mean by a *visual, audible,* or *legible medium* (para. 4)?
3. What is an *acronym* (para. 13)? What acronym is mentioned in this essay?

DISCUSSING MAIN POINT AND MEANING

1. In the essay, which examples are given of language that has been subverted from its true meaning?
2. How do the news media and politicians manipulate language? Why do they do this?

3. Does Sanders feel we are at the mercy of lies in our language? Explain your answer using evidence from the essay.

EXAMINING SENTENCES, PARAGRAPHS, AND ORGANIZATION

1. How does Sanders begin the essay? How does he end it? Explain how the author gets from his original to his final subject.
2. What does the inclusion of George Orwell's essay add to this argument? Why is it important?
3. The essay begins as a personal essay, but it does not end as one. What are the benefits of beginning this way? Are there drawbacks?

THINKING CRITICALLY

1. What is the origin of the word *euphemism*? Are the words *euphemism* and *verbal chicanery* (para. 9) interchangeable in your mind? Why or why not?
2. Do we think that a dishwashing liquid called Joy will bring us joy? How do words and how does advertising sway us?
3. What elements of ourselves are lost when we start losing the true meanings of words? Do we become different? How? Do you believe that advertising dehumanizes us? Why or why not?

WRITING ACTIVITIES

1. Write a brief essay about a time in your life when you realized that what was said was not what was actually meant. Try to write anecdotally, as Sanders does in his introduction.
2. Research one of the political events mentioned in the essay, and write down all of the euphemistic language you can find that was used to describe it or that was used to sway public opinion about it. Once you have at least five to ten euphemisms, try to convert them into truthful statements. For example, if you are researching the plight of Japanese Americans in World War II (para. 9), you might jot down "Relocation Centers" = prisons. Write a brief essay that shares your findings and what effect these euphemisms may have had on public opinion at the time.
3. Consider an advertising campaign either on the screen or on the page. Identify the language being used to sell you something, and explain why an advertiser would anticipate that that language would be effective.

Langston Hughes

That Word *Black*

[*The Chicago Defender,* November 3, 1951]

When the following short essay first appeared in 1951, it was considered an insult to call an African American "black." The acceptable and respectful word at the time — the one Langston Hughes himself would have used — was Negro. *But by August 1963, when Martin Luther King Jr. delivered his famous "I Have a Dream" speech, the terms used to describe African Americans were changing. King favored the term* Negro, *but in a speech that preceded his that historic day, the twenty-three-year-old John Lewis (now a congressional leader) repeatedly used the word* black *instead of* Negro. *By the late 1960s, the word* black *had grown more popular, a result of movements like the Black Panthers and such expressions as "black is beautiful," a sentiment Hughes anticipates at the conclusion of the essay.*

One of the nation's most prolific writers, Langston Hughes (1902–1967) was born in Joplin, Missouri, but traveled east as a young man and became a leading, multitalented figure of the Harlem Renaissance. A poet, novelist, essayist, dramatist, short story writer, and journalist who also wrote many children's books, Hughes is still widely read today. In 1943, he created in his newspaper columns for the Chicago Defender *the memorable character Jesse B. Semple ("Simple"), a plain-speaking, working-class man from Harlem. The character was so engaging that Hughes went on to publish five collections of sketches:* Simple Speaks His Mind *(1950),* Simple Takes a Wife *(1953),* Simple Stakes a Claim *(1957),* The Best of Simple *(1961), and* Simple's Uncle Sam *(1965). Hughes said he based "Simple" on an actual factory worker he met in a Harlem bar in 1942.*

"This evening," said Simple, "I feel like talking about the word *black.*"   1

"Nobody's stopping you, so go ahead. But what you really ought   2
to have is a soap-box out on the corner of 126th and Lenox where
the rest of the orators hang out."

"They expresses some good ideas on that corner," said Simple,   3
"but for my ideas I do not need a crowd. Now, as I were saying, the

word *black*, white folks have done used that word to mean something bad so often until now when the N.A.A.C.P. asks for civil rights for the black man, they think they must be bad. Looking back into history, I reckon it all started with a *black* cat meaning bad luck. Don't let one cross your path!

"Next, somebody got up a *black-list* on which you get if you   4
don't vote right. Then when lodges come into being, the folks they didn't want in them got *black-balled*. If you kept a skeleton in your closet, you might get *black-mailed*. And everything bad was *black*. When it came down to the unlucky ball on the pool table, the eight-rock, they made it the *black* ball. So no wonder there ain't no equal rights for the *black* man."

"All you say is true about the odium attached to the word *black*," I   5
said. "You've even forgotten a few. For example, during the war if you bought something under the table, illegally, they said you were trading on the *black* market. In Chicago, if you're a gangster, the *Black Hand Society* may take you for a ride. And certainly if you don't behave yourself, your family will say you're a *black* sheep. Then if your mama burns a *black* candle to change the family luck, they call it *black* magic."

"My mama never did believe in voodoo so she did not burn no   6
black candles," said Simple.

"If she had, that would have been a *black* mark against her."   7

"Stop talking about my mama. What I want to know is, where do   8
white folks get off calling everything bad *black*? If it is a dark night, they say it's *black* as hell. If you are mean and evil, they say you got a *black* heart. I would like to change all that around and say that the people who Jim Crow me have got a *white* heart. People who sell dope to children have got a *white* mark against them. And all the white gamblers who were behind the basketball fix are the *white* sheep of the sports world. God knows there was few, if any, Negroes selling stuff on the black market during the war, so why didn't they call it the *white* market? No, they got to take me and my color and turn it into everything *bad*. According to white folks, black is bad.

"Wait till my day comes! In my language, bad will be *white*. Blackmail will be *white* mail. Black cats will be good luck, and *white* cats will be bad. If a white cat crosses your path, look out! I will take the black ball for the cue ball and let the *white* ball be the unlucky eight-rock. And on my blacklist — which will be a *white* list then — I will put everybody who ever Jim Crowed me from Rankin to Hitler, Talmadge to Malan, South Carolina to South Africa.

"I am black. When I look in the mirror, I see myself, daddy-o, but I am not ashamed. God made me. He did not make us no badder than the rest of the folks. The earth is black and all kinds of good things comes out of the earth. Everything that grows comes up out of the earth. Trees and flowers and fruit and sweet potatoes and corn and all that keeps mens alive comes right up out of the earth — good old black earth. Coal is black and it warms your house and cooks your food. The night is black, which has a moon, and a million stars, and is beautiful. Sleep is black which gives you rest, so you wake up feeling good. I am black. I feel very good this evening. 10

"What is wrong with black?" 11

BACKGROUND AND CONTEXT

1. Words have denotations (their literal, explicit meanings) and connotations (their range of associations). For example, to call something "cool" doesn't necessarily mean that it's cold or chilly. What connotations does Hughes use to characterize the word *black*? How embedded are these expressions in the English language? Would a foreign speaker know these connotations?

2. What does the essay tell you about how "black" was thought of sixty years ago? What is Hughes saying about the use of the word through his invented character Simple? Within twenty years the word *black* became accepted usage and the word *Negro* was considered unacceptable. What do you think caused this change?

STRATEGY, STRUCTURE, AND STYLE

1. Note that the essay takes the form of a dialogue and that both characters are "black." But in what ways do the characters differ in speech and style of address? What advantages does Hughes gain through the use of dialogue? What would the essay be like if it took the form of an address by a single speaker?

2. How would you describe Simple's basic argument? How does he arrive at his conclusion? How important are examples to his point of view? Would you argue that these are all just words and common expressions, or that these words have an impact on ways we think and feel?

COMPARISONS AND CONNECTIONS

1. Compare the way Hughes explores the word *black* to the way Deborah Tannen writes about *bossy* (p. 63). Does *bossy* have only negative connotations? Which essay do you think does a better job of helping readers understand the power of certain words?

2. Try doing what Hughes does. Take a common word (such as *boy* or *girl*), and in a short essay examine its various connotations, looking at both negative and positive aspects of its use. You might look at the word from the perspective of different cultures and ethnic groups.

Discussing the Unit

SUGGESTED TOPIC FOR DISCUSSION
Each of these authors explores the importance of words. After reading these essays, consider what choices are made when deciding what to call — or how to describe — anyone or anything, and all that a word comes to stand for.

PREPARING FOR CLASS DISCUSSION
1. What sorts of associations get caught up in a word, and why might one word be preferable to another? How do you sort through all of the factors and feelings that end up connected to a word?
2. We often think of words as solid, solitary, and unchangeable. When are you sure a word "fits" its subject? Can a time or a sports team or a person take on many names and still be "named"? Consider examples of this from the essays in this chapter.

FROM DISCUSSION TO WRITING
1. How do we know when a word or a name is "right"? Which arguments in this chapter were particularly compelling about when a word does or doesn't fit? Write an essay that explains why one discussion or story was more compelling than another.
2. Compare the different reasons one might choose one word over another as outlined in this chapter. Does Tannen's essay have anything in common with Sanders's essay? Does the naming that happens in "America Then" share any similarity to the naming in "Washington, Yay! Redskins, Boo!"? Explain in a brief essay.

TOPICS FOR CROSS-CULTURAL DISCUSSION
1. Does gender or race play a part in how these authors approach the question of words and names? How so? Cite examples from at least three of the essays you read in this chapter, and explain how gender and race come into play in the discussion.
2. What happens when one ethnic group has control over the names of other people or things? What happens when it does not? Did the essays by Greg Nasif and Langston Hughes change your perspective? Why or why not?

3

Free Speech: Is It Endangered on Campus?

Free expression is such a fundamental liberty that many national charters, including the U.S. Constitution, have made it among the first rights they've expressly numbered. On college campuses, the right to hold and express dissenting views has always been considered not only an important personal freedom but also a critical component of healthy academic discourse and diversity. What happens, though, when one student's right starts to infringe on another student's well-being? Where should we draw the line?

A major battlefield in the academic free-speech wars has been what to do about content that, while it might be important to understanding a particular field or discipline, upsets students exposed to it. Some students have recently called for professors to confront this problem head-on by adopting the Internet trend of appending their courses with *trigger warnings*, explicit alerts that certain material on a syllabus may be upsetting, or "triggering," especially to students with past traumas.

This chapter examines the trigger warning debate in the larger context of freedom of expression. In a *New York Times* article summarizing both sides of the issue, Jennifer Medina traces the history of the trigger warning, and presents its pros and cons. Students, especially those with difficult events in their past, have long kept silent about upsetting course material, and in "Warning: The Literary Canon Could Make Students Squirm," Medina suggests that their speaking out might be the very heart of free speech. However, some professors tell her that the trigger warnings stifle, rather than encourage, debate by effectively censoring important texts, perhaps arbitrarily. Sometimes, according to these students and professors, such warnings affect the open mind that students, especially in the humanities, are expected to bring to the material. In Medina's summary, the warnings "suggest a certain fragility of mind that higher learning is meant to challenge, not embrace."

Two student essays from the University of Iowa debate the merits of these warnings. In "Colleges Should Adopt Trigger Warnings," Brianne Richson argues the issue isn't freedom vs. repression, but the protection of people suffering from severe traumas, who have every right to share a classroom with the majority. She focuses on victims of post-traumatic stress disorder, who may be especially upset by course material that touches on their traumas, while there's little benefit to teaching it. These victims, Richson writes, "do not have more to learn about the academic subject matter that is traumatic for them; they have lived it." In a rebuttal, Jon Overton asserts the importance of absolutely unrestrained conversation. Trigger warnings threaten to turn the classroom into "a horrific nightmare of political correctness on steroids," he writes in "Beware the Trigger Warning."

"Isn't the purpose of a university to stir discussion, not silence it?" former New York mayor Michael Bloomberg asks in the 2014 Harvard commencement address that rounds out this chapter. Bloomberg isn't speaking of trigger warnings, but of a broader issue of academic freedom. He warns against a "groupthink" mentality, in which only certain views are accepted on campus, and others—especially conservative ones—have to be checked at the classroom door.

This chapter's "America Then" comes from a liberal academic, law professor Wendy Kaminer, who nonetheless seems to agree with Bloomberg in spirit, albeit nearly twenty years ago. In "A Civic Duty to Annoy," Kaminer reacts to what she sees as the problem of coddled students—long before the trigger warning—demanding comfort at the expense of the rights of others. She reminds us that "everyone is bound to feel silenced, invisible, or unappreciated at least once in a while." But is Kaminer's outlook fading as the university becomes ever more diverse? Can we, and should we, sacrifice a bit of our ability to say whatever we want for the sake of others' well-being?

Jennifer Medina

Warning: The Literary Canon Could Make Students Squirm

[*The New York Times*, May 17, 2014]

BEFORE YOU READ

Why might some students want to be warned if they will encounter disturbing or graphic material in the classroom? Should literature come with a warning label?

WORDS TO LEARN

forewarn (para. 1): to warn in advance (verb)

misogynistic (para. 1): indicating a dislike or hatred of women (adjective)

explicit (para. 2): leaving nothing implied (adjective)

ideological (para. 3): pertaining to beliefs that guide an individual or group (adjective)

traction (para. 3): the power used to pull something (noun)

mandate (para. 4): official order or authorization to do something (noun)

provocative (para. 4): thought-provoking; stimulating discussion (adjective)

fragility (para. 4): frailty or delicacy (noun)

inimical (para. 5): harmful (adjective)

inevitable (para. 10): sure to happen (adjective)

vandalism (para. 13): deliberate destruction or damage to property (noun)

inferiority (para. 14): lowness in rank; the state of being lesser (noun)

tortuous (para. 20): winding or crooked (adjective)

SANTA BARBARA, Calif. — Should students about to read "The Great Gatsby" be forewarned about "a variety of scenes that reference gory, abusive and misogynistic violence," as one Rutgers student proposed? Would any book that addresses racism — like "The Adventures of Huckleberry Finn" or "Things Fall Apart" — have to be preceded by a note of caution? Do sexual images from Greek mythology need to come with a viewer-beware label?   1

Jennifer Medina is an education reporter for the New York Times. *She was the recipient of a Front Page Award from the Newswomen's Club of New York for her stories on the aftermath of Hurricane Katrina in 2006. She has served as Hartford bureau chief since July 2006.*

Colleges across the country this spring have been wrestling with   2
student requests for what are known as "trigger warnings," explicit alerts
that the material they are about to read or see in a classroom might upset
them or, as some students assert, cause symptoms of post-traumatic
stress disorder in victims of rape or in war veterans.

The warnings, which have their ideological roots in feminist thought,   3
have gained the most traction at the University of California, Santa Barbara, where the student government formally called for them. But there
have been similar requests from students at Oberlin College, Rutgers
University, the University of Michigan, George Washington University
and other schools.

| The warnings have been widely debated |

The debate has left many academics   4
fuming, saying that professors should be
trusted to use common sense and that being
provocative is part of their mandate. Trigger
warnings, they say, suggest a certain fragility
of mind that higher learning is meant to challenge, not embrace. The warnings have been widely debated in intellectual circles and largely criticized
in opinion magazines, newspaper editorials and academic email lists.

"Any kind of blanket trigger policy is inimical to academic freedom,"   5
said Lisa Hajjar, a sociology professor at the university here, who often
uses graphic depictions of torture in her courses about war. "Any student
can request some sort of individual accommodation, but to say we need
some kind of one-size-fits-all approach is totally wrong. The presumption there is that students should not be forced to deal with something
that makes them uncomfortable is absurd or even dangerous."

Bailey Loverin, a sophomore at Santa Barbara, said the idea for   6
campuswide trigger warnings came to her in February after a professor
showed a graphic film depicting rape. She said that she herself had been
a victim of sexual abuse, and that although she had not felt threatened
by the film, she had approached the professor to suggest that students
should have been warned.

Ms. Loverin draws a distinction between alerting students to mate-   7
rial that might truly tap into memories of trauma — such as war and torture, since many students at Santa Barbara are veterans — and slapping
warning labels on famous literary works, as other advocates of trigger
warnings have proposed.

"We're not talking about someone turning away from something   8
they don't want to see," Ms. Loverin said in a recent interview. "People
suddenly feel a very real threat to their safety — even if it is perceived.
They are stuck in a classroom where they can't get out, or if they do try to
leave, it is suddenly going to be very public."

The most vociferous criticism has focused on trigger warnings for   9
materials that have an established place on syllabuses across the country. Among the suggestions for books that would benefit from trigger
warnings are Shakespeare's "The Merchant of Venice" (contains anti-
Semitism) and Virginia Woolf's "Mrs. Dalloway" (addresses suicide.)

"Frankly it seems this is sort of an inevitable movement toward peo-   10
ple increasingly expecting physical comfort and intellectual comfort in
their lives," said Greg Lukianoff, president of the Foundation for Individual Rights in Education, a nonprofit group that advocates free speech. "It
is only going to get harder to teach people that there is a real important
and serious value to being offended. Part of that is talking about deadly
serious and uncomfortable subjects."

The term "trigger warning" has its genesis on the Internet. Feminist   11
blogs and forums have used the term for more than a decade to signal
that readers, particularly victims of sexual abuse, might want to avoid
certain articles or pictures online.

On college campuses, proponents say similar language should be used   12
in class syllabuses or before lectures. The issue arose at Wellesley College
this year after the school installed a lifelike statue of a man in his under-
wear, and hundreds of students signed a petition to have it removed. Writing in The Huffington Post, one Wellesley student called it a "potentially
triggering sculpture," and petition signers cited that "concerns that it has
triggered memories of sexual assault amongst some students."

Here at the University of California, Santa Barbara, in March there   13
was a confrontation when a group of anti-abortion protesters held up
graphic pictures of aborted fetuses and a pregnant professor of feminist
studies tried to destroy the posters, saying they triggered a sense of fear
in her. After she was arrested on vandalism, battery and robbery charges,
more than 1,000 students signed a petition of support for her, saying
the university should impose greater restrictions on potentially trigger-
inducing content. (So far, the faculty senate has promised to address the
concerns raised by the petition and the student government but has not
made any policy changes.)

At Oberlin College in Ohio, a draft guide was circulated that would   14
have asked professors to put trigger warnings in their syllabuses. The
guide said they should flag anything that might "disrupt a student's learning" and "cause trauma," including anything that would suggest the inferiority of anyone who is transgender (a form of discrimination known as
cissexism) or who uses a wheelchair (or ableism).

"Be aware of racism, classism, sexism, heterosexism, cissexism,   15
ableism, and other issues of privilege and oppression," the guide said.
"Realize that all forms of violence are traumatic, and that your students

have lives before and outside your classroom, experiences you may not expect or understand." For example, it said, while "Things Fall Apart" by Chinua Achebe — a novel set in colonial-era Nigeria — is a "triumph of literature that everyone in the world should read," it could "trigger readers who have experienced racism, colonialism, religious persecution, violence, suicide and more."

After several professors complained, the draft was removed from a campus website, pending a more thorough review by a faculty-and-student task force. Professors and campus administrators are expected to meet with students next fall to come up with a more comprehensive guide. 16

Meredith Raimondo, Oberlin's associate dean of the College of Arts and Sciences, said the guide was meant to provide suggestions, not to dictate to professors. An associate professor of comparative American studies and a co-chairwoman of the task force, Ms. Raimondo said providing students with warnings would simply be "responsible pedagogical practice." 17

"I quite object to the argument of 'Kids today need to toughen up,'" she said. "That absolutely misses the reality that we're dealing with. We have students coming to us with serious issues, and we need to deal with that respectfully and seriously." 18

But Marc Blecher, a professor of politics and East Asian studies at Oberlin and a major critic of trigger warnings at Oberlin, said such a policy would have a chilling effect on faculty members, particularly those without the job security of tenure. 19

"If I were a junior faculty member looking at this while putting my syllabus together, I'd be terrified," Mr. Blecher said. "Any student who felt triggered by something that happened in class could file a complaint with the various procedures and judicial boards, and create a very tortuous process for anyone." 20

VOCABULARY/USING A DICTIONARY

1. What is a *presumption* (para. 5)?
2. What part of speech is *vociferous* (para. 9)? What is a synonym for *vociferous*?
3. What language does the word *genesis* (para. 11) come from?

RESPONDING TO WORDS IN CONTEXT

1. Are the words *graphic* (para. 5) and *explicit* (para. 2) similar? Both are used in ways that suggest similarity (*"explicit* alerts," *"graphic* depictions").
2. What is the difference between reading a book in *private* and being in a situation in which it will be discussed in *public* (para. 8)?

3. The essay speaks of a group that *advocates* (para. 10) free speech. What part of speech is the word in the essay? How else can *advocate* be used and what does it mean?

DISCUSSING MAIN POINT AND MEANING

1. Who do trigger warnings protect? According to this essay, whom might trigger warnings *not* protect?
2. What are some examples of issues that trigger warnings might cover if they are used in literature?
3. What are some of the arguments *against* the use of trigger warnings that Medina includes in her essay?

EXAMINING SENTENCES, PARAGRAPHS, AND ORGANIZATION

1. Look at Medina's opening paragraph. How is it structured? Is the structure effective?
2. How does Medina express opposing viewpoints in her essay?
3. What do Medina's quotations throughout the essay add to the piece?

THINKING CRITICALLY

1. A sociology professor is quoted in the essay as stating, "The presumption that students should not be forced to deal with something that makes them uncomfortable is absurd or even dangerous." Do you agree or disagree with this statement? Why?
2. Do you think people should be protected from ideas that might remind them of real-world trauma? Why or why not? Who should be protected? Where should you draw the line?
3. Do you think any of the examples Medina gives of students in favor of trigger warnings show that some students have taken their cause too far, or do you believe that all of the examples are valid? Choose one example from the essay and explain your position.

WRITING ACTIVITIES

1. Chinua Achebe's book *Things Fall Apart* has been called "a triumph of literature that everyone in the world should read," yet it is filled with potentially triggering material (introducing or reintroducing trauma). Can you think of another book you have read with such potentially "dangerous" material? Were you glad you read it? Answer these questions in a short essay, and argue whether such a book needs a "trigger warning." If you have read Achebe's book, you are welcome to choose that book as your topic. (Or you may choose a film if you prefer.)

2. Does it make sense that groups involved in feminist blogs and forums used the term "trigger warning" long before the term made its way onto the college campus? Explain in writing what ways those groups might have made use of the term.

3. Read other articles on the debate about adding "trigger warnings" to literature in the classroom. Compile a list of reasons for and against such labels (these reasons should be drawn from the article, but they can also be your reasons for or against the labels, based on what you've read). Include a short "Works Cited" page at the end of your list.

STUDENT DEBATE

Brianne Richson

Colleges Should Adopt Trigger Warnings

[*The Daily Iowan,* University of Iowa, May 6, 2014]

Jon Overton

Beware the Trigger Warning

[*The Daily Iowan,* University of Iowa, May 7, 2014]

BEFORE YOU READ

What sort of precautions should we take to protect people suffering from post-traumatic stress disorder (PTSD) from reexperiencing their trauma? Should our concern for them extend into the classroom? Is it the responsibility of a student with PTSD to discuss that condition with his or her professor?

WORDS TO LEARN

vague (Richson, para. 1): indefinite; indistinct (adjective)

adverse (Richson, para. 2): unfavorable in effect (adjective)

prominent (Richson, para. 2): standing out (adjective)

affinity (Richson, para. 3): attraction to a person or thing (noun)

sensory (Richson, para. 5): relating to the senses (adjective)

antithetical (Richson, para. 6): directly opposed (adjective)

obligation (Richson, para. 8): something that must be done because it is right (noun)

Brianne Richson and Jon Overton are students at the University of Iowa.

gripe (Overton, para. 1): complaint (noun)

predict (Overton, para. 2): to foretell (verb)

recently (Overton, para. 4): lately (adverb)

motivations (Overton, para. 7): incentives (noun)

empathy (Overton, para. 7): identification with the feelings and thoughts of another (noun)

initiate (Overton, para. 7): to begin (verb)

Brianne Richson

Colleges Should Adopt Trigger Warnings

[*The Daily Iowan,* University of Iowa, May 6, 2014]

We all have that one memory we'd prefer people not bring up because we want to block it from our consciousness forever. Hopefully, such memories become more vague as we grow further removed from them with time, but what about a memory that has legitimately traumatized a person? A memory that has even made its holder a victim of post-traumatic stress disorder (PTSD)?

Students at colleges across the country are taking a term originating from the world of blogs, "trigger warning," and calling for its direct use on class syllabi, to alert them to potential adverse reactions to sensitive academic material. This might include anything from sexual assault — a prominent issue on college campuses — to eating disorders, violent graphic content, or topics of race. The list goes on.

One might consider such measures dramatic and symptomatic of what I have often heard my father refer to as the "every kid gets a trophy" generation: a generation full of coddling and cushioning when things go wrong. It isn't fair, however, to compare modern parents' affinity for sheltering their children from failure with the generation's demand to be protected from reliving that which was traumatic.

Is it too much to ask that a rape survivor be forewarned when a professor is about to cover material on the topic or to ask that a person who was confronted with a racial slur and beaten up be allowed to leave the lecture hall before course material sends her or him into a tizzy of hypervigilance, a hallmark characteristic of PTSD?

A great difficulty of PTSD is that it can surface at any given time following a traumatic event — in weeks or years. It is one thing to be aware of what sensory elements could trigger an episode for you, but it is another to have the ability to actively avoid these potentially toxic situations.

University of California-Santa Barbara has passed a resolution that professors should indicate in syllabi when emotionally or physically stressful material would be presented in class, prompting a Los Angeles Times editorial to stamp the measure as "antithetical to college life." The same editorial suggests that trigger warnings are a cop-out for students not wishing to engage with a diverse set of subject material or to face traditionally uncomfortable issues head-on.

Victims of PTSD do not have more to learn about the academic subject matter that is traumatic for them; they have lived it. Not everyone has the luxury of dealing with issues upfront and immediately after a trauma. And no one has the right to force you to do so. In Ohio, Oberlin College has gone so far as to suggest that trigger material should not even be included in a course if it is not clear how the students might learn from the material.

> Victims of PTSD do not have more to learn about the academic subject matter that is traumatic for them; they have lived it.

Such measures certainly have a potential to be taken too far, but our obligation to prevent a trauma survivor's class time becoming a living hell outweighs concerns about a stunted learning environment.

Jon Overton

Beware the Trigger Warning

[*The Daily Iowan,* University of Iowa, May 7, 2014]

Brianne Richson suggests that U.S. colleges and universities should adopt trigger warnings on syllabi, on the grounds that people who've suffered traumatic experiences may be exposed to course material that would trigger memories of those events.

I agree that we should be considerate toward people who suffer from psychological illnesses. My main gripe with trigger warnings more broadly, however, is that while they aim to be sensitive to people suffering from afflictions like post-traumatic stress disorder, they threaten to stifle some of the most important conversations and lessons in college.

Trigger warnings run into the same problem as proposed hate-speech 3 laws: Where do they stop? Anything can be a trigger, from hot dogs to Nazis to Mike Tyson to the color yellow. The right smell, sound, word, or image can initiate a painful flashback for a particular person, who can't always antici-pate them. The triggers don't have to be traditionally traumatic words, phrases, or concepts, so you can't easily predict what will set someone off.

> Trigger warnings run into the same problem as pro-posed hate-speech laws: Where do they stop?

And yet in Ohio, Oberlin College re- 4 cently issued a policy that advised instruc-tors to "remove triggering material when it does not contribute directly to the course learning goals." This implies that professors ought to go through their syllabi line by line to consider what might trigger a traumatic memory for some students.

Students at the University of California-Santa Barbara also passed 5 a resolution encouraging faculty to include a list of potential triggers on course syllabi and not punish students for leaving early if triggering con-tent arises. Some of the most extreme trigger warning advocates have even attacked classical literature like *Things Fall Apart* and *The Great Gatsby*.

Thanks to some highly vocal faculty at Oberlin, the attack on aca- 6 demic freedom there was shot down, but these examples illustrate perfectly what is so dangerous about trigger warnings. They threaten to transform higher education into a horrific nightmare in which political cor-rectness on steroids allows students to avoid any information with which they disagree. One of the great things about colleges and universities is that they challenge your worldview. They force you to confront information that makes you rethink cherished beliefs. This can be distressing, but that's the point: to expose yourself to new ideas and points of view.

The motivations behind trigger warnings are undoubtedly admi- 7 rable. They reflect the pinnacle of empathy and compassion. However, it's up to the students who suffer from PTSD to tell their instructors in advance if they're concerned about a potential trigger from specific course material. As much as we'd like to help trauma victims, we can't know what's going to initiate a panic attack, and trying to prevent any and all of them endangers academic discourse.

VOCABULARY/USING A DICTIONARY

1. What part of speech is *stifle* (Overton, para. 2)? What does it mean?

2. What is the difference between the words *advise* (Overton, para. 4) and *advice*?

3. What is *vigilance*? What is *hypervigilance* (Richson, para. 4)?

RESPONDING TO WORDS IN CONTEXT

1. What is a *slur* (Richson, para. 4)? What part of speech is it?
2. Can you think of some of the *traumatic* (Overton, para. 4) issues trigger warnings might cover for students?
3. How might trigger warnings lead to *"a stunted learning environment"* (Richson, para. 8)?

DISCUSSING MAIN POINT AND MEANING

1. What opposition to the idea of trigger warnings does Richson consider in her essay?
2. What point of Richson's does Overton agree with?
3. Does Overton think trigger warnings have come about for worthy or unworthy reasons?

EXAMINING SENTENCES, PARAGRAPHS, AND ORGANIZATION

1. Why does Richson include a sentence with dashes in the second paragraph?
2. How does Overton indicate that his essay is a response to another's work? Is that indication necessary to the essay?
3. Do you think Richson could go further in her conclusion? Why or why not?

THINKING CRITICALLY

1. Overton writes, "I agree that we should be considerate toward people who suffer from psychological illnesses." Do you think from his essay that this statement is true? Explain.
2. Do you think the generation of students considering trigger warnings for their material has grown accustomed to "coddling and cushioning" (Richson, para. 3)? How might trigger warnings be an extension of that?
3. What are some alternatives to trigger warnings for students with PTSD? Are there any alternatives or are trigger warnings the best solution for them?

WRITING ACTIVITIES

1. Read some of the arguments for and against trigger warnings that have surfaced recently in the news. Do you find their arguments more or less compelling than Richson's? Why or why not?
2. In an exercise, respond to Overton's essay. Try to address his points one by one (paragraph by paragraph). When you have finished, try to craft your exercise into an essay that is a rough response to Overton.
3. Research the rise of interest in trigger warnings at Oberlin College. What led to the interest in having warnings there? What led to the policy that was "shot down" (Overton, para. 6)? What do you think of the debate Oberlin College is having there?

Moving from General to Specific

A common and effective way to develop an essay is to move from a general point to a specific instance. A writer may open an essay by claiming that ever since its beginnings the English language has undergone incessant change: The original Old English of the Anglo Saxons is unreadable today. That could prepare the way for the following paragraph to show specifically how the new social media — text-messaging, tweeting, etc. — are also changing the English language and that such changes are natural and inevitable.

Notice how University of Iowa student Brianne Richson, who makes a case for including trigger warnings in academic syllabi, begins with a firm, strong argument about PTSD and then moves into a paragraph giving specific instances of students who might be affected by triggering material. She not only supports her argument with concrete examples but also brings it to a startling life in this paragraph, which forces us to confront particular instances that may challenge the notions of victims we brought to her argument.

1
Strong examples make the best possible case

2
A technical term shows depth of understanding

Is it too much to ask that a rape survivor be forewarned when a professor is about to cover material on the topic or to ask that <u>a person who was confronted with a racial slur and beaten up</u> (1) be allowed to leave the lecture hall before course material sends her or him into a tizzy of <u>hypervigilance</u> (2), a hallmark characteristic of PTSD?

Michael Bloomberg

On the Repression of Free Expression (from Commencement Speech at Harvard University)

[*MikeBloomberg.com*, May 29, 2014]

BEFORE YOU READ

Do you think your government practices a tolerance of all viewpoints, including those that go deeply against the grain of those held by the majority? What about your university? Should a government and university be tolerant and protective of everyone's views?

WORDS TO LEARN

prestigious (para. 1): esteemed (adjective)
viewpoint (para. 3): perspective (noun)
manifest (para. 5): to make clear; to show (verb)
ardent (para. 8): passionate (adjective)
denounce (para. 9): to condemn (verb)
vigilance (para. 13): watchfulness (noun)
ensure (para. 14): to guarantee (verb)
censorship (para. 23): the act of suppressing something (noun)
irony (para. 24): use of words to convey a meaning opposite to the literal meaning (noun)
monopoly (para. 27): the exclusive possession or control of something (noun)

homogenous (para. 29): made up of the same kind (adjective)
tenure (para. 29): the amount of time a person holds a job (in this essay, referring to academic tenure, which is the right to keep a teaching job as long as you want it) (noun)
pedagogically (para. 41): relating to how things are taught (adverb)
posterity (para. 42): all future generations (noun)
hypocrisy (para. 45): pretending to be or believe something that isn't what one actually is or believes (noun)
bastion (para. 45): a fortified area (noun)
rescind (para. 47): to take back (verb)

T he good news is, Harvard remains what it was when I first arrived on campus 50 years ago: America's most prestigious university. And, like other great universities, it lies at the heart of the American experiment in democracy.

1

Michael Bloomberg served three terms as the 108th mayor of New York. He is the founder of the global company Bloomberg LP, and is an entrepreneur and philanthropist. He attended Johns Hopkins University as well as Harvard University, where he received his master of business administration.

Their purpose is not only to advance knowledge, but to advance the ideals of our nation. Great universities are places where people of all backgrounds, holding all beliefs, pursuing all questions, can come to study and debate their ideas — freely and openly. 2

Today, I'd like to talk with you about how important it is for that freedom to exist for everyone, no matter how strongly we may disagree with another's viewpoint. 3

Tolerance for other people's ideas, and the freedom to express your own, are inseparable values at great universities. Joined together, they form a sacred trust that holds the basis of our democratic society. 4

But that trust is perpetually vulnerable to the tyrannical tendencies of monarchs, mobs, and majorities. And lately, we have seen those tendencies manifest themselves too often, both on college campuses and in our society. 5

That's the bad news — and unfortunately, I think both Harvard, and my own city of New York, have been witnesses to this trend. 6

First, for New York City. Several years ago, as you may remember, some people tried to stop the development of a mosque a few blocks from the World Trade Center site. 7

It was an emotional issue, and polls showed that two-thirds of Americans were against a mosque being built there. Even the Anti-Defamation League — widely regarded as the country's most ardent defender of religious freedom — declared its opposition to the project. 8

The opponents held rallies and demonstrations. They denounced the developers. And they demanded that city government stop its construction. That was their right — and we protected their right to protest. But they could not have been more wrong. And we refused to cave in to their demands. 9

The idea that government would single out a particular religion, and block its believers — and only its believers — from building a house of worship in a particular area is diametrically opposed to the moral principles that gave rise to our great nation and the constitutional protections that have sustained it. 10

Our union of 50 states rests on the union of two values: freedom and tolerance. And it is that union of values that the terrorists who attacked us on September 11th, 2001 — and on April 15th, 2013 — found most threatening. 11

To them, we were a God-less country. 12

But in fact, there is no country that protects the core of every faith and philosophy known to human kind — free will — more than the United States of America. That protection, however, rests upon our constant vigilance. 13

We like to think that the principle of separation of church and   14
state is settled. It is not. And it never will be. It is up to us to guard it
fiercely — and to ensure that equality under the law means equality
under the law for everyone.

If you want the freedom to worship as you wish, to speak as you   15
wish, and to marry whom you wish, you must tolerate my freedom to do
so — or not do so — as well.

> Attempting to restrict my freedoms — in ways that you would not restrict your own — leads only to injustice

What I do may offend you. You may   16
find my actions immoral or unjust. But
attempting to restrict my freedoms — in
ways that you would not restrict your
own — leads only to injustice.

We cannot deny others the rights and   17
privileges that we demand for ourselves.
And that is true in cities and it is no less true
at universities, where the forces of repres-
sion appear to be stronger now than they have been since the 1950s.

When I was growing up, U.S. Senator Joe McCarthy was asking: 'Are   18
you now or have you ever been?' He was attempting to repress and crimi-
nalize those who sympathized with an economic system that was, even
then, failing.

McCarthy's Red Scare[1] destroyed thousands of lives, but what was   19
he so afraid of? An idea — in this case, communism — that he and others deemed dangerous.

But he was right about one thing: Ideas can be dangerous. They can   20
change society. They can upend traditions. They can start revolutions.
That's why throughout history, those in authority have tried to repress
ideas that threaten their power, their religion, their ideology, or their
reelection chances.

That was true for Socrates and Galileo, it was true for Nelson Man-   21
dela and Václav Havel, and it has been true for Ai Wei Wei, Pussy Riot,
and the kids who made the 'Happy' video in Iran.

Repressing free expression is a natural human weakness, and it is up   22
to us to fight it at every turn. Intolerance of ideas — whether liberal or
conservative — is antithetical to individual rights and free societies, and
it is no less antithetical to great universities and first-rate scholarship.

There is an idea floating around college campuses — including here   23
at Harvard — that scholars should be funded only if their work conforms

---

[1] McCarthy's Red Scare (para. 19): Also known as "McCarthyism," a fear of
communism in the United States, during which time the House Committee on
UnAmerican Activities was formed and investigated people in this country who
were accused of being Communist or Communist supporters.

to a particular view of justice. There's a word for that idea: censorship. And it is just a modern-day form of McCarthyism.

Think about the irony: In the 1950s, the right wing was attempting to repress left wing ideas. Today, on many college campuses, it is liberals trying to repress conservative ideas, even as conservative faculty members are at risk of becoming an endangered species. And perhaps nowhere is that more true than here in the Ivy League. 24

In the 2012 presidential race, according to Federal Election Commission data, 96 percent of all campaign contributions from Ivy League faculty and employees went to Barack Obama. 25

Ninety-six percent. There was more disagreement among the old Soviet Politburo than there is among Ivy League donors. 26

That statistic should give us pause — and I say that as someone who endorsed President Obama for reelection — because let me tell you, neither party has a monopoly on truth or God on its side. 27

When 96 percent of Ivy League donors prefer one candidate to another, you have to wonder whether students are being exposed to the diversity of views that a great university should offer. 28

Diversity of gender, ethnicity, and orientation is important. But a university cannot be great if its faculty is politically homogenous. In fact, the whole purpose of granting tenure to professors is to ensure that they feel free to conduct research on ideas that run afoul of university politics and societal norms. 29

When tenure was created, it mostly protected liberals whose ideas ran up against conservative norms. 30

Today, if tenure is going to continue to exist, it must also protect conservatives whose ideas run up against liberal norms. Otherwise, university research — and the professors who conduct it — will lose credibility. 31

Great universities must not become predictably partisan. And a liberal arts education must not be an education in the art of liberalism. 32

The role of universities is not to promote an ideology. It is to provide scholars and students with a neutral forum for researching and debating issues — without tipping the scales in one direction, or repressing unpopular views. 33

Requiring scholars — and commencement speakers, for that matter — to conform to certain political standards undermines the whole purpose of a university. 34

This spring, it has been disturbing to see a number of college commencement speakers withdraw — or have their invitations rescinded — after protests from students and — to me, shockingly — from senior faculty and administrators who should know better. 35

It happened at Brandeis, Haverford, Rutgers, and Smith. Last year, it happened at Swarthmore and Johns Hopkins, I'm sorry to say. 36

In each case, liberals silenced a voice — and denied an honorary 37
degree — to individuals they deemed politically objectionable. That is
an outrage and we must not let it continue.

If a university thinks twice before inviting a commencement speaker 38
because of his or her politics censorship and conformity — the mortal
enemies of freedom — win out.

And sadly, it is not just commencement season when speakers are 39
censored.

Last fall, when I was still in City Hall, our Police Commissioner was 40
invited to deliver a lecture at another Ivy League institution — but he
was unable to do so because students shouted him down.

Isn't the purpose of a university to stir discussion, not silence it? 41
What were the students afraid of hearing? Why did administrators not
step in to prevent the mob from silencing speech? And did anyone consider that it is morally and pedagogically wrong to deprive other students
the chance to hear the speech?

I'm sure all of today's graduates have read John Stuart Mill's *On Lib-* 42
erty. But allow me to read a short passage from it: 'The peculiar evil of
silencing the expression of an opinion is, that it is robbing the human
race; posterity as well as the existing generation; those who dissent from
the opinion, still more than those who hold it.'

He continued: 'If the opinion is right, they are deprived of the 43
opportunity of exchanging error for truth: if wrong, they lose, what is
almost as great a benefit, the clearer perception and livelier impression of
truth, produced by its collision with error.'

Mill would have been horrified to learn of university students silencing 44
the opinions of others. He would have been even more horrified that faculty
members were often part of the commencement censorship campaigns.

For tenured faculty members to silence speakers whose views they 45
disagree with is the height of hypocrisy, especially when these protests
happen in the northeast — a bastion of self-professed liberal tolerance.

I'm glad to say, however, that Harvard has not caved in to these com- 46
mencement censorship campaigns. If it had, Colorado State Senator
Michael Johnston would not have had the chance to address the Education School yesterday.

Some students called on the administration to rescind the invitation 47
to Johnston because they opposed some of his education policies. But to
their great credit, President Faust and Dean Ryan stood firm.

As Dean Ryan wrote to students: 'I have encountered many people 48
of good faith who share my basic goals but disagree with my own views
when it comes to the question of how best to improve education. In my
view, those differences should be explored, debated, challenged, and
questioned. But they should also be respected and, indeed, celebrated.'

He could not have been more correct, and he could not have pro-   49
vided a more valuable final lesson to the class of 2014.

As a former chairman of Johns Hopkins, I strongly believe that a uni-   50
versity's obligation is not to teach students what to think but to teach students how to think. And that requires listening to the other side, weighing
arguments without prejudging them, and determining whether the other
side might actually make some fair points.

If the faculty fails to do this, then it is the responsibility of the admin-   51
istration and governing body to step in and make it a priority. If they do
not, if students graduate with ears and minds closed, the university has
failed both the student and society.

And if you want to know where that leads, look no further than   52
Washington D.C.

Down in Washington, every major question facing our country —   53
involving our security, our economy, our environment, and our health — is
decided.

Yet the two parties decide these questions not by engaging with one   54
another, but by trying to shout each other down, and by trying to repress
and undermine research that runs counter to their ideology. The more
our universities emulate that model, the worse off we will be as a society.

VOCABULARY/USING A DICTIONARY

1. What part of speech is the word *tyrannical* (para. 5)? What is a *tyrant*?
2. What is a *mosque* (para. 7)?
3. What part of speech is *diametrically* (para. 10)? What is a *diameter*?

RESPONDING TO WORDS IN CONTEXT

1. Bloomberg uses the words *separation* and *inseparable*, and *tolerance* and
   intolerance in this essay (paras. 4, 14, and 22). Given your understanding of
   the words, what do you think the prefix *in-* indicates?
2. The idea of "forces of repression" and people who "repress" others (paras. 17,
   18, and 20) are introduced throughout. What does it mean to *repress* someone
   or something? What are some of the forms *repression* takes in this essay?
3. Bloomberg writes, "Intolerance of ideas . . . is *antithetical* to individual rights
   and free societies." What do you think *antithetical* means here?

DISCUSSING MAIN POINT AND MEANING

1. What does Bloomberg mean when he suggests the need for "*tolerance for
   other people's ideas*" (para. 4)? How is that tolerance exhibited?
2. According to Bloomberg, what is the role professors and universities play in
   terms of their general purpose and dissemination of different viewpoints?
3. How has Harvard acted, in Bloomberg's opinion, in regard to conformity and
   censorship, and what message has it sent its students?

EXAMINING SENTENCES, PARAGRAPHS, AND ORGANIZATION

1. What does the introductory paragraph of the excerpt tell you about what will follow in the body of the speech?
2. What sort of examples does Bloomberg insert to make the essay feel most relevant to current events and to the lives of the students in his audience?
3. How does Bloomberg connect ideas about the government's role in supporting individual freedoms to the idea of supporting individual freedoms in universities, and back again to the government's role?

THINKING CRITICALLY

1. Even in a country that values free speech, how are people kept from voicing opinions? What power structures are in place that have control over who gets heard and why?
2. Do you agree that universities have the same obligation to uphold diverse voices that you might expect of our government? Why or why not?
3. Bloomberg states, "When 96 percent of Ivy League donors prefer one candidate to another, you have to wonder whether students are being exposed to the diversity of views that a great university should offer." Do you think this idea of Bloomberg's is true or false? Why?

WRITING ACTIVITIES

1. Bloomberg recounts a story about the New York police commissioner who was invited to give a lecture at a university but was shouted down, unable to speak. He asks, "Isn't the purpose of a university to stir discussion, not silence it? . . . did anyone consider that it is morally and pedagogically wrong to deprive other students the chance to hear the speech?" (para. 41). Do you agree? Write a short paper with arguments that support your position.
2. Do you think a professor can support a particular ideology without "repressing unpopular views" (para. 33)? How do ideologies get expressed in university settings? And do you think this is appropriate use of systems of higher education? Write an op-ed piece, perhaps to submit to your student newspaper, that expresses your thoughts on the matter.
3. Look into the proposed building of an Islamic community center and mosque near the site of the World Trade Center in New York. Read articles that express a variety of opinions or news sources that quote a variety of opinions on the building of the mosque in that area. Do you understand why some people felt the way they did? Do you understand why Bloomberg supported the building of the mosque there? Write a brief essay that explores how different viewpoints were expressed about this proposition, how all of these viewpoints relate to the comments Bloomberg makes about tolerance and freedom, and their importance in this country.

Wendy Kaminer

A Civic Duty to Annoy

Although many Americans say they applaud diversity (see Chapter 4), they also often prefer to be among people who think and feel the same way they do. Given the choice, most people would rather be around those who agree with them politically, culturally, and socially. Yet, in the following short essay that appeared in the Atlantic *in September 1997, the best-selling social critic Wendy Kaminer argues that a healthy civic life demands a great deal of disagreement, and that people should be much less sensitive about expressions that may offend them. Resisting the complaints of her privileged students about being "marginalized" or "oppressed," she maintains that "sometimes nurturing students means challenging their complaints instead of satisfying their demands for sympathy."*

What is there about being in a room filled with people who agree with me that makes me want to change my mind? Maybe it's the self-congratulatory air of consensus among people who consider themselves and one another right-thinking. Maybe it's the consistency of belief that devolves into mere conformity. Maybe it's just that I can no longer bear to hear the word "empower."

At self-consciously feminist gatherings I feel at home in the worst way. I feel the way I do at family dinners, when I want to put my feet up on the table and say something to provoke old Uncle George. To get George going, I defend affirmative action or the

An attorney, author, and social critic, Wendy Kaminer has won many awards, including a Guggenheim Fellowship in 1993, and has served as president of the National Coalition against Censorship. Her numerous articles and reviews have appeared in such publications as the New York Times, *the* New Republic, *and the* Nation. *She is the author most recently of* Worst Instincts: Cowardice, Conformity, and the ACLU *(2009). Other books include* Sleeping with Extra-Terrestrials: The Rise of Irrationalism and Perils of Piety *(2000),* True Love Waits: Essays and Criticism *(1997), and* It's All the Rage: Crime and Culture *(1996).*

capital-gains tax. To irritate my more orthodox feminist colleagues, I disavow any personal guilt about being born white and middle-class. I scoff every time I hear a Harvard student complain that she's oppressed.

I'm not alone in my irreverence, but feminist pieties combined   3
with feminine courtesy keep most of us in line. Radcliffe College[1], where I am based, is devoted to nurturing female undergraduates. We're supposed to nod sympathetically, in solidarity, when a student speaks of feeling silenced or invisible because she is female, of color, or both. We're not supposed to point out that Harvard students are among the most privileged people in the universe, regardless of race or sex.

I don't mean to scoff at the discrimination that a young woman   4
of any color may have experienced or is likely to experience someday. I do want to remind her that as a student at Harvard/Radcliffe or any other elite university she enjoys many more advantages than a working-class white male attending a community college. And the kind of discrimination that students are apt to encounter at Harvard — relatively subtle and occasional — is not "oppression." It does not systematically deprive people of basic civil rights and liberties and is not generally sanctioned by the administration.

Besides, everyone is bound to feel silenced, invisible, or unap-   5
preciated at least once in a while. Imagine how a white male middle manager feels when he's about to be downsized. Like laments about dysfunctional families, complaints about oppression lose their power when proffered so promiscuously. Melodramatic complaints about oppression at Harvard are in part developmental: students in their late teens and early twenties are apt to place themselves at the center of the universe. But their extreme sensitivity reflects frequently criticized cultural trends as well. An obsession with identity and self-esteem has encouraged students to assume that every insult or slight is motivated by racist, sexist, or heterosexist bias and gravely threatens their well-being. What's lost is a sense of perspective. If attending Harvard is oppression, what was slavery?

---

[1] Founded in 1879 in Cambridge, Radcliffe served as the woman's college of the then all-male Harvard University. It didn't fully merge with Harvard until 1999, two years after Kaminer's essay.

Sometimes nurturing students means challenging their com- 6
plaints instead of satisfying their demands for sympathy. I've heard
female students declare that any male classmate who makes deroga-
tory remarks about women online or over the telephone is guilty of
sexual harassment and should be punished. What are we teaching
them if we agree? That they aren't strong enough to withstand a few
puerile sexist jokes that may not even be directed at them? That their
male classmates don't have the right to make statements that some
women deem offensive? There would be no feminist movement if
women never dared to give offense.

When nurturing devolves into pandering, feminism gives way to 7
femininity. Recently a small group of female students called for disci-
plinary proceedings against males wearing "pornographic" T-shirts in a
dining hall. They found it difficult to eat lunch in the presence of such
unwholesome, sexist images. Should we encourage these young
women to believe that they're fragile creatures, with particularly delicate digestive systems? Should we offer them official protection from
T-shirts? Or should we point out that a group of pro-choice students
might someday wear shirts emblazoned with words or images that pro-
life students find deeply disturbing? Should we teach them that the art
of giving and taking offense is an art of citizenship in a free society?

That is not a feminine art. Radcliffe, for example, is an unfail- 8
ingly polite institution. Criticism and dissatisfaction are apt to be
expressed in a feminine mode, covertly or indirectly. It's particularly
hard for many of us not to react with great solicitude to a student
who declares herself marginalized, demeaned, or oppressed, even if
we harbor doubts about her claim. If she seeks virtue in oppression,
as so many do, we seek it in maternalism.

We tend to forget that criticism sometimes expresses greater 9
respect than praise. It is surely more of an honor than flattery. You
challenge a student because you consider her capable of learning.
You question her premises because you think she's game enough
to re-examine them. You do need to take the measure of her self-
confidence, and your own. Teaching — or nurturing — requires that
you gain students' trust and then risk having them not like you.

Sometimes withholding sympathy feels mean, insensitive, and 10
uncaring; you acquire all the adjectives that aren't supposed to attach
to women. You take on the stereotypically masculine vices at a time

when the feminine virtue of niceness is being revived: Rosie O'Donnell[2] is the model talk-show host, civility the reigning civic virtue, and communitarianism the paradigmatic political theory. Communities are exalted, as if the typical community were composed solely of people who shared and cared about one another and never engaged in conflict.

In fact communities are built on compromise, and compromise   11
presupposes disagreement. Tolerance presupposes the existence of people and ideas you don't like. It prevails upon you to forswear censoring others but not yourself. One test of tolerance is provocation. When you sit down to dinner with your disagreeable relations, or comrades who bask in their rectitude and compassion, you have a civic duty to annoy them.

BACKGROUND AND CONTEXT

1. According to Kaminer's title, it is our "civic duty to annoy." Explain what you think she means by this. What examples from her essay support your opinion?
2. How would you describe Kaminer's general attitude toward the way people think? What do you make of her opening sentence? How does it help characterize her as an author? What tends to annoy her about conversations she reports in her second paragraph?

STRATEGY, STRUCTURE, AND STYLE

1. Do you agree with Kaminer's statement that "teaching — or nurturing — requires that you gain students' trust and then risk having them not like you" (para. 9)? Have you ever had an experience with a teacher who was similar to this? If so, what did it mean to you?
2. What do you make of the phrase "If she seeks virtue in oppression . . . " (para. 8)? What can make oppression virtuous? Examine the entire sentence: Who is "she" and who is "we"?

COMPARISONS AND CONNECTIONS

1. Kaminer seems to believe that our society has gone too far to protect people from criticism and disappointment in college and social life. Do you agree with her? The essay was published back in 1997 — do you think her point is still relevant? Give a few examples of why or why not.
2. Have you ever exercised your "civic duty to annoy" as Kaminer did when "to irritate. . . [her] more orthodox feminist colleagues," she would "disavow any

---

[2] Comedian and LGBT activist Rosie O'Donnell (b. 1962) hosted a popular television show from 1996 to 2002.

personal guilt about being born white and middle class" and "to provoke old Uncle George," she would "defend affirmative action or the capital-gains tax" (para. 2)? If so, write a short essay describing a time you've exercised this duty. Or if not, explain what held you back.

Discussing the Unit

SUGGESTED TOPIC FOR DISCUSSION

Should a university be the place for uncensored dialogue on social issues? What about when some of that dialogue harms students, especially those living with past trauma? Have the readings in this chapter affected your views on the subject? If so, in what ways? If not, why not?

PREPARING FOR CLASS DISCUSSION

1. What does each writer see as the problems confronting American classrooms? How significant are those problems?
2. Having read the essays in this chapter, what do you think should be done to improve dialogue on college campuses in this country?

FROM DISCUSSION TO WRITING

1. In their respective looks at trigger warnings on campus, Richson and Overton each acknowledge the importance of accommodating students who may need additional help. But they differ on key points from there. Where do they differ? Do you find yourself agreeing with Richson, with Overton, or a little with both?
2. Compare and contrast how any two works in this chapter speak to the significance of free speech on campus. Why, according to the selections, is freedom of speech in a college setting important? Do you agree? Why or why not?

TOPICS FOR CROSS-CULTURAL DISCUSSION

1. Using either the Internet for research or your own experience, describe the higher education system of a country other than the United States. What ideas might be brought to the United States to improve its system? What aspects of our own higher education system might benefit another country's?
2. Based on research or your own experience, how do you think freedom of expression in the United States compares with other countries? For example, what might Michael Bloomberg have addressed if he were speaking to students in China? Or the Middle East? Do you think European students enjoy more or less freedom of speech than do American students?

Diversity: How Is the Face of America Changing?

For centuries, Americans have referred to their country — most often but not always proudly — as a "melting pot," a place where people of all backgrounds, colors, and creeds come to live and work together freely and harmoniously. Today, in what some regard as a "postracial" society, is diversity still a relevant category of discourse? Or should Americans be focusing on what brings us together more than on what separates us?

This chapter examines the voices of immigrants and minorities in America and begins by taking stock of the shifts in American demographics the last few years have wrought. In "The Changing Face of America," Haya El Nasser presents statistics that show us how much the country is changing, on paper at least. The biggest difference? Hispanics have far greater numbers — and political power — than ever before. Coupled with a shift from rural to urban concentration and a "baby bust" owing to the recent recession, El Nasser urges us to "wake up to the new face of America."

Christine Granados bears direct witness to the struggles and triumphs of this growing Latino population in an essay reminiscing on a multicultural childhood in El Paso, Texas. In "True Colors," Granados recounts her mother's efforts to reconcile Latin American roots with her U.S. setting, in particular by painting her bland Texan home a vibrant Mexican yellow. Readers get the feeling that when her mother decides "she would make her mark with color," she means on more than just the house's exterior.

"True Colors" avoids the uglier sides of the minority experience in America, especially the bigotry and generalizations to which many people of color are subjected based on their background. We all know that stereotypes can be hurtful and unpleasant, but sometimes we fail to think about the damage done by "positive" stereotypes — sweeping notions of people based on alleged advantages. In this chapter's student essay, "Positive Stereotypes Are Hurtful, Too," Hailey Yook examines the burden of living in a community in which East Asians are presumed to be smarter than everyone else. Yook contends this stereotype is just as detrimental as a negative one, asking, "Will my capabilities and successes always be defined entirely by my race? What if I feel that I don't meet these expectations, standards and pressures that my race imposes on me . . . Am I not truly Asian?"

Many people confuse arguments like Yook's for advocacy of total assimilation — public blindness to ethnic background and cultural traditions. In an impassioned argument against conflating diversity with assimilation, Barry Lopez's "Six Thousand Lessons" celebrates the cultural diversity of people not just as an interesting spice-of-life difference, but also as an essential component to our survival as human beings. Taking its title from the approximate number of human languages on Earth, Lopez argues that every culture has something vital to teach us, and rails against the "heresy of believing one place is finally not so different from another somewhere, because in the moment he is weary of variety or otherwise not paying attention."

For a sense of what Lopez is fighting against, this chapter's "America Then" looks back to 1891, when immigrants were pouring into the United States. After a wave of violence against Italian Americans, the *Nation* magazine editorialized that recent arrivals needed to do more to adopt American customs. "The Proper Sieve for Immigrants" certainly condemns acts of racist aggression; it also shifts the onus onto the immigrants, notably to become fluent in English: "As a cohesive force there is nothing that can compare to language," the editors write. Today we may find the argument quaint or even offensive, but many of our politicians are advancing similar logic as you read this. What do you think of it?

Haya El Nasser

The Changing Face of America

[*USA Weekend*, January 18-20, 2013]

BEFORE YOU READ

How is the face of America changing? Do you think the makeup of the United States would feel different to someone who time-traveled from 1950 to today? From 1960 to today? From 1995?

WORDS TO LEARN

demographic (para. 1): pertaining to social statistics, such as the number of births and deaths in a population (adjective)

diverse (para. 2): multiform (adjective)

median (para. 5): middle; average in a number sequence (adjective)

adapt (para. 7): to adjust (verb)

unprecedented (para. 12): never done or experienced before (adjective)

clout (para. 12): the power of influence (noun)

fertility (para. 19): the ability to reproduce (noun)

longevity (para. 21): the length of life (noun)

I f Rip Van Winkle[1] had slipped into his deep sleep 20 years ago and awakened today, he would have missed a stunning American revolution — a demographic one.   1

The USA now is: 2

- Led by a biracial president who will be sworn in Monday for a second term.
- More crowded (88 million more people).
- More diverse (Hispanics[2] have surpassed blacks as the largest minority).

---

[1] In Washington Irving's well-known tale "Rip Van Winkle" (written in 1818), an inebriated Rip falls asleep in the Catskill mountains and wakes up twenty years later to find a drastically changed world.

[2] Hispanics (para. 2): A name given to those descended from a group of people with a connection to Spain, but not necessarily of a particular *race*. The term may be used to include Cubans, Mexicans, Puerto Ricans, and South and Central Americans.

Haya El Nasser is a Los Angeles–based digital reporter for Aljazeera America. Formerly, she was a demographics reporter for USA Today. Her writing focuses on issues of business and finance, U.S. politics, and demographics.

- More urban (more than 80% live in or near cities).
- More settled in the Sun Belt (growth in the South and West accounted for 85% of the gains in the last decade).

Van Winkle probably would be even more slack-jawed at the cultural upheaval before his eyes. 3

There are "childless cities" and even more childless neighborhoods because people are having fewer babies. 4

There are more single people. The median age of marriage is at a new high (28.6 for men and 26.6 for women). More people are living alone or with unmarried partners, and less than half of households are traditional husband-and-wife arrangements. 5

What may shock our folk hero more: The latest Census data count same-sex couples and people who are multiracial. 6

"What's constant in this country is its ability to adapt — adapt to people with changing backgrounds, people with changing attitudes," says William Frey, demographer at the Brookings Institution. 7

For most of the nation's history, black-white race relations have dominated. Now, the surge in the number of Hispanics — who can be of any race but are counted as a group — has changed the equation. So has the rapid growth of Asians. 8

"But Hispanics really are a very big part of America's present and future," Frey says. "And they're not clustered in one area. They've been fanning out to all parts of the United States, and by moving into new parts of the country . . . they're becoming accepted by these communities." 9

Fueled by immigration and births to immigrants, diversity truly is at a tipping point. 10

"When one demographic group reaches one-third of the population, the group — if united — becomes very powerful and large enough to affect the election outcome," says demographer Cheryl Russell, former editor in chief of *American Demographics* and now editorial director of New Strategist Publications. "This is what happened in the last election." 11

Consider: Republican presidential candidate Mitt Romney gained an unprecedented advantage among whites but lost largely by underestimating the political clout of blacks, Asians and Hispanics, according to a Brookings analysis of the 2012 election. President Obama carried those groups by a margin of 80%. 12

"The role of minority groups, especially Hispanics, has, frankly, shocked a lot of people when they looked at the result of this election," Frey says. "People thought this was going to happen 20 years from now." 13

Change is happening fast. Just since 2000, the percentage of non-whites 14
went from 31% to 37%. But among the under-45 group, share of whites will
slip under 50% in 15 years. Among kids, it will happen in six years.

The way we live has been reshaped not just by this growing diversity 15
but also by the aging of the population and by the Great Recession that
the nation is emerging from.

Average household size is at a record low of 2.55 people. At the same 16
time, the number of homes where several generations live under one roof
is going up — a reaction to unemployment and the housing meltdown.

Yes, crowded homes are up and average household size is down. It 17
seems anything goes today. There's a hodgepodge of living arrangements,
from grandparents, kids and grandkids living under one roof to same-sex
couples, blended families and living solo.

Even though the Millennial generation that follows Gen X is even 18
bigger than the Baby Boomers, we're in the thick of a baby bust. Births
are down 9% from their peak just five years ago, a decline attributed to
a poor economy that has kept immigrants
away and forced others to postpone starting families.

> Change is
> happening fast.

"The fertility rate has fallen among 19
young women in particular," Russell says.
"The economy is driving more young people into school, causing men
and women to delay marriage."

If more opt for academia over matrimony, the result is predict- 20
able: Education levels are soaring and women are making great strides.
Women now are top degree earners at every level of higher education.
More than half of PhDs are earned by women.

Men may be losing ground in the diploma race, but they're gaining 21
on the longevity front. Although still trailing that of women, men's life
expectancy is rising at a faster rate, thanks largely to healthier living (less
smoking, more exercise) and medical advances.

The 2010 Census found that 80% of the 53,364 people age 100 and 22
up are women. Centenarians are up 5.8% in the past decade.

So, to all those who may have slept through this demographic revo- 23
lution, wake up to the new face of America. Says Russell: "We are going
through a major transformation."

VOCABULARY/USING A DICTIONARY

1. What does it mean if someone is *biracial* (para. 2)?
2. What does a *demographer* (para. 7) do?
3. What part of speech is *opt* (para. 20)?

RESPONDING TO WORDS IN CONTEXT

1. El Nasser writes that due to increased immigration and births to immigrants, diversity has hit its *tipping point*. Can you tell what a *tipping point* is (para. 10) from the context of the essay?
2. What does *slack-jawed* (para. 3) look like? Is El Nasser using the term figuratively or literally?
3. If a variety of living situations can be termed a *hodgepodge* (para. 17), how would you define *hodgepodge*?

DISCUSSING MAIN POINT AND MEANING

1. If Rip Van Winkle woke up today after a twenty-year sleep, what sort of things would have changed in the United States?
2. Diversity has reshaped the way we live and what we look like, but according to El Nasser, what other two factors have played a role in changing the American demographic?
3. In the 2012 election, which group was hugely supportive of Mitt Romney? Which groups helped win the election for President Obama with their support by coming out in numbers to vote?

EXAMINING SENTENCES, PARAGRAPHS, AND ORGANIZATION

1. How is paragraph 2 structured? Why does El Nasser organize it that way?
2. Can you think of any words related to the word *centenarians* (para. 22)? Where in the paragraph does El Nasser define it for you?
3. El Nasser could have started the essay with paragraph 2. Why does El Nasser structure the opening as she does?

THINKING CRITICALLY

1. How do you think minority groups are influencing politics, in terms of the types of candidates running for office and winning?
2. What other things besides increased diversity would shock Rip Van Winkle if he woke up after twenty years?
3. What are some of the reasons for delaying having children that might not have been true twenty years ago?

WRITING ACTIVITIES

1. El Nasser discusses the Obama/Romney presidential race and suggests reasons for its outcome. Research the election and describe a handful of typical voters in a short essay.
2. America has always been a country of immigrants. What is different about the experiences of immigrants who came to this country from the turn of the century to around 1930 and the immigrants who are coming here now? Write a profile of a typical immigrant of an earlier period, and research

where he or she might have come from, what hardships were faced once here, where he or she might have lived, and any other information that would distinguish that individual. Then, write a profile of a typical immigrant today, answering the same questions.

3. Research President Obama's parentage. Who were his parents? What can you say about their race and how differences in their race might have influenced Obama? Do you think he brings the influence of his parents, in terms of racial influence or any other factors, into his life as President of the United States? Explain.

Christine Granados

True Colors

[*Texas Monthly*, May 2014]

BEFORE YOU READ

Have you ever felt ashamed of your family or wished you were living someone else's life? What about your heritage or family would you have changed?

WORDS TO LEARN

homogeneous (para. 2): composed of all the same kind (adjective)

xeriscaped (para. 2): (refers to landscaping) designed to minimize need for water (adjective)

innocuous (para. 3): harmless (adjective)

larceny (para. 11): the wrongful taking of someone's possessions for one's own (noun)

accomplice (para. 15): someone who helps another commit a crime (noun)

gaudy (para. 19): tastelessly showy or flashy (adjective)

devoid (para. 20): not possessing (adjective)

Christine Granados is a Mexican American writer, whose fiction and nonfiction have appeared in Texas Monthly, Evergreen Review, Callaloo, *and National Public Radio's* Latino USA, *among others. She has worked as a journalist for the* El Paso Times, Austin American-Statesman, Rockdale Reporter, *and* People.

As a teenager, I held firm to the notion that I was as American as apple pie — even though, growing up on the border, I ate apple pie once a decade or less. The closest I came to the classic dessert were the empanadas[1] we got from the vendor who happened into Moe's, a Mexican restaurant in El Paso's Lower Valley. My favorite was the *piña*, or pineapple. It had the word "apple" in it, which made it more American. After my father forked over the change for our pastries, I would cry, "*¡Joven!*" ("Young man!"), like a preppy *fresa* from Juárez. Simon or Manny or one of the other waiters would come to the table and say, "*A sus órdenes.*" I would order "*más e*Sprite, please," then wash down my Mexican-style apple pie.

The minute we left the restaurant and headed home was when my fantasy truly began. Home was on the east side of El Paso, a majority Anglo, suburban neighborhood of homogeneous, earth-toned brick houses and xeriscaped yards. We had moved there from the Lower Valley, where Mexican Americans outnumbered Anglos ten to one and Pepto-Bismol–pink cinder-block homes and yards covered with corn and sunflowers were the norm. Our new community embodied the American sensibility I had acquired through a steady diet of eighties television and Tab cola. In my teenage imagination, my life was a *Family Ties* episode, and I was Alex P. Keaton's fair-haired girlfriend. So what if I had a Mexican last name and kinky brown hair? I had no trouble pretending that my parents were Elyse and Steven Keaton, without the college degrees and fancy jobs, and that we lived in a middle-class Ohio enclave with neoclassical architecture and shade trees. Our cement patio, overlooking acres of sand and tumbleweeds, was my mudroom.

The inside of our house presented more of a challenge. While the Keatons lived among innocuous beige walls with framed artwork hung in neat rows, the walls of our home were each painted a different color — peach, powder-blue, brown, midnight-blue — and bedizened with what can best be described as Mexican-style Applebee's decor. My mother — who, like me and her mother before her, was born and raised in El Paso — collected knickknacks. But she didn't focus on a single theme, like owls or roosters. Instead, she hoarded a little of everything: dried flowers, miniature elephant heads, a yard-long No. 2 pencil, baskets, coffee trays, flea-market paintings, candlesticks, clocks, rolling pins, plates, artificial wreaths, tin signs, and bird's nests, cages, and houses, all mounted to the walls. Our home disrupted my all-American fantasy, but I could live with it, as long as my mother's Mercado Juárez taste was confined to the interior.

[1] Empanadas (para. 1): A turnover or pastry of Latin American origins

By contrast, I was proud of our front yard, with its non-native ever-green shrubs, imported oleander bushes, and white glitter rocks that sparkled in the sun. At its center was a five-by five-foot plot of Bermuda grass that my mother kept a rich green year-round. The yard was identical to our neighbors' yards — a tidy, respectable garden, not embarrassing in the least. 4

That is, until my mother decided to ruin it. One day she made a special trip to a Mexican artist's workshop across town, near the Border Highway, and came home with three handcrafted and painted cement frog statues, which she described as "lifelike." 5

"I don't think real frogs hold umbrellas," I said, as we unloaded them from the car. 6

As if she hadn't heard me, she held up a frog that was in a reclining position, with its hands behind its head and its legs crossed, and said, "Look, this one could be your dad — this is exactly how his belly sticks out when he lies down." 7

This time it was me who pretended not to hear. Then she said, "Help me put these little guys in the front yard, yah?" 8

I couldn't walk away and act as though we weren't related, like I did at the mall or the mercado, so I had to think fast. "Do you really think we should put them out here?" I said, as she arranged the *ranas*. "They're so cute somebody might steal them." 9

She brushed off my comment. "Don't be silly. We left *that* neighborhood to come here." 10

That evening I called my boyfriend, Kiki, and asked him to steal my mother's yard art under the cover of night. The next day, as I was eating breakfast, my mother walked in and said, "The frogs are gone." I wondered if my television-show sweetheart Alex would have committed petty larceny for me like Kiki had — no questions asked. My mother interrupted my thought. 11

"You were right, Chris," she said. "I should have listened to you. There goes thirty dollars down the drain." 12

My sense of triumph was dampened by the sad look on her face. I tried to cheer her up. "I'll bet someone else is enjoying them in their own yard." 13

She said, "You might be right. After I drop you off at school, I'm going to drive around the neighborhood and look for them." 14

My mother spent several years scanning East Side yards for her "froggies." I never had the heart to tell her that Kiki and an accomplice had tossed her three friends out of a pickup truck in the desert near the airport, where they met a fatal and crumbly end. 15

But the frogs' disappearance didn't keep my mother down long. A 16 week later she decided to try again at giving our yard a face-lift. This time she would make her mark with color.

I got my first glimpse of her handiwork 17 from the back seat of a classmate's car as we turned onto my street. "Wow, that's *really* yellow," my friends laughed. My mother had painted our double garage doors, but it wasn't the sun-kissed yellow of the homes in El Paso's Kern Place neighborhood. It was highway-warning-sign yellow. It literally glowed in the dark.

> It was highway-warning-sign yellow. It literally glowed in the dark.

I wanted to drown myself in sand. There was no way I could con- 18 tinue my urbane fantasy life in a house that slapped people to attention. My brothers, however, kept their senses of humor. "You can take the Mexican out of the barrio, but you can't take the barrio out of the Mexican," one said. The other remarked that he knew we were in trouble when our neighbor's Mexican maid, Tencha, said, "What a beautiful color."

I nearly bit through my retainer — fashioned for me across the river 19 in Mexico — when I heard my father's friend marveling at my mother's ability to match the color of the Save 'N Gain so exactly. My mother conceded, "Well, I guess it *is* a little bright. Maybe you men can paint over it after work someday." I wasn't about to stand still while someone likened our house to a discount grocery, nor did I live my life by Mexican time. That weekend I put on a black lace headband, a Bonjour crop top, parachute pants — good for holding paintbrushes — and leg warmers, then set about making our lives less gaudy. I was finished painting by Sunday evening.

The garage doors remained white until I left for college, after which 20 my mother painted the ribbed doors with the leftover yellow paint to make them look paneled. When I saw them, I thought the fluorescent highlights stood out in a tasteful way. Our neighborhood, I'd started to realize, was indeed devoid of color.

Now, as a mother myself, those white garage doors of my adoles- 21 cence remind me of my teenage son's room. Two years ago, I had each room of our house painted a different color, and I even mounted a typewriter to the wall. When I asked my son what color he wanted, he said, "White. Leave my walls white, Mom." Then one day I brought home a three-foot-high wrought-iron Tyrannosaurus rex from a street vendor outside Cuero for our front yard. My son suggested I put it in the back because it might get stolen. Unlike my own mother, I listened.

VOCABULARY/USING A DICTIONARY

1. What is an *enclave* (para. 2)?
2. How do you think the *mudroom* (para. 2) got its name?
3. What part of speech is *urbane* (para. 18)? How is it similar to the word *urban*?

RESPONDING TO WORDS IN CONTEXT

1. What is *neoclassical* (para. 2) architecture?
2. What does it mean if something is *bedizened* with a certain décor (para. 3)?
3. When Granados's mother *concedes* something in paragraph 19, what is she doing?

DISCUSSING MAIN POINT AND MEANING

1. To whom does Granados compare her life and lifestyle?
2. What is it that Granados objects to about her mother's taste in decorating?
3. Is Granados different from her mother? How is she different *as* a mother?

EXAMINING SENTENCES, PARAGRAPHS, AND ORGANIZATION

1. How does Granados use Spanish in the essay? Is it effective?
2. What sort of details does Granados include about her childhood? Does it place her in a particular time?
3. How does the ending of Granados's essay mimic the beginning? How does it differ?

THINKING CRITICALLY

1. Why does Granados compare her life with Alex P. Keaton's? What does he represent?
2. What does "American as apple pie" mean to Granados? Is there such a thing?
3. How is Granados's life typically American? How is it not?

WRITING ACTIVITIES

1. Write a paragraph that gives some indication of where your family is from or what your family is like by including particular phrases or details that are specific to your family. Look at Granados's opening paragraphs as an example of how this is done.
2. Granados writes that she grew up on the east side of El Paso. Research El Paso and describe the city and anything that differentiates it from other cities. Where did she move from, and what community did she move into? Does Granados's description fit with the lifestyle you have researched?
3. In pairs, discuss the changes Granados's mother made to their lawn. Do you think anyone cared what the lawn looked like? Why or why not? Why do you think Granados was concerned about what it looked like? Discuss your group's thoughts with the class.

Hailey Yook (student essay)

Positive Stereotypes Are Hurtful, Too

[*The Daily Californian*, University of California–Berkeley, March 10, 2014]

BEFORE YOU READ
Are stereotypes always bad? Why might someone feel hindered by a stereotype even if it's a positive one?

WORDS TO LEARN
criteria (para. 1): standards used to judge (noun)
versatility (para. 2): ability to adapt (noun)
detrimental (para. 3): harmful (adjective)
trite (para. 5): overused (adjective)

impose (para. 5): to force something on someone (verb)
endeavor (para. 6): determined effort (noun)
oppressive (para. 7): burdensome (adjective)

For the love of everything that's good and pure, can someone please explain to me what the phrase "You're so Asian" means? And while you're at it, let me know what criteria, scale and measurements one might use for determining my degree of "Asian-ness." Maybe there's a panel of judges involved? 1

The stereotype is an interesting concept, particularly in its versatility. It can be comic and satirical and, at the same time, offensive and humiliating. My ethnicity mostly experiences positive, or "model-minority" stereotypes. But just like their negative counterparts, positive stereotypes strip people of their individuality and alienate them for not meeting the standards that are imposed upon them. 2

Negative stereotypes are widely acknowledged as harmful, so they're often effectively rejected. But positive stereotypes, which are widely embraced and even considered flattering, can be equally detrimental. One particularly harmful positive stereotype of Asians is that they are all smart. A 2010 study about the model-minority stereotype showed that Asian Americans are most likely to be perceived as nerds. OK, so a lot of people think we're smart, and of course, it's good to be smart. But this positive prejudice is just as threatening to my identity. 3

First off, like other stereotypes, it's obviously false and easily ignorable. But because it is considered more socially acceptable, intelligence in Asians 4

Hailey Yook is a student at the University of California–Berkeley.

is regarded as the result of having Asian genes[1]. The stereotype that "Asians are smart" becomes "Asians are smart only because they are Asian." Therefore, no matter how much effort, studying or practice an Asian person puts in, when he or she achieves academic excellence, it's likely that the common reaction will be along the lines of "Asians are so

> The stereotype that "Asians are smart" becomes "Asians are smart only because they are Asian."

smart" or, you guessed it, "You're so Asian." Such a person's achievement and intelligence will likely be attributed to one thing and one thing only — race.

Well, at least we're not being called stupid, right? Despite how trite this may sound, it truly is a blessing and a curse. If my race is taking all of the credit for my efforts and accomplishments, what am I as an individual? Will my capabilities and successes always be defined entirely by my race? What if I feel that I don't meet these expectations, standards and pressures that my race imposes on me . . . Am I not truly Asian? 5

I've never had that perfect 4.0, and I'm not the type to strive for absolute perfection in every academic endeavor. So yes, I'm personally victim to the pressures of this stereotype — to make sure I'm staying on top of my studies because if I ever show signs of struggle, I'm not being "Asian enough." I've witnessed during all of my years in the public school system how parents, classmates and even teachers expect the Asian student to excel and even unknowingly guide them in math and science without considering the individual student's interests and abilities. These pressures can cause some to crack. The model-minority stereotype creates unnecessary stress, prevents students from acknowledging problems with stress and seeking help and generates feelings of shame and reluctance in seeking academic assistance. 6

Out of all of the stereotypes about my race, I find this one to be the most limiting and oppressive. Although it's easy to ignore assumptions that I'm as smart as I'm "supposed" to be, it's hard to ignore that my success is attributed to my background. And it's even harder to ignore that I'm not "Asian enough" if I struggle academically. Stereotypes are inevitable, but something like intelligence can be so important to a person's life that attributing it merely to race and disguising it as a compliment is more than a stereotype — it's an outright insult. 7

VOCABULARY/USING A DICTIONARY
1. What is a *stereotype* (para. 2)?
2. What does it mean to *alienate* (para. 2) someone?
3. What is the opposite of *excel* (para. 6)?

---

[1] genes (para. 4): Genes determine heredity in living things.

RESPONDING TO WORDS IN CONTEXT

1. Yook says Asian stereotypes may cause someone feelings of *reluctance* (para. 6) in seeking academic help with studies. What does it mean if someone is *reluctant* to do something?
2. What does Yook mean when she states intelligence is sometimes mistakenly *attributed* (para. 4) to race?
3. How are Asian Americans sometimes *perceived* (para. 3) due to the stereotype she is discussing?

DISCUSSING MAIN POINT AND MEANING

1. Why is it hurtful to say, "Asians are so smart!"?
2. Does Yook think it's bad to be thought of as smart? Where does she state her opinion about that?
3. How is Yook personally affected by the stereotyping of Asian Americans?

EXAMINING SENTENCES, PARAGRAPHS, AND ORGANIZATION

1. Does the author's race (self-identification as an Asian) have any influence on how the essay affects you? Explain your answer.
2. What would happen to the essay if Yook brought in more "evidence" for her argument?

THINKING CRITICALLY

1. Do you think you excel at something or lag behind in a certain area because of your race or ethnicity? What about gender?
2. What sort of positive stereotypes do you hold about people who are Asian? Who are African American? White? Hispanic? Can you see how such stereotypes deny a person's individuality and achievement?
3. Do you think, after reading this essay, that you will think twice before you group someone into a stereotype (before you say, "You're so Asian," for example)? Which part of the essay was most compelling to you?

WRITING ACTIVITIES

1. Look on the Internet for articles written about positive stereotypes. In a short report, decide whether the majority of information out there about positive stereotyping is in line with Yook's argument. Discuss what races are being stereotyped and what the stereotypes are.
2. Consider the term *positive stereotype* in paragraph 3. In a freewriting exercise, define, in your own words, what each word means to you. Then, move on to a discussion of what positive prejudice might be — since this is a freewriting, writing can be in flashes or imagery of what comes to mind.
3. In pairs, speak with another student about what pressures are on students for academic success. Are any pressures brought about because of some sort of

stereotyping, racial or otherwise? Consider all the different ways someone can be stereotyped as you talk. Speak from personal experience if you wish.

Establishing Your Main Point

As you learn to express opinions clearly and effectively, you need to ask yourself a relatively simple question: Will my readers understand my main point? In composition, a main point is sometimes called a thesis or a thesis statement. It is often a sentence or two that summarizes your central idea or position. It need not include any factual proof or supporting evidence — that can be supplied in the body of your essay — but it should represent a general statement that clearly shows where you stand on an issue, what you are attacking or defending, and what exactly your essay is about. Although main points are often found in opening paragraphs, they can also appear later on in an essay, especially when the writer wants to set the stage for his or her opinion by opening with a topical reference, an emotional appeal, or a general observation.

For instance, University of California–Berkeley student Hailey Yook begins her essay on positive stereotypes with a humorous reflection on what it can possibly mean to be "so Asian." But in her third paragraph, having planted that idea, she states her point explicitly. Notice how she creates a context by beginning this paragraph with the given that negative stereotypes are harmful and then moves in a direction parallel with her essay, to show that it's no better to have an entire ethnicity pegged down positively.

1

States the main point of the essay

Negative stereotypes are widely acknowledged as harmful, so they're often effectively rejected. But positive stereotypes, which are widely embraced and even considered flattering, can be equally detrimental. (1) One particularly harmful positive stereotype of Asians is that they are all smart. A 2010 study about the model-minority stereotype showed that Asian Americans are most likely to be perceived as nerds. OK, so a lot of people think we're smart, and of course, it's good to be smart. But this positive prejudice is just as threatening to my identity. (2)

2

Summarizes the main reasoning

STUDENT WRITER AT WORK
Hailey Yook

R.A. What inspired you to write this essay? And publish it in your campus paper?

H.Y. Very early on in grade school, I learned from my classmates and friends that I was "lucky" to be Asian because it meant that I was smart. I went through life knowing that if I ever accomplished something that made me feel proud, the rest of the world would merely attribute these achievements to my ethnicity. It felt unfair and wrong, and I was baffled to find that such stereotypical remarks were still widely regarded as compliments when I came to college. So, as a social issues columnist for the *Daily Californian*, I felt it was right for me to write this piece.

R.A. What response have you received?

H.Y. UC Berkeley is home to so many outspoken, socially and politically active students. I love the variety of opinions present on campus and the respect we give one another despite differences in beliefs. This piece sparked both praise and backlash, both of which revealed a lot to me. For example, I learned there were many readers out there who had similar issues with their own ethnicity's associated stereotypes. Others told me that it was silly to complain about these positive stereotypes since they could actually be advantageous in the hiring process. Much of the feedback made me realize that this was a topic that readers had a lot of trouble relating to if they had never experienced it themselves.

R.A. Do you generally show your writing to friends before submitting it? Do you collaborate or bounce your ideas off others?

H.Y. I'll talk to a couple of my friends and my editor about an idea in mind before I start writing. They'll help me brainstorm about how to flesh out my thoughts onto paper. After I write, my editor and I collaborate on how to better get my message across and how to clarify certain things that may be confusing to readers. Discussion with my friends and with my editor helps immensely when it comes to developing my point of view. They help me see that others could interpret what I say a bit differently than how I think it sounds, which is useful to keep in mind as I'm writing.

R.A. What do you like to read?

H.Y. The main publications that I enjoy reading include the *Washington Post* (so much love for my hometown, Washington D.C.!), the *New Yorker*, *Wired* (I'm a bit of a tech geek), and of course, the *Daily Californian*. My absolute favorite blog is Longform.org. Longform articles are so underappreciated or skipped over by many due to the length. Whenever I have free time or am in the mood for some thought-provoking nonfiction and fiction longform pieces, I go to this blog.

R.A. What topics most interest you as a writer?

H.Y. I'm primarily interested in contemporary social issues, especially regarding inequality based on gender, race, sexual orientation, and socioeconomic status. Inequality tests the foundation of our society, and I'm fascinated in studying and writing about how reducing various forms of inequality could strengthen social cohesion and allow communities to reach their full potential.

R.A. What advice do you have for other student writers?

H.Y. Don't be afraid to write about things that you feel strongly about, even if it's likely that others might disagree. The world needs more opinionated and informed people. If you can back up your argument with the same support and evidence that made you feel strongly about it in the first place, put it on paper and share it with everyone else! If even one person has learned something interesting and new from your writing (even if that one person is yourself), keep writing!

Barry Lopez

Six Thousand Lessons

[*Prairie Schooner,* Summer 2013]

BEFORE YOU READ

Have you ever considered how many different countries and cultures there are in the world? How many have you yourself encountered?

WORDS TO LEARN

aspiration (para. 2): longing or ambition (noun)

disparate (para. 3): dissimilar (adjective)

heresy (para. 3): something at variance with accepted doctrine (noun)

persistent (para. 4): tenaciously enduring (adjective)

unpredictable (para. 4): not able to be foreseen (adjective)

copses (para. 5): thickets of trees (noun)

inutility (para. 6): uselessness (noun)

justifiably (para. 6): defensibly (adverb)

intuition (para. 7): insight (noun)

perilous (para. 7): dangerous (adjective)

profound (para. 7): going far beyond the superficial or obvious (adjective)

autonomy (para. 7): independence (noun)

deference (para. 7): respectful submission (noun)

strife (para. 7): conflict (noun)

When I was a boy I wanted to see the world. Bit by bit it happened. In 1948, at the age of three, I left my home in Mamaroneck, New York, just north of New York City, and flew with my mother to a different life in California's San Fernando Valley, outside Los Angeles. I spent my adolescent summers at the Grand Canyon and swam in the great Pacific. Later, when my mother married again, we moved to the Murray Hill section of Manhattan. Another sort of canyon. I traveled across Europe by bus when I was seventeen. I went to Mexico. In 1970 I moved to rural Oregon. I camped in the desert in Namibia and on the polar plateau, twenty kilometers from the South Pole. I flew to Bangkok and Belém, to Nairobi and Perth, and traveled out into the country beyond.

1

Barry Lopez is an author, essayist, and fiction writer. The themes of his work are humanitarian and environmental concerns. He won the National Book Award for Nonfiction for Arctic Dreams, *and his* Of Wolves and Men *was a National Book Award finalist. The* San Francisco Chronicle *has described him as "the nation's premier nature writer."*

Over the years I ate many unfamiliar meals, overheard arguments 2
on town and city streets conducted in Pashto, Afrikaans, Cree, Flemish, Aranda, and other tongues unknown to me. I prayed in houses of worship not my own, walked through refugee camps in Lebanon, and crossed impossible mountain passes on the Silk Road. Witness was what I was after, not achievement. From the beginning, I wanted to understand how very different each stretch of landscape, each boulevard, each cultural aspiration was. The human epistemologies embedded in the six thousand spoken ways of knowing God compare with the six thousand ways a river can plunge from high country to low, or the six thousand ways dawn might break over the Atacama, the Tanami, the Gobi, or the Sonora.

Anyone determined to see so many of the world's disparate faces 3
might easily succumb to the heresy of believing one place is finally not so different from another somewhere, because in the moment he is weary of variety or otherwise not paying attention. I have found myself there. But each place is itself only, and nowhere repeated. Miss it and it's gone.

Of the six thousand valuable lessons that might be offered to a per- 4
sistent traveler, here is one I received. Over the years, in speaking with Eskimo people — Yup'ik and Inupiat in Alaska and Inuit in Canada — I came to understand that they prefer to avoid the way we use collective nouns in the West to speak about a species. Their tendency is not to respond to a question about what it is that "caribou" do, but to say instead what an individual caribou once did in a particular set of circumstances — in that place, at that time of year, in those weather conditions, with these other animals around. It is important to understand, they say, that on another, apparently similar occasion, the same animal might do something different. All caribou, despite their resemblance to each other, are not only differentiated, one from the other, but are in the end unpredictable.

In Xian once, where Chinese archeologists had uncovered a march- 5
ing army of terra-cotta horses and soldiers, and where visitors could view them in long pits in situ, I studied several hundred of each with a pair of binoculars. The face of each one, men and horses alike, was unique. Itself only. I've watched hundreds of impala bounding away from lions on the savannah of Botswanan Africa, and flocks of white corellas roosting at dusk in copses of gum trees at the edge of the Great Sandy Desert in Western Australia, and I have had no doubt in those moments that, with patience and tutoring, I would learn to distinguish one animal from another.

It is terrifying for me to consider, now, how television, a kind of cul- 6
tural nerve gas, has compromised the world's six thousand epistemologies,

generalizing them into the inutility of "what we all know" and "what we all believe." To consider the campaigns mounted for all to speak Mandarin or English in order "to make life easier." To consider how a stunning photograph of a phantom orchid can be made to stand today for all phantom orchids through time. To consider how traveling to Vienna can signify for some that you've more or less been to Prague. How, if you're pressed for time, one thing can justifiably take the place of another.

During these years of travel, my understanding of what diversity 7
means has changed. I began with an intuition, that the world was, from place to place and from culture to culture, far more different than I had been led to believe. Later, I began to understand that to ignore these differences was not simply insensitive but unjust and perilous. To ignore these differences does not make things better. It creates isolation, pain, fury,

> To ignore these differences does not make things better.

despair. Finally, I came to see something profound. Long-term, healthy patterns of social organization, among all social life forms, it seemed to me, hinged on work that maintained the integrity of the community while at the same time granting autonomy to its individuals. What made a society beautiful and memorable was some combination of autonomy and deference that, together, minimized strife.

It is now my understanding that diversity is not, as I had once 8
thought, a characteristic of life. It is, instead, a condition necessary for life. To eliminate diversity would be like eliminating carbon and expecting life to go on. This, I believe, is why even a passing acquaintance with endangered languages or endangered species or endangered cultural traditions brings with it so much anxiety, so much sadness. We know in our tissues that the fewer the differences we encounter in our travels, the more widespread the kingdom of Death has become.

VOCABULARY/USING A DICTIONARY
1. What is an *epistemology* (para. 2)?
2. What does it mean to *succumb* to something (para. 3)?
3. How is something positioned *in situ* (para. 5)?

RESPONDING TO WORDS IN CONTEXT
1. What do you think a *polar plateau* (para. 1) looks like?
2. What do you think a *collective noun* (para. 4) is, based on Lopez's examples?
3. Lopez says, in paragraph 4, that caribou are *differentiated* from each other. What does that mean?

DISCUSSING MAIN POINT AND MEANING

1. What does Lopez's sentence "When I was a boy I wanted to see the world," tell you about him and the essay?
2. How do Lopez's travels shape his picture of the world? What does he learn from visiting so many places?
3. What happens when we rid the world of its diversity?

EXAMINING SENTENCES, PARAGRAPHS, AND ORGANIZATION

1. What do you think Lopez means when he says, "Witness was what I was after, not achievement" (para. 2)?
2. How do you understand the simile Lopez incorporates into his last paragraph?
3. What does the title "Six Thousand Lessons" refer to?

THINKING CRITICALLY

1. Do you think "each place is itself only, and nowhere repeated" (para. 3) is a true statement? What do you think that means?
2. Think about how television might be a "kind of cultural nerve gas" (para. 6). Is that metaphor meaningful to you?
3. Diversity is definitely a characteristic of life. Do you agree with Lopez that it is also a condition necessary for life?

WRITING ACTIVITIES

1. Research two of the places Lopez discusses in his essay. Write a brief essay comparing the two locations in terms of people, language, culture, terrain, and any other distinguishing characteristics. How are they different from each other?
2. In small groups, explore the language of the Eskimo people. Lopez remarks on their dislike of collective nouns. Are there any other differences between their language and our own? What do those differences tell us about how they see the world, compared with our worldview?
3. In a short essay, examine the campaign in this country to make English the national language. What would we lose by instituting a national language?

The Nation **Editorial Staff**

The Proper Sieve for Immigrants

The diversity that many Americans loudly applaud has largely come about through immigration. As America was being explored and settled, from the sixteenth century and well into the birth of the Republic, many nations contributed to its development — England, Spain, Holland, France, Portugal, and Sweden, to list prominent European countries only. Many immigrants came here to farm, and for many of them America did seem to be a land of opportunity. This concept of America received some of its earliest depictions in the writings of explorers such as Captain John Smith, who promoted immigration to New England in the first decade of the seventeenth century, and a French writer living in New York state, St. Jean de Crevecoeur, who in

ELLIS ISLAND IMMIGRATION STATION-NEW YORK HARBOR

© Michael Maslan Historic Photographs/Corbis

Immigrants preparing to leave Ellis Island for other destinations in the United States, circa late nineteenth century.

1782 famously created the image of America as a great melting pot: "Here individuals of all nations are melted into a new race of men, whose labors and posterity will one day cause great changes in the world."

But the history of the United States has long shown a divided attitude over immigration, which has for many decades been one of our most hotly debated issues. It's virtually impossible to turn on the evening news, visit a political site, or pick up a newspaper without encountering a range of conflicting opinions on the topic of immigration. Yet, this was also the case over a century ago, as the following editorial indicates. "The Proper Sieve for Immigrants" appeared in The Nation *magazine on April 16, 1891, during a period when immigrants, largely from Italy and Germany, were pouring into America in unprecedented numbers, causing widespread concern for health and public safety. The editorial was triggered by a New Orleans mob that earlier that March had lynched eleven Italian immigrants.*

We do not pretend to be wiser on this subject than any one else, but if it be decided that unrestricted immigration, as at present carried on, is dangerous to American institutions and ideals, it is very odd that the value of language as a political and moral test of fitness should be overlooked. Nearly all the really secure or progressive modern States are based on community of language — France, England, Russia, Germany, and Italy. The only two in Europe about whose future there are serious doubts are the polyglot States of Austria and Turkey. All European nationalities have in fact been built up on language. As a cohesive force there is nothing that can compare to language. How a democratic state governed by opinion expressed through universal suffrage could last for any considerable length of time without community of language, it is hard to conceive, for it is through community of language that men are able to feel and think the same way about public affairs, and cherish the same political ideals. Every immigrant who comes to this country speaking or understanding the English language becomes, from the day he lands, exposed to all the moral and social influences and agencies on which we rely for the maintenance and preservation of the American nationality. Everything he hears every hour helps to make him a good citizen. Every man who lands ignorant of English, on the other hand, if an ignorant man generally, is absolutely shielded for an indefinite period against all the instrumentalities of American

1

civilization. No American ideas reach him. American persuasion does not touch him. He remains a foreigner in spite of himself, outside all the great currents of popular thought and sentiment. To feel the pulse or tap the chest of such a man, therefore, in order to ascertain his probable value as a citizen, when he does not know one word of the medium in which the national life, in all fields of activity, is carried on, seems an absurdity on its face.

Moreover, the test of language would be more easily applied   2
than any other. Every immigrant who got in without ability to answer a question in English would be a witness of the inspecting officer's dishonesty, for any one could apply the test. Of course, it would have to be applied under various restrictions. It would hardly do to cut off the relatives and friends of non-English foreigners now resident in this country. Nor would it do to treat ignorance of English as a disqualification in the case of skilled or educated foreigners, for they would be sure to acquire the language promptly after settling here. But, taken for all in all, this test would shut out more of the undesirable element in immigration, and would be easier of application, and would have more practical advantages, than any other that could be devised. It is true, it would to a great extent confine immigration to English, Scotch, and Irishmen, but why not, if the restriction be really undertaken in the interest of American civilization? We are under no obligation to see that all races and nations enjoy an equal chance of getting here. This legislation, as we understand it, is to be for the benefit of the United States; and if the United States is desirous of admitting some Europeans, but only those easiest of absorption, the ones to choose are those who, when they land, can at once enter into intellectual relations with the community at large.

BACKGROUND AND CONTEXT

1. Consider the opening sentence of the editorial. Why would the massacre of Italians in New Orleans be a reason to place a restriction on immigration? Why not, say, restrict lynchings?

2. Much of the tone and language of the editorial would sound offensive to many Americans today, even though the opinion appeared in a prominent progressive journal. Can you identify some words and phrases that you would not expect to see in our media now? What does that language suggest about the attitudes of those who wrote the opinion and their audience?

STRATEGY, STRUCTURE, AND STYLE

1. What do you think the editorial writers mean by a "community of language" (para. 1)? Why is it important to them? How would they make sure immigrants will be better able to assimilate? What exceptions do they allow when it comes to language?

2. Note that the editorial assumes the nation is seeking a way to stem the tide of immigration. The argument is not a proposal to restrict immigration. What is *The Nation*'s argument about?

COMPARISONS AND CONNECTIONS

1. Note the role that diversity plays in the essays included in this chapter. That term, however, does not appear in the *Nation* editorial. Why do you think that is the case? How do you think the editorial writers would respond to the concept of diversity as the word is used today?

2. In a short essay, consider the main points of the editorial. Do you think it represents obsolete and offensive ideas? Do you see any points in the editorial that would be relevant to today's immigration debate? Single out what you think are some outdated ideas and others that could pertain to today. Explain why you think some ideas are outdated and others, if any, are still relevant.

Discussing the Unit

SUGGESTED TOPIC FOR DISCUSSION

Is cultural unification a goal worth achieving? Or is it actually problematic? Could downplaying one's membership in a particular ethnic group have negative consequences, both for individuals and society? Why or why not?

PREPARING FOR CLASS DISCUSSION

1. Do you pay attention in your daily life to the diversity around you? How does being around different kinds of people influence your life? Did the readings in this chapter change your perspective? If so, how?

2. Considering the essays in this chapter, list some circumstances in which identifying with a specific ethnic or racial group might be beneficial to an individual or to society. Conversely, list circumstances when such identification might be problematic. What do these distinctions say about the importance of race and ethnicity in modern society?

FROM DISCUSSION TO WRITING

1. Write an essay in which you compare and contrast how any two readings in this chapter examine diversity. What does each writer consider diversity to be? As you consider this question, look for points of similarity and difference in the writers' responses.

2. Imagine that you are the parent of children who are members of more than one racial or ethnic group. (And if you already are the parent of children of mixed races or ethnicities, consider them in particular.) Then, describe how you would prefer them to identify themselves, racially or ethnically, both privately and in the larger culture. Explain the reasons for your decision. If you think it would be better that your children not focus too much on their racial or ethnic identity, explain why.

TOPICS FOR CROSS-CULTURAL DISCUSSION

1. Describe the immigration challenges the United States faces today. How would you address them? What impact would your choices have on the country's diversity and character? Its history and traditions surrounding immigration?

2. What are the major ethnic or religious groups in another country you are familiar with? Are there tensions between these groups? Does one group hold more power than the others? What effect does the situation have on the well-being of the country?

5

Race: Does It Still Matter?

The previous chapter mainly examined the immigrant experience in America, but the discussion of our differences goes far beyond recent arrivals. For as long as America has existed, race has been one of its most challenging issues. In the era of the first mixed-race president, some observers say we can finally shelve it — they claim we're living in a "postracial" America, in which systematic oppression of certain ethnic groups by others is no longer a serious problem, in which Martin Luther King Jr.'s dream of a society that judges its individuals "not by the color of their skin but by the content of their character" has come true.

Not everyone agrees with this vision of progress. Some cultural critics argue that racial injustice still plagues American society, and in particular that African Americans and other minorities are the persistent victims — sometimes unknowingly — of "institutional racism," persecution that's not direct (like segregation) but systemic. Naomi Zack lays out the case for the existence of this kind of hidden racism in "More Than Skin Deep." Race, she says, is an artificial idea rather than a biological reality, and in turn racism is not just a matter of prejudging someone with different skin tone. Most minorities, she argues, suffer from a system in which they are disadvantaged from the beginning — a person whose grandparents were discriminated against directly "starts out in life without an economic and mainstream cultural foundation." Zack makes the case that we must correct imbalances early in life to reach true equality.

Jana King, a student at Louisiana State University, agrees that race in today's discussions of justice is not so much about skin color as it is about social standing; disadvantage carries down from generation to generation, she writes, maintaining segregation in practice even when it isn't legally sanctioned. In "In Living Color," King argues strongly for affirmative action, a form of positive discrimination to close the gap between privileged and disadvantaged communities. The point is not, she says, to discriminate against whites but "to allow a candidate for any position, job or education a fighting chance when up against someone who was given more opportunities."

Opponents of affirmative action, of course, point to what they consider the hypocrisy of fighting inequality with more inequality. Isn't it possible, many of them ask, to create a racially just society simply by ignoring racial differences all around? Ben Carson draws from his experience as an African American neurosurgeon to make the case for shifting our focus away from race altogether. Carson writes that accusations of racism often distract from the real socioeconomic issues at hand, and suggests that the structural racism outlined by Zack and Jana King is overblown. What really counts is what's inside each of us, he says in "Gray Matter, the Stuff That Really Matters." Racial and cultural variety are part of what make life interesting, he says, but shouldn't be regarded as a political issue anymore: "Maybe 2014 can be a new beginning when we can stop judging people based on superficial characteristics."

Over both sides of the issue lingers the reality that race identity is far more complicated than black, white, and the shades in between. In this chapter's "Spotlight on Research," author W. Ralph Eubanks explores the way that DNA testing can identify the complex ethnic identities that underlie simplistic identifications. Eubanks describes the epiphany of having his own mixed background traced through his blood, concluding that "our society's generally accepted racial categories cannot begin to address the complexity and nuance of our heritage."

No discussion of race in America can be complete without references to the legacy of slavery. Although abolished by Lincoln with the Emancipation Proclamation that took effect in the midst of the Civil War on January 1, 1863, slavery has had an enduring impact on American society. The horrific daily facts of slavery and its human abuses were commonly witnessed by millions of earlier Americans and they were especially felt by those living in the volatile years leading up to the Civil War. One of America's most influential anti-slavery advocates was himself a former slave who taught himself to read and write and eventually escaped to New York City. Frederick Douglass became perhaps the nation's most prominent orator of his time, and this chapter's "America Then" features the most famous portion of his most famous speech, called "What, to the American Slave, Is Your Fourth of July?" Hardly a rhetorical question, it was one Douglass was fully prepared to answer: To the slave it was "a day that reveals to him, more than all other days in the year, the gross injustice and cruelty to which he is the constant victim."

Naomi Zack

More Than Skin Deep

[*Oregon Humanities,* Summer 2013]

BEFORE YOU READ

What is the history behind the experience of race in this country? How did we come to our ideas about race, and how are different people affected by those ideas?

WORDS TO LEARN

provocative (para. 2): tending to provoke a reaction (adjective)

shorthand (para. 2): a simplified system of communication (noun)

foundation (para. 2): basis (noun)

determinant (para. 3): a factor that influences something (noun)

destabilize (para. 5): to make unstable (verb)

laud (para. 7): praise (verb)

heyday (para. 12): a time of success and good fortune (noun)

quota (para. 14): allotment (noun)

enclaves (para. 14): distinct, isolated areas or groups (noun)

predominantly (para. 15): chiefly (adverb)

disproportionately (para. 18): unequally (adverb)

gerrymandering (para. 19): a practice that establishes a political advantage for a party, dividing election districts unfairly to give one party a majority in many districts (noun)

implementation (para. 19): execution (noun)

accessible (para. 20): attainable (adjective)

In 2008, when Italy's Prime Minister Silvio Berlusconi referred to President Barack Obama as "sun-tanned," Italians and Americans considered it a racist gaffe. Obama's skin hue could be identical to that of a white person who has a suntan, but calling Obama "sun-tanned" disregards an ancestry and self-identification that has resulted in his African American identity.

It is provocative to refer to race simply in regards to skin color. Skin color does have a lot to do with race, but skin color differences aren't socially neutral variations in the same way that differences in hair or eye

---

Naomi Zack is a philosophy professor at the University of Oregon. She is the author of seven books and numerous papers on the topics of race, feminism, and disaster ethics. In addition, she is a member of the editorial boards of several academic journals.

color often are. Instead, skin color can be used as shorthand for the idea of race as a system of biological human types. People think that race must be biological because members of different races have different physical traits that they inherit from their parents, and biology includes the study of heredity. However, if by the term *race* we mean a system of human types that differ in objective physical ways that scientists can study, this system has no foundation in biology.

There is no single gene that determines a person's race, and the 3 combinations of genes that are more frequent in each of the major racial groups are not present in all members of those groups. Scientists have in the past differed on where to draw the line between races, coming up with anywhere between three and sixty human races. The mapping of the human genome[1] in the early twenty-first century yielded no data about race. In short, as far as biological science is concerned, there are no general physical determinants that line up with each of the major races.

What it comes down to is that people resemble their parents if their 4 parents resemble one another. If parents have different skin colors associated with different races, the child is multiracial and may not resemble either parent. The possibility that people could identify as more than one race was officially ignored by the US Census Bureau until 2000, which was the first year that respondents were allowed to check as many boxes for race as applied to them. But ever since 1967 when the Supreme Court, in *Loving v. Virginia*,[2] struck down antimiscegenation laws that prohibited racial intermarriage, mixed-race babies have been the fastest growing racial segment in national birth rates.

The growth and official recognition of multiracial populations desta- 5 bilize older beliefs that only three or four human races exist. All of the possible permutations of racial identity afforded by the census results in more than sixty different racial identities — far more than the average person can easily use when trying to identify the race of another person. Yet, the complexity of what it means to be multiracial has not dislodged commonly held ideas about race as an objective biological foundation for human difference. But although race is not a legitimate subject for biological study, it remains an important and legitimate subject for the social sciences and humanities.

Race is a social construction, or a changing idea and system of 6 behavior that human beings invent and reinvent about themselves

---

[1] Human genome (para. 3): The complete set of human genetic information, determined by DNA sequencing.

[2] *Loving v. Virginia* (para. 4): 1967 Supreme Court case and ruling that struck down laws prohibiting interracial marriage as unconstitutional.

and others, usually to organize society for their own benefit. The irony is that groups that have been racialized and who have been harmed by racism — African Americans, Latinos, and Native Americans, for example — sometimes use, as a source of pride and protest, the very identities that were originally imposed to crush them and keep them down. For instance, W. E. B. DuBois, who founded the National Association for the Advancement of Colored People in 1909, wrote about the "destiny of the Negro race" to demonstrate the excellence of black people in the face of the extreme racism of his day, which included lynching and segregation. Today, some people of color strongly resist giving up the idea of race and may remain deeply suspicious of the idea of a color-blind society because they are concerned that they will have no basis, no identity, from which to resist or politically protest racial discrimination by white people.

Because ideas about differences in race continue to have powerful   7 effects in ordinary life, it is important to know the history of these ideas. With the European colonization of other parts of the world beginning in the early 1400s, race as a form of human difference became attached to heredity. This attachment offered justification for why it was acceptable to enslave people who were seen as inferior and ineligible for freedom and equality — beliefs in universal human equality were lauded during the seventeenth and eighteenth centuries' Age of Enlightenment. Europeans and Americans who economically benefitted from colonizing Africa, India, the Americas and parts of Southeast Asia — and slave owners and their advocates — all found this justification useful. Although for many years historians lamented that blacks were enslaved because they were a different race, systematic ideas of black racial inferiority actually developed concurrently with the period of American slavery. It is more accurate to say that blacks in America became known as a different race because of the institution of slavery. Under slavery, the children of slaves were automatically slaves, even if only one parent, almost always the mother, was a slave.

The full-blown theory of human race came into existence only when   8 biology emerged as a science in the eighteenth and nineteenth centuries. Samuel George Morton in the early 1800s built on a long tradition of racial pseudoscience (which included works by the philosopher Immanuel Kant and the French writer Arthur de Gobineau) and developed a complex system based on the skull and brain sizes of different races, concluding blacks had the smallest brains, thus making them inferior to other races. His ideas were later supported by speculations about white racial superiority and ideologies of white supremacy, such as Madison Grant's 1916 book, *The Passing of the Great Race*.

By the 1940s, such theories were discredited by American cul-   9
tural anthropologist Franz Boas and in the 1950s, by his students, who
included Claude Levi-Strauss and Margaret Mead. Ideas of racial biological inferiority were further challenged after World War II through
the *Statement on the Nature of Race and Race Differences* published by
the United Nations Educational, Scientific, and Cultural Organization
(UNESCO) and *Heredity, Race, and Society* by Theodosius Dobzhansky
and L. C. Dunn. And Stephen Jay Gould, in his 1981 book, *The Mismea-
sure of Man*, explains how Morton had falsified his data. The main idea
shared in these works is that social differences among human groups are
the result of culture and history, not biology.

The racialization of blacks was not a unique historical phenomenon.   10
For instance, Arab Americans and Middle Eastern Americans were officially categorized as racially white in the census during the twentieth
century, but after the events of 9/11, fear of terrorist acts by members
of these groups led some people to think about them as a race, based
on the color of their skin. In another example, Mexican Americans are
an ethnic or cultural group and not a race, according to the US Census
Bureau. But fear of illegal immigrants has led to some police in south-
western border states profiling people who "look Mexican" and request-
ing proof of legal residence without evidence of criminal behavior.

Patterns of racialization in the United States have not been limited   11
to those who are today considered racial or ethnic minorities. When
English colonizers and settlers were the dominant group in the American
colonies, Irish immigrants were disparaged as members of a less-refined
race. Benjamin Franklin expressed fear of the cultural influence of German immigrants, referring to the dark complexions of those from southern Germany. At the turn of the twentieth century, even Franz Boas, the
progressive Jewish American anthropologist who spread the idea that
culture is not inherited and did so much to debunk old theories of racial
hierarchies, warned his colleagues about the effects on US society of a
huge influx of immigrants from eastern and southern Europe, referring
to the new arrivals as "types distinct from our own."

Italians, Poles, Germans, and some Scandinavian groups were all   12
considered dangerous nonwhites at different times and were feared by
"native-born" Americans as job competitors or proponents of socialism,
communism, and other radical ideas. For instance, the Socialist Party
of Oregon was formed in 1904, but by 1908 to 1910 — the heyday of
the national Socialist Party — the federal government investigated the
so-called Red Finns of Astoria for their dangerous, radical ideas; all
"dangerous radicals" were at that time subject to being rounded up and
deported. On the eve of World War I, President Woodrow Wilson and

members of Congress spoke out against foreign language newspapers, cultural organizations, and schools, many of which were German American. Under that pressure, most of those presses and the ethnic organizations they represented quietly folded. Second- and third-generation European immigrants then focused their energy on full cultural assimilation to dominant Anglo-America.

By World War II, most descendants of the European so-called non-   13
white races had assimilated to the dominant Anglo-American culture. Their parents and grandparents had worked hard and long at jobs that native-born Americans did not want, and they made sure that their off-spring had good educations. Fearing integration, many third-generation European immigrants left American cities to live in the suburbs after racial segregation in schools became illegal with the 1954 US Supreme Court decision in *Brown v. Board of Education*. There they often shed their ethnic backgrounds to become not only fully American, but generically white.

This process of white flight intensified after the Civil Rights legisla-   14
tion of the 1960s. Blacks moved from the South to the large northern cities of New York, Philadelphia, and Chicago, as did recent immigrants from Asia and South and Central America (after quotas on immigration were relaxed in 1965), who set up ethnic enclaves in the more impoverished areas of inner cities. Skin color, combined with poverty and cultural difference, continues to set racial and ethnic minorities apart from the more affluent society.

This economic separation of racial and ethnic minorities from what   15
is a predominantly white middle-class and/or affluent population can be explained by what is called *structural racism* in sociology and *institutional racism* in the humanities. It works like this: If someone's family is poor because his or her parents, grandparents, and great-grandparents were not permitted, because of racially discriminatory policies, to attain college degrees or work in professions that would allow them to accumulate wealth, that person starts out in life without an economic and main-stream cultural foundation. Similarly, if discriminatory housing practices like redlining[3] have prevented a person's parents or grandparents from buying a home in neighborhoods populated by whites, that creates residential segregation with people of color living in poorer neighborhoods.

The United States has a higher rate of residential racial segregation   16
in the early twenty-first century than it did in the 1970s; this matters

---

[3] Redlining (para. 15): A discriminatory practice in particular geographic areas used by employers, healthcare providers, real estate agents, and others to deny jobs, services, and houses to people based on race.

because K–12 schools in the United States are funded on a local level through property taxes, which are based on property values. Simply put, school districts with more funding can provide better educational opportunities than those that are underfunded. The funding for schools in rich white neighborhoods, where every child has a computer and there are opportunities for foreign travel, may be a thousand times greater than that for schools in poor neighborhoods where many residents are people of color.

Equal educational opportunities are important because, since the late twentieth century, the single most reliable predictor of an individual's socioeconomic success relative to his or her parents' is standardized test scores in middle school. It doesn't matter whether the tests are measuring the right things in human value terms or even in broad cognitive skills. In our present system, although race influences a young person's chances in life, high scores on standardized tests matter more. Higher scores open the doors of socioeconomic mobility more effectively than privilege because of race (being white) or gender (being male) because high school teachers and college admissions officers tend to favor and support students with high test scores. Yet, because of factors attributable to institutional racism, racial minorities are disproportionately represented in low scores on standardized tests.

Institutional racism can explain why blacks are more than twice as likely to be poor than whites in the United States, even though numerically, there are more poor whites than blacks. It can also explain why blacks also disproportionately populate the criminal justice system. In every measure of human well-being — health, life expectancy, infant survival, education, employment, and stress — blacks and Hispanics fare poorly compared to whites.

The mainstream press has made a big deal of the fact that Hispanics are the fastest growing minority and that at some time in the twenty-first century, whites will be a numerical minority in the United States. However, the term *minority* can be misleading. *Minority* means a smaller number, but throughout history, small, powerful elites have oppressed a larger number of citizens or residents (for instance, in South Africa during apartheid or in parts of the US South during slavery). Population numbers alone may seem to represent power in a democracy, but this is true only if those large in number understand their political system and can vote together for the benefit of their group. Before the Voting Rights Act of 1965, whites in some parts of the United States feared the impact of high numbers of minority voters, so they instituted poll taxes, burdensome literacy requirements, and gerrymandering. In the twenty-first century, there has been fraud in counting votes from districts largely occupied by racial minorities. In other words, the right to vote is a powerful tool for racial minorities but the implementation of this right has been an ongoing struggle.

> Institutional racism and its impact on the quality of life and political power of people of color is evidence that race still matters.

Institutional racism and its impact on the quality of life and political power of people of color is evidence that race still matters. Some believe that racial equality is apparent in the success of some blacks and Hispanics in politics, entertainment, and sports. These critics have a point. Although race matters in terms of the kind of success that most Americans value, it is not the only thing that matters. Upward socioeconomic mobility is of course possible and accessible to those who begin life with disadvantages associated with minority racial identity, but such individuals are numerical minorities in any racial group.

What this means in terms of social justice is that if our society values equal opportunity so individuals can strive for the American Dream — whatever its specific forms — then we need to fully support equality in K–12 education. This does not mean, of course, that we should ignore real differences in IQ and aptitude, but it does mean that we have to correct those inequalities in grade school that are unfairly associated with race. We like to say that every adult who makes a mistake and wants to change deserves a second chance, but we also need to remember that every child deserves a first chance.

VOCABULARY/USING A DICTIONARY

1. What part of speech is *biological* (para. 2)? What kind of science is *biology*?
2. What does the word *multiracial* (para. 4) mean? How can you guess at the meaning of the word based on what its parts mean?
3. If something develops *concurrently* (para. 7) with something else, how does it develop?

RESPONDING TO WORDS IN CONTEXT

1. The word *antimiscegenation* is used in paragraph 4. What is *miscegenation*? How does adding *anti-* change the definition?
2. What is a census (para. 5)? What did it record?
3. Zack writes that inherited differences (in this case, race) were pointed to as a justification of slavery — "why it was acceptable to enslave people who were seen as *inferior* and *ineligible* for freedom and equality" (para. 7). What does *inferior* mean? How do you define *ineligible*?

DISCUSSING MAIN POINT AND MEANING

1. How have ideas of race changed over the last 100 years in the United States?
2. What does "white flight" (para. 14) mean? When did it take place, and why?
3. According to Zack, how are children most affected by racialization in the United States today?

EXAMINING SENTENCES, PARAGRAPHS, AND ORGANIZATION

1. How does Zack incorporate the history of race in her essay? Is it important to the essay?
2. Why does Zack begin with an anecdote about the president? How does the anecdote in the introduction connect to where she ends up in her conclusion?
3. One paragraph in the essay begins, "Race is a social construction, or a changing idea and system of behavior that human beings invent and reinvent about themselves and others, usually to organize society for their own benefit." What information does Zack include in this paragraph? How is this idea pivotal to her essay?

THINKING CRITICALLY

1. Should people identify by race? What is important about such identification? Why might someone *not* want to identify by race?
2. If more people are born identifying as multiracial, what happens to the idea of race in the United States?
3. How do inequalities in grade school get associated with race? Does Zack think it's possible to avoid such seeming inequalities?

WRITING ACTIVITIES

1. Read about the Supreme Court case *Loving v. Virginia*. What does it tell you about race and how the law has approached race? Do you think the Supreme Court ruled correctly? Explain how the Supreme Court viewed the law in 1967 and the implications of the ruling for people today.
2. Using Zack's model of racial history, outline an experience of race in this country beginning with the United States' origins (I. might be "Colonial History," A. "Whites" (with subheadings), B. "Blacks" (with subheadings), and C. "Native Peoples" (with subheadings)). Plot the circumstances and interactions of different races in the outline as U.S. history progresses, ending with Zack's information about racial experience today.
3. Consider the comments of Italy's Prime Minister Berlusconi about President Obama. Discuss why calling Obama "sun-tanned" might be considered insensitive or racist. Write a short essay on whether you think race is important to mention. How should Obama have been introduced — should remarks have been made about race at all?

Jana King (student essay)

In Living Color

[*The Daily Reveille,* Louisiana State University, March 14, 2014]

BEFORE YOU READ

Have you ever heard the term *affirmative action*? Why is it used? Who benefits from it?

WORDS TO LEARN

denial (para. 1): refusal to believe or acknowledge something (noun)

judicial (para. 2): pertaining to the courts (adjective)

indicator (para. 2): something that points to something else (noun)

gradient (para. 3): an inclined surface (noun)

hyphenated (para. 3): pertaining to people of mixed origin or identity (adjective)

supremacist (para. 7): someone who believes in the superiority of a particular group (noun)

I've spent my life feeling uncomfortable when talking about race, struggling over the choice between "African-American" and "black," followed by the guilt of pointing out race at all. The arguments that we don't need to talk about race and that any effort to is laced with white guilt turned into charity have skewed racial ideologies into denial of race as an issue. Political commentator and comedian Bill Maher said it best: "The new racism is the denial of racism." As a country, we have abolished slavery, granted voting rights to everyone and elected a black president for two terms. Yet we still don't see the problem in claiming to be "color-blind." The denial of someone's ethnicity is not an acceptance of that person. Claiming to be color-blind is saying you are not comfortable accepting other people as they are, and you would feel more comfortable if they had the same background as you. 1

This is a relevant argument in the political and judicial systems in America. When Barack Obama was elected in 2008, there was an uproar over having a black president, but there were also people who claimed he was not the first black president because he is half-white. In fact, when Bill Clinton was elected in 1993, some called him the first black president, not because of his skin color but because of his birth into a single 2

Jana King is a student at Louisiana State University.

parent working class household, ability to play the saxophone and love of fast-food. The comparison of these presidents points out a truth — race isn't all about skin color in America. Sure, it's an obvious indicator of difference, but there is a set of ideas attached to the racial group that can make one person "blacker" than another.

The idea of the black race being a gradient in which one person can be blacker than another makes it apparent that "whiteness" is something that can be achieved. Indeed, white is a central point that we use to measure other races. White people don't even think of being white as a race. Race is everyone else. Nobel prize-winning author Toni Morrison touched on the idea of hyphenated identities when it comes to race: "In this country, American means white. Everybody else has to hyphenate."

> White people don't even think of being white as a race. Race is everyone else.

3

Civil rights leaders would have been disappointed to see the hyphenated identity of an African-American. In an interview with an assistant professor in the Department of Communication Studies, Bryan McCann posited that if Martin Luther King Jr. were to walk around Baton Rouge, he would see the racial divide. "He would look at the neighborhoods, poverty rates and see Baton Rouge as segregated. It's not legally sanctioned, but functionally we are an incredibly segregated society," McCann said.

4

In recognition of this segregation, several institutions have put codes in place to encourage ethnic diversity. The most popular and controversial is affirmative action. The opposition believes affirmative action is a punishment for the majority's white, slave-owning ancestors and a reward for ancestral black slaves. They cling to the belief that America is no longer racist because we are finished with slavery and everyone can vote. Let me be clear. This is not the point of affirmative action. Affirmative action covers a wide range of policies. When LSU is performing a job search, it may state women and members of minority groups are encouraged to apply. This is a weak version of affirmative action that gives LSU a cover, should anyone question the disproportionately low number of ethnically diverse employees. The point of affirmative action is to allow a candidate for any position, job or education a fighting chance when up against someone who was given more opportunities.

5

There may be a white applicant with more opportunities and probably more successes and a longer resume. Then there could be a minority applicant who works harder but has had fewer opportunities. That candidate seems like a risk to an employer, but not through any fault of their own. "To oppose affirmative action is to assume that racism is self-correcting or done. Neither is true," McCann says.

6

Those who claim affirmative action is not effective have a point, 7
though. Historically, the group that has benefited the most from the
policies are white women. The oppressive history of America can only
be interrupted by affirmatively helping those from previously excluded
groups into positions that give them the opportunity to succeed. Otherwise we could create a permanent white supremacist society. We have
overcome much in the fight against racism, but we still have a long way to
go before we are a post-racial America.

VOCABULARY/USING A DICTIONARY

1. If something is *skewed* (para. 1), what does it look like?
2. What does it mean if something is *controversial* (para. 5)?
3. A *saxophone* (para. 2) is what sort of instrument?

RESPONDING TO WORDS IN CONTEXT

1. What does it mean to be *color-blind* (para. 1)? What does Jana King
   mean?
2. If Martin Luther King Jr. would see Baton Rouge as *segregated* (para. 4), what
   would he see?
3. King refers to a reward for ancestral black slaves in paragraph 5. What does
   she mean by that? Who are the *ancestral black slaves*?

DISCUSSING MAIN POINT AND MEANING

1. What is the problem with claiming to be to color-blind, according to King?
2. If race isn't only about skin color in America, what else is it about?
3. What is affirmative action supposed to do?

EXAMINING SENTENCES, PARAGRAPHS, AND ORGANIZATION

1. If you think of this essay as being about "color," what does King say about
   color in her first three paragraphs?
2. How does King use quotations to support her ideas?
3. King uses a transition at the end of her essay to switch the direction of her
   essay. What idea has she been following that she then reverses?

THINKING CRITICALLY

1. Do you understand King's supportive stance for affirmative action? Do you
   believe that America is no longer racist?
2. What is the difference between segregation before and segregation after
   the civil rights movement?
3. Would it be difficult to choose between a white applicant with more opportunities and successes and a minority applicant who works harder but has
   had fewer opportunities?

WRITING ACTIVITIES

1. As a class, create three resumes for fictional job applicants (or school applicants. One is a privileged white applicant, one is an applicant of color (privileged or underprivileged), and the third is either white or of color (underprivileged). Once you have their backgrounds and experiences in writing, work in small groups to discuss your candidates and make a hiring decision.

2. Research Bill Clinton and Barack Obama. Write a short essay on their similarities and differences. At the end of your essay, touch on this idea of "blackness," and consider if this idea holds any weight given the portraits you've just presented.

3. King states: "Claiming to be color-blind is saying you are not comfortable accepting other people as they are, and you would feel more comfortable if they had the same background as you." Write a response to this statement. If you are white, is it important to your identity? If you are African American, is it important to your identity? If you are of another ethnicity, is it important to your identity? Try to determine why or why not.

LOOKING CLOSELY

Integrating Quotations

It's important to maintain a voice in persuasive writing, but most of the time a quotation from an authority gives your own words both extra power and validation. An expert might say something you're not entirely qualified to say, or might express ideas that correlate with yours in a way that complements your own writing but adds a different voice. Typically, writers quote specialists in the fields they're discussing, often from a published work. Louisiana State University student Jana King goes one step further, quoting an authority on race she's interviewed. The professor she cites advances her argument in a novel way; he also speaks for Martin Luther King Jr., which a professor can do far more credibly than a college student could have. The quotation shows that Jana King has put real research into her writing and shows us that it's not just her opinion we're hearing.

1 *Introduces the source* 2 *Quotation complements the argument*	In an interview with <u>an assistant professor in the Department of Communication Studies, Bryan McCann</u> (1) posited that if Martin Luther King Jr. were to walk around Baton Rouge, he would see the racial divide. <u>"He would look at the neighborhoods, poverty rates and see Baton Rouge as segregated. Its not legally sanctioned, but functionally we are an incredibly segregated society," McCann said.</u> (2)

STUDENT WRITER AT WORK
Jana King

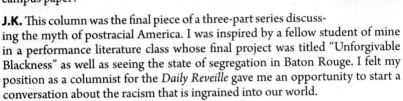

R.A. What inspired you to write this essay? And publish it in your campus paper?

J.K. This column was the final piece of a three-part series discussing the myth of postracial America. I was inspired by a fellow student of mine in a performance literature class whose final project was titled "Unforgivable Blackness" as well as seeing the state of segregation in Baton Rouge. I felt my position as a columnist for the *Daily Reveille* gave me an opportunity to start a conversation about the racism that is ingrained into our world.

R.A. Are your opinions unusual or fairly mainstream given the general climate of discourse on campus?

J.K. It varies. I'm on campus with 30,000 other individuals, and I receive a mixture of negative and positive feedback on most of my columns. Usually, the ones who agree with me are liberally minded, whereas the majority of disagreement comes from conservatives. However, I don't believe those labels are all-inclusive, and I have been surprised by some of the responses I have gotten.

R.A. How long did it take for you to write this piece? Did you revise your work? Work on multiple drafts? If so, how many drafts did you create? What were your goals as you revised?

J.K. It took me three weeks to write the entire series that this essay was a part of. That included interviews, research, writing rough drafts, and going through the editing process. I produced one column a week, with "In Living Color" taking the longest. I am lucky enough to be under student editors and faculty advisors who gave insight and edits both on form and content. Dealing with such a delicate and sensitive subject as a student writer was frightening, and I owe any positive feedback on the column to those who helped me.

R.A. What topics most interest you as a writer?

J.K. I've always had an interest in social issues. I believe that they are the first and foremost issues an individual will deal with, and because of that it is important to be aware of any rising problems. I've always been fascinated by the rise of oppressed groups and demands of power (female voting rights, civil rights movement) and the later denial of any such issues by their oppressors.

R.A. What advice do you have for other student writers?

J.K. The biggest problem I have is putting my fingers on the home keys of the keyboard and starting a column. The white blank screen is intimidating, and it's almost too much for me to get my point across. But every single time I remind myself that it is okay to fail. It is okay to write a bad column that no one likes. Because for every time I have had someone tell me that I should give up writing, that my opinions are stupid, that I have no idea what I am talking about, I have three stories of people who have felt so strongly about something I wrote that they have contacted me and expressed appreciation of my views being published in the paper. In order to write the good pieces, you also have to write the jumbled words and run on sentences. You just have to give yourself the option to fail. It's way too much pressure to expect each column to be a hit. Simply put, just keep writing.

Ben Carson

Gray Matter, the Stuff That Really Matters

[*The Washington Times*, January 7, 2014]

BEFORE YOU READ

What part does race play in your experience of politics and society? Should race be considered relevant or irrelevant to one's political life?

WORDS TO LEARN

entity (para. 5): living being (noun)

superficial (para. 6): on or affecting only the surface (adjective)

ignite (para. 8): to set on fire (verb)

hypersensitive (para. 8): excessively sensitive (adjective)

unwarranted (para. 13): without justification or authorization (adjective)

dispel (para. 13): to disperse or alleviate (verb)

foster (para. 13): to encourage (verb)

segregation (para. 14): the act of isolating or separating (noun)

default (para. 18): a failure to act (noun)

adhere (para. 24): to stay attached (verb)

prescribed (para. 24): dictated or defined (adjective)

Ben Carson is a former neurosurgeon, credited as being the first surgeon to separate conjoined twins at the head. He is a weekly columnist at The Washington Times, *and has published six best-selling books. He was awarded the Presidential Medal of Freedom in 2008, the nation's highest civilian honor.*

A few years ago, I was participating in a national radio interview when the questioner asked me, "Dr. Carson, I notice that you don't speak very often about race. Why is that?" 1

I replied, "It's because I'm a neurosurgeon." 2

The puzzled look on her face demanded further clarification. 3

I proceeded to explain that when I take a patient to the operating room and open the cranium, exposing the brain, I am operating on the actual thing that makes that person who they are. 4

The hair, scalp and skull bones are merely external coverings of the critical entity — namely, the brain — which determines all the most important things about us as human beings. 5

We have a choice of concentrating on superficial characteristics, which mean little or nothing, or concentrating on the source of our humanity, our intellect, our personality and the content of our character. 6

A few weeks ago, during her television program on the Fox News Channel, Megyn Kelly made reference to the racial makeup of Jesus Christ and Santa Claus. She indicated that in American culture they are usually portrayed as Caucasian. 7

This ignited a firestorm of protests and disagreement as do many innocent remarks in today's hypersensitive culture. There was little discussion of who Jesus Christ was or his message, nor was there much reference to the symbolism of Santa Claus. 8

> Why do we in America, almost half a century after the death of Martin Luther King, still continue to make judgments based on the color of one's skin rather than the content of one's character?

Instead, accusations of racist tendencies were leveled. 9

In the Bible, many characters are described in some detail when it is relevant to the story being told. The fact that there is little or nothing describing the physical appearance of Jesus should serve as an indicator of the irrelevance of racial descriptions for someone with such an important mission. 10

Why do we in America, almost half a century after the death of Martin Luther King, still continue to make judgments based on the color of one's skin rather than the content of one's character? 11

Those who seem most concerned about race are the so-called progressives, some of whom claim that if we stop fanning the flames of racial injustice, we will return to the days racial prejudice was acceptable. 12

This kind of pessimism is unwarranted, and we need to remember that a great deal of the racism in the past was based on total ignorance, 13 which bred fear and hatred. Those wishing to maintain the unjust status quo were in no hurry to allow the truth to be revealed to whites or blacks about the other side, since such revelations would dispel myths and foster harmony.

Thus, segregation and blissful ignorance were maintained at all costs. The fear and loathing that characterizes the political atmosphere in America today is also based on ignorance.   14

Too many people are willing to listen to the inflammatory rhetoric of the dividers who happily toss out accusations of racism against critics of the president of the United States whenever people disagree with his policies.   15

Rather than acting like third-graders and calling each other names, why not actually discuss the policies themselves?   16

Why not have a discussion about the gigantic issues facing our society, such as whether we want the government to control our lives and the lives of everyone around us, as opposed to the original vision for this country, of individual independence and self-determination?   17

If we are to thrive, we must be able to see the big-picture issues and not get bogged down with superficial, peripheral problems. The direction of our country is a very big deal, and if we don't have a serious discussion about it, the nature of our society will change by default.   18

I am very grateful that God gave us racial variety. Who would want to go to the National Zoo if every animal was a Thompson's gazelle?   19

Who would visit the national aquarium if every fish was a goldfish? Who would want to get up in the morning if everybody looked exactly like them?   20

In an episode of "The Twilight Zone"[1] many years ago, a very beautiful and smart young woman was regarded as unsuitable for society. It was revealed at the end of the episode that everyone else was quite ugly, which, for that society, was the norm.   21

They judged the woman harshly because her external appearance was different. Obviously, creator Rod Serling was ahead of his time with his social commentary.   22

Maybe 2014 can be a new beginning when we can stop judging people based on superficial characteristics.   23

We will know that America has made substantial social progress when black Americans are not expected to adhere to any particular political philosophy, just as white American do not have a prescribed political doctrine to which they must adhere.   24

---

[1] *The Twilight Zone* (para. 21): Popular fantasy/science fiction television series created by Rod Serling that ran in the 1950s. It was hugely popular and led to a number of spin-offs.

Fortunately, we get to choose whether we are going to use the mag-   25
nificent gray matter that sits between our ears as opposed to our skin
color to determine who we are and our course of action.

VOCABULARY/USING A DICTIONARY

1. What is a *cranium* (para. 4)?
2. What does the prefix *ir-* mean? What is *relevance*? What is the definition of *irrelevance* (para. 10)?
3. If you didn't know the meaning of the word *inflammatory* (para. 15), what words, located within *inflammatory*, might lead you toward a definition?

RESPONDING TO WORDS IN CONTEXT

1. What does someone who is *Caucasian* (para. 7) look like?
2. What is *pessimism* (para. 13)? What might its opposite be?
3. What part of speech is the word *peripheral* (para. 18)? What does it mean to be *peripheral* or on the *periphery* of something?

DISCUSSING MAIN POINT AND MEANING

1. Carson writes, "When I take a patient to the operating room and open the cranium, exposing the brain, I am operating on the actual thing that makes that person who they are" (para. 4). What sort of a characteristic is race, in Carson's opinion?
2. In this essay, who are the "dividers" (para. 15) in this country, and what are they saying?
3. What three things does Carson name as the most important aspects of who we are? Are these things superficial or essential?

EXAMINING SENTENCES, PARAGRAPHS, AND ORGANIZATION

1. Is this essay about "gray matter" and what really matters? Where in the essay does Carson talk about "gray matter"?
2. Where does Carson incorporate an allusion into his text? What is alluded to? Why is it effective?
3. Does Carson clarify which policies are being overlooked or underdiscussed due to race? Where might these policies have been brought into the essay or looked at in more detail?

THINKING CRITICALLY

1. Carson writes, "Maybe 2014 can be a new beginning when we can stop judging people based on superficial characteristics" (para. 23). Is race irrelevant? Do you think it is possible for a society to be color-blind when it comes to race?

2. Carson comes to the opinions he expresses first through his work as a doctor — he deals with people's internal organs, and race plays no part in his work. The essay moves into a discussion of politics. Should race play no part in political discussions? Where do the realms of politics and medicine differ and where are they the same?

3. Does Megyn Kelly's comment about the racial make-up of Jesus Christ and Santa Claus seem racist to you? Why might it have been construed that way?

WRITING ACTIVITIES

1. Write a response to Megyn Kelly's references about Jesus and Santa Claus (you should research the incident on the Fox News Channel first). Before you write, outline a list of points you want to make in support of her comments as innocent or against her comments as having a racist tone to clarify your position.

2. Create a short screenplay or play dialogue similar to Rod Serling's *The Twilight Zone* episode referenced in this essay. It should be a form of social commentary — consider some aspect of society that can be explored in a conversation between characters or "types." Be sure to include a character list at the beginning of the script that briefly identifies the speakers.

3. Read Frederick Douglass' "Fourth of July" speech on p. 164. With that text and Ben Carson's essay in mind, write briefly about issues of race and your feelings about how far this country has come, or how little things have changed, in 2015 in the way we deal with race and racial inequality.

Spotlight on Research

W. Ralph Eubanks

Color Lines

[*The American Scholar,* Spring 2013]

W. Ralph Eubanks is an author, journalist, professor, and public speaker. He served as the director of publishing of the Library of Congress in Washington, D.C., from 1995 to 2013. Currently, he is the editor of the Virginia Quarterly Review. *In 2007, he was the recipient of a Guggenheim Fellowship for his memoir,* Ever Is a Long Time: A Journey Into Mississippi's Dark Past.

My family's complex racial history, filled as it is with myths and truths, led me 1 to DNA ancestry testing. I had begun writing a book on the life and times of my maternal grandparents, whose marriage around 1915 was an act of defi-

continued

ance in a part of the South governed by Jim Crow laws. In that book, *The House at the End of the Road,* my purpose had been to tell the little-known story of mixed-race families in the American South, like my mother's, that prevailed in spite of Jim Crow and laws against interracial marriage. As the book took shape, a scientific study caught my eye.

In late 2005, scientists reported the discovery of a gene mutation that   2 had led to the first appearance of white skin in humans. Other than this minor mutation — just one letter of DNA code out of 3.1 billion letters in the human genome — most people are 99.9 percent identical genetically. And yet, what divisions have arisen as a result of such a seemingly inconsequential genetic anomaly. Moreover, this mutation had separated members of my family along tightly demarcated racial lines for three generations. As this discovery became known, I was invited to join a class on race relations at Pennsylvania State University in which all the students participated in DNA ancestry testing as a way of discussing contemporary attitudes about race and cultural identity.

Through the DNA tests, students came to realize that the racial or ethnic   3 identities they grew up with were sometimes in conflict with their genetic material, belying the notion of racial purity. In class, I listened to students talk about racial labels and identities, and whether ancestry testing had changed their perceptions of themselves. Most embraced the newly found diversity that their DNA test revealed, and none felt that ancestry testing had changed their personal identities. Still, the discovery of mixed ancestry was a struggle for a few. One white student wondered whether her African heritage came from "a rape in my past," and another thought that her African DNA must have come from "promiscuous family members." These comments were indicative of the stigma that any hint of African ancestry carries for many white Americans. No one suggested that racial passing — which I'd immediately brought up in the discussion — might explain some of these traces of mixed heritage. Only one student even seemed to understand the idea of racial passing. He grew up in an interracial home, with a father of Jamaican descent and an Irish mother, and he was close to both sides of his family. Although issues of race were discussed openly at home, he told me, no one ever forced him to choose between being black and being white. And in spite of having fair skin, he did not claim to be white, choosing instead to forge his own identity as multiracial, thus embracing his phenotypic ambiguity.

When the instructor, sociologist Sam Richards, asked whether I would   4 be interested in taking my own DNA ancestry test, as part of a larger DNA study being conducted by anthropologist Mark Shriver, I did not hesitate to say yes. Given that I already knew my mixed-race background, the results weren't shocking: 60 percent West African ancestry combined with 32 percent European, six percent East Asian, and two percent Native American. The East Asian ancestry was the only surprise, but Mark explained that Asians and Native Americans are closely related evolutionarily. (Several years later, I took a second and more sophisticated DNA test that revealed slightly different results: 50 percent African, 44 percent European, and six percent Asian. These two sets of results are within the margin of error.)

Outside Mark's office at Penn State, I studied a wall of photographs 5 showing the faces of various people from his DNA study, from Penn State and around the world, each image accompanied by the ethnic designation that person identified with. Beside the photograph was a paper flap, which, when lifted, showed what a DNA sample revealed about that person's ethnic background. As I went through photograph after photograph, few of the personal ethnic identities matched the DNA profiles. Most people had some mixture of DNA from at least two groups; many, like me, had genetic ancestry from Europe, East Asia, West Africa, and Native American groups. Blond people had African and Asian ancestry, and several dark-skinned people had more than half of their DNA from Europe.

What we see when we look at a person may or may not correlate to his 6 or her ancestral and ethnic background. DNA results confirmed for me that identity cannot be constructed based on a "percentage" of African ancestry, and that our society's generally accepted racial categories cannot begin to address the complexity and nuance of our heritage. I soon began to think about race only in terms of culture and biology together. And as race became an abstract rather than a concrete concept, the categorical ways in which I had thought about race in the past were quickly broken down. Once we see how small the differences are that bring about the characteristics we think of as racial — hair, skin color, eyes, facial features — in relation to the entire human genome, it's hard to make a fuss about them. Our differences are astonishingly slight.

DRAWING CONCLUSIONS

1. Does this essay qualify as a personal essay? Why or why not?
2. Why did Eubanks decide to test his own DNA? What do Eubanks's students learn from studying their own genetic material?
3. What do most people think *race* is? Does this essay challenge that assumption?

Frederick Douglass

From "What to a Slave, Is the Fourth of July?"

One of America's greatest public figures, Frederick Douglass (1817–1895), was born into slavery in Maryland and worked as a field hand and servant until he managed to escape to New York City in 1838 at the age of twenty-one. Self-educated (he taught himself to read and write) and fiercely determined, Douglass transformed himself into one of the nation's most formidable intellectuals and writers of his time. He served in a number of government positions, published his own periodicals, and was known as an outstanding orator and eloquent civil-rights advocate. His life and career became a model for such powerful African American leaders as W. E. B. Du Bois and Martin Luther King Jr. Besides a large number of famous speeches (such as his 1852 Fourth of July oration), Douglass is also the author of the enduring American memoir, The Life and Times of Frederick Douglass, which first appeared in 1881.

Douglass delivered his best-known speech on July 5, 1852 in Rochester, New York, where he was invited to help celebrate the nation's seventy-sixth birthday. The speech is very long and for those interested the full text can easily be found online. Early in the speech, Douglass makes his position clear when he famously says: "This Fourth of July is yours, not mine. You may rejoice, I must mourn." It must be remembered that the address is being delivered in an era when slavery was not only still widely practiced in America but also had many defenders. Although Abolitionism — the movement to abolish slavery — was gaining ground in northern states, the Civil War and Lincoln's Emancipation Proclamation were years away. In the following excerpt that demonstrates the intricate art of persuasion, Douglass passionately argues not about the evils of slavery but about why arguments to abolish it are needed at all.

Fellow-citizens; above your national, tumultuous joy, I hear the   1
mournful wail of millions! whose chains, heavy and grievous yesterday, are, today, rendered more intolerable by the jubilee shouts that reach them. If I do forget, if I do not faithfully remember those

bleeding children of sorrow this day, "may my right hand forget her cunning, and may my tongue cleave to the roof of my mouth!"[1] To forget them, to pass lightly over their wrongs, and to chime in with the popular theme, would be treason most scandalous and shocking, and would make me a reproach before God and the world. My subject, then fellow-citizens, is AMERICAN SLAVERY. I shall see, this day, and its popular characteristics, from the slave's point of view. Standing, there, identified with the American bondman, making his wrongs mine, I do not hesitate to declare, with all my soul, that the character and conduct of this nation never looked blacker to me than on this 4th of July! Whether we turn to the declarations of the past, or to the professions of the present, the conduct of the nation seems equally hideous and revolting. America is false to the past, false to the present, and solemnly binds herself to be false to the future. Standing with God and the crushed and bleeding slave on this occasion, I will, in the name of humanity which is outraged, in the name of liberty which is fettered, in the name of the constitution and the Bible, which are disregarded and trampled upon, dare to call in question and to denounce, with all the emphasis I can command, everything that serves to perpetuate slavery — the great sin and shame of America! "I will not equivocate; I will not excuse;"[2] I will use the severest language I can command; and yet not one word shall escape me that any man, whose judgment is not blinded by prejudice, or who is not at heart a slaveholder, shall not confess to be right and just.

But I fancy I hear some one of my audience say, it is just in this circumstance that you and your brother abolitionists fail to make a favorable impression on the public mind. Would you argue more, and denounce less, would you persuade more, and rebuke less, your cause would be much more likely to succeed. But, I submit, where all is plain there is nothing to be argued. What point in the anti-slavery creed would you have me argue? On what branch of the subject do the people of this country need light? Must I undertake to prove that the slave is a man? That point is conceded already. Nobody doubts it. The slaveholders themselves acknowledge it in the enactment of laws for their government. They acknowledge it when they punish disobe-

2

---

[1] Biblical quotation, from *Psalm 137*.

[2] Douglass quotes noted abolitionist William Lloyd Garrison (1805-1879)

dience on the part of the slave. There are seventy-two crimes in the State of Virginia, which, if committed by a black man, (no matter how ignorant he be), subject him to the punishment of death; while only two of the same crimes will subject a white man to the like punishment. What is this but the acknowledgment that the slave is a moral, intellectual and responsible being? The manhood of the slave is conceded. It is admitted in the fact that Southern statute books are covered with enactments forbidding, under severe fines and penalties, the teaching of the slave to read or to write. When you can point to any such laws, in reference to the beasts of the field, then I may consent to argue the manhood of the slave. When the dogs in your streets, when the fowls of the air, when the cattle on your hills, when the fish of the sea, and the reptiles that crawl, shall be unable to distinguish the slave from a brute, *then* will I argue with you that the slave is a man!

For the present, it is enough to affirm the equal manhood of the   3
Negro race. Is it not astonishing that, while we are ploughing, planting and reaping, using all kinds of mechanical tools, erecting houses, constructing bridges, building ships, working in metals of brass, iron, copper, silver and gold; that, while we are reading, writing and cyphering, acting as clerks, merchants and secretaries, having among us lawyers, doctors, ministers, poets, authors, editors, orators and teachers; that, while we are engaged in all manner of enterprises common to other men, digging gold in California, capturing the whale in the Pacific, feeding sheep and cattle on the hill-side, living, moving, acting, thinking, planning, living in families as husbands, wives and children, and, above all, confessing and worshipping the Christian's God, and looking hopefully for life and immortality beyond the grave, we are called upon to prove that we are men!

Would you have me argue that man is entitled to liberty? that he   4
is the rightful owner of his own body? You have already declared it. Must I argue the wrongfulness of slavery? Is that a question for Republicans?[3] Is it to be settled by the rules of logic and argumentation, as a matter beset with great difficulty, involving a doubtful application of the principle of justice, hard to be understood? How should I look to-day, in the presence of Americans, dividing, and subdividing a discourse, to show that men have a natural right to

---

[3] He means citizens of a republic, not the political party that Lincoln belonged to.

freedom? speaking of it relatively, and positively, negatively, and affirmatively. To do so, would be to make myself ridiculous, and to offer an insult to your understanding. — There is not a man beneath the canopy of heaven that does not know that slavery is wrong *for him*.

What, am I to argue that it is wrong to make men brutes, to rob   5
them of their liberty, to work them without wages, to keep them ignorant of their relations to their fellow men, to beat them with sticks, to flay their flesh with the lash, to load their limbs with irons, to hunt them with dogs, to sell them at auction, to sunder their families, to knock out their teeth, to burn their flesh, to starve them into obedience and submission to their masters? Must I argue that a system thus marked with blood, and stained with pollution, is *wrong*? No! I will not. I have better employments for my time and strength than such arguments would imply. What, then, remains to be argued? Is it that slavery is not divine; that God did not establish it; that our doctors of divinity are mistaken? There is blasphemy in the thought. That which is inhuman, cannot be divine! Who can reason on such a proposition? They that can, may; I cannot. The time for such argument is passed.

At a time like this, scorching irony, not convincing argument, is   6
needed. O! had I the ability, and could I reach the nation's ear, I would, today, pour out a fiery stream of biting ridicule, blasting reproach, withering sarcasm, and stern rebuke. For it is not light that is needed, but fire; it is not the gentle shower, but thunder. We need the storm, the whirlwind, and the earthquake. The feeling of the nation must be quickened; the conscience of the nation must be roused; the propriety of the nation must be startled; the hypocrisy of the nation must be exposed; and its crimes against God and man must be proclaimed and denounced.

What, to the American slave, is your Fourth of July? I answer: a   7
day that reveals to him, more than all other days in the year, the gross injustice and cruelty to which he is the constant victim. To him, your celebration is a sham; your boasted liberty, an unholy license; your national greatness, swelling vanity; your sounds of rejoicing are empty and heartless; your denunciations of tyrants, brass fronted impudence; your shouts of liberty and equality, hollow mockery; your prayers and hymns, your sermons and thanksgivings, with all your religious parade, and solemnity, are, to him, mere bombast, fraud, deception, impiety, and hypocrisy — a thin veil to cover up

crimes which would disgrace a nation of savages. There is not a nation on the earth guilty of practices, more shocking and bloody, than are the people of the United States, at this very hour.

Go where you may, search where you will, roam through all the monarchies and despotisms of the old world, travel through South America, search out every abuse, and when you have found the last, lay your facts by the side of the everyday practices of this nation, and you will say with me, that, for revolting barbarity and shameless hypocrisy, America reigns without a rival.

8

BACKGROUND AND CONTEXT

1. Although Douglass realizes his audience is gathered to celebrate Independence Day, why do you think he brings up the unpleasant subject of slavery? How is slavery related to the festive occasion?
2. Who are the "millions" Douglass refers to in the opening line of this portion of his speech? What is their relation to his audience and how is it expressed in sound?

STRATEGY, STRUCTURE, AND STYLE

1. Note Douglass's question about argument: "What point in the anti-slavery creed would you have me argue?" How does he use the claim that there is nothing to argue about as a way to help him organize his argument?
2. What does Douglass mean when he says "Must I undertake to prove that the slave is a man? That point is conceded already. Nobody doubts it. The slaveholders themselves acknowledge it in the enactment of laws for their government." How does the slaveholder's enactment of laws "acknowledge" that slaves are human beings?

COMPARISONS AND CONNECTIONS

1. A decade after Douglass delivered his address, Abraham Lincoln would issue the Emancipation Proclamation that legally ended the institution of slavery. How does that historical fact affect your response to the July Fourth oration? Would Douglass's speech still be relevant after Lincoln's act? In a short essay discuss how relevant you think Douglass's address is today. Does it possess only historical interest to twenty-first century readers or do parts still resonate?
2. Read Douglass's address in the context of the other selections in this unit. In a short essay, describe how you think Douglass might respond to current thinking on the topic of race. As an ardent abolitionist who advocated for the elimination of slavery, how do you think he would perceive race relations today?

Discussing the Unit

SUGGESTED TOPIC FOR DISCUSSION

Some authors in this unit illustrate their point through personal experience, and others through data and historical analysis. With that in mind, which essays did you find most interesting? Which arguments seemed the most sound? Why?

PREPARING FOR CLASS DISCUSSION

1. The authors in this chapter assert that race is a social construct, meaning that it is created by social or cultural practices — not something fixed in nature. Could any other aspects of who we are or what is important to us, such as gender or religious belief, also be considered social constructs? Why or why not?

2. How would you compare these authors' different recommendations for dealing with racial issues? Are some more practical than others?

FROM DISCUSSION TO WRITING

1. What images of race do these authors discuss and challenge in their essays? Make a list of perceptions or misperceptions about African Americans. Where do these ideas about what it means to be African American come from?

2. Although the works in this unit address similar issues, Frederick Douglass' medium, the speech, differs significantly from the others. Write an analysis of how the medium makes a difference in how Douglass delivered his message. How does the medium affect an author's language or structure?

TOPICS FOR CROSS-CULTURAL DISCUSSION

1. America has a particularly deep history of racial division, but other countries have been in the news in recent years for their internal racial tensions. Research another country that has recently experienced conflict over race. What is the nature of the conflict? What, if anything, is being done about it?

2. In the United States, race has long been portrayed as divided between whites and African Americans, but the increasing Hispanic population is challenging this. How do you think it is changing or complicating discussions of race in the United States?

Guns: Can the Second Amendment Survive?

To the perpetual confusion of this country, its founders wrote in the Second Amendment to the Constitution that "A well regulated Militia, being necessary to the security of a free State, the right of the people to keep and bear Arms, shall not be infringed." The precise meaning of this right, and whether it still applies to modern society, has been the subject of heated debate. In particular, tragic public events like the 2012 school shooting in Newtown, Connecticut, have raised the question of whether public safety trumps an antiquated liberty to own guns.

In the poignant essay that provides a backdrop for this chapter, Brian Doyle reminds us of what happened that horrible day at Sandy Hook Elementary School. "Dawn and Mary" recounts the heroism of two staffers at the school who, according to the media reports he cites, "jumped, or leapt, or lunged out of their chairs and ran toward the bullets," ignoring their instincts for self-preservation to try to save children. Doyle frames the shooting in an entirely human way, from the point of view of its victims, barely alluding to the attacker. Whatever our view of the social ills at play in Newtown, Doyle reminds us that we can't forget the bravery of the victims.

Doyle does not propose anything we might have done to prevent their killing, though, or otherwise make a political argument in his essay. Advocates of gun control — government efforts to ban or restrict private ownership of guns—often respond to terrible events like the one Doyle describes by declaring that tighter control of firearms in Connecticut might have averted the tragedy. In "Kids and Guns and Public Safety," columnist Diane Dimond takes on the argument for government control with an appeal for personal responsibility. If the Newtown killer's mother had done more to secure her dangerous weapons, Dimond argues, she could have created a stronger deterrent than any public restriction. Public safety, she writes, relies not on the state to ban guns but on "every adult who owns guns to step up and be accountable for it."

This chapter's student debate, from the pages of the *Loyola Phoenix* (from Loyola University in Chicago), begins with a similar plea for responsible gun ownership rather than regulation. Christina Tenuta focuses on moments in which armed citizens have, rather than causing violence, contained and even prevented it. In "Responsible Gun Ownership Saves Lives," Tenuta echoes Dimond's case that gun control can be costly and ineffective, whereas an armed public can keep shootings at bay. Tenuta criticizes the media, which, she says, have focused on armed killers but "have largely ignored cases in which private individuals, not police officers, have been the first responders to a shooting."

James Stancliffe provides Tenuta's counterpoint in "Guns Act As Force Multiplier, Endangering Everyone." Stancliffe views guns not as a way to prevent violence, but as its central and most deadly cause in today's society. "When an unarmed person gets into a fight with another unarmed person there is the smallest risk of serious injury or death," he writes. "Throw guns into that mix and the risk greatly increases, not just to those involved but also to any bystanders." Stancliffe makes an appeal for gun control on the grounds that our laws must respect public safety before they consider the individual right to own a gun.

Two works in other media round off this exploration of a complex intersection of safety and liberty. Cartoonist Matt Bors skewers our dialogue on guns by considering what else we might blame for violence—at which both gun control advocates and opponents can comfortably laugh. Jane Vincent Taylor's poem "New Law Makes Local Poet Nervous," meanwhile, tells a subtle story of fear and surprise in consequence of an "open carry" law allowing private citizens to carry unconcealed guns.

The amendment that started the gun control debate in America remains itself a matter of debate. What does the Constitution mean by "a well regulated Militia" or "keep and bear Arms"? In this chapter's "America Then," literary critic Paul Fussell examines the question with detailed attention to language. He concludes that while the authors of the amendment might not have approved of banning guns, they weren't setting out a provision for complete freedom, either; they intended government to control the use of deadly weapons to keep it orderly. "If interstate bus fares can be regulated," Fussell says, "it's hard to see why the Militia can't be, especially since the Constitution says it must be." As you read through this chapter, keep in mind this essential tension between freedom and public safety — a common theme in our public affairs.

Brian Doyle

Dawn and Mary

[*The Sun,* August, 2013]

BEFORE YOU READ

Who comes to mind when you hear the word *hero*? What comes to mind when you hear the word *courage*? Who are our modern-day heroes and what do they teach us about ourselves?

WORDS TO LEARN

staffer (para. 1): a member of a staff or group of employees (noun)

fiber (para. 8): something fine and threadlike; a filament (noun)

E arly one morning several teachers and staffers at a grade school[1] are in a meeting. The meeting goes for about five minutes when the teachers and the staffers hear a chilling sound in the hallway. *We heard pop pop pop,* said one of the staffers later.   1

Most of the teachers and the staffers dove under the table. That is the reasonable thing to do and that is what they were trained to do and that is what they did.   2

But two of the staffers jumped, or leapt, or lunged out of their chairs, and ran toward the bullets. *Jumped* or *leapt* or *lunged* — which word you use depends on which news account of that morning you read. But the words all point in the same direction — toward the bullets.   3

One of the staffers was the principal. Her name was Dawn. She had two daughters. Her husband had proposed to her five times before she said yes and finally she said yes and they had been married for ten years.   4

---

[1] Sandy Hook Elementary School: The events described in this essay took place at Sandy Hook Elementary School on December 14, 2012, in Newtown, Connecticut. Twenty-year-old Adam Lanza shot and killed twenty children and six adults at the school. Dawn Hochsprung and Mary Sherlach approached the gunman, as did Natalie Hammond, who survived.

Brian Doyle is editor of Portland *magazine at the University of Portland in Oregon. He is the author of more than a dozen books and was a finalist for an Oregon Book Award in two categories. His most recent book is the sea novel* The Plover, *which was published in 2014.*

They had a cabin on a lake. She liked to get down on her knees to work with the littlest kids in her school.

The other staffer was named Mary. She had two daughters. She was a crazy football fan. She had been married for thirty years. They had a cabin on a lake. She loved to go to the theater. She was going to retire in one year. She liked to get down on her knees to work in her garden.

The principal told the teachers and the staffers to lock the door behind her and the other staffer and the teachers and the staffers did that. Then Dawn and Mary ran out into the hall.

You and I have been in that hallway. You and I spent years in that hallway. It's friendly and echoing and when someone opens the doors at the end of the hallway a wind comes and flutters through all the kids' paintings and posters on the tile walls.

The two women jumped, or leapt, or lunged, toward the bullets. Every fiber in their bodies, bodies descended from millions of years of bodies leaping away from danger, must have wanted to dive under the table. That's what you are supposed to do. That's what you are trained to do. That's how you live another day. That's how you stay alive to paint with the littlest kids and work in the garden and hug your daughters and drive off laughing to your cabin on the lake.

> The two women jumped, or leapt, or lunged, toward the bullets.

But they leapt for the door, and the principal said *lock the door after us,* and they lunged right *at* the boy with the rifle.

The next time someone says the word *hero* to you, you say this: There once were two women. One was named Dawn and the other was named Mary. They both had two daughters. They both loved to kneel down to care for small holy beings. They leapt out of their chairs and they ran right at the boy with the rifle, and if we ever forget their names, if we ever forget the wind in that hallway, if we ever forget what they did, if we ever forget how there is something in us beyond sense and reason that snarls at death and runs roaring at it to defend children, if we ever forget that all children are our children, then we are fools who allowed memory to be murdered too, and what good are we then? *What good are we then?*

VOCABULARY/USING A DICTIONARY

1. What does a *principal* (para. 4) do?
2. A *lunge* (para. 3) is what sort of an action?
3. What is a *rifle* (para. 9)? In what way is it different from a *gun*?

RESPONDING TO WORDS IN CONTEXT

1. What do the words "jumped, or leapt, or lunged" indicate about the action happening in the essay?
2. The writer describes a *chilling* (para. 1) sound heard in the hallway. What does *chilling* mean when used in a literal way? What might the figurative sense mean?
3. What does it mean to *snarl* at death (para. 10)? Why does this verb fit so well with the action taking place in the essay?

DISCUSSING MAIN POINT AND MEANING

1. What event is being described in this essay? How can you tell?
2. What details do we know about the women, Dawn and Mary? Are they similar or different people?
3. How does this essay act as a memorial for the two women? How can you tell the writer wants to memorialize them?

EXAMINING SENTENCES, PARAGRAPHS, AND ORGANIZATION

1. The first names of two women are prominent in this essay, but the writer never uses their last names. Why do you think the writer skips this seemingly important detail?
2. The writer circles back to certain details over the course of the essay. Which details get repeated? What is the effect of repeating them?
3. The essay slips into second person and first person plural at times. Why do you think the author made this choice?

THINKING CRITICALLY

1. How was Mary and Dawn's behavior drastically different from what anyone would have expected?
2. What are your associations with the word *hero*? Are Mary and Dawn typical heroes? Why or why not?
3. Why is memory important in this essay? What role does it play?

WRITING ACTIVITIES

1. Research the Newtown, Connecticut, school shooting. Write a brief article about Dawn Hochsprung and Mary Sherlach based on what you learn. It should be a more formal and factual article, the kind you would find in a newspaper. How is your article different from Doyle's essay? What does that tell you about your intentions in writing versus Doyle's?
2. With a partner, come up with a list of ten heroes. They can be famous or people connected to you in some personal way. Discuss each hero's attributes. As a class, discuss what traits groups felt were heroic, and consider whether the two women in the essay share those attributes. Try to formulate a definition of the word *hero* based on class discussion.

3. In a freewriting exercise, write about a school shooting — this one, or one of the many others that have taken place (including Columbine or Virginia Tech) in the last fifteen years. What do you know about the people involved (victims and perpetrators)? Describe them as best as you can without researching them. Can you recall names, ages, and interests? Discuss your freewritings as a class.

Diane Dimond

Kids and Guns and Public Safety

[*Rockland County Times,* January 25, 2014]

BEFORE YOU READ

Who is responsible for keeping kids safe from guns? Gun owners? Schools?

WORDS TO LEARN

herd (para. 1): to gather and move a group (verb)

anticipation (para. 1): a feeling of excitement (noun)

mantra (para. 4): word or phrase repeated often, indicative of someone's beliefs (noun)

accountability (para. 10): state of being responsible for something (noun)

resolve (para. 16): determination (noun)

divert (para. 16): to turn from one course to another (verb)

Uncle Jim used to herd a group of us kids into the car on a sunny Saturday morning and head to an isolated area outside town. His son, little Jim, my two cousins Sandy and Terry and I were full of anticipation. We were going target shooting — with a real gun — guided every step of the way in gun safety by Uncle Jim. I was about 10 or 11 years old, the oldest kid in the group. 1

"Always keep a gun pointed toward the ground until you are ready to shoot," Uncle Jim would say as he set up soda cans on a fence post about 20 yards away. "Never, ever point a gun toward another person." 2

Diane Dimond is an investigative reporter and television journalist. She is a special correspondent for Newsweek *and* TheDailyBeast.com. *She has also worked as a correspondent for* Hard Copy, Extra, Entertainment Tonight, *and* Court TV. *She has authored two books,* Be Careful Who You Love: Inside the Michael Jackson Case *(2005) and* Cirque Du Salahi: Be Careful Who You Trust *(2010).*

There on the southwest mesa outside Albuquerque, we would wait   3
patiently until it was our turn to handle the pistol. Uncle Jim would stand
right behind us and guide the gun into our hands, showing us the proper
technique of cradling the hands around the bottom of the gun while
placing an index finger on the trigger. Then he'd take a step back as we
raised our arms and tell us to shoot when we were ready.

While in an outstretched-arms position, I once turned slightly to   4
ask him a question and he urgently leapt forward repeating the mantra,
"Never, ever point a gun toward another person." He steered my arms
back to the target.

If only there were an Uncle Jim inside every house with a kid and a   5
gun.

I've been thinking about my young gun training ever since hearing   6
news about the school shooting in Roswell, New Mexico — just two
hundred miles from where I learned to handle a gun. The first thought
that popped into my head was, "Where did that child get access to a
gun?"

The 12-year-old got the shotgun from his home and used it to shoot   7
two of his classmates inside a crowded gymnasium at the Berrendo
Middle School. Thankfully, the result was not as devastating as some
other recent school shootings but, at this writing, one of the wounded
children, a 12-year-old boy, is still hospitalized in critical but stable condition. The second victim, a 13-year-old girl, is home now but still has
limited use of one arm.

According to police, a search of the boy's home revealed several fire-   8
arms were kept there — none stored in a lock box.

Police revealed that the boy actually took time to saw off the stock of   9
the shotgun, making it easier to conceal. Again I thought, "Where were
the parents while he was doing this?"

Some will say it's not fair to question what the parents did or didn't   10
do. Know that my heart aches for them, as well as the wounded and their
families. But who else was responsible for that child getting a gun? Who
else was responsible for the safekeeping of that weapon? It's easy to say
that placing blame solves nothing but without accountability, where are
we? After the next school shooting involving a minor do we just shrug
our shoulders and say nothing different could have been done?

Reader Alice Benson of Tijeras Canyon, New Mexico, wrote me   11
after the Roswell shooting. She helps newly released parolees navigate
the court system and Benson asked, why don't schools have just one
entrance, manned by an armed guard and a metal detector?

"One might ask: When was the last time we heard of someone get-   12
ting shot in a courtroom?" Benson wrote. "Why do we guarantee the

safety of criminals in a courtroom and not the safety of our most vulnerable resource — our children?"

Good question, Alice. Let's do the math. 13

After a school shooting in Cleveland, Ohio, a few years ago, city 14
fathers set aside 3.3 million dollars to put metal detectors in all 111 public schools and to hire guards to man them. Can your state afford that?

The average cost of a good metal detector is upwards of $7,000. Multiply that by the approximately 100,000 public schools in this country. 15
Then, of course, there would be the cost of each guard's salary. If he or she is armed, they would have to be state certified and trained and would certainly ask for more than minimum wage, say, $40,000 or $50,000, per school, per year.

So, I'd say the bottom-line answer to the question, Alice, is that there is 16
not enough money in the school budget. And not enough resolve to divert funds from other sources to provide such security at the entrance to every single public school. Right or wrong, it is the reality.

> A much easier solution would be for every adult who owns guns to step up and be accountable for it.

Also, let's ask ourselves: Is that the 17
atmosphere we want while educating children? Think of the tension and anxiety surrounding airport security checkpoints. Will the kids have to take off their shoes and belts and empty their pockets every morning? Is that how we want our kids to start each day?

A much easier solution would be for every adult who owns guns to 18
step up and be accountable for it. Even if there is no child in the home, firearms are tops on the list of items robbers look for when they break into a house. Every gun owner should have conscience enough to secrete their gun or, preferably, buy a locked cabinet in which to store every weapon they own. I'm not talking about gun control here. I'm talking personal responsibility.

I wonder what Uncle Jim, a life-long resident of New Mexico, would 19
have said about the Roswell school shooting? He's no longer with us, but I bet he'd hang his head, let out a big sigh, and say, "Never, ever point a gun towards another person."

VOCABULARY/USING A DICTIONARY

1. What is a *lock box* (para. 8)?
2. What might *safekeeping* (para. 10) mean, even if you've never looked it up in the dictionary?
3. What does it mean to be *accountable* (para. 18) for something? What part of speech is it?

RESPONDING TO WORDS IN CONTEXT

1. What part is the *stock* (para. 9) on a shotgun?
2. When Dimond speaks of school shootings *involving a minor* (para. 10), what does she mean?
3. What does it mean to *secrete their gun* (para. 18)?

DISCUSSING MAIN POINT AND MEANING

1. Who does Dimond wish would be a role model for children today in order to avoid gun violence?
2. What does Alice Benson suggest is the appropriate response to make children safer from guns?
3. Why is Benson's idea rejected by Dimond?

EXAMINING SENTENCES, PARAGRAPHS, AND ORGANIZATION

1. What is the framing Dimond uses for this essay?
2. What do you notice about the paragraphs in this piece? What does this tell you about the medium in which it was published?
3. Why do you think Dimond responds directly to Benson in the piece?

THINKING CRITICALLY

1. Do you think Benson has a good idea about how to prevent school shootings? Do you think Dimond has a better one? Explain.
2. Where do you think Dimond falls on the question of gun control after hearing her thoughts on public safety and knowing her familiarity with guns?
3. Do you think a responsible adult can prevent school shootings? Is that enough to affect the outcome if a child has access to a gun?

WRITING ACTIVITIES

1. Research the Roswell, New Mexico, school shooting. How is this shooting similar to or different from other school shootings that have been in the news? Write an essay that compares the shooting at Roswell to another shooting.
2. Write an article for a paper that offers your opinion on kids and guns and public safety. What do you think can be done to avoid the sort of shootings that have become more and more common since the Columbine shooting in 1999?
3. Has an adult in your life ever helped you maneuver through some of the most complicated situations you've encountered as a young adult? Write a personal essay that begins with an anecdote from the past (either recent or from childhood) that eventually offers an explanation of how that adult helped guide your choices in life for the better, or how you have been affected by that person's words or actions.

Christina Tenuta (student essay)

Responsible Gun Ownership Saves Lives

[*The Loyola Phoenix,* Loyola University, Chicago, October 2, 2013]

James Stancliffe (student essay)

Guns Act As a Force Multiplier, Endangering Everyone

[*The Loyola Phoenix,* Loyola University, Chicago, October 23, 2013]

BEFORE YOU READ

There is a gun debate raging in this country. Tenuta and Stancliffe's essays show two sides of that debate. Ask yourself how you feel about the public's access to guns, and consider which argument you agree with and why.

WORDS TO LEARN

stalemate (Tenuta, para. 1): a position in which no action can be taken (noun)

scrutiny (Tenuta, para. 2): a close and searching look (noun)

infringe (Stancliffe, para. 2): to encroach upon (verb)

ensure (Stancliffe, para. 4): to guarantee (verb)

imposition (Stancliffe, para. 6): the putting on of something as a burden; something imposed (noun)

legacy (Stancliffe, para. 6): something handed down from the past (noun)

Christina Tenuta and James Stancliffe are students at Loyola University, Chicago.

181

Christina Tenuta (student essay)

Responsible Gun Ownership Saves Lives

[*The Loyola Phoenix,* Loyola University, Chicago, October 2, 2013]

In the past few years, the United States has seen some of the deadliest 1
mass shootings in American history. As Democratic and Republican
lawmakers are stuck in a stalemate over gun control laws, the rest of
the nation remains perplexed over many factors that have caused these
awful and random acts of violence. It's easy to look at these mass shootings and become solely involved with the complexity of the gun control
debates, but reflection on these mass shootings begs the question: Do
Americans really need guns?

And that answer is simple. The Second Amendment promises 2
Americans the right to bear arms. Over the course of the past few years,
this amendment has been under intense scrutiny after instances such as
the Columbine, Virginia Tech, Newtown and, most recently, the Washington Naval Yard shootings. Obviously, these random acts of violence
do not represent the ultimate goal of the Second Amendment, which is
protection.

Americans, through the Second Amendment, reserve the right to 3
protect themselves using any means necessary. Modern technology has
given us the best weapon for protection: the firearm. Are lawmakers to
ignore the basic right of protecting oneself
or one's family? Absolutely not. Most people might argue that the police force is the
only protection citizens need and on some
level, these people are right. But as great as
the police force is, it is not always the first
responder in a dire situation.

> Are lawmakers to
> ignore the basic
> right of protecting
> oneself or one's
> family?

Mass killings from guns have been the 4
focus of today's media, but the media have largely ignored cases in which
private individuals, not police officers, have been the first responders to
a shooting. They have prevented countless innocent deaths by stopping
shooters using their own privately owned and licensed guns. In the Trol-
ley Shooting of February 2007, Sulejman Talovic killed five people and
wounded four more in Salt Lake City before an off-duty cop, Kenneth
Hammond, distracted him before police arrived. As an off-duty cop,

Hammond had the same limited rights as a civilian, and was in no way responsible for subduing Talovic or using his authoritative police power. He acted like an average citizen, using safe gun ownership in order to prevent a shooter from doing any more damage.

Gunfire broke out in the Clackamas County Mall in Oregon in December 2012, where two people were fatally shot and one wounded when Jacob Roberts opened fire. A mallgoer, Nick Meli, drew his own gun on Roberts, but did not fire it being fully aware he might accidentally hit one of the shoppers trying to escape Roberts' gunfire. Meli not only prevented what could have been an even greater tragedy, but also illustrated smart and responsible gun safety amidst the chaos of the shooting. 5

These shootings and dozens of others could have potentially been far more deadly. However, thanks to the Second Amendment, the shooters were stopped by people with privately owned firearms before any more deaths were caused. Cases like these have been largely ignored in the Great Gun Debate. 6

Most recently, gun control advocates looked at Europe's strict gun control policies as the answers to the United States' firearm problems. The United Kingdom has one of the strictest gun control policies in the world, which makes it very difficult for individuals to own guns and easy for the authorities to revoke gun rights from those who already own them. The United Kingdom requires a lengthy application process in which the applicant needs a substantial reason for acquiring a gun, as well as a character evaluation from family members or friends. The United Kingdom has even proposed the idea that policemen should not carry firearms on their person. 7

In 2011 England saw some of the worst riots in its history. What started as a peaceful march to protest police force after Mark Duggan was killed by a policeman earlier that April soon turned violent. Storefronts in the Tottenham area of London were lit on fire after being looted, and Tottenham's Bruce Grove Post Office was burned down. These riots soon spread to other London neighborhoods and the police force failed to control them. The riots lasted several days and caused massive amounts of damage. Unable to defend themselves against violent protesters and looters, many property owners had to watch their livelihood being taken from them. Perhaps if the United Kingdom's gun laws permitted more citizens to carry guns, the looters could have been stopped and less damage done. Should Americans really use this as their model for gun reform? 8

The United States' gun policies are much more lenient in comparison. Gun policies vary from state to state, but most states require a permit or license and registration. The United States' seemingly lenient 9 gun policies, however, offer no proof that firearms are misused. Statistics show that homicides from firearms have, in fact, steadily decreased since 1993. The gun laws already put in place aim to serve the purpose of the Second Amendment — the right of Americans to own a firearm and the right to protect themselves and others. The gun debate, as it stands, incorporates a number of different issues that have created an entirely complex argument. New regulations, like the New York state SAFE Act, have been proposed throughout many states to curb gun sales by requiring background checks that would restrict purchases by both the mentally disabled and those with a criminal record. But one thing is certain: Americans should have the basic right to keep their guns.

James Stancliffe (student essay)

Guns Act As a Force Multiplier, Endangering Everyone

[*The Loyola Phoenix*, Loyola University, Chicago, October 23, 2013]

One of the things that I had to consider in coming to a university in Chicago was the threat of gun violence. This is not just because of the homicide rate in Chicago, but also because it is a completely alien idea to a foreign national. I went from a nation where virtually no one owns a gun to a nation where gun ownership is glorified. Many of my friends in Australia asked me why I was putting my safety at risk coming to the United States for college. I still believe that it was a great decision, but I would be lying if I said that the danger of guns was not a concern. The basic thrust of Christina Tenuta's argument is that Americans should be able to keep their guns. I have to respect that the United States has a long and proud culture of gun ownership, with many seeing the acquisition of a firearm as a rite of passage. However, I don't believe that significant actions to reduce gun violence infringe on the ability of law-abiding citizens to own guns in a safe and responsible way. I also don't believe that the current situation is at all acceptable — it must change.

I disagree with the interpretation of the Second Amendment to the Constitution that many pro-gun Americans hold to. The full text reads, "A well regulated Militia, being necessary to the security of a free State, the right of the people to keep and bear Arms, shall not be infringed." This "well regulated Militia" was not designed to protect citizens, as it makes explicitly clear. Instead, it is "necessary to the security of a free State." In an era when the United States possessed an army comprised solely of people who had to bring their own weapons to battles and had to police their own streets after the departure of the occupying British forces, this was seen as essential. But this does not mean that they wanted to guarantee the right of every person to own any weapon they desire. Nor did they anticipate the incredible advances in technology that modern firearms represent. The problem with these advances is that they are used to such destructive capacities in modern life.

> This does not mean that they wanted to guarantee the right of every person to own any weapon they desire.

My main issue with guns is that they act as a force multiplier. When an unarmed person gets into a fight with another unarmed person there is the smallest risk of serious injury or death. Throw guns into that mix and the risk greatly increases, not just to those involved but also to any bystanders. For example, Nick Meli did not open fire in the 2012 Clackamas County Mall shooting because he realized the risk of hitting bystanders due to the limitations of his marksmanship skills. However, in many situations, an intervening third party does not consider the risk of firing. 3

The Congressional Research Service estimated that there were more than 310 million guns in the United States that did not belong to the military. That's barely less than the population of the country — America has a population of 314 million. According to the Centers for Disease Control, in 2010 there were 11,078 firearm-related murders in the United States, along with more than 19,000 other gun deaths. While in a few situations private citizens have reduced casualties by intervening, one must remember that almost all of the perpetrators are private citizens as well. In many cases, they purchase the guns and ammunition completely legally, load and carry the guns under the protection of the law, and only when they open fire on crowds of innocents do they commit crimes. I cannot see a legal system that allows this to happen as one that should be defended. I believe that serious efforts must be made to ensure that people who would use these weapons in an offensive manner can never purchase them. 4

Many European nations, along with other countries, such as Australia, New Zealand and Canada, have implemented some degree of gun control. In Britain most police officers do not even carry guns. Yes, there were huge riots in London in 2011. However, it should be noted that 5 during this incredible and violent confrontation, only five people were killed. Instead of high death tolls, there was significant property damage. But property can be rebuilt. Glass can be reset. Stores can be restocked. Lives cannot be restarted after death.

I have the highest respect for law-abiding gun owners in the United   6
States and admire the familial tradition of hunting. Indeed, I look forward to being able to hunt during my time in this country. But because guns are so widely and freely available in the United States, and unfortunately find their way into the hands of criminals and maniacs, tens of thousands of people die every year. Without guns those lives would not have ended. To stand for reform in this situation is not to stand for an imposition of government or the death of a cultural legacy. It is to take a stand for life.

VOCABULARY/USING A DICTIONARY
1. What happens when something is *revoked* (Tenuta, para. 7)?
2. What is the opposite of *lenient* (Tenuta, para. 9)?
3. What verb does *acquisition* (Stancliffe, para. 1) come from?

RESPONDING TO WORDS IN CONTEXT
1. Why did Stancliffe need to consider the *homicide* (para. 1) rate before coming to school in Chicago?
2. What do you think *marksmanship* (Stancliffe, para. 3) means, given the story that Tenuta and Stancliffe relate about Nick Meli?
3. Can you guess what a *perpetrator* (Stancliffe, para. 4) is, given the context of Stancliffe's paragraph?

DISCUSSING MAIN POINT AND MEANING
1. Do Tenuta and Stancliffe have any places of common ground in their essays?
2. Which two situations in both essays are pointed to as examples in which gun control is at issue?
3. What is different about Tenuta's and Stancliffe's interpretations of the Second Amendment?

EXAMINING SENTENCES, PARAGRAPHS, AND ORGANIZATION
1. How does Stancliffe arrange his ideas in certain sentences to support an idea and then show his disagreement with some aspect of it?
2. Tenuta introduces short narratives that describe recent events in which having a gun was important, in her opinion. How do these effectively vary the writing in the paper?
3. How does Stancliffe's essay pattern itself on Tenuta's?

THINKING CRITICALLY

1. Should a citizen, a bystander, a victim, be the "first responder in a dire situation" (para. 3, Tenuta) if his or her response is with a firearm? Why or why not?

2. What do you think of Tenuta's idea that the London riots and lootings of 2011 could have been stopped by property owners carrying guns? Do you agree with Stancliffe's idea that it was better for no one in that situation to have had guns?

3. Do you think Stancliffe's perspective is important because he does *not* come from a country with the same approach to guns found in the United States? Are his views similar to those held by Americans who are for gun control in this country?

WRITING ACTIVITIES

1. Look at the situations described in the Clackamas County mall and the London riots. Write your own response to either Tenuta's or Stancliffe's essay, outlining your own thoughts about the availability of guns in those situations.

2. Look into the Columbine, Virginia Tech, Newtown, and Washington Navy Yard shootings mentioned in Tenuta's essay. Again, write a response to Tenuta's essay (or Stancliffe's, which doesn't mention those incidents explicitly), and outline your own thoughts about the availability of guns in those situations.

3. Research the United Kingdom's position on guns. What are its gun laws? Do you think they would work in the United States (Tenuta asks, rhetorically: "Should Americans really use this as their model of gun reform?") Write a short explanation of why they would or would not.

LOOKING CLOSELY

The Art of Argument: Summarizing an Opposing Position

When making a case for or against a position, writers should let the reader know in advance the arguments on the other side. In this way, the reader will clearly understand the major points or positions the writer disagrees with. Once the writer has offered a summary of an opponent's position, he or she can then go on to state their disagreement. In a short essay, however, the writer will not have the space to offer a fully detailed summary of his or her opponent's position. Note how Loyola University student James Stancliffe succinctly summarizes the position he opposes in one sentence. He is then able to demonstrate very clearly his own position: Although he respects the views of many responsible gun owners, he does not believe that taking action to reduce gun violence violates Second Amendment rights. He will then argue this case in the body of his essay.

1 *Concisely summarizes opposing view*	<u>The basic thrust of Christina Tenuta's argument is that Americans should be able to keep their guns.</u> (1) I have to respect that the United States has a long and proud culture of gun ownership, with many seeing the acquisition of a firearm as a rite of passage. <u>However, I don't believe</u>
2 *Counters with his own argument*	<u>that significant actions to reduce gun violence infringe on the ability of law-abiding citizens to own guns in a safe and responsible way. I also don't believe that the current situation is at all acceptable — it must change.</u> (2)

Matt Bors

Guns and Butter(ed) Popcorn

[*The Nation*, January 22, 2014]

© Matt Bors/Universal Uclick

VISUAL DISCUSSION AND PERSUASION

1. What current issue is this comic about? Is it about more than one?
2. How does the joke unfold in the cartoon — the joke about the fact that no one wants to blame gun violence on a lack of gun control laws?
3. How does Bors emphasize the absurdity of the words in his pictures?

Matt Bors is a nationally syndicated editorial cartoonist and editor and the comics journalism editor for Cartoon Movement. *In 2012, he was a finalist for the Pulitzer Prize and became the first alt-weekly cartoonist to win the Herblock Prize for excellence in cartooning. His work has appeared in the* Los Angeles Times, *the* Nation, Village Voice, *and the* Daily Beast, *among others.*

Jane Vincent Taylor

New Law Makes Local Poet Nervous

[*This Land,* February 1, 2013]

On November 1, 2012, Oklahoma passed an "open carry" law allowing people to carry guns in public. According to the on-line journal *thinkprogress*, "Oklahoma's new "open carry" law allows individuals with permits to openly carry guns in public and into many types of businesses including restaurants, grocery stores and banks, unless they post a sign prohibiting guns."

Writing in the Oklahoma literary journal, *This Land*, the poet, Jane Vincent Taylor, described one of the effects the new law had on her while visiting a local coffee shop. Do you think her first reaction of fear was justified? What do you think is her personal response to the new law?

Taylor's work has appeared in This Land, Nimrod, *and* Still Point Quarterly, *among other periodicals. Her most recent book of poetry is* The Lady Victory *(2012). She teaches creative writing at Ghost Ranch, a retreat and education center in New Mexico.*

Others have book fests, opera
and garden expos.
We have gun shows. Ammo.
Freedom
and now more freedom: open carry.

Like an old decoy I sit in my local coffee shop.
Post-holiday parents, toddlers in tow, order the special –
peppermint pancakes, dollar-size.

Megan fills the ketchup bottles.
Poinsettias wrinkle and curl. The radio plays Reba.
In walks a vested cowboy sporting a leather holster.

I react the way a gun insists: with fear. But nearer now,
I see his fancy shoulder bag
holds only oxygen,

precious sips of life — protection,
safety — openly carried, so we can all
breathe a little easier.

Paul Fussell

A Well-Regulated Militia

The Second Amendment to the U.S. Constitution consists of a fairly brief sentence: "A well regulated Militia, being necessary to the security of a free State, the right of the people to keep and bear Arms, shall not be infringed." For centuries, this Amendment seemed straightforward and was rarely a legal issue. Yet in the politically turbulent 1960s, following the shooting deaths of President John F. Kennedy, his brother Senator Robert Kennedy, and civil rights leader Martin Luther King Jr., an anti-gun sentiment began growing. The anti-gun movement gained momentum with the attempted assassination of President Ronald Reagan in 1981, when one of the men also shot in the incident, James Brady, initiated a congressional bill that would subject gun buyers to a federal background check. Hotly contested by such pro-gun organizations as the National Rifle Association (founded in 1871 but not an influential lobbying group until 1975), the Brady Act was finally enacted in 1993. Today, with an estimated 300,000 firearm-related deaths a year—and with one highly publicized school shooting following right on the heels of another—an accurate understanding of the Second Amendment has become more important than ever: What did the framers mean by a militia and by the phrase "to keep and bear Arms," and does the Second Amendment guarantee the right of individual citizens to own weapons or only those who are part of a "militia"? Many legal scholars, historians, and journalists have covered this issue but few with the concision, wit, and irony of Paul Fussell. At a time when many believe the Second Amendment

---

An eighteenth-century scholar who taught for many years at Rutgers University before moving to the University of Pennsylvania, Fussell wrote numerous academic studies—on such topics as poetic meter, rhetoric, and eighteenth-century literature. But after winning the National Book Award in nonfiction for The Great War and Modern Memory *in 1975 (Fussell served in the infantry in World War II), he began writing essays on a variety of topics for a general public. One of those essays, "A Well-Regulated Militia," was published in the* New Republic *in 1981.*

should itself be amended, given its increasingly costly consequences, Fussell argues that it should not be revised or abolished but just taken literally and enforced.

In the spring Washington swarms with high school graduating   1
classes. They come to the great pulsating heart of the Republic —
which no one has yet told them is Wall Street — to be impressed by
the White House and the Capitol and the monuments and the
Smithsonian and the space capsules. Given the state of public sec-
ondary education, I doubt if many of these young people are at all
interested in language and rhetoric, and I imagine few are fascinated
by such attendants of power and pressure as verbal misrepresenta-
tion and disingenuous quotation. But any who are can profit from a
stroll past the headquarters of the National Rifle Association of
America, its slick marble façade conspicuous at 1600 Rhode Island
Avenue, NW.

There they would see an entrance flanked by two marble panels   2
offering language, and language more dignified and traditional than
that customarily associated with the Association's gun-freak constituency, with its T-shirts reading GUNS, GUTS, AND GLORY ARE
WHAT MADE AMERICA GREAT and its belt buckles proclaiming
I'LL GIVE UP MY GUN WHEN THEY PRY MY COLD DEAD
FINGERS FROM AROUND IT. The marble panel on the right
reads, "The right of the people to keep and bear arms shall not be
infringed," which sounds familiar. So familiar that the student
naturally expects the left-hand panel to honor the principle of sym-
metry by presenting the first half of the quotation, namely: "A well-
regulated Militia, being necessary to the security of a free state, . . ."
But looking to the left, the inquirer discovers not that clause at all but
rather this lame list of NRA functions and specializations: "Firearms
Safety Education. Marksmanship Training. Shooting for Recreation."
It's as if in presenting its well-washed, shiny public face the NRA
doesn't want to remind anyone of the crucial dependent clause of the
Second Amendment, whose latter half alone it is so fond of invoking
to urge its prerogatives. (Some legible belt buckles of members
retreat further into a seductive vagueness, reading only, "Our American Heritage: the Second Amendment.") We infer that for the Association, the less emphasis on the clause about the militia, the better.

Hence its pretence on the front of its premises that the quoted main clause is not crucially dependent on the now unadvertised subordinate clause — indeed, it's meaningless without it.

Because flying .38- and .45-caliber bullets rank close to cancer, heart disease, and AIDS as menaces to public health in this country, the firearm lobby, led by the NRA, comes under liberal attack regularly, and with special vigor immediately after an assault on some conspicuous person like Ronald Reagan or John Lennon. Thus the *New Republic,* in April 1981, deplored the state of things but offered as a solution only the suggestion that the whole Second Amendment be perceived as obsolete and amended out of the Constitution. This would leave the NRA with not a leg to stand on.

But here as elsewhere a better solution would be not to fiddle with the Constitution but to take it seriously, the way we've done with the First Amendment, say, or with the Thirteenth, the one forbidding open and avowed slavery. And by taking the Second Amendment seriously I mean taking it literally. We should "close read" it and thus focus lots of attention on the grammatical reasoning of its two clauses. This might shame the NRA into pulling the dependent clause out of the closet, displaying it on its façade, and accepting its not entirely pleasant implications. These could be particularized in an Act of Congress providing:

(1) that the Militia shall now, after these many years, be "well-regulated," as the Constitution requires.

(2) that any person who has chosen to possess at home a gun of any kind, and who is not a member of the police or the military or an appropriate government agency, shall be deemed to have enrolled automatically in the Militia of the United States. Members of the Militia, who will be issued identifying badges, will be organized in units of battalion, company, or platoon size representing counties, towns, or boroughs. If they bear arms while not proceeding to or from scheduled exercises of the Militia, they will be punished "as a court martial may direct."

(3) that any gun owner who declines to join the regulated Militia may opt out by selling his firearms to the federal government for $1,000 each. He will sign an undertaking that if he ever again owns firearms he will be considered to have enlisted in the Militia.

(4) that because the Constitution specifically requires that the Mili- 8
tia shall be "well regulated," a regular training program, of the
sort familiar to all who have belonged to military units charged
with the orderly management of small arms, shall be instituted.
This will require at least eight hours of drill each Saturday at
some convenient field or park, rain or shine or snow or ice.
There will be weekly supervised target practice (separation
from the service, publicly announced, for those who can't hit a
barn door). And there will be ample practice in digging simple
defense works, like foxholes and trenches, as well as necessary
sanitary installations like field latrines and straddle trenches.
Each summer there will be a six-week bivouac (without
spouses), and this, like all the other exercises, will be under the
close supervision of long-service noncommissioned officers of
the United States Army and the Marine Corps. On bivouac,
liquor will be forbidden under extreme penalty, but there will
be an issue every Friday night of two cans of 3.2 beer, and feeding will follow traditional military lines, the cuisine consisting
largely of shit-on-a-shingle, sandwiches made of bull dick (balo-
ney) and choke-ass (cheese), beans, and fatty pork. On Sundays
and holidays, powdered eggs for breakfast. Chlorinated water
will often be available, in Lister Bags. Further obligatory exercises designed to toughen up the Militia will include twenty-
five-mile hikes and the negotiation of obstacle courses. In
addition, there will be instruction of the sort appropriate to
other lightly armed, well-regulated military units: in map-
reading, the erection of double-apron barbed-wire fences, and
the rudiments of military courtesy and the traditions of the
Militia, beginning with the Minute Men. Per diem payments
will be made to those participating in these exercises.

(5) that since the purpose of the Militia is, as the Constitution 9
says, to safeguard "the security of a free state," at times when
invasion threatens (perhaps now the threat will come from
Nicaragua, national security no longer being menaced by
North Vietnam) all units of the Militia will be trucked to the
borders for the duration of the emergency, there to remain in
field conditions (here's where the practice in latrine-digging
pays off) until Congress declares that the emergency has
passed. Congress may also order the Militia to perform other

duties consistent with its constitutional identity as a regulated volunteer force: for example, flood and emergency and disaster service (digging, sandbag filling, rescuing old people); patrolling angry or incinerated cities; or controlling crowds at large public events like patriotic parades, motor races, and professional football games.

(6) that failure to appear for these scheduled drills, practices, bivouacs, and mobilizations shall result in the Militiaperson's dismissal from the service and forfeiture of badge, pay, and firearm.

Why did the Framers of the Constitution add the word *bear* to the phrase "keep and bear arms?" Because they conceived that keeping arms at home implied the public obligation to bear them in a regulated way for "the security of" not a private household but "a free state." If interstate bus fares can be regulated, it is hard to see why the Militia can't be, especially since the Constitution says it must be. The *New Republic* has recognized that "the Second Amendment to the Constitution clearly connects the right to bear arms to the eighteenth-century national need to raise a militia." But it goes on: "That need is now obsolete, and so is the amendment." And it concludes: "If the only way this country can get control of firearms is to amend the Constitution, then it's time for Congress to get the process under way."

I think not. Rather, it's time not to amend Article II of the Bill of Rights (and Obligations) but to read it, publicize it, embrace it, and enforce it. That the Second Amendment stems from concerns that can be stigmatized as "eighteenth-century" cuts little ice. The First Amendment stems precisely from such concerns, and no one but Yahoos wants to amend it. Also "eighteenth-century" is that lovely bit in Section 9 of Article I forbidding any "Title of Nobility" to be granted by the United States. That's why we've been spared Lord Annenberg and Sir Leonard Bernstein, Knight.[1] Thank God for the eighteenth century, I say. It understood not just what a firearm is and what a Militia is. It

---

[1] *Lord Annenberg . . . Knight:* Walter H. Annenberg (1908–2002) was a controversial billionaire publisher, known both for his philanthropy and for using his publication for direct personal or political ends; Leonard H. Bernstein (1919–1990) was a massively influential composer whose many works include the score for *West Side Story*.

also understood what "well regulated" means. It knew how to compose a constitutional article and it knew how to read it. And it assumed that everyone, gun lobbyists and touring students alike, would understand and correctly quote it. Both halves of it.

BACKGROUND AND CONTEXT

1. Why does Fussell mention that at the National Rifle Association's entrance, the panels cite only one part of the Second Amendment? What part is that? How does the complete sentence alter the way someone, like Fussell, may interpret the Amendment?

2. Much of what Fussell writes about the duties of a "militia" can be found in the National Guard — regular training periods, disaster service, etc. But does Fussell equate the National Guard with a militia? Why would the National Guard — given Fussell's point of view — not be equivalent to the militia Fussell calls for? Describe what you think Fussell means by a "militia" and why it is central to his argument.

STRATEGY, STRUCTURE, AND STYLE

1. Although he never claims it directly, how can you tell Fussell supports gun control? Why doesn't he believe the Second Amendment should be repealed or revised? Do you think pro-gun proponents would endorse Fussell's proposal? Why or why not? For Fussell, how would a militia work as a form of gun control?

2. Can you find any examples of humor in Fussell's proposal? Look carefully at his six suggestions on how Congress should proceed. What details do you think he means to be comic? What makes them funny?

COMPARISONS AND CONNECTIONS

1. How do you evaluate Fussell's main point: that we can understand the meaning of the Second Amendment only if we take into account both halves of the sentence? In a short essay, provide your own interpretation of the Amendment: Do you think the true meaning of the Amendment rests on the second part alone? Or does Fussell get it right?

2. Compare Fussell's essay to Wendy Kaminer's "A Civic Duty to Annoy" (p. 109). What do they have in common? How does each writer set forward an argument against an opposing view? How does each use humor to make a point?

Discussing the Unit

SUGGESTED TOPIC FOR DISCUSSION

Deciding what place guns should have in American life requires us to make many personal and public decisions. Would you let your child play with toy guns? Would you own a gun to protect yourself in your home? Would you support candidates who favor gun control?

PREPARING FOR CLASS DISCUSSION

1. Consider the issue of guns in American life from a historical perspective. To do so, analyze the meaning of the Second Amendment (see p. 171). What do you think the framers of the Constitution had in mind when they wrote those words? How did the colonists use guns in Revolutionary War America? Does the Second Amendment apply today?

2. How much control should the government have over the firearms industry? In answering this question, think about the arguments put forth in the selections in this chapter.

FROM DISCUSSION TO WRITING

1. Assume you are tasked with writing a proposal to improve the gun laws in the United States. What are your top three priorities? Why? Find statistics to support your recommendations, and be sure to cite your sources.

2. Consider a common position that isn't your own about the role guns should have in American life. Write an essay that examines why others may feel the way they do, and consider the possible pros or benefits to society behind their reasoning. Refer to at least one selection from this chapter in your response.

TOPICS FOR CROSS-CULTURAL DISCUSSION

1. Research the rules regulating the firearms industry and gun ownership in a country other than America. Does the country's constitution provide any specific right to bear arms? Do you think the United States would benefit from following the other country's approach to guns? Would the other country benefit from the United States' approach to guns?

2. Choose a country other than the United States and research its violent crime rates. How does the violence compare to that of American culture? What are some factors that promote or curb violence in that country?

7

College Sports: Should Student Athletes Be Paid?

Few issues present a set of circumstances as uniquely American as college sports. The National Collegiate Athletic Association, or NCAA, had $913 million in total revenue in 2013 — dwarfing university athletics in other nations and even some professional sports here in the United States. But unlike professional athletes, student athletes in America play for free. Is that right? Should the massive college sports industry be compensating its players, or should players be motivated only by the team spirit and love of sport that's always kept them on the fields and courts?

Political sportswriter Dave Zirin believes that, all tradition aside, the time has come for a change. In "The Shame of the NCAA" he argues emphatically that colleges (and moreover the NCAA itself) needs to start giving back to the athletes who make its money. Zirin emphasizes the exploitation of those college athletes who bring in huge profits to their schools but receive little or nothing in return. Writing just as the annual basketball ritual known as March Madness has begun, Zirin points out that, despite all the media attention and promotional hoopla, one thing will "go largely unnoticed": "the fact that kids, ranging in age from 18 to 22 and branded with corporate logos, are producing this tidal wave of revenue — and they're not receiving a dime of it." At the conclusion of his essay, Zirin offers several suggestions on how to reform "this warped system."

Still, the idea of compensation remains highly controversial. A Washington Post-ABC News poll in March 2014 found that the general public

overwhelmingly opposed compensating athletes, with only a small fraction of Americans supporting any plan to pay college athletes. The polling
results confirmed the stance of NCAA President Mark Emmert, who claims
that Americans expect athletes to "play college athletics as part of their educational experience and for the love of their sport — not to be paid a salary."
Yet public opinion does not tell the whole story, and many sports writers and
commentators have been highly vocal in their support of compensation, as
have many athletes. The matter will ultimately be decided not by public opinion but by the courts.

Moreover, even proponents of paying athletes can't agree on how exactly
it would work. Would students playing the less profitable sports get the same
wage? Would women get equal pay as men? And would student athletes form
unions to bargain collectively for better working conditions? A *New York Daily
News* cartoon suggests some of the extreme possibilities a paycheck for athletes would entail. Finally, this chapter's student essay explores the issue from a
fellow student's point of view: Pensacola State College's Tim Ajmani considers
the ways compensating players could improve not only his classmates' lives but
also their grades. Where many athletes leave school prematurely, Ajmani writes
in "Compensation for College Athletes?" pay "could provide a little more incentive to stay in school and get their degrees."

Of course, unequal academic performance is another issue that
affected athletes in college for years before the subject of financial compensation was opened. Our "In Brief" feature consists of an old joke about
college football players (you can substitute whatever college you wish) that
pokes fun at the stereotypical athlete. Yet the joke has an unexpected twist.
This sort of joke is then examined seriously in Red Smith's "The Student Athlete," an "America Then" classic that calls our universities to task for dropping
the ball with their athletes' education. Writing in 1979, Smith quotes the
astoundingly poor writing of a football player at an elite university to suggest that he hasn't received the same education as his peers. Smith claims
that the student's writing "makes it achingly clear how some institutions of
learning use some athletes" for their skills on the field without attention to
their education. Since this education is often what universities — and the
NCAA — claim athletes get in return for their play, consider as you read this
chapter whether they are exploited by the system, or whether the majority
of Americans are right in thinking they get a fair shake already.

Dave Zirin

The Shame of the NCAA

[*The Nation,* April 1, 2013]

BEFORE YOU READ

What are some of the controversies surrounding the National Collegiate Athletic Association?

WORDS TO LEARN

bracketology (para. 1): a new word for picking winning college basketball teams based on the scheduling match-ups (or brackets) determined by the NCAA (noun)

hysteria (para. 1): an uncontrollable outburst of emotion (noun)

palatial (para. 2): resembling a palace (adjective)

tantamount (para. 2) equal (adjective)

austerity (para. 3): severity (noun)

stark (para. 4): grim (adjective)

agitated (para. 6): disturbed (adjective)

impediment (para. 8): obstruction (noun)

shilling (para. 9): promoting for purposes of swindling (verb)

carnally (para. 9): physically, bodily (adverb)

embezzlers (para. 9): trusted people who take money for their own use (noun)

lucrative (para. 9): profitable (adjective)

manifestly (para. 12): clearly apparent; obviously (adverb)

confections (para. 12): skillfully crafted devices (noun)

chattel (para. 16): property, slave (noun)

afoul (para. 17): into conflict with, up against (preposition)

cartel (para. 17): organizations conspiring together to regulate and control production and costs (noun)

I t's time for that period of breathless college-hoops hysteria known as March Madness. It's time for bracketology, Final Four predictions, office pools and the gambling of billions of dollars, legal and illegal. What will go largely unnoted is the fact that kids, ranging in age from 18 to 22 and branded with corporate logos, are producing this tidal wave of revenue — and they're not receiving a dime of it.

1

Dave Zirin is the sports editor for the Nation, *and the first sportswriter at the publication in 150 years. He is a columnist for* SLAM *magazine and the* Progressive, *and is the author of eight books on the topics of American sports and politics. He was named one of* UTNE Reader's *"50 Visionaries Who Are Changing Your World."*

Welcome to the National Collegiate Athletic Association (NCAA)   2
in the twenty-first century, about as corrupt and mangled an institution as
exists in the United States. At palatial college stadiums across the country,
players are covered in more ads than stock cars and generate billions of
dollars, all to the roar of millions of fans for whom college sports are tantamount to religion. One problem cannot be tackled without the other:
the same system that spends so much on revenue-generating sports and is
the stage of the sports world's most egregious scandals, from Notre Dame
to Penn State, also exploits athletes to a degree that renders such scandals
inevitable.

A constant refrain by the yipping heads of the sports world is that   3
the NCAA is on a toboggan ride toward change, which is being driven
by financial pressures. In 2010, only twenty-two of the 120 football
bowl subdivision schools made money from campus athletics, up from
only fourteen the previous year. In a time of austerity, public universities preach, with a catch in their throat, that the revenue just isn't there.
So schools are realigning into different mega-conferences with the hope
that this will provide enough money to maintain the status quo. But even
the revenue-producing sport of football loses money.

If you look at top salaries, though, it's hard to see much austerity.   4
The numbers are mindboggling: according to *USA Today*, salaries of
new head football coaches at the bowl-eligible schools increased by
35 percent from 2011 to 2012. Average annual pay has ballooned to
$1.64 million, an astonishing increase of more than 70 percent since
2006. This is all as tuition hikes, furloughs, layoffs and cuts in student aid
have continued unabated. In an era of stagnating wages, compensation
for coaching a college football team has risen like a booster's adrenaline
during bowl season. The question is how—not just how is this possible, given the stark economic realities of most universities, but how can
schools be this shameless?

The question is increasingly relevant as the organization's crisis spills   5
into open view. "I don't recall a time when there has been less optimism
about the NCAA and how it operates," said Josephine Potuto, the former
chair of the NCAA's committee on infractions and a law professor at the
University of Nebraska, speaking to *The New York Times* recently.

After he became NCAA president in 2010, Mark Emmert had to   6
be shamed into the idea of considering basic fairness to the athletes
who generate all this wealth. In an interview on a PBS *Frontline* special,
"Money and March Madness," a visibly agitated Emmert refused to
reveal his own seven-figure salary on camera and insisted that it would
"be utterly unacceptable . . . to convert students into employees. . . .
I can't say it often enough, obviously, that student athletes are students.

They are not employees." He quickly backpedaled, though, telling *USA Today* that at the April 2011 NCAA board meeting, he would "make clear . . . that I want [paying players] to be a subject we explore."

After Emmert revealed that he was "justice-curious," the NCAA 7 quickly issued a statement that this kind of "exploration" was consistent with previous statements. Sure enough, the April meeting produced a proposal for a stipend. Even though it was quickly rescinded, the issue will not go away. In fact, just in time for the NCAA finals, we seem to have reached a tipping point on the issue of compensating college athletes. As former Syracuse all-American linebacker Dave Meggyesy said, "These are more than full-time jobs. When I played at Syracuse in the early 1960s, it wasn't like that. We had a regular season and twenty days of spring practice. Now it's year-round. It's a more cynical system now than when I played, starting with those one-year renewables. That's a heavy hammer. You get hurt, tough shit, you're out. And there's no worker's comp for injuries."

> We seem to have reached a tipping point on the issue of compensating college athletes.

The biggest impediment to reform, however, is the greed of those in 8 power. Even as schools are losing money, even as "student-athletes" put themselves at risk for free, those running the NCAA have never had it better. March Madness, the sixty-eight-team elimination basketball tournament, generates at least 90 percent of the NCAA's operating budget. That included, for 2009, a total compensation for the fourteen top executives of nearly $6 million, with the president earning $1.1 million. The association has lavished $35 million on a 130,000-square-foot expansion of its headquarters in Indianapolis. Other revenue streams come from video games, posters, jerseys and boutique credit cards featuring images of popular amateur athletes.

The corruption extends to the college sports media industry. Over 9 the past decade, the number of college football and basketball games broadcast on ESPN channels has skyrocketed from 491 to 1,320. ESPN now happens to be both the number-one broadcaster of college football and basketball and those sports' number-one news provider. Covering sports and shilling for the industry have become carnally intertwined. Nationally credited journalists from ESPN and other media outlets reportedly show up at the Fiesta Bowl a week in advance, where they stay at the finest resorts and receive a different expensive present every day, courtesy of the tournament's corporate sponsors. As DC sports radio host Steve Czaban said, "It sounds like sports-media Hannukah." The Fiesta Bowl was an embezzler's paradise awash in scandal for years, with no one the wiser until Fiesta Bowl CEO John Junker pleaded guilty to fraud last year. Then there's March Madness on CBS and its neat $1-million-per-commercial rates for the Final Four. Eight hours of coverage, with all those lucrative commercial breaks, are the cure for media recession blues.

And all that's apart from the multibillion-dollar gambling industry. 10 March Madness is now officially a busier time in Vegas than the Super Bowl. No other event unites sports fans with non–sports fans in offices and factory break rooms quite like it. Every year, overheated articles from the business press rail about declining productivity as employees fill out their brackets and lodge their bets. More than $100 billion passes through Sin City at that time — and that's chicken feed compared with the money changing hands under the table and online.

For the "student-athletes," though, there is nothing. As former LSU 11 coach Dale Brown said, "Look at the money we make off predominantly poor black kids. We're the whoremasters." Desmond Howard, who won the 1991 Heisman Trophy while playing for the Michigan Wolverines, call the system "wicked," telling *USA Today*, "You see everybody getting richer and richer. And you walk around and you can't put gas in your car? You can't even fly home to see your parents?"

This is a civil rights issue, a fact that was made manifestly clear by 12 one of the great chroniclers of the civil rights movement, Taylor Branch. The Pulitzer Prize–winning author of a magisterial three-volume series on Martin Luther King Jr., Branch also has roots in the sports world, as the co-author of Bill Russell's memoir, *Second Wind*. In October 2011, in an article for *The Atlantic*, "The Shame of College Sports," Branch sparked a discussion that has been amplified by the recent scandals. "For all the outrage," he wrote, "the real scandal is not that students are getting illegally paid or recruited, it's that two of the noble principles on which the NCAA justifies its existence — 'amateurism' and the 'student-athlete' — are cynical hoaxes, legalistic confections propagated by the universities so they can exploit the skills and fame of young athletes. . . . The NCAA makes money, and enables universities and corporations to make money, from the unpaid labor of young athletes."

Branch added that "slavery analogies should be used carefully. Col- 13 lege athletes are not slaves. Yet to survey the scene — corporations and universities enriching themselves on the backs of uncompensated young men, whose status as 'student-athletes' deprives them of the right to due process guaranteed by the Constitution — is to catch an unmistakable whiff of the plantation."

The injustice is outrageous. It's time for a change. 14

The arguments against issuing a stipend or work-study to scholar- 15
ship athletes wither at the slightest touch. The best that critics can come
up with is that the free room and board players get should be enough, or
that paying them would ruin their "spirit" and "love of the game."

Comparisons to the Old South have come not just from those branded 16
as "outsiders," like Branch. Walter Byers, the association's executive director
from 1951 to 1987 and the man most responsible for the modern NCAA,
has seen the light. After his retirement, he told the great sportswriter Steve
Wulf: "The coaches own the athletes' feet, the colleges own the athletes'
bodies, and the supervisors retain the large rewards. That reflects a neo-
plantation mentality on the campuses." In a year when we are celebrating
a film about Abraham Lincoln's struggle to pass the constitutional amendment that abolished slavery, there is still some emancipating to be done on
college campuses, where young men are employees but are treated like an
uneasy combination of chattel and gods.

We need a massive reformation of this warped system. Here are a 17
few suggestions:

- So-called "student-athletes" should have workers' compensation protections.
- Scholarships should be guaranteed for four years, so players
  can't be dismissed from school if they run afoul of their coaches.
- Ceilings should be put on coaching salaries, with the money
  saved in revenue-producing sports used to pay stipends to
  athletes.
- The NBA and NFL should fund their own minor leagues, so
  universities don't have that responsibility.
- The corrupt cartel otherwise known as the NCAA should be
  abolished.

Any one of the above would make the current system more just, less 18
rife with hypocrisy and more able to handle the challenges of intercollegiate sports.

VOCABULARY/USING A DICTIONARY
1. What does *egregious* (para. 2) mean?
2. What is the *status quo* (para. 3)?
3. How do you feel if you are *cynical* (para. 7)?

RESPONDING TO WORDS IN CONTEXT
1. What, literally, is a *toboggan ride* (para. 3)?
2. What does Zirin mean by *stagnating wages* (para. 4)?
3. If something is less *rife* (para. 18), what does that mean?

DISCUSSING MAIN POINT AND MEANING

1. What are some of the problems with the NCAA, according to Zirin?
2. What apparent discrepancy causes Zirin to ask if schools have no shame?
3. What is the biggest problem that keeps the NCAA from changing its ways?

EXAMINING SENTENCES, PARAGRAPHS, AND ORGANIZATION

1. How does Zirin work the word *shame* into his essay (titled The *Shame* of the NCAA)?
2. How are quotations worked into the essay to show contrasting points of view?
3. How does Zirin use March Madness as an effective introduction to his thesis?

THINKING CRITICALLY

1. Are football and basketball important to your school? How is your campus life influenced by sports?
2. Why are football coaches paid so much money? Should players be paid as much as their coaches?
3. Do you agree with Mark Emmert that "student athletes are students. They are not employees"? Explain what he means. If you disagree, explain how they *are* employees.

WRITING ACTIVITIES

1. What are some of the scandals that have recently rocked the NCAA? Are any of them connected to the problems Zirin mentions? Address these in a short report.
2. What is March Madness? Zirin describes it this way: "Players are covered in more ads than stock cars and generate billions of dollars, all to the roar of millions of fans for whom college sports are tantamount to religion." In a brief essay, explain what it is, and explore the role advertising and student athletes play in it.
3. Do you think student athletes should be compensated? In an essay state your opinion and offer reasons why you think they should or should not. Do you think college athletes are exploited? Where would the money come from if most college sports programs, such as swimming, tennis, crew, field hockey, and even baseball are not profitable for the schools? Should only football and basketball players (mostly male) be compensated? In your essay consider how compensation could be distributed fairly or why it should not be enacted.

Bill Bramhall

Northwestern University Football Players Unionize

[*New York Daily News,* March 28, 2014]

© Daily News, L.P. (New York) Used with permission.

VISUAL DISCUSSION AND PERSUASION

1. How do you know, without the title, what Bramhall's cartoon is about?
2. How are words used to express the joke within the cartoon?
3. Can you tell from the drawing how Bramhall feels about the unionization?

Bill Bramhall is a cartoonist at New York Daily News. *His work appears frequently in such newspapers as the* Wall Street Journal, *the* New York Times, *and the* Los Angeles Times. *His debut picture book,* Hep Cat, *was published in 2004.*

Tim Ajmani (student essay)

Compensation for College Athletes?

[*The Corsair*, Pensacola State College, April 25, 2012]

BEFORE YOU READ
Do you believe that college athletes should be compensated for their time in addition to receiving scholarships? Why or why not?

O ne of the biggest issues involving the NCAA today is whether or not student athletes should be compensated for their services to their school's athletic programs. A highly debated subject, the topic has perhaps gained more and more controversy due to recent support by high-profile coaches. The NCAA has also been negatively perceived for its strict and sometimes questionable enforcement of its policies involving extra benefits for student athletes.

Scandals like the ones at Miami and Ohio State haven't helped its case. A big part of why student athletes are involved in receiving improper benefits is the nature of college athletics. If you compare the NFL or the NBA to college football or basketball, what is the difference between them? Both are high-revenue-producing businesses. Both make their players famous. Both tempt their players to participate in questionable activities. In some ways, college sports are just as, if not more, popular and successful than their professional counterparts.

Consider the situation that the University of Kentucky basketball program is in. It just won a national championship. Its entire starting lineup, including three true freshman players,[1] declared for the NBA draft afterwards. Critics of Kentucky and Head Coach John Calipari harp on the fact that his so-named "one-and-dones" have ruined the landscape of college basketball. But they are missing the point.

Calipari isn't doing anything illegal. He is abiding by the current system set in place by the NCAA and succeeding at an extremely high

---

[1] true freshman players (para. 3): College athletes who compete the first year they enter college. Many college freshmen choose to "red shirt," which means they sit out competition, but are able to practice with the team in order to develop their skills.

Tim Ajmani attended Pensacola State College, where he was a writer and a section editor for The Corsair.

level (it also helps that he is a superb coach with a knack for producing NBA-ready talent). The NBA's policy for players entering the draft centers on the fact that they have to be at least one year out of high school. And remember, many of these basketball players, as well as many college athletes, come from places where they have experienced financial hardship.

It shouldn't be a surprise to anyone that these athletes want to make a good income as soon as they can. However, would they be as eager to leave school if they were being compensated for competing on their college teams? I understand that college athletes already (for the most part) are on scholarship and receive many benefits because of their campus celebrity. But if they were to be given a little income for themselves, which they could use for their individual purposes, it could provide a little more incentive to stay in school and get their degrees.

And this brings me back to NCAA violations involving supposed illegal benefits. These same players and programs that the NCAA is punishing for violations are being taken advantage of, far worse than they would like to admit. You have street agents[2] providing favors for these athletes and expecting the athletes to give favors in return (which is how most violations come out in the news).

Then you have the colleges themselves. Think of the Reggie Bush saga years ago at the University of Southern California. The school distanced themselves from Bush because of the sanctions that the NCAA put on their athletic programs because of violations that Bush committed while at USC. But do you hear them apologizing for all of the money that Bush made them during his time there?

> College athletes are pawns in a huge chess game.

In today's world, college athletes are pawns in a huge chess game. These are young men and women that are still finding their way in the world. And as much as the NCAA, colleges, and universities want to deny, they do take advantage of them. They reap the benefits of the athletes competing in their sports. But they also punish them to protect their institutions' integrity and character. They are just as at fault as their athletes at times, particularly in some of their strange rulings of cases that arise.

The reality is that the notion of compensating student athletes isn't as cut-and-dry as people believe it is.

[2] street agents (para. 6): Middlemen who sell signatures and camp visits of high school athletes to interested parties.

VOCABULARY/USING A DICTIONARY

1. What does the word *controversy* mean (para. 1) and what are the word's origins?
2. What is the definition of the word *revenue* (para. 2), and from what language does the word come?
3. The word *sanction* has two very different meanings (para. 7). Provide both definitions and indicate which definition is applicable to this essay.

RESPONDING TO WORDS IN CONTEXT

1. What does Ajmani mean by the phrase "In today's world, college athletes are pawns in a huge chess game"? How is the word *pawn* being used?
2. What does the term *starting lineup* mean (para. 3), and why would Ajmani emphasize that the starting lineup left?
3. In the sentence "Critics of Kentucky and Head Coach John Calipari harp on the fact that his so-named 'one-and-dones' have ruined the landscape of college basketball" (para. 3), how is the word *harp* being used? What do you think the coach means by the phrase "one-and-dones"?

DISCUSSING MAIN POINT AND MEANING

1. Does Ajmani have a clear argument in this essay? If so, what is it?
2. What does Ajmani believe about NCAA violations and illegal benefits?
3. How does Ajmani portray Kentucky head coach John Calipari?

EXAMINING SENTENCES, PARAGRAPHS, AND ORGANIZATION

1. What is the purpose of the Reggie Bush example in paragraph 7?
2. What point does Ajmani illustrate in paragraph 3, when he discusses the University of Kentucky?
3. Ajmani uses several rhetorical questions throughout his essay. Cite at least two and explain their meaning within the context of the argument.

THINKING CRITICALLY

1. What assumptions does Ajmani make about his readers, and where are these assumptions made apparent? Cite specific examples from the text.
2. In paragraph 2, Ajmani states, "In some ways, college sports are just as, if not more, popular and successful than their professional counterparts." Do you agree with this statement? Why or why not?
3. Can you think of any other activities or jobs that create massive revenue that the workers or players do not see the benefits of? Be as specific as possible.

WRITING ACTIVITIES

1. College athletes undoubtedly help earn money for the universities they play for. Keeping in mind both sides of the argument and the essays you've read on the topic, write a short essay in which you argue that it is or is not ethical to not pay college athletes.

2. Whether you agree with Ajmani or not, write a short essay in which you argue against paying college athletes. Cite specific reasons as to why college athletes should *not* be paid, and reference at least one claim made in Ajmani's essay.

3. The final line of Ajmani's essay is: "The reality is that the notion of compensating student athletes isn't as cut-and-dry as people believe it is." Maintaining Ajmani's argument, write three alternate final lines and provide a brief explanation of why each closing line would function well within Ajmani's argument.

LOOKING CLOSELY

The Art of Argument: Anticipating Opposition

When you take a position you think will be unpopular or controversial, an effective strategy is to anticipate the objections you may receive. In this way, you indicate that you have thought carefully about your position, and you make it more difficult for those who resist your argument to reject your claims outright. In nearly all effective argument and debate, the writer or speaker will attempt to anticipate arguments likely to be made by the other side. This doesn't mean that you have answered the opposing arguments satisfactorily, but it does mean that the opposing side will need to take into account your awareness of its position.

In "Compensation for College Athletes?" Tim Ajmani, a student at Pensacola State College, realizes that one objection readers may have to his opinion that college athletes should be paid for their services is that most of these athletes are already being compensated in the form of scholarships and other benefits. By mentioning this, Ajmani shows his readers that he is aware that those who might disagree with him would object to his position: They would argue that college athletes are already obtaining payment in other forms. Note that he makes his awareness clear by stating "I understand that college athletes. . . ." After showing his understanding of this key fact, Ajmani then goes on to say why "a little income for themselves" could "provide a little more incentive to stay in school and get their degrees."

1 *Recognizes the financial motive to leave school*	It shouldn't be a surprise to anyone that these athletes want to make a good income as soon as they can. However, would they be as eager to leave school if they were being compensated for competing on their college teams? (1) I understand that college athletes already (for the most part) are on scholarship and receive many benefits because of their campus celebrity.(2) But if they were to be given a little income for themselves, which they could use for their individual purposes, it could provide a little more incentive to stay in school and get their degrees. (3)
2 *Acknowledges that many already receive scholarships*	
3 *Counters that position by claiming that some income would offer incentive to stay in school*	

STUDENT WRITER AT WORK
Tim Ajmani

R.A. What inspired you to write this essay? And publish it in your campus paper?

T.A. As a Community Conversations Editor, most of my inspiration for columns and blogs came from discussions and debates on campus between students.

R.A. What response have you received to this piece? Has the feedback you have received affected your views on the subject?

T.A. We actually put out a poll for feedback on the topic, and based on the results, most readers generally disagreed with the argument that athletes should be compensated in some way. I was a little surprised because of recent events that have transpired, but it really didn't change my views on the subject.

R.A. Have you written on this topic since? Have you read or seen other work on the topic that has interested you?

T.A. I have not written on the topic since I published the column. But I'm seeing more and more debate regarding the stance that athletes should be financially compensated for their participation in their school's athletics, particularly from sports networks like ESPN.

R.A. How long did it take for you to write this piece? Did you revise your work? What were your goals as you revised?

T.A. It probably took me about two to three hours in terms of a draft, with another one to two revising. I usually write a column in one sitting when I have a clear head with clear focus. Writing a piece in spurts doesn't work for me. I made three complete revisions checking over the work, looking for content and grammatical errors.

R.A. What topics most interest you as a writer?

T.A. As a writer, I'd definitely have to say any debate regarding sports. I love expressing my views and ideas on anything regarding issues in the collegiate and professional sports world.

R.A. Are you pursuing a career in which writing will be a component?

T.A. Yes, writing is a very important component in the engineering field.

R.A. What advice do you have for other student writers?

T.A. When writing, don't rush things. Take the time and effort to proofread your work again after your final revision. You wouldn't believe how many times I've spotted things that needed to be corrected after I thought I was finished.

The Football Star's Final Exam

[*Desert Exposure,* August 2014]

Many jokes depend on stereotypes. The following is based on the stereotype of the academically challenged college football star. But is the joke on Bubba or not?

Bubba went to LSU on a football scholarship. He was a great running back, but a poor student.

Come graduation day, Bubba didn't have enough credits. But he was a great football star and the students held a rally and demanded the dean give him a diploma anyway. They were so insistent that the dean agreed if Bubba could answer one question correctly, he would give him a diploma.

The one-question test was held in the auditorium and all students packed the place. It was standing room only. The dean was on the stage and told Bubba to come up. The dean had the diploma in his hand and said, "Bubba, if you can answer this question correctly, I'll give you your diploma.

Bubba said he was ready and the dean asked him the question: "Bubba," he said, "how much is three times seven?"

Bubba looked up at the ceiling and then down at his shoes, just pondering the question. The students began chanting, "Graduate him anyway? Graduate him anyway!"

Then Bubba held up his hand and the auditorium became silent. Bubba said: "I think I know the answer. Three times seven is 21."

A hush fell over the auditorium and then students began another chant: "Give him another chance! Give him another chance!

Red Smith

The Student Athlete

The complaint that our university system exploits athletes is not a recent one. On November 12, 1979, the prominent sportswriter Red Smith published the following column in the New York Times *criticizing both the NCAA and the colleges for the way they glowingly promote the ideal of a "student athlete," especially when that student is far less likely to be a serious student than a serious athlete. Smith does not believe all colleges are exploitative, but sees a growing trend for schools to admit academically unqualified students in order to enhance their athletic programs. He writes: "Some colleges recruit scholar athletes in the hope that the scholar can spare enough time from the classroom to help the team. Others recruit athletes and permit them to attend class if they can spare the time from the playing field." To prove his point that college athletes may be academically unqualified, Smith quotes an ungrammatical answer from a star wide receiver at a "major university" in response to a question from one of his professors, a football fan. To show the level of inability, the professor forwarded the answer to Smith, who cites the clumsily written remarks without naming the college, the student, or the professor. Smith's main point in sharing this example of what he believes is embarrassingly poor writing is to show that the student "is only a victim." "The culprit," Smith concludes, "is the college, and the system."*

A native of Green Bay, Wisconsin, Walter Wellesley "Red" Smith (1905–1982) studied journalism at Notre Dame and then embarked on a celebrated career as a sportswriter that would last a lifetime. Considered one of the nation's most "literary" sportswriters, Smith joined the New York Times *in 1971 and won a Pulitzer Prize for commentary in 1976. His writing on a variety of sports can be found in several of his collections, including* The Red Smith Reader *(1983), and in 2013 the prestigious Library of America honored his work by releasing* American Pastimes: The Very Best of Red Smith.

Some edifying words about student athletes were heard on the air   1
over the weekend. Whenever a college football game is on radio or
television, it is accompanied by edifying words about student athletes, about the importance of intercollegiate athletics in a rounded
educational program and about the vital role played by the National
Collegiate Athletic Association. The edifying words are composed
by writers for the N.C.A.A.

Student athlete is a term susceptible to various definitions. It can   2
mean a biochemistry major who participates in sports, or a Heisman
Trophy candidate who is not necessarily a candidate for a bachelor's
degree. Some student athletes are more studious than athletic, and
vice versa.

There is at hand a piece written by a student athlete in his senior   3
year at a major university that has been polishing young intellects for
more than a century. He is an attractive young man, short months
away from graduation, the best wide receiver in the school. One of
his professors, who happens to be a football buff, asked him why his
teammate, John Doe, never played first string although he was a better passer than Richard Spelvin, the starting quarterback. The young
man said he would write the answer "like it was a quiz."

What follows is an exact copy of the young man's answer. That is,   4
it is exact except for the names. The quarterbacks are not really
named John Doe and Richard Spelvin and the university's athletic
teams are not known as the Yankees.

"People (Some) feel that Doe did not have the ability to run the   5
type of offense that the yankys ran. He also made some mistakes
with the ball like fumbling."

"As a wide receiver it didn't make me any different who quar-   6
terback. But I feel he has the best arm I ever saw or play with on a
team. Only why I feel the I do about the quarter-back position is
because I am a receiver who came from J.C. out of state I caught a
lot of pass over 80 and I did not care a damn thing but about 24 in
one year."

"Spelvin is my best friend and quarterback at my J.C. school.   7
Spelvin has an arm but when you don't thrown lot of half the time I
dont care who you are you will not perform as best you can. Spelvin
can run, run the team and most of all he makes little mistakes."

"So since they didn't pass Spelvin was our quarterback. But if we   8
did pass I feel Spelvin still should of start but Doe should have play a

lot. Tell you the truth the yanky's in the pass two years had the best combination of receivers in a season that they will ever have. More — ask to talk about politics alum Doe problems just before the season coaches hate?"

The last appears to be a suggestion that alumni politics may have   9
played a part in the coaches' decision on which quarterback would play first string. However, the professor who forwarded this material did so without comment or explanation.

The importance of disguising the names of these student ath-   10
letes and the identity of the university is obvious. It would be unforgivable to hold a kid up to public ridicule because his grip on a flying football was surer than his grasp of the mother tongue. He is only a victim. The culprit is the college, and the system.

The young man's prose makes it achingly clear how some institu-   11
tions of learning use some athletes. Recruiters besiege a high school senior with bulging muscles and sloping neck who can run 40 yards in 4.3 seconds. The fact that he cannot read without facial contortions may be regrettable, but if his presence would help make a team a winner, then they want his body and are not deeply concerned about his mind.

Some colleges recruit scholar athletes in the hope that the   12
scholar can spare enough time from the classroom to help the team. Others recruit athletes and permit them to attend class if they can spare the time from the playing field. If the boy was unprepared for college when he arrived, he will be unqualified for a degree four years later, but some culture foundries give him a degree as final payment for his services.

One widely accepted definition of the role of a college is "to pre-   13
pare the student for life after he leaves the campus." If the young man quoted above gets a job as wide receiver for the Green Bay Packers, then perhaps the university will have fulfilled its purpose. However, only a fraction of college players can make a living in the National Football League. Opportunities are even more limited for college basketball players, for pro basketball employs fewer players.

Where outside of pro football can our wide receiver go? He can   14
pump gas. He can drive a truck. He has seen his name in headlines, has heard crowds cheering him, has enjoyed the friendship and admiration of his peers and he has a diploma from a famous university. It is unconscionable.

BACKGROUND AND CONTEXT

1. In what ways does Smith's "The Student Athlete" cover the controversies surrounding the academic "pass" today's colleges appear to be offering their athletes? Do you think Smith's column is relevant to the issue today? Explain what has changed since Smith wrote his column in 1979.

2. Oddly, neither Smith nor the professor explains why a verbally challenged student would volunteer to write out his answer "like it was a quiz." Remember, this was long before e-mail or text messaging was possible. Do you think it makes a difference how Smith received this information? Explain why you think the student decided to write out an answer to his professor's apparently simple question. What might be the student's motive to do so?

STRATEGY, STRUCTURE, AND STYLE

1. Smith speaks of "edifying words" in the opening sentence of his column and then repeats that phrase twice again in the opening paragraph. What do you think he means by that phrase, and why is he giving those words such prominence? In what tone of voice do you think they are meant to be read? How do they help establish Smith's point of view?

2. What is your opinion of the student quotation Smith includes to show deficient writing? Do you think he's being too hard on the student? Do you think he might have paid more attention to what the student was saying? In your opinion, do you agree with Smith that unless that student found a position in pro football his employment future was very limited? Explain why or why not.

COMPARISONS AND CONNECTIONS

1. The idea of paying student athletes was practically unthinkable at the time Smith wrote his column. Why do you think that was the case? After carefully rereading the essay in the light of the selections in this unit, consider how you think Smith would respond to paying student athletes. In a short essay, summarize Smith's point of view on the student athletes and explain what you think his opinion would be about their being paid.

2. Try this exercise: Take the passage of student writing that Smith cites and rewrite it so that you think it would be acceptable to Smith. In revising the passage, what do you think were the student's most common mistakes? Which errors struck you as most serious and which ones as minor?

Discussing the Unit

SUGGESTED TOPIC FOR DISCUSSION

This unit explores the effect of money on college sports programs and the way in which college sports programs can distract everyone from academics. Are institutions of higher learning selling out by focusing on their sports programs? Are they harming their student bodies by doing so? Where do you draw the line between enthusiasm for football games and the commercialization of college football?

PREPARING FOR CLASS DISCUSSION

1. Do you believe college athletes should be paid? How have the arguments found in this chapter influenced your answer?
2. What is the role of sports in higher education? Why has such importance been placed on how sports teams represent a particular school? Do you feel that importance is misplaced? Why or why not?

FROM DISCUSSION TO WRITING

1. What is the least appealing aspect of college sports today? Using the essays in this chapter, write a brief essay that outlines what is most disappointing or contemptible about how college sports operate in the current climate.
2. Who do you believe benefits from college sports programs the most? Looking at all the answers provided in this chapter, write an essay that compares their responses to your own.

TOPICS FOR CROSS-CULTURAL DISCUSSION

1. American colleges are the only ones in the world that include athletic programs, the most successful and influential of which are hyped to the point of being broadcast across the nation by major sponsors. What does that suggest about cultural differences between the United States and other countries? Does that mean other countries don't value sports the way Americans do? Explain.
2. Schools in several states are mentioned in the essays in this chapter. Do the states mentioned reflect a particular region of the country? Which regions are more affected by the money poured into sports programs, based on the schools pointed out in these essays? Do you imagine the culture of sports is different in these regions?

8

Marriage: What Does It Mean Today?

Why do we still get married? Is the institution simply a doomed vestige of an earlier age, or does it take meaning and power from the centuries of tradition it draws on and continues? As America continues to debate marriage equality for gay and lesbian couples — and as divorce rates continue to jump to alarming levels — some critics argue for throwing out the whole notion of a legally sanctioned love relationship. Others, meanwhile, urge us to hold on tight to an important cultural construct we may be at risk of losing.

In "Modern Family," conservative columnist Mona Charen advances an impassioned argument for the improving power formal marriage has on both of its members. A critic of same-sex marriage, Charen concentrates in this essay on straight marriage. Her central claim is that "the 'piece of paper' matters" — in other words, the formal institution brings together two people with fundamentally different strengths, which they combine in a single life-long effort.

Charen's conservative premise that men and women bring different things to the table is not without its critics. The implication of traditional gender roles — that men are better at bringing home bread and women at cooking it — irks many who believe these roles are nothing more than a construct.

Prominent feminist critic Rebecca Solnit agrees fundamentally that the face of marriage is changing, and is also optimistic about the shifts. Solnit concentrates on same-sex marriage, which some on the right claim could do serious damage to the majority institution of heterosexual marriage. But rather than taking the common liberal view that gay marriage poses no threat to straight people, Solnit surprises us by surmising that "maybe the conservatives are right, and maybe we should celebrate that threat rather than denying it." In "More Equal Than Others" she argues that so-called traditional marriage is based on fundamental imbalances of power, and is tainted by the oppression of women that sustained it for hundreds of years. The best way to save marriage, Solnit claims, is to make it a more equal partnership — and legally sanctioning same-sex couples as equals is an indispensable part of that process.

If Solnit is right that marriage is a traditional tool of domination rather than a union of love, why not toss out the whole thing altogether? What's the point of continuing a government recognition of what's supposed to be first and foremost an intimate, personal relationship? Some point out that, only a half-century ago, conservatives opposed mixed-race relationships; today only a fringe disapproves of them. Holly Nall, however, has faced subtle, indirect objections to her boyfriend who is older and of a different racial background. In her student essay "Mixed Relationships Offer Diversity" she describes a loving and enriching partnership with her boyfriend. But she is careful to put her relationship in context — Americans required their Supreme Court to strike down laws that would have made her and her boy-friend criminals for being together today. "Nearly 50 years after that court ruling, same-sex couples are still fighting for the right to marry the people they love," she writes. Nall suggests that the discrimination against gay and lesbian couples is not a defense of tradition, but an indefensible bigotry.

Still, despite the wars waged on behalf of and in opposition to marriage today, for many married couples it continues to be a way of life fraught with obstacles yet not without its rewards. In "Married Life" Tim Aubry, an award-winning essayist, engages in a brief though complex meditation on the way the "endlessness" of marriage affects us psychologically.

At the heart of the argument, in some ways, is the value of traditional marriage itself. Before gay, or even interracial, marriage was an issue on America's radar, were marriages actually loving institutions? Or were they ways of legalizing the ownership of women by men? For a historical perspective on the question, this chapter's America Then comes from one of the most influential voices in American radicalism, author and self-professed agitator Emma Goldman. "That marriage is a failure none but the very stupid will deny," Goldman writes in 1910. Consider why she thinks that, and whether her arguments still hold for marriages — of all new shapes, sizes, and colors — today.

Mona Charen

Modern Family?

[*Townhall.com*, February 28, 2014]

BEFORE YOU READ

What does the modern family look like? Is it any different from the older "traditional" family?

WORDS TO LEARN

cohabitation (para. 1): situation in which people are living together (noun)

controversy (para. 1): contention (noun)

dirge (para. 2): funeral song (noun)

hubbub (para. 3): a noisy situation (noun)

disparage (para. 7): to belittle (verb)

provenance (para. 8): place of origin (noun)

The traditional family is dead, so we've been informed. It's been replaced by blended families, cohabitation, single-parent families, and, if the latest scientific controversy regarding mitochondrial DNA pans out, multiple biological parents for a single child.

It's not wrong to declare that the face of the American family is changing (even if most of the changes have been for the worse), but it may be overwrought. The only way to sing a dirge for the "traditional" family is to define it exceedingly narrowly — and even then, it's not dead, just diminished. If you define "traditional" as a father working and mother not working outside the home, and 2.4 children (OK, kidding about the .4), then yes, only about 23 percent of families fit that model today. But if you broaden the definition a bit to include households in which one spouse, usually the husband, works full time and the other, usually the wife, works only part time in order to care for children, then you get a majority of married couples. Among parents of children younger than 6, married mothers

---

Mona Charen is a columnist and political analyst based in Washington, D.C. Her writing centers on the topics of foreign policy, terrorism, politics, and culture. She is the author of two books, and was a weekly panelist on CNN's Capital Gang. *Her work has appeared in more than 200 papers, including the* Boston Globe, Baltimore Sun, St. Louis Post-Dispatch, Atlanta Journal-Constitution, *and* Washington Times.

are less likely to be working at all, according to the U.S. Department of Labor, making those families look very traditional indeed.

The mode for married parents today is supposed to be egalitarian — that is, mom and dad sharing equally in the tasks of breadwinning, housework and child care. Remember the great hubbub about the rise of so-called breadwinner moms? That was much less than it appeared, a case of media exuberance untethered to facts. They counted, for example, single moms on welfare as "breadwinners," which is quite a stretch of the definition.   3

Examining married parents, Brad Wilcox of the Institute for Family Studies finds that most are following a "neo-traditional" pattern. Mothers do nearly 70 percent of the child care and housework in these households, while fathers do 65 percent of the breadwinning. Though scorned as outmoded, this pattern actually matches women's preferences. Fifty-three percent of married mothers say that part-time work is ideal, and another 23 percent prefer to be stay-at-home moms.   4

Surveys consistently find that women do much more housework than men, even in cohabiting relationships. Feminists howl at the injustice of it, and economists attempt to measure and quantify it. It's really no mystery. Men do less housework because they don't care! Is the sink getting rust stains around the drain? Are the potatoes in the pantry sprouting green shoots? Does the TV screen have fingerprints on it? How many men would notice, and what percentage of those would care?   5

> Feminists howl at the injustice of it, and economists attempt to measure and quantify it. It's really no mystery.

After my first year of marriage, I suggested that the best place to hide jewels would be in the back of the refrigerator since most thieves are men, and men can never find anything in the back of the refrigerator. Raising three sons confirms that it's testosterone-induced blindness.   6

This is not to disparage the stronger sex. Married men tend to earn more money than single men — as much as 44 percent more after controlling for age, IQ, education, experience, race and number of children. Economists call it the marriage premium.   7

Speculation as to the provenance of this bounty includes "ability bias," i.e., those men who are able to earn more money are better able to attract spouses; "signaling," meaning that being married signals reliability and other valuable traits to employers; and "human capital," i.e., being married makes men work harder, curb their tempers, and otherwise perform better at work.   8

I lean to the human capital explanation. Brain research has shown 9 that, on average, women are better at understanding emotions than men. Married men have advantage over their single coworkers, in that they can consult their wives regarding interpersonal conflicts and questions. Their wives can help them to understand what's really going on. My mother performed this function for my dad for years.

This is only part of the explanation (which is pure speculation I freely 10 admit). By itself, this feminine psychological insight would suggest that women should earn more than men, and that isn't the case. No, the other piece of the puzzle regarding married men and work is love and appreciation. Married men work harder because they know they are working for the welfare of those they love. Married women probably convey their gratitude to their husbands for providing the security they and the children need, and this cements a man's place in the world.

The "marriage premium" doesn't work for cohabitating men, nor for 11 those who father children they don't raise. The "piece of paper" matters. Something to consider the next time someone celebrates the decline of "traditional" marriage.

VOCABULARY/USING A DICTIONARY

1. What is a *breadwinner* (para. 3)?
2. What is *capital* (para. 8)?
3. Is it odd that *economists* (para. 5) are looking at what happens in a marriage?

RESPONDING TO WORDS IN CONTEXT

1. What does the word *neo* mean when combined with *traditional* (para. 4)?
2. When Charen writes, "Feminists *howl* at the injustice of it" (para. 5), does she mean that they really *howl*?
3. When Charen says that men can never find anything at the back of the refrigerator because of *testosterone-induced blindness* (para. 6), what does she mean?

DISCUSSING MAIN POINT AND MEANING

1. What is one enticing reason for people to prefer a neo-traditional marriage, according to Charen?
2. Why, according to Charen, do women do more of the housework in the neo-traditional family than men?
3. How is a traditional family structured?

EXAMINING SENTENCES, PARAGRAPHS, AND ORGANIZATION

1. What facet of the modern family gets the most consideration from Charen in this essay?
2. Is Charen's essay about the death of the traditional family? Why might one think it will be about that topic?
3. Does Charen's essay rely on factual or personal information?

THINKING CRITICALLY

1. Do you think you have a good picture of a traditional family after reading this essay? What has changed about the traditional family?
2. Do you wish there were less speculation in this essay? If so, where is the speculation problematic for you? If not, which conjectures are strongest in your opinion?
3. Is this piece about the way traditional families have or have not changed, or an incentive for men to marry to earn more money? Explain your answer.

WRITING ACTIVITIES

1. What does today's family look like? In a short personal essay, describe your family. Does it sound like the picture Charen presents?
2. Google "breadwinner moms" (Charen alludes to them in paragraph 3 in her essay). What sort of information comes up? Do they exist? Are they important to the picture of the modern family? Who qualifies for the appellation "breadwinner mom"?
3. Write a spoof of a domestic situation—a marriage in which husbands do housework because they care, and women don't because they don't care. Or a spoof in which a millionaire works around the clock because he feels so loved and appreciated by his wife. Or a family in which there are multiple parents for one child. Think about the tone you will use and how greatly you will have to exaggerate the situation.

Rebecca Solnit

More Equal Than Others

[*Financial Times*, May 24, 2013]

BEFORE YOU READ

Have you ever considered the purpose of marriage? What is marriage between a man and a woman all about — and how is it different from same-sex marriage? How is it the same?

WORDS TO LEARN

metaphysically (para. 1): in a way dealing with the abstract (adverb)

dissemble (para. 2): to conceal true motives and thoughts, in some way (verb)

disposition (para. 4): emotional outlook; mood (noun)

prosecute (para. 5): to institute legal proceedings against (verb)

throttle (para. 6): to choke or strangle (verb)

anomaly (para. 7): an exception (noun)

quotidian (para. 8): usual (adjective)

hierarchical (para. 8): characterized by a ranking system (adjective)

inherently (para. 8): innately (adverb)

mount (para. 12): to put on a platform (verb)

boon (para. 14): a blessing (noun)

For a long time, the advocates of same-sex marriage have been saying that such unions pose no threat, contradicting the conservatives who say such unions are a threat to traditional marriage. Maybe the conservatives are right, and maybe we should celebrate that threat rather than denying it. The marriage of two men or two women doesn't impact any man-and-woman marriage directly. But metaphysically it could. 1

To understand how, you need to look at what traditional marriage is. And at the ways in which both sides are dissembling: the advocates by denying, or more likely overlooking the threat, and the conservatives by being coy about what it's a threat to. 2

Rebecca Solnit is a San Francisco–based writer whose work focuses on topics such as environment, politics, art, and activism. She is the author of thirteen books, and her writing has appeared in numerous online and print publications. Her book The Faraway Nearby *(2013) was nominated for a National Book Award.*

Recently a lot of Americans have swapped the awkward phrase   3
"same-sex marriage" for the term "marriage equality." The phrase is ordinarily employed to mean that same-sex couples have the rights different-
sexed couples do. But it could also mean that marriage is between equals.
That's not what traditional marriage was. Throughout much of its history
in the west, the laws defining marriage made the husband essentially an
owner and the wife a possession.

The British judge William Blackstone wrote in 1765, "By marriage,   4
the husband and wife are one person in law: that is, the very being or
legal existence of the woman is suspended during the marriage, or at
least is incorporated and consolidated into that of the husband . . . "
Under such rules, a woman's life was dependent on the disposition of her
husband, and though there were kind as well as unkind husbands then,
rights are more reliable than the kindness of someone who holds absolute power over you. And rights were a long way off.

Until Britain's Married Women's Property Acts of 1870 and 1882,   5
everything belonged to the husband; the wife was penniless on her own
account, no matter her inheritance or her earnings. Laws against wife
beating were passed around that time in both England and the US but
rarely enforced until the 1970s. That domestic violence is now prose-
cuted hasn't cured the epidemic of such violence in both countries.

The novelist Edna O'Brien's recent memoir has some blood-curdling   6
passages about her own journey through what appears to have been a
very traditional marriage. Her first husband was withering about her literary success and obliged her to sign over her cheques to him. When she
refused to sign over a large film-rights cheque, he throttled her, but when
she went to the police they were not much interested. That was a half a
century ago, but in the US, a woman is still beaten every nine seconds
by an intimate partner or former partner, and about three a day are murdered by that category of guy. The violence horrifies me, but so does the
underlying assumption that the abuser has the right to control and punish his victim and the way such violence is used to that end.

The recent case in Cleveland, Ohio, of Ariel Castro, accused of   7
imprisoning, torturing and sexually abusing three young women for a
decade, is extreme, but it may not be the anomaly it is portrayed as. For
one thing, Castro is claimed to have been spectacularly and openly violent to his now-deceased common-law wife. And what lay behind Castro's alleged actions must have been a desire for a situation in which he
held absolute power and the women were absolutely powerless, a vicious
version of the traditional arrangement.

This is the tradition feminism protested and protests against — not   8
only the extremes but the quotidian situation. Feminists in the 19th

century made some inroads, those of the 1970s and 1980s made a great many more, which every woman in the US and UK has benefited from. And feminism made same-sex marriage possible by doing so much to transform a hierarchical relationship into an egalitarian one. Because a marriage between two people of the same gender is inherently egalitarian — one partner may happen to have more power in any number of ways,

> It's a relationship between people who have equal standing and who are free to define their roles themselves

but for the most part it's a relationship between people who have equal standing and who are free to define their roles themselves.

Gay men and lesbians have already opened up the question of what qualities and roles are male and female in ways that can be liberating for straight people. When they marry, the meaning of marriage is likewise opened up. No hierarchical tradition underlies their union. Some people have greeted this with joy. A Presbyterian pastor who had performed a number of such marriages told me, "I remember coming to this realisation when I was meeting with same-sex couples before performing their ceremonies when it was legal in California. The old patriarchal default settings did not apply in their relationships, and it was a glorious thing to witness." 9

American conservatives are frightened by this egalitarianism, or maybe just appalled by it. It's not traditional. But they don't want to talk about that tradition or their enthusiasm for it, though if you follow their assault on reproductive rights, women's rights and, all last winter, renewing the Violence Against Women Act, it's not hard to see where they stand. However, they dissembled on their real interest in stopping same-sex marriage. 10

Those of us following the court proceedings around, for example, California's marriage-equality battle have heard a lot about how marriage is for the begetting and raising of children, and certainly reproduction requires the union of a sperm and an egg — but those unite in many ways nowadays, including in laboratories and surrogate mothers. And everyone is aware that many children are now raised by grandparents, stepparents, adoptive parents and other people who did not beget but love them. 11

Many heterosexual marriages are childless; many with children break up: they are no guarantee that children will be raised in a house with two parents of two genders. The courts have scoffed at the reproduction and child-raising argument against marriage equality. And the conservatives have not mounted what seems to be their real objection: that they wish to preserve traditional marriage and more than that preserve traditional gender roles. 12

I know lovely and amazing heterosexual couples who married in the 1940s and 1950s and every decade since. Their marriages are egalitar- 13 ian, full of mutuality and generosity (and of course I've known nice men married to unbearable human beings too: being a jerk knows no gender, though power relations do, and the law reinforced that until very recently). But even people who weren't particularly nasty were deeply unequal in the past. I also know a decent man who just passed away, aged 91: in his prime he took a job on the other side of the country without informing his wife that she was moving or inviting her to participate in the decision. Her life was not hers to determine. It was his.

It's time to slam the door shut on that era. And to open another 14 door, through which we can welcome equality: between genders, among marital partners, for everyone in every circumstance. Marriage equality is a threat: to inequality. It's a boon to everyone who values and benefits from equality. It's for all of us.

VOCABULARY/USING A DICTIONARY
1. What is an *inroad* (para. 8)?
2. What is the past tense of the word *beget* (para. 11)? What does *beget* mean?
3. If you take apart the word *heterosexual*, what does *hetero* add to the compound word?

RESPONDING TO WORDS IN CONTEXT
1. How are both sides *dissembling* (para. 2) about traditional marriage in this essay?
2. What did it mean in 1765 for a woman to be *incorporated and consolidated* (para. 4) into the husband?
3. In what way are conservatives being *coy* (para. 2) about what same-sex marriage might threaten?

DISCUSSING MAIN POINT AND MEANING
1. What, according to Solnit, does the phrase "marriage equality" really mean in the discussion of traditional and same-sex marriage?
2. What is Solnit's take on the argument about the importance of procreation in marriage?
3. What is the main problem of traditional marriage, according to Solnit?

EXAMINING SENTENCES, PARAGRAPHS, AND ORGANIZATION
1. Do you know Solnit's position on marriage equality at the outset of her essay? How does her opening seem to contradict her ultimate position on marriage?
2. How does Solnit's conclusion return full circle to her introductory paragraph?
3. How does Solnit use evidence to establish the long tradition of inequality in traditional marriage?

THINKING CRITICALLY

1. What are traditional gender roles in this country? How have they manifested themselves in the traditional marriage?

2. Do you think, as Solnit does, that getting rid of "old patriarchal default settings" via same-sex marriage alleviates inequality in those marriages? Explain.

3. What are some of the arguments for and against the legal establishment of same-sex marriage that Solnit does *not* cover in her essay?

WRITING ACTIVITIES

1. In this essay, Solnit makes a distinction between "hierarchical" and "egalitarian" relationships. In a freewriting exercise, come up with as many examples of "egalitarian" relationships (and/or marriages) as you can. What do they look like?

2. Follow the freewriting about "egalitarian" relationships with a freewriting about "hierarchical" relationships (and/or marriages). Try to write about more than one. What do they look like?

3. Drawing from the two freewritings above for material, write a short essay that compares and contrasts different kinds of relationships (and/or marriages). How do they fit into the model provided by Solnit of the traditional marriage? How do they fit into her model of the same-sex (more equal) marriage? Discover as you write what makes a marriage more or less equal than another.

Holly Nall (student essay)

Mixed Relationships Offer Diversity

[*Golden Gate Xpress*, San Francisco State University, April 1, 2013]

BEFORE YOU READ

Have you ever noticed a relationship between two people who couldn't be more different, for whatever reason? Did you form judgments about that relationship, or could you find a way to celebrate their differences?

WORDS TO LEARN

assumption (para. 2): the belief that something is true (noun)

fetish (para. 2): a strong, unusual need or desire for something (noun)

patently (para. 4): obviously (adverb)

Holly Nall is a student at San Francisco State University.

My boyfriend is full of surprises. He's equal parts rock star, Prince Charming and ridiculous nerd. He treats me like a queen, even though I repeatedly insist otherwise, and makes me laugh until my sides hurt. He's also 16 years older than me, and black.

I'm well aware of the assumptions being made. I have daddy issues, he has money, or there must be some other shallow fetish at play. If not, then I must be settling, because clearly the only older men worth dating are George Clooney clones. The really negative stuff doesn't reach my ears, but I've overheard enough nasty conversations about similar relationships to know what some people are really thinking. I couldn't care less.

Nothing about this pairing was deliberate. In fact, it developed about as naturally as it could. Ron was my singing teacher and one of my closest friends. Once I started falling for him, I realized I didn't know how old he was, and I couldn't seem to find the right moment to ask. On one of our first dates, as we were carded for our beers, he asked to see my license photo. We traded, and my eyes went straight to his birth year: 1970. I was mortified when I did the math. He looked great for his age, but he was a lot older than I had guessed. Was this a deal breaker?

As the night went on, I decided that it was not. On the surface we were opposites, but at the core we were such a perfect match that I had to see it through. I will never regret throwing that stigma out the window. My family adores Ron. The color of his skin was never an issue, despite his being the first black person anyone in my patently Caucasian family has dated. For Ron, the warm welcome was unfamiliar territory. His last two relationships both ended because the girlfriend's family refused to accept him. They never even met, but they knew he was black and that was enough. Their loss was our gain.

> We've come a long way since the civil rights movement, but prejudice is far from extinct.

There has been some talk of marriage, and when the time comes, there is no one I would rather take that step with. I'm grateful that we have the option. Interracial marriage was illegal in many states until 1967, when the Supreme Court finally declared the bans to be unconstitutional. Mixed-race marriages have been on the rise ever since. Fortunately we won't have to fly to another state just to walk down the aisle, but many couples still don't have that luxury. Nearly 50 years after that court ruling, same-sex couples are still fighting for the right to marry the people they love.

We've come a long way since the civil rights movement, but prejudice is far from extinct. It may have departed from most of our laws, but it still lingers in the silent judgements we all make about people we don't even know. If you wouldn't date or marry someone of the same gender, or outside your own race, ethnicity, generation, religion, political party or income bracket, that's perfectly fine. What you can't do is expect everyone else to do the same. Dating someone who differs greatly from yourself is an opportunity to learn from each other and grow together. We live in a brilliantly diverse society, and allowing others the freedom to live and love as they choose is just the kind of liberty we should be known for.

VOCABULARY/USING A DICTIONARY

1. What part of speech is *shallow* (para. 2)? How do you define it?
2. What might you be feeling if you are *mortified* (para. 3)?
3. What does it mean if something *lingers* (para. 6)?

RESPONDING TO WORDS IN CONTEXT

1. What is a "deal breaker" (para. 3)?
2. Since Nall has been speaking about race, what do you think *Caucasian* (para. 4) means?
3. When Nall says, "prejudice is far from *extinct*" (para. 6) what does she mean?

DISCUSSING MAIN POINT AND MEANING

1. What kinds of judgments does Nall expect of her relationship? Why?
2. Why is Ron surprised by the way Nall's parents react to him?
3. What is Nall grateful for, if she and Ron settle down together in the future?

EXAMINING SENTENCES, PARAGRAPHS, AND ORGANIZATION

1. Consider Nall's first sentence. Does it in any way allude to the content of the essay that follows?
2. Does Nall's switch from personal argument in the beginning to impersonal argument in her last two paragraphs work in this essay? Why or why not?
3. How does Nall change her writing perspective in her final paragraph? Is it effective?

THINKING CRITICALLY

1. What are some of the differences Nall and her boyfriend must surmount to have their relationship work?
2. Nall seems to embrace differences fully in her relationship and for other people. Why do some people object to relationships that seem different, even when they are not in them?
3. Can you imagine back to a time (say, 1967) when interracial marriage was illegal? Do you think the struggle to legalize it was similar to the struggle to legalize same-sex marriage?

WRITING ACTIVITIES

1. Read about the Supreme Court decision that legalized interracial marriage (*Loving v. Virginia*). Write a short news report as if you were reporting from 1967. Write about the victory for some people and the continued opposition by others. Will you applaud diversity as Nall does as you write your report, or will you write from a different position?

2. Have you ever had a relationship or friendship with someone who was different from you in some way that allowed you to learn from each other and grow together? Write a short personal essay that explores that relationship.

3. Do some research on affirmative action. What have some of the reactions been to it? Who is largely in favor, and who is opposed? Write a brief essay and offer some of your opinions on affirmative action as you understand its benefits and pitfalls.

LOOKING CLOSELY

Varying Sentences

The rhythm of prose is very important in keeping a reader engaged with your voice and your argument. Good writers vary long and compound sentences with simple ones. Variation serves two purposes: It keeps writing from sounding dull and monotone, and it adds additional emphasis to short sentences. Holly Nall, a student at San Francisco State, employs a masterful use of variation. Notice in the two examples below how she alternates between short, simple sentences (those with one subject and one verb) and more complex ones. In particular, pay attention to the ways the short sentences are punchy and emphatic.

1 *Longer sentences pack more information*	My boyfriend is full of surprises. <u>He's equal parts rock star, Prince Charming and ridiculous nerd.</u> (1) He treats me like a queen, even though I repeatedly insist otherwise, and makes me laugh until my sides hurt. <u>He's also 16 years older than me, and black.</u> (2)
2 *Shorter sentences provide emphasis*	. . . There has been some talk of marriage, and when the time comes, there is no one I would rather take that step with. <u>I'm grateful that we have the option.</u> (2)

STUDENT WRITER AT WORK
Holly Nall

Courtesy of Holly Nall

R.A. What inspired you to write this essay? And publish it in your campus paper?

H.N. This was my first op-ed piece, and it was inspired by gossip I overheard about another girl who was dating an older man. Most people in the room didn't know me or my dating situation, and I was hurt by their comments. It made me wonder what people might say about my relationship behind my back, so I pitched a piece about it.

R.A. What was your main purpose in writing this piece?

H.N. I suppose I was defending my unconventional relationship, and putting any potential rumors or questions to rest. But I was also standing up for all relationships that may seem out of the norm to some, because the only thing that matters is how happy two people are together.

R.A. What response have you received to this piece?

H.N. The response was very positive and supportive.

R.A. Do you generally show your writing to friends before submitting it? Do you collaborate or bounce your ideas off others?

H.N. Writing is usually a solitary process for me, but when I'm struggling I benefit from discussing my work with friends and fellow writers. Since this was such a personal piece, I wrote it all from my heart, and the only collaboration was with the editors, who helped me to clarify my more emotional opinions.

R.A. What do you like to read?

H.N. As of late, my favorite online source for reading has been *Hello Giggles,* because it covers so many issues from a female twenty-something perspective and is always an engaging read. I also enjoy local publications such as the *San Francisco Chronicle* and *SF Weekly,* as well as a bunch of food blogs and magazines, because cooking is my passion.

R.A. What topics most interest you as a writer?

H.N. In terms of journalism, I really enjoy telling human stories—any assignments that have allowed me to spend a lot of time with one person and tell their story. On my personal blog, I write a lot about cooking, technology, and conservation.

R.A. Are you pursuing a career in which writing will be a component?

H.N. I've ventured more into visual journalism over the course of my college career, specifically video and design. I'm sure writing will always be a part of what I do, but I think the emphasis will be on the visuals.

R.A. What advice do you have for other student writers?

H.N. Join the student publication, ASAP. Put in the time as a reporter, become an editor, and see how the whole process works. It's difficult work, but you will learn more than you ever knew possible, and you will spend time working with talented people who become friends for life.

IN BRIEF: ESSAY

Timothy Aubry

Married Life

[*The Point*, Issue 7, November 2013]

A *l onger version of the following reflections on marriage was first published in a Chicago-based literary journal,* The Point, *and was selected for* The Best American Essays 2014. *Timothy Aubry is an English professor at Baruch College in New York City and the author of* Reading as Therapy: What Contemporary Fiction Does for Middle-Class Americans *(2011). His essays have appeared in* n+1, Paper Monument, *and the* Millions. *He lives with his wife in Brooklyn, New York.*

You might want to consider Aubry's thoughts about marriage in connection with Emma Goldman's classic 1910 essay on the topic, "Marriage and Love" on p. 240.

The problem with marriage, we all know, is the endlessness of it. Plenty   1
of things we do will have long-term repercussions, but in what other situation do you promise to do something for the rest of your life? Not when you choose a college. Not when you take a job. Not when you buy a house. During childhood, you pick up many habits that are probably going to be lifelong, like walking, talking, reading, and sleeping, but once you've got those down, you start to feel like you're at greater liberty to decide what things you want to do and what things you want to stop doing. Especially when you're a young adult the apparently infinite multiplicity of possible choices — possible jobs, possible friends, possible cities, possible girlfriends or boyfriends — can sometimes fool you into thinking you have an infinite amount of time to try out everything. But once you're married, you've significantly cut down the options, and it suddenly makes your life feel shorter — like now there's a direct line between you and your own death. You've just gotten on a train and you

continued

won't get off until the very end of the track. In your final moments, if you stick to your promise, you'll still be doing the same thing you're doing now, dealing with the same person, possibly having the same arguments. And that commonality between now and then makes that far-off time, when you're old and sick and about to die, a little more imaginable. Which is scary.

Apparently even my father didn't quite escape this predicament. Although they were no longer married, my mother was still there with him in the hospital on the day he died of lung cancer at age sixty. And she even managed to subject him to one of their old familiar rituals, though he wasn't exactly in a condition to notice. Apparently after the nurse declared him dead and shepherded me, my sister and my two aunts out into another room, while we were all hugging and crying, my mother stayed in the room with my father's body in order to give him a final piece of her mind. "How *could* you?" she asked him. "How could you take such bad care of yourself and abandon your two kids like this?" My parents had been divorced for over fifteen years, and my father was dead, but my mother wanted to get in one last good fight.

I was stunned when my mother told me afterwards what she had just done. You had to have some pretty strong feelings, after all, to stand there yelling at a corpse. Did my mother still love my father? Perhaps, but I also think his death had taken something important from her — something distinct from love that marriage offers to us all. Watching her two kids collapse into sobs, she'd looked at their faces and thought about how they'd have to spend the rest of their lives fatherless, with one less person really looking out for them. Though they were both technically adults, one pregnant with her first child, they'd seemed to her especially vulnerable and helpless, and she wanted someone to blame. The causes of their distress were too big to comprehend and pretty much beyond anyone's control: disease, aging and death. So my dad, who could at least have tried to quit smoking, represented a much more tangible and more satisfying target for her grievances.

Marriage gives you someone to blame — for just about everything. Before you get married, when you feel depressed, you think to yourself, "Is this it?" And by "it" you mean life. Is this all life has to offer? Just one day followed by another? The same dreary routine? Etc. But after you get married, you think to yourself, "Is *this* it?" And by "it" you mean marriage. If your life feels monotonous, devoid of possibilities, static, two-dimensional, whatever, you don't blame your life; you blame your marriage. As a thing that's supposed to fill up your days until you die,

2

3

4

continued

your marriage becomes like an emblem of your life, like a kind of plastic insulation that's pressed all the way up against the very borders of your existence. It's much easier to blame the stuff lining the walls than the room itself. And there is, you sometimes remind yourself, just a little space between the lining and the outer boundaries, and thus it allows you to trick yourself into thinking if you could just get into that space between where your marriage ends and your life continues, or if you could somehow tear down the plastic, escape the confines of your marriage, life would suddenly be vibrant and rich and unexpected and mysterious again. So maybe the greatest gift marriage gives us is the chance to fantasize, to imagine that there's more to life than there actually is, and it accomplishes this by assuming responsibility for all the misery and dullness that we would otherwise equate with life itself.

Emma Goldman

Marriage and Love

By the end of the nineteenth century and the early decades of the twentieth, the United States had entered the modern world. Industry and manufacturing transformed cities nearly overnight; inventors like Thomas Edison unprecedentedly altered the expectations of average people; newly formed advertising firms promoted the first brand-name goods with logos and created a new type of American — the consumer — and amidst these rapid changes artists, novelists, and dramatists began to challenge long-standing societal and cultural norms. One sacred institution revered by religion and society that activists and intellectuals attacked in many different ways was marriage. By the outbreak of the First World War in 1914 and the raucous era of the 1920s that F. Scott Fitzgerald named "The Jazz Age," only fairy tales would end ". . . and they lived happily ever after."

Marriage, of course, is still a respected institution, and a thriving business, if we look at the costs of a traditional wedding. Yet, despite the alarming divorce rate and the economic difficulties many couples experience today, people still debate the value of marriage and many still believe it is an institution worth saving. Over one hundred years ago, the following essay, "Marriage and Love," appeared on the same topic, yet this one (shockingly for its time) did not offer advice on how to save the institution of marriage; instead, it severely criticized marriage and suggested the lives of both women and men would be better if it were abolished. The author of the essay was the political activist and anarchist Emma Goldman (1869–1940). One of the leading figures in the history of radical American politics, the Lithuanian-born Goldman came to the United States in her teens, where she soon embraced the causes of women and laborers. Goldman founded the magazine Mother Earth *in 1906 and in 1910 published her influential book,* Anarchism and Other Essays, *from which the following selection is taken. A popular lecturer on politics and literature, Goldman was imprisoned in 1917 and two years later deported to the Soviet Union.*

The popular notion about marriage and love is that they are synony-   1
mous, that they spring from the same motives, and cover the same
human needs. Like most popular notions this also rests not on actual
facts, but on superstition.

Marriage and love have nothing in common; they are as far   2
apart as the poles; are, in fact, antagonistic to each other. No doubt
some marriages have been the result of love. Not, however, because
love could assert itself only in marriage; much rather is it because
few people can completely outgrow a convention. There are today
large numbers of men and women to whom marriage is naught but
a farce, but who submit to it for the sake of public opinion. At any
rate, while it is true that some marriages are based on love, and
while it is equally true that in some cases love continues in married
life, I maintain that it does so regardless of marriage, and not
because of it.

On the other hand, it is utterly false that love results from mar-   3
riage. On rare occasions one does hear of a miraculous case of a married couple falling in love after marriage, but on close examination it
will be found that it is a mere adjustment to the inevitable. Certainly
the growing-used to each other is far away from the spontaneity, the
intensity, and beauty of love, without which the intimacy of marriage
must prove degrading to both the woman and the man.

Marriage is primarily an economic arrangement, an insurance   4
pact. It differs from the ordinary life insurance agreement only in that
it is more binding, more exacting. Its returns are insignificantly small
compared with the investments. In taking out an insurance policy
one pays for it in dollars and cents, always at liberty to discontinue
payments. If, however, a woman's premium is a husband, she pays for
it with her name, her privacy, her self-respect, her very life, "until
death doth part." Moreover, the marriage insurance condemns her to
life-long dependency, to parasitism, to complete uselessness, individual as well as social. Man, too, pays his toll, but as his sphere is
wider, marriage does not limit him as much as woman. He feels his
chains more in an economic sense.

Thus Dante's motto over Inferno applies with equal force to mar-   5
riage: "Ye who enter here leave all hope behind."[1]

---

[1] Dante's motto (para. 5): Famous line from *Inferno* (*hell* in Italian), the long
poem by Dante Alighieri (1265–1321).

That marriage is a failure none but the very stupid will deny. One 6
has but to glance over the statistics of divorce to realize how bitter a
failure marriage really is. Nor will the stereotyped Philistine argument that the laxity of divorce laws and the growing looseness of
woman account for the fact that: first, every twelfth marriage ends in
divorce; second, that since 1870 divorces have increased from 28 to
73 for every hundred thousand population; third, that adultery, since
1867, as ground for divorce, has increased 270.8 per cent.; fourth,
that desertion increased 369.8 per cent.

Added to these startling figures is a vast amount of material, dra- 7
matic and literary, further elucidating this subject. Robert Herrick, in
Together; Pinero, in *Mid-Channel;* Eugene Walter, in *Paid in Full,*[2] and
scores of other writers are discussing the barrenness, the monotony,
the sordidness, the inadequacy of marriage as a factor for harmony
and understanding.

The thoughtful social student will not content himself with the 8
popular superficial excuse for this phenomenon. He will have to dig
down deeper into the very life of the sexes to know why marriage
proves so disastrous.

Edward Carpenter[3] says that behind every marriage stands the life- 9
long environment of the two sexes; an environment so different from
each other that man and woman must remain strangers. Separated by
an insurmountable wall of superstition, custom, and habit, marriage has
not the potentiality of developing knowledge of, and respect for, each
other, without which every union is doomed to failure.

In our present pygmy state love is indeed a stranger to most peo- 10
ple. Misunderstood and shunned, it rarely takes root; or if it does, it
soon withers and dies. Its delicate fiber can not endure the stress and
strain of the daily grind. Its soul is too complex to adjust itself to the
slimy woof of our social fabric. It weeps and moans and suffers with
those who have need of it, yet lack the capacity to rise to love's summit.

Some day, some day men and women will rise, they will reach 11
the mountain peak, they will meet big and strong and free, ready to
receive, to partake, and to bask in the golden rays of love. What fancy,

---

[2] Herrick, Pinero, Walter (para. 7): Popular literary figures of the day who challenged conventional morals.

[3] Carpenter (para. 9): Highly influential author of many books on marriage and
human sexuality who was considered one of the earliest champions of gay rights
and lived 1844–1929.

what imagination, what poetic genius can foresee even approximately the potentialities of such a force in the life of men and women. If the world is ever to give birth to true companionship and oneness, not marriage, but love will be the parent.

BACKGROUND AND CONTEXT

1. A popular Frank Sinatra song said that "love and marriage go together like a horse and carriage." How does Emma Goldman's opinion differ? Which does she value and why?

2. Goldman partly makes a case against marriage by citing divorce statistics. Do you think that the likelihood a marriage will end in divorce acts as a deterrent to a couple deciding to get married? Explain why or why not.

STRATEGY, STRUCTURE, AND STYLE

1. Note Goldman's analogy of a marriage to a life insurance policy. According to her, what do they have in common? What differences does she acknowledge? Evaluate her analogy. Explain whether or not you think it works as a description of marriage.

2. Consider Goldman's reference to Edward Carpenter's view of the "two sexes." Do you think it is applicable even today, or in your opinion do boys and girls grow up understanding each other better than they did a hundred years ago? How does Carpenter's view help support her argument?

COMPARISONS AND CONNECTIONS

1. Read Goldman's 1910 essay together with Rebecca Solnit's "More Equal Than Others." Based on Goldman's reasoning about marriage, what do you think her opinion would be on same-sex marriage? Or you may also want to compare Goldman's essay to Judy Brady's "I Want a Wife" on p. 330. How does Goldman's older feminist position contrast to Brady's 1970's feminism and to today's feminism voiced by Solnit?

2. In a brief essay, compare Goldman's essay to Frederick Douglass's "What to a Slave, Is the Fourth of July?" address (p. 164). Although Goldman does not address the subject of race relations, can you find any points in common? Any similar images or metaphors? Compare how each author and activist concludes his or her argument.

Discussing the Unit

SUGGESTED TOPIC FOR DISCUSSION

Is a lifelong, monogamous commitment to another person — the traditional ideal for a marriage — a goal worth upholding or a fairy-tale notion, both unrealistic and limiting? Do individuals and society pay any price when marriage rates decline? Or do the benefits of marriage alternatives, such as cohabitation or a decision to remain single, potentially outweigh the costs? If so, for whom, and under what circumstances?

PREPARING FOR CLASS DISCUSSION

1. At a time of greater financial and reproductive independence for women, what benefits might women still see in marriage? What are the benefits for men? How might these have changed over the past fifty years? Consider these questions with this chapter's essays in mind.
2. What assumptions about marriage do the selections in this chapter consider? Did the essays challenge your own assumptions about marriage? In what ways?

FROM DISCUSSION TO WRITING

1. Considering the essays in this chapter, discuss how the definition of a "good marriage" has changed over time and how it has remained the same.
2. People who prefer cohabitation to marriage often say that marriage is "only a piece of paper." Drawing on your own experiences and observations and the essays in this chapter, discuss whether you agree or disagree with this statement. Also, consider whether the "piece of paper" itself might have any social or economic value.

TOPICS FOR CROSS-CULTURAL DISCUSSION

1. Research another country where same-sex couples can legally marry. When and how did they gain the right to do so?
2. In some countries and cultural groups, especially in South Asia, arranged marriages are common. In these marriages, parents choose spouses for their children, considering such factors as a potential mate's religion, socioeconomic background, and reputation. In modern Western cultures, however, most people choose their own spouses, usually placing romantic feelings over other considerations. Taking into account the benefits and limitations of marriage as discussed in this chapter, what might be some advantages of an arranged marriage over a "love marriage"? What are some possible drawbacks? Do you think arranged marriages could ever become popular in the United States? Why or why not?

9

The Environment:
Is the Crisis Overblown?

In 2013, the United Nations Intergovernmental Panel on Climate Change concluded that: (1) the past three decades have almost certainly been the hottest in nearly 1,000 years and (2) that humans — through our insatiable appetite for the burned carbon that lights our cities and powers our vehicles — are almost certainly to blame. The report is nothing all that new, but headlines like it throw us now and then into a frenzy: What can we do to stem rising temperatures and the global calamities that might accompany them? Vociferous proposals ranging from a tax on carbon to a complete rewiring of the nation's power infrastructure speak to the urgency with which some people greet climate-change facts and figures.

The news throws some on the right, however, into a different kind of frenzy. Many conservatives believe that reports of a warming world — or at least of mankind's responsibility for turning up the heat — are exaggerated. Some directly accuse the science establishment of flubbing the numbers or misinterpreting the data in order to push a radical environmentalist agenda. In "The Myth of 'Settled Science,'" columnist Charles Krauthammer announces immediately that he is neither a climate-change "believer" nor a "denier." But he chides the believers for an arrogant know-it-all attitude about what will happen to the Earth in the next half century when the evidence is in some cases unclear. In fact, he says, many indicators suggest the alleged crisis is nonexistent. "None of this is dispositive," Krauthammer says after citing some challenging data, "It doesn't settle the issue. But that's the point." The piece urges us to keep an open mind about a future nobody can forecast precisely.

In an aside, Krauthammer also faults President Obama for evangelizing for the environment from "carbon-belching Air Force One." Indeed, a common comeback from skeptics of environmentalism is that their opponents behave just as badly—in many cases more badly—than they do. Are you a hypocrite if you argue for a carbon tax from the front seat of an SUV? Activist Bill McKibben takes on that question frankly and thoroughly in "A Moral Atmosphere." McKibben is a conservationist deeply troubled by what he sees as the depletion of dirty fossil fuels, but he also admits that he's part of the problem, trying to make climate-conscious lifestyle changes but ultimately putting gas in his tank like everyone else. McKibben argues that individual conservation efforts, while they might make one feel good, don't compare to the real collective action the government can spearhead. In fact, they can distract us from what he says will really save the planet: changing the laws, not the lightbulbs. To critics who point out that he and his fellow environmentalists drive on a gas-guzzling bus, McKibben writes, "If those of us who are trying really hard are still fully enmeshed in the fossil fuel system, it makes it even clearer that what needs to change are not individuals but precisely that system."

McKibben works from the assumption that climate change is real, and is a threat to the planet. Laying out that cause in this chapter—as well as proposing a possible solution—is pioneering scientist James Hansen. His 2013 acceptance speech for the liberal Nation Institute's Ridenhour Courage Prize employs unequivocal language about the danger he believes we're in: "The irrefutable scientific conclusion is that we cannot burn all of the fossil fuels without handing our children, grandchildren and future generations a situation that is out of their control, with enormous consequences for their well-being and for the very existence of many of the other species on our planet." Hansen believes humanity must transition to cleaner sources of energy, and attempts to bridge the political gap with what he calls a "progressive conservative approach" to incentivizing that shift.

If the climate crisis is so gallingly, perilously apparent, why do so many Americans doubt its existence? More than a third of Americans don't believe man-made climate change exists at all. While Krauthammer would argue that the science isn't settled, some climate-change believers have taken to analyzing the sources of this disbelief critically. In a "Spotlight on Research," Judith Shulevitz asks, "Why Do People Deny Science?" Shulevitz argues that, despite Krauthammer's assertions, the scientific community is more or less agreed on the threat. She considers poll data on the public's perception of the issue and concludes that Americans are not, generally, antiscience. Rather, she writes, "What they disagree about is what the science says. People assimilate the data and choose the experts that fit most neatly with their and their peers' values." Shulevitz tries to tease out the values that line up with skepticism toward environmental crisis.

This chapter's student essay turns away from climate change specifically, to another major issue facing the environment and our collective response. Hydraulic fracking, a controversial way of extracting fuel from the ground, has spurred protests and demonstrations from the public for years. Binghamton University student Macon Fessenden, though, says the outrage about fracking he sees on campus is woefully uninformed. In "Hydrofracking: Getting the Facts Straight," he suggests this outrage may be emblematic of the one-sided environmentalist view in general, and reminds us that there are two sides to the issue. Uncommitted himself, Fessenden lays out elegantly "the foundation of the environment vs. big business problem. What's more important, growth or conservation? Jobs or water quality?"

The questions Fessenden poses, of course, have been around for a long time. One seminal source for them was Rachel Carson's 1962 classic *Silent Spring*, a book which some call the foundational text of the environmentalist movement. This chapter's America Then comes from her introductory chapter, "A Fable for Tomorrow." Carson imagines a bleak future, many years after we have neglected our environment and overexploited our natural resources. "No witchcraft, no enemy action had silenced the rebirth of new life in this stricken world," she writes. "The people had done it themselves." As you read consider whether you agree, 50 years later, that this kind of future could await us on our current path. What can we do to swerve out of its way?

Charles Krauthammer

The Myth of "Settled Science"

[*The Washington Post,* February 20, 2014]

BEFORE YOU READ

Is there any such thing as "settled science"? Or are the findings of science meant to be always changing?

WORDS TO LEARN

static (para. 2): fixed (adjective)

impervious (para. 2): impenetrable (adjective)

randomized (para. 4): in a random order (adjective)

dynamics (para. 6): motivating or driving forces (noun)

concede (para. 7): admit (verb)

ostentatiously (para. 8): in a manner intended to attract notice (adverb)

dispositive (para. 12): often used in law to mean facts or data that in themselves can decide a case (adjective)

contemptibly (para. 12): despicably (adverb)

malevolent (para. 12): evil or harmful

I repeat: I'm not a global warming believer. I'm not a global warming denier. I've long believed that it cannot be good for humanity to be spewing tons of carbon dioxide into the atmosphere. I also believe that those scientists who pretend to know exactly what this will cause in 20, 30 or 50 years are white-coated propagandists. 1

"The debate is settled," asserted propagandist-in-chief Barack Obama in his latest State of the Union address. "Climate change is a fact." Really? There is nothing more anti-scientific than the very idea that science is settled, static, impervious to challenge. 2

Take a non-climate example. It was long assumed that mammograms help reduce breast cancer deaths. This fact was so settled that Obamacare requires every insurance plan to offer mammograms (for free, no less). 3

Now we learn from a massive randomized study — 90,000 women followed for 25 years — that mammograms may have no effect on breast 4

Charles Krauthammer is a Pulitzer Prize–winning columnist, political commentator, author, and physician. He currently serves as a contributor for FOX News Channel, and frequently appears on Special Report with Bret Baier, The O'Reilly Factor, *and* FOX News Sunday.

cancer deaths. Indeed, one out of five of those diagnosed by mammogram receives unnecessary radiation, chemo or surgery.

So much for settledness. And climate is less well-understood than breast cancer. If climate science is settled, why do its predictions keep changing? And how is it that the great physicist Freeman Dyson, who did some climate research in the late 1970s, thinks today's climate-change Cassandras are hopelessly mistaken?

They deal with the fluid dynamics of the atmosphere and oceans, argues Dyson, ignoring the effect of biology, i.e., vegetation and topsoil. Further, their predictions rest on models they fall in love with: "You sit in front of a computer screen for 10 years and you start to think of your model as being real." Not surprisingly, these models have been "consistently and spectacularly wrong" in their predictions, write atmospheric scientists Richard McNider and John Christy — and always, amazingly, in the same direction.

Settled? Even the U.K.'s national weather service concedes there's been no change — delicately called a "pause" — in global temperature in 15 years. If even the raw data is recalcitrant, let alone the assumptions and underlying models, how settled is the science?

Last Friday, Obama ostentatiously visited drought-stricken California. Surprise! He blamed climate change. Here even The New York Times gagged, pointing out that far from being supported by the evidence, "the most recent computer projections suggest that as the world warms, California should get wetter, not drier, in the winter."

How inconvenient. But we've been here before. Hurricane Sandy was made the poster child for the alleged increased frequency and strength of "extreme weather events" like hurricanes.

Nonsense. Sandy wasn't even a hurricane when it hit the U.S. Indeed, in all of 2012, only a single hurricane made U.S. landfall. And 2013 saw the fewest Atlantic hurricanes in 30 years. In fact, in the last half-century, one-third *fewer* major hurricanes have hit the U.S. than in the previous half-century.

Similarly tornadoes. Every time one hits, the climate-change commentary begins. Yet last year saw the fewest in a quarter-century. And the last 30 years — of presumed global warming — has seen a 30 percent *decrease* in extreme tornado activity (F3 and above) versus the previous 30 years.

None of this is dispositive. It doesn't settle the issue. But that's the   12
point. It mocks the very notion of settled science, which is nothing but
a crude attempt to silence critics and delegitimize debate. As does the
term "denier" — an echo of Holocaust denial, contemptibly suggesting
the malevolent rejection of an established historical truth.

Climate-change proponents have made their cause a matter of fealty   13
and faith. For folks who pretend to be brave carriers of the scientific
ethic, there's more than a tinge of religion in their jeremiads. If you whore
after other gods, the Bible tells us, "the Lord's wrath be kindled against
you, and he shut up the heaven, that there be no rain, and that the land
yield not her fruit" (Deuteronomy 11).

Sounds like California. Except that today there's a new god, the   14
Earth Mother. And a new set of sins — burning coal and driving a fully
equipped F-150.

But whoring is whoring, and the gods must be appeased. So if Cali-   15
fornia burns, you send your high priest (in a carbon-belching Air Force
One, but never mind) to the bone-dry land to offer up, on behalf of the
repentant congregation, a $1 billion burnt offering called a "climate resil-
ience fund."

Ah, settled science in action.   16

VOCABULARY/USING A DICTIONARY

1. If someone is *recalcitrant* (para. 7), what is he or she like?
2. What is *fealty* (para. 13)?
3. If something increases in *frequency* (para. 9), what happens?

RESPONDING TO WORDS IN CONTEXT

1. What is the difference between *legitimized* and *delegitimized* (para. 12) debate?
2. How does a climate-change *proponent* (para. 13) feel about climate change?
3. What is the history of the word *jeremiad* (para. 13), and how does it explain Krauthammer's invocation of religion ("there's more than a tinge of religion in their jeremiads") in his sentence?

DISCUSSING MAIN POINT AND MEANING

1. What example is used to show the danger of simply accepting one account for climate change?
2. Why might President Obama have been wrong, according to Krauthammer, in saying the droughts in California were caused by climate change?
3. What does Krauthammer suggest is behind the climate-change proponents' adherence to their cause?

EXAMINING SENTENCES, PARAGRAPHS, AND ORGANIZATION

1. How does Krauthammer describe his position on the subject in his first paragraph?
2. How can you tell from his paragraphs that this essay is written for a newspaper? Can you find any paragraphs you would combine?
3. How does Krauthammer use figurative speech to ridicule the idea of "settled science" at the end of his essay?

THINKING CRITICALLY

1. Does Krauthammer have an open mind about the reality or unreality of climate change? Do you think he is truly "not a global warming denier"?
2. Do you think that hurricanes and tornadoes are becoming more violent in recent years? Why or why not?
3. Do you think climate science can be worked out via computer? Why are computers important in the investigation of climate change?

WRITING ACTIVITIES

1. Research Hurricane Sandy. Do you think it is important for Krauthammer to say, "Nonsense. Sandy wasn't even a hurricane when it hit the U.S."? Why was Sandy so destructive? Does Krauthammer minimize its force? Can you find any information about climate change and its possible connections to Sandy?
2. Complete a short writing exercise in which you consider all the effects of a drought in California. Then read a few reports on the most recent droughts in that region. Write a short essay that combines your ideas about drought with evidence from recent droughts to describe its effects on the land and people.
3. Consider your own feelings about climate change. If necessary, read a few more articles — both scientific and op-ed — on the subject. Write an essay that states your opinion about the validity of climate change science and research, and back up your position with evidence from your reading.

Bill McKibben

A Moral Atmosphere

[*Orion*, March/April 2013]

BEFORE YOU READ
What can be done to stall or reverse climate change? Are we doing enough?
What actions are truly effective?

WORDS TO LEARN
vital (para. 3): essential (adjective)
strenuous (para. 4): vigorous or overly active (adjective)

trajectory (para. 4): the curve that describes the path of a projectile (noun)
bogus (para. 8): not genuine (adjective)

The list of reasons for not acting on climate change is long and ever-shifting. First it was "there's no problem"; then it was "the problem's so large there's no hope." There's "China burns stuff too," and "it would hurt the economy," and, of course, "it would hurt the economy." The excuses are getting tired, though. Post Sandy (which hurt the economy to the tune of $100 billion) and the drought ($150 billion), 74 percent of Americans have decided they're very concerned about climate change and want something to happen. 1

But still, there's one reason that never goes away, one evergreen excuse not to act: "you're a hypocrite." I've heard it ten thousand times myself — how can you complain about climate change and drive a car / have a house / turn on a light / raise a child? This past fall, as I headed across the country on a bus tour to push for divestment from fossil fuels, local newspapers covered each stop. I could predict, with great confidence, what the first online comment from a reader following each account would be: "Do these morons not know that their bus takes gasoline?" In fact, our bus took biodiesel[1] — as we headed down the 2

---

[1] biodiesel (para. 2): Vegetable oil–or animal fat–based diesel fuel that powers automobiles.

Bill McKibben is an environmentalist and author of what is widely regarded as the first book on climate change, The End of Nature *(1989). In addition to having written a dozen books, he is the founder of 350.org, an international grassroots climate change movement.*

East Coast, one job was watching the web app that showed the nearest station pumping the good stuff. But it didn't matter, because the next comment would be: "Don't these morons know that the plastic fittings on their bus, and the tires, and the seats are all made from fossil fuels?"

Actually, I do know — even a moron like me. I'm fully aware that we're embedded in the world that fossil fuel has made, that from the moment I wake up, almost every action I take somehow burns coal and gas and oil. I've done my best, at my house, to curtail it: we've got solar electricity, and solar hot water, and my new car runs on electricity — I can plug it into the roof and thus into the sun. But I try not to confuse myself into thinking that's helping all that much: it took energy to make the car, and to make everything else that streams into my life. I'm still using far more than any responsible share of the world's vital stuff.

And, in a sense, that's the point. If those of us who are trying really hard are still fully enmeshed in the fossil fuel system, it makes it even clearer that what needs to change are not individuals but precisely that system. We simply can't move fast enough, one by one, to make any real difference in how the atmosphere comes out. Here's the math, obviously imprecise: maybe 10 percent of the population cares enough to make strenuous efforts to change — maybe 15 percent. If they all do all they can, in their homes and offices and so forth, then, well . . . nothing much shifts. The trajectory of our climate horror stays about the same.

> If those of us who are trying really hard are still fully enmeshed in the fossil fuel system, it makes it even clearer that what needs to change are not individuals but precisely that system.

But if 10 percent of people, once they've changed the light bulbs, work all-out to change the system? That's enough. That's more than enough. It would be enough to match the power of the fossil fuel industry, enough to convince our legislators to put a price on carbon. At which point none of us would be required to be saints. We could all be morons, as long as we paid attention to, say, the price of gas and the balance in our checking accounts. Which even dummies like me can manage.

I think more and more people are coming to realize this essential truth. Ten years ago, half the people calling out hypocrites like me were doing it from the left, demanding that we do better. I hear much less of that now, mostly, I think, because everyone who's pursued those changes in good faith has come to realize both their importance and their limitations. Now I hear it mostly from people who have no intention of changing but are starting to feel some psychic tension. They feel a little guilty, and so they dump their guilt on Al Gore because he has two houses. Or they find even lamer targets.

For instance, as college presidents begin to feel the heat about divest- 7 ment, I've heard from several who say, privately, "I'd be more inclined to listen to kids if they didn't show up at the college with cars." Which in one sense is fair enough. But in another sense it's avoidance at its most extreme. Young people are asking college presidents to stand up to oil companies. (And the ones doing the loudest asking are often the most painfully ideal- istic, not to mention the hardest on themselves.) If as a college president you *do* stand up to oil companies, then you stand some chance of changing the outcome of the debate, of weakening the industry that has poured bil- lions into climate denial and lobbying against science. The action you're demanding of your students — less driving — can't rationally be expected to change the outcome. The action they're demanding of you has at least some chance. That makes you immoral, not them.

Yes, they should definitely take the train to school instead of drive. 8 But unless you're the president of Hogwarts, there's a pretty good chance there's no train that goes there. Your students, in other words, by advocat- ing divestment, have gotten way closer to the heart of the problem than you have. They've taken the lessons they've learned in physics class and politi- cal science and sociology and economics and put them to good use. And you — because it would be uncomfortable to act, because you don't want to get crosswise with the board of trustees — have summoned a basically bogus response. If you're a college president making the argument that you won't act until your students stop driving cars, then clearly you've failed morally, but you've also failed intellectually. Even if you just built an energy-efficient fine arts center, and installed a bike path, and dedicated an acre of land to a college garden, you've failed. Even if you drive a Prius,[2] you've failed.

Maybe especially if you drive a Prius. Because there's a certain sense 9 in which Prius-driving can become an out, an excuse for inaction, the twenty-first-century equivalent of "I have a lot of black friends." It's nice to walk/drive the talk; it's much smarter than driving a semi-military vehicle to get your groceries. But it's become utterly clear that doing the right thing in your personal life, or even on your campus, isn't going to get the job done in time; and it may be providing you with sufficient psy- chic comfort that you don't feel the need to do the hard things it will take to get the job done. It's in our role as citizens — of campuses, of nations, of the planet — that we're going to have to solve this problem. We each have our jobs, and none of them is easy.

---

[2] Prius (para. 8): Hybrid car manufactured by Toyota.

VOCABULARY/USING A DICTIONARY

1. What is a *divestment* (para. 2)? What are we doing when we *divest* of something?
2. What part of speech is *curtail* (para. 3)? What does it mean?
3. What's the definition of *imprecise* (para. 4)? How is it different from *precise*?

RESPONDING TO WORDS IN CONTEXT

1. If we could *convince our legislators* (para. 5) to do something, what are we doing?
2. What does McKibben mean by *psychic tension* (para. 6) and *psychic comfort* (para. 9)?
3. If one gets *crosswise* (para. 8) with someone, what does that mean?

DISCUSSING MAIN POINT AND MEANING

1. Why is McKibben's essay titled "A Moral Atmosphere"? What is the moral course of action in regard to climate change, according to his argument?
2. What is the problem facing those, like McKibben, who individually do what they can to reduce climate change?
3. Why does McKibben applaud those who may still drive to school while advocating to college presidents that they divest from their connections to businesses that produce or profit from fossil fuel consumption?

EXAMINING SENTENCES, PARAGRAPHS, AND ORGANIZATION

1. What does the phrase *evergreen excuse* mean in paragraph two? How does the phrase connect back to the topic at hand?
2. Why is the word *moron* repeated in paragraphs 2, 3, and 5? How does the word change meaning with each use?
3. Why does McKibben refer to Hogwarts in paragraph 8? What does the writer achieve by including the reference?

THINKING CRITICALLY

1. Why is it hard to reach consensus about what to do about climate change?
2. What sort of difficulties do organizations face when they divest from fossil fuels?
3. Do you think it is important to take part in individual acts to curtail climate change—the ones that may not have the most impact? Why or why not?

WRITING ACTIVITIES

1. Investigate the number of hybrid automobiles currently being manufactured. Who makes them? What claims are being made about them? How and to whom are they being marketed? Write a short article, as if you were reporting for *Consumer Reports* or an environmentally conscious magazine, that compares these cars to each other and to standard automobiles, and give some information about them to the general public.

2. What are your school's connections to and policies about fossil fuels and the companies that produce them? Write a research article about your university's investments and where their endowments come from. Was your information public or did you have to ask for it? How do your findings link up with McKibben's points being made about the role of campuses in the reduction of climate change?

3. McKibben is no "moron" about climate change. He has been very active as a writer and environmental campaigner. Find out more about McKibben through Internet research, and write a short essay about his life and his work in this area. Do you feel his essay is more credible now that you know more about him? Is knowing more about him unnecessary? Explain your answer, drawing other materials by or about McKibben in to strengthen your argument.

James Hansen

Acceptance Speech for the 2013 Ridenhour Courage Prize

[*The Nation*, May 27, 2013]

BEFORE YOU READ
How will we meet the challenges of climate control? What are some alternative solutions, beyond the ones you might ordinarily hear from the proponents of climate change?

WORDS TO LEARN
persistence (para. 1): perseverance (noun)
inertia (para. 4): inactivity (noun)
irrefutable (para. 5): undeniable (adjective)
inevitable (para. 6): unavoidable (adjective)
fringe (para. 13): margin or periphery (noun)

James Hansen is director of NASA's Goddard Institute for Space Studies. He is an adjunct professor at Columbia University in the Department of Earth and Environmental Sciences and is best known for his work in the field of climatology. He was the first scientist to warn the U.S. Congress of the dangers of climate change.

Thanks, Joe, for your kind words and especially for the huge 1
amount of important and effective work that you have done in
informing the public about climate change. And thanks to the
Ridenhour organization for their persistence in offering me this prestigious award.

I would like to use my several minutes here to summarize the truth 2
about our current predicament with human-made climate change and
the opportunity that this presents for dealing with fundamental problems faced by people in the United States and the rest of the world.

I must emphasize the threat posed by our current energy pathway 3
and the fact that we are rapidly running out of time for changing our
course. Yet I should emphasize equally that a sensible course toward
abundant clean energy is not only possible, but could yield stronger
economies with more equitable opportunities for all. Such a course is
needed if we are to preserve and enjoy the remarkable life on our planet.

The carbon dioxide, CO_2, that we put in the air by burning fossil 4
fuels will stay in the climate system for millennia. We have only felt part
of the climate response from the CO_2 already in the air — the climate
responding only slowly because of the great inertia of the massive global
ocean and ice sheets.

The irrefutable scientific conclusion is that we cannot burn all of 5
the fossil fuels without handing our children, grandchildren and future
generations a situation that is out of their control, with enormous consequences for their well-being and for the very existence of many of the
other species on our planet. We must leave most of the remaining coal in
the ground, as well as the carbon-intensive, highly polluting unconventional fossil fuels such as tar sands and tar shale.

The task of leaving these dirty fuels in the ground and moving on 6
to a bright future for today's young people cannot be accomplished by
trickery and gimmicks, such as carbon cap-and-trade and offsets, with
their inevitable horse-trading and lobbying.

We must have a simple, honest, across-the-board carbon fee col- 7
lected from the fossil fuel companies at the small number of domestic
mines and ports of entry. All of that money should be distributed to the
public — 100 percent of it — with equal amounts going to all legal residents. The fee must continue to rise gradually, so the public, businesses
and entrepreneurs have the incentive to make choices and develop products that reduce and eventually eliminate fossil fuel use.

This will stimulate the economy as we develop more carbon-efficient 8
products and energy sources. About 60 percent of the people will get
more money in their monthly dividend than they pay in increased prices,
but to stay on the positive side, they must make wise choices. Yes, this

implies some wealth redistribution. Low-income people, if they try, can gain somewhat. Rich people who have multiple houses and fly around the world will pay more than they receive in their dividend, but they can afford it.

This approach can be made international via an agreement between the United States and China. China has many reasons to join, as climate disruption will hit the Chinese hard, and they need to solve their severe pollution problems. Other nations will then join in order to avoid border duties on their products and in order to gain the clean energy benefits.   9

The United States must exercise leadership. This is the last chance for the liberal left and the conservative right to cooperate for the good of the nation and the world, for the good of young people, future generations and nature.   10

> This is the last chance for the liberal left and the conservative right to cooperate for the good of the nation and the world, for the good of young people, future generations and nature.

What I have described is a progressive conservative approach. It puts an honest price on fossil fuels, making them pay their costs to society. It allows all alternatives to compete on a level playing field.   11

We must demand that the liberal left keep their hands off of our wallets. Not one dime of the carbon fee should be used to make the government bigger. One hundred percent of the money must go to the public. Nor should any of this money be used for subsidizing research on specific government-selected industries. The government is not competent to choose the best technologies — let them all compete. There are existing government resources and departments for research, development and demonstration, which can assist early development of candidate technologies.   12

The public is fed up with self-indulgent partisanship. If today's parties cannot cooperate on such a simple, honest approach that would stimulate our economy, provide millions of good jobs, a clean environment and a stable climate, then in 2016 there should be a new party — not a fringe party on the left or right, but a centrist party, an American Party, a party that will take Washington back from the lobbyists and give it to the American people.   13

VOCABULARY/USING A DICTIONARY

1. Is a *prestigious* (para. 1) award distinctive or not?

2. Is a *predicament* (para. 2) a situation you'd want to be in?

3. What does *equitable* mean (para. 3)? Does it mean the same thing as *equal*?

RESPONDING TO WORDS IN CONTEXT

1. How is climate change a *fundamental* (para. 2) problem?
2. What might a source of *abundant clean energy* (para. 3) be?
3. What is *partisanship* (para. 13)? Why does Hansen say we are fed up with it?

DISCUSSING MAIN POINT AND MEANING

1. What does Hansen's progressive conservative approach toward climate change consist of?
2. Does Hansen find the issue of climate change particularly pressing?
3. Where must the money go when it is collected as a carbon fee?

EXAMINING SENTENCES, PARAGRAPHS, AND ORGANIZATION

1. Do you think this piece works equally well as a speech and as an essay? What gives it its particular strengths, one way or another?
2. What indicators do you have that this is a speech (if you were reading it as an essay and didn't know)?
3. How does Hansen call on every potential player to participate in the healing of this crisis in the body of the speech?

THINKING CRITICALLY

1. Are you persuaded of the dangers of climate change by Hansen's words? Where does he persuade you most effectively?
2. Does Hansen's suggested fee make sense? What about his restrictions on who uses the money?
3. Do you see a time in which people can get over their particular allegiances and partisanship in order to work together in the manner Hansen describes? Why or why not?

WRITING ACTIVITIES

1. Listen to James Hansen's TED talk on climate change. Write a response to the talk and to the speech that you read. In what ways is he convincing? Is it more convincing to hear him or to read his words?
2. Write a brief report on the work Hansen has done in his lifetime. In what ways is he an expert on climate change? Do you think his work is worthy of the awards he has received for it?
3. Explore the idea of a carbon fee. What do you think possible objections to it will be? Who would be in favor of it, and why?

Spotlight on Research

Judith Shulevitz

Why Do People Deny Science?

[*The New Republic,* October 21, 2013]

Judith Shulevitz is a columnist for, and the science editor of the New Republic. *Her writing has appeared in* Slate, *the* New York Times Book Review, *and the* New Yorker, *and her 2010 book,* The Sabbath World: Glimpses of a Different Order of Time, *was lauded as being "a swift, penetrating book intent on shattering the habits of mindless workaholism" by the* New Yorker.

If you read the non-enthralling 36-page summary of a report about to come   1
out from the U.N. Intergovernmental Panel on Climate Change, as I did last
week, you may have been struck by something faintly odd. Most news stories
interpreted the communiqué as the strongest statement yet from the world's
top climate experts — more than 800 from 39 countries — that human-
induced global warming will irreversibly transmogrify earth, sea, and sky
unless carbon emissions are capped soon. The reporters weren't wrong, but
they missed something, perhaps because it was so obvious it slipped beneath
notice. It was the tone. The document made heavy use of italics (*"virtually
certain," "very likely"*) and language ("unequivocal," "unprecedented") not
usually stooped to by scientists. The writers focused on their "confidence in
the validity" of their findings rather than on the findings themselves. In short,
this was no neutral act of scientific communication. It was a rebuttal to those
who have done nothing to mitigate the risks of climate change, because they
refuse to admit its plain facts.

Why *do* people persist in underestimating risk in the face of a clear sci-   2
entific consensus? I don't think I exaggerate when I say that lack of belief in
climate change is the main obstacle to keeping the planet a place on which
humans and other species can live comfortably. Do the skeptics (roughly
a third of all Americans) act in bad faith, or do they just think badly? Are
they cynical, ill-educated, innumerate, distrustful of science, or pawns of the
merchants of doubt? Do they watch too much Fox News, whose website,
predictably, called the report "an embarrassment, self-serving and beyond
misleading"?

The conundrum encompasses more than global warming. Scientists,   3
politicians, and regulators are constantly trying to figure out which risks will
alarm people. Why is bioengineering, the crossbreeding of biology with technology, scary, but nanotechnology, the manipulation of tiny particles that
can change the fundamental properties of things, not scary — at least not so
far? Why did we stop holding protests about nuclear power? Why was the
human papillomavirus vaccine anathematized when given to teenage girls,

continued

even though we've been giving another vaccine for a sexually transmitted disease — hepatitis B — to infants for years?

Clearly, scientists can't manage public reactions to risk as well as they'd   4
like. History has made fools of environmentalists who believed that people would change their behavior if they only knew how bad global warming could be. Some psychologists, such as Daniel Kahneman, say that most people just aren't very good at deliberation; they process difficult scientific material too quickly and emotionally to estimate risk accurately. Another hypothesis targets the right-wing personality, claiming that it is close-minded, complexity-averse, and prone to forcing all evidence into a partisan framework.

Lately, though, an explanation of flawed risk assessment has become   5
popular that has the virtue of not dismissing half the population as ignorant, stupid, or biased by temperament. It's called the cultural cognition of risk, and its best-known advocate is a handsome, puckish law and psychology professor at Yale named Dan Kahan. He thinks misperceptions of risk make perfect sense if you view them in a social context. First, says Kahan, rid yourself of the thought that Americans distrust science, scientists, or the scientific consensus. Consider this line from a 2009 Pew Research report: "Overwhelming majorities say that science has had a positive effect on society and that science has made life easier for most people." What they disagree about is what the science says. People assimilate the data and choose the experts that fit most neatly with their and their peers' values. Kahan and colleagues like to plot these worldviews on charts that illustrate how certain sociocultural tendencies — hierarchical-individualist   and   egalitarian-communitarian are the two big ones — consistently correlate to the same judgments about what's worrisome and what isn't.

Risk assessment by groupthink is reasonable, if not rational, because, at   6
the personal level, it costs nothing. If you misconstrue the nature of a global threat, your mistake won't hurt you much, because you can't save yourself anyway. But if you contradict your friends or powerful members of your group — that could cost you dearly. (Incidentally, Kahan sees evidence of scientific groupthink on both sides of the ideological spectrum.) Kahan's most provocative finding, though, is that people better at "cognitive reflection," or slow, probing thought, are actually *more* likely to arrive at predetermined conclusions about risk, not less. The urge to maintain status within one's social network is so powerful, Kahan told me, that well-educated people will use their information-gathering and computational skills to marshal a more impressive body of evidence in support of whatever identity it is (free-thinking skeptic, caring mother hen) that earns them brownie points in their troop. On his blog, he once called these strong in-group effects "tapeworms of cognitive illiberalism" and a dispiriting omen for democracy.

Kahan's conclusions wouldn't surprise anyone who has spent her life   7
studying politics. Political theorists have been working out for decades how the interests of individuals and small groups obstruct the interests of the

continued

collective and why it's so hard to get people to act on threats they can't see or feel. According to Kahan, what cultural cognition theory has to add is the science of science communication. He and his kind conduct research on how to present science so that it won't be entangled with issues of "membership and loyalty to a group."

So what would he tell the environmentalists? The key is "not to use language or modes of communication that convey animosity, contempt, and hostility," he told me, because then "the signal that will come through is . . . that our group is under assault." I wasn't able to force any good examples out of him, though I couldn't help suspecting that one tactic would be to play down the words "United Nations," since that body, as everybody knows, flies black helicopters and encroaches on U.S. sovereignty. But I'd guess that Harvard political scientist and sociologist Theda Skocpol, for one, wouldn't think Kahan could tell the environmentalists much. In a recent and devastating post-mortem on the failed attempt to pass cap-and-trade legislation in President Obama's first term, she was contemptuous of the kind of politics that relies on "messaging campaigns," as she calls them. "The new vogue to pay psychological researchers to come up with phrases that subliminally appeal to individuals," she wrote, is "a waste of resources." She'd rather have green groups put their money into boots-on-the-ground, precinct-by-precinct, Tea Party-style organizing. I read Kahan that passage and he countered by asking what message Skocpol's organizers would offer up, and how they'd know whether it would work if they didn't test it with "evidence-based methods." 8

Skocpol may have a message — she prefers cap-and-dividend to cap-and-trade, since those dividends mean money in voters' pockets — and, presumably, she'd know she was right if that legislation passed. But Kahan and Skocpol aren't as far apart as they seem. Both consider group identity as important, politically, as individual acts of cognition, and both know that groups are not static. If you need a group's approval to get your warnings heard, then your job is to get that group on your side, whether by sloganeering or knocking on doors or — preferably — both. Sometimes democracy is less a matter of thinking well than of choosing your friends wisely. 9

DRAWING CONCLUSIONS

1. Why do people deny science, according to Shulevitz?
2. What does Shulevitz notice about the report issued by the UN Intergovernmental Panel on Climate Change? Should we be surprised by the tone of the document?
3. Is Shulevitz's article helpful to those who might want to approach people who deny climate change? Explain.

Macon Fessenden (student essay)

Hydrofracking: Getting the Facts Straight

[*Pipe Dream,* Binghamton University, November 8, 2013]

BEFORE YOU READ

What do you think about the issue of fracking? What are some of its positives and negatives?

WORDS TO LEARN

woefully (para. 1): unhappily (adverb)

provision (para. 1): supply or stock (noun)

perpetuation (para. 2): continuation (noun)

disclose (para. 2): to expose to view (verb)

anthropogenic (para. 3): relating to the influence of humans on nature (adjective)

conglomerate (para. 4): something composed of many parts (noun)

Hydrofracking is one of the most controversial issues in the country and perhaps the most widely discussed topic on campus. I purposefully don't call the topic "controversial" at Binghamton University because that would mean there is a two-sided debate on the issue. There isn't. There is woefully little pro-fracking rhetoric on campus. If you travel to the relatively rural streets behind the Nature Preserve, you will find as many pro-fracking signs as anti-fracking ones. The area isn't as resoundingly anti-fracking as campus. We, on the other hand, screen "Gasland" at least once a semester and hold protests against Halliburton. I am not against protests or documentary screenings, but I am against a one-sided provision of information. 1

Let's get some facts straight. Hydraulic fracturing (hydrofracking) has been occurring in New York state to extract oil and natural gas for decades. So why have we been hearing so much about it in the past few years? Relatively recent advancements in the industry have brought about the ability for horizontal drilling, which opens up the Marcellus 2

Macon Fessenden is a student at Binghamton University.

Shale[1] for high-volume natural gas extraction. So, besides the perpetuation of non-renewable, carbon-producing energy sources, what is wrong with hydrofracking? It's all in the fluids, baby. A high-pressure solution of water, sand and toxic chemicals is pumped through highly reinforced pipes that eventually break up rock to release the gas that is stored in pockets in the shale. The composition of the solution used to be a "trade secret" due to "Halliburton loopholes" passed under President George W. Bush, but now many companies, including Halliburton, publicly disclose the chemicals in their "frack fluid." There are two major problems with this fluid: The high pressure can crack the pipes and release fluid and methane into the water table, and storage and disposal of the fluid is expensive and can result in disastrous leaks and spills.

The popular documentary "Gasland," which helped launch horizontal hydrofracking onto the national stage, is an anecdotal film about a few isolated cases of water poisoning. The primary sob story in the movie, the water of Dimock, Pa., has since been researched and cleared of well-poisoning. The most shocking image of the movie is a family lighting their tap water on fire due to the abundance of methane in the wells. However, the Marcellus Shale is so full of gas that some leaks out into the water table without anthropogenic influence. There has been enough gas in the water table to light tap water on fire for as long as there's been a water table (probably since the last Ice Age). 3

So with the chance of major catastrophe, why is this a discussion? There is a ridiculous amount of money to be made in this business, and not just for big, bad oil and gas conglomerates. Landowners who lease their land for natural gas extraction may be looked down upon in the community, but many of them are farmers paying off tens of thousands of dollars of debt. Some of these families will be above water for the first time in their 4

> So with the chance of major catastrophe, why is this a discussion?

lives and will be able to pump their own money into the local economy. These companies may be bad, but it's not Walmart driving out local businesses and paying rotten money for rotten jobs. They're paying hard-working, salt-of-the-earth people big bucks to lease out a few acres of their land.

There are very few EPA-substantiated claims of water poisoning from hydraulic fracturing. These major incidents have occurred because of human error and failure to follow regulations. Fracking is an inher- 5

---

[1] Marcellus Shale (para. 2): A rock formation found in eastern North America.

ently safe process; it's the scary possibility of an accident that makes fracking such a big issue. And if accidents were common, then I would understand. But research shows that the stories you hear are insubstantial and sensationalized.

Anecdotes dominate the debate at the state and national level. The gas companies are guilty of many bad things, but what matters to the struggling landowners is that they are willing to shell out millions of dollars to drill. And here lies the foundation of the environment vs. big business problem. What's more important, growth or conservation? Jobs or water quality? I am fully ambivalent (not apathetic) on the issue and refuse to get behind either side until the state runs an Environmental Impact Statement on the combined impact of the wells in New York state. But until then, look at information from both NYPIRG (New York Public Interest Research Group) and Friends of Natural Gas with equally skeptical eyes as you remember both of them have their own agendas.

6

VOCABULARY/USING A DICTIONARY
1. What is *methane* (para. 3)?
2. What direction is *horizontal* (para. 2)?
3. What verb is contained in the word *extraction* (para. 4)?

RESPONDING TO WORDS IN CONTEXT
1. What is meant by the word *rhetoric* (para. 1)?
2. Fessenden exhorts us to be *skeptical* (para. 6) of both sides in the fracking debate. What is he asking of us?
3. When Fessenden says the companies are willing to *shell out* (para. 6) money to landowners, what does he mean?

DISCUSSING MAIN POINT AND MEANING
1. What does Fessenden object to on his college campus?
2. What was the documentary *Gasland* about? What purpose did the movie serve?
3. Why does Fessenden think fracking is safe?

EXAMINING SENTENCES, PARAGRAPHS, AND ORGANIZATION
1. Fessenden makes statements like this in paragraph 5: "Fracking is an inherently safe process; it's the scary possibility of an accident that makes fracking such a big issue. And if accidents were common, then I would understand." How might Fessenden include more examples in this portion of the essay to strengthen his own points?
2. Can you point to specific passages in the essay that show where Fessenden's tone leans towards the colloquial?

3. Fessenden writes, "Let's get some facts straight" (para. 2). Which facts does he use to organize his essay?

THINKING CRITICALLY

1. Does Fessenden sound like he wants to hear a debate about hydrofracking, or does it sound like he has chosen a side? Why do you think so?
2. Why do you think students at Binghamton are so much against hydrofracking? Why is there a significant difference between the school and the community?
3. Would you be okay with "frack fluid" near your water supply? Do you think anti-fracking fears are unfounded? Do you think pro-fracking interest looks beyond the money to be made?

WRITING ACTIVITIES

1. Where is Marcellus Shale located? How have communities in those regions been affected by fracking? What did those communities look like before fracking became part of the business of their region?
2. Imagine a debate about fracking. What are the pros? What are the cons? List as many possibilities as you can imagine. Does Fessenden look at the most important issues about fracking in his essay? Does he present a debate or a "one-sided provision of information"? Explain your answer in writing.
3. What do you think about "fracking fluid" being a "trade secret" of Halliburton for so long? Research Halliburton and the George W. Bush presidency, and write a report on the company's practices at that time. Was President Bush a protector of Halliburton? How were people affected by the company's and the president's decisions?

LOOKING CLOSELY

Effective Openings: Establishing a Clear Context for an Argument

When writing an essay that advances an opinion about a current issue, one of the best approaches a writer can take is to clearly summarize the general context or situation that gave rise to the issue. This approach is effectively demonstrated in Macon Fessenden's "Hydrofracking: Getting the Facts Straight." Note how his opening paragraph sets out in a clear and direct way the situation that has prompted his essay — the lack of real debate on the controversial environmental issue of hydrofracking. Fessenden begins by observing the differences between how the campus and off campus community are dealing with the controversy, and wonders why both sides of this debate are "woefully" absent on campus. Off campus he sees a true "controversy" with people on both sides of the issue; but on campus he finds no controversy and comes out against the "one-sided provision of information."

1 *Contrasts situation on and off campus*	Hydrofracking is one of the most controversial issues in the country and perhaps the most widely discussed topic on campus. <u>I purposefully don't call the topic "controversial" at Binghamton University because that would mean there is a two-sided debate on the issue. There isn't. There is woefully little pro-fracking rhetoric on campus. If you travel to the relatively rural streets behind the Nature Preserve, you will find as many pro-fracking signs as anti-fracking ones.</u> (1) The area isn't as resoundingly anti-fracking as campus. We, on the other hand, screen "Gasland" at least once a semester and hold protests against Halliburton. I am not against protests or documentary screenings, but <u>I am against a one-sided provision of information.</u> (2)
2 *Clearly states his main point*	

STUDENT WRITER AT WORK
Macon Fessenden

R.A. What inspired you to write this essay? And publish it in your campus paper?

M.F. I have learned a lot about hydrofracking in my time at Binghamton, it's one of the major topics on campus and in the surrounding area. There is misinformation everywhere, and there are many people, especially in my old department, that blindly hate hydrofracking for the sole purpose that it isn't solar or wind, so they cling to any and all negative information that comes out about it, while completely ignoring the other side. The confirmation bias is astounding on both sides of the political spectrum, and if I can somehow contribute to bringing both sides down a few notches, I will be a very happy person.

R.A. Are your opinions unusual or fairly mainstream given the general climate of discourse on campus?

M.F. My opinions are relatively unusual for my environment, but not radical by any means.

R.A. What advice do you have for other student writers?

M.F. Read a lot, and see what kind of writing style you like. There are so many amazing writers out there and they all have different styles, and it's best to find one you like and stick to it. Not all amazing writers write fiction books either. Read reputable movie reviewers, short stories, poetry, human interest articles, anything. Good writers are everywhere and they write about everything. Also, don't be too pretentious in your writing. Everyone has access to a thesaurus, and the sign of good writing isn't how many big words you can stuff into a sentence. It's about flow, sentence structure, rhythm, syntax and, lastly, diction. Good writing is about how it sounds in your head or out loud, not how many people you can confuse.

Rachel Carson

A Fable for Tomorrow

In the early summer of 1962, a series of articles began appearing in the New Yorker *that would help transform the way the American public understood the toxic impact of synthetic chemicals in the form of pesticides on humans, animal life, and the natural environment. Later that year, the articles were collected, expanded, and published in a best-selling book,* Silent Spring. *Written by Rachel Carson, a marine biologist and author of several highly successful books on nature, the book achieved an enormous influence; in fact, it is credited with initiating the modern environmental movement. Celebrating the book's fiftieth anniversary in 2012, the* Atlantic *reported: "Reading* Silent Spring *today, it is disquieting to realize how much was already known in 1962 about the environmental health impacts of petrochemicals. Even more shocking is to recognize how little our regulatory response to these chemicals' effects has changed, despite the past five decades' great advances in scientific understanding." The lyrical opening chapter of the book included here, "A Fable for Tomorrow," was written last and served as a prologue to alert readers to the impending environmental disasters her book would describe and explain.*

There was once a town in the heart of America where all life seemed   1
to live in harmony with its surroundings. The town lay in the midst
of a checkerboard of prosperous farms, with fields of grain and hill-
sides of orchards where, in spring, white clouds of bloom drifted
above the green fields. In autumn, oak and maple and birch set up a

---

After receiving a master's degree in zoology at Johns Hopkins University, Rachel Carson (1907–1964) spent a few years teaching and then took a position in marine biology with the U.S. Department of Fisheries. In the 1930s, she partly realized her early ambition to be a poet when she began publishing literary essays on the sea that would lead to a best-selling trilogy: Under the Sea-Wind *(1941),* The Sea Around Us *(1951), and* The Edge of the Sea *(1955). While writing* Silent Spring, *Carson was battling breast cancer, and she died within two years of the book's completion.*

blaze of color that flamed and flickered across a backdrop of pines. Then foxes barked in the hills and deer silently crossed the fields, half hidden in the mists of the fall mornings.

Along the roads, laurel, viburnum and alder, great ferns and wild- 2
flowers delighted the traveler's eye through much of the year. Even in winter the roadsides were places of beauty, where countless birds came to feed on the berries and on the seed heads of the dried weeds rising above the snow. The countryside was, in fact, famous for the abundance and variety of its bird life, and when the flood of migrants was pouring through in spring and fall people traveled from great distances to observe them. Others came to fish the streams, which flowed clear and cold out of the hills and contained shady pools where trout lay. So it had been from the days many years ago when the first settlers raised their houses, sank their wells, and built their barns.

Then a strange blight crept over the area and everything began to 3
change. Some evil spell had settled on the community: mysterious maladies swept the flocks of chickens; the cattle and sheep sickened and died. Everywhere was a shadow of death. The farmers spoke of much illness among their families. In the town the doctors had become more and more puzzled by new kinds of sickness appearing among their patients. There had been several sudden and unexplained deaths, not only among adults but even among children, who would be stricken suddenly while at play and die within a few hours.

There was a strange stillness. The birds, for example — where 4
had they gone? Many people spoke of them, puzzled and disturbed. The feeding stations in the backyards were deserted. The few birds seen anywhere were moribund; they trembled violently and could not fly. It was a spring without voices. On the mornings that had once throbbed with the dawn chorus of robins, catbirds, doves, jays, wrens, and scores of other bird voices there was now no sound; only silence lay over the fields and woods and marsh.

On the farms the hens brooded, but no chicks hatched. The 5
farmers complained that they were unable to raise any pigs — the litters were small and the young survived only a few days. The apple trees were coming into bloom but no bees droned among the blossoms, so there was no pollination and there would be no fruit.

The roadsides, once so attractive, were now lined with browned 6
and withered vegetation as though swept by fire. These, too, were silent, deserted by all living things. Even the streams were now lifeless. Anglers no longer visited them, for all the fish had died.

In the gutters under the eaves and between the shingles of the roofs, a white granular powder still showed a few patches; some weeks before it had fallen like snow upon the roofs and the lawns, the fields and streams. 7

No witchcraft, no enemy action had silenced the rebirth of new life in this stricken world. The people had done it themselves. 8

This town does not actually exist, but it might easily have a thousand counterparts in America or elsewhere in the world. I know of no community that has experienced all the misfortunes I describe. Yet every one of these disasters has actually happened somewhere, and many real communities have already suffered a substantial number of them. A grim specter has crept upon us almost unnoticed, and this imagined tragedy may easily become a stark reality we all shall know. 9

What has already silenced the voices of spring in countless towns in America? This book is an attempt to explain. 10

BACKGROUND AND CONTEXT

1. When Carson's book appeared, many chemical companies and scientists affiliated with them condemned her approach and professional knowledge. What part of "A Fable for Tomorrow" do you think adversaries of her position would point to critically? Explain what you think they would object to.

2. Consider the book's title, *Silent Spring*. What do you think it refers to specifically? Explain what larger significance the title suggests.

STRATEGY, STRUCTURE, AND STYLE

1. Why do you think Carson begins her short prologue by describing an American town and then ends it by claiming that the "town does not actually exist"? As you read, did you think she was describing a particular town? Why or why not? How did you feel as a reader when you discovered she has imagined this town?

2. How would you explain Carson's decision not to include specific details in the prologue? For example, why do you think she uses expressions such as "a strange blight," "evil spell," and "mysterious maladies"? Identify similar words and expressions that appear in her description. How does this language establish a tone and a mood? How do you think her essay would differ if she mentioned chemicals and pesticides right off?

COMPARISONS AND CONNECTIONS

1. In the chapter's "Spotlight on Research" by Judith Shulevitz, we meet a psychology professor who tries to explain why people deny science. He suggests, in one example, that environmentalists should not "use language or modes of communication that convey animosity, contempt, and hostility" because then "the signal that will come through is . . . that our

group is under assault." How do you think he would react to Carson's style of communication in her prologue? In a short essay that refers to the psychologist's advice, explain how effective Carson's approach is in terms of convincing readers about environmental dangers.

2. Carson's book is specifically about the dangers of pesticides. How might one use her method of writing as seen in her prologue to describe the environmental hazards many people worry about today: Global warming? Fracking? Pollution? Nuclear energy? In a brief essay try adopting Carson's style to warn readers about any particular hazard that concerns you.

Discussing the Unit

SUGGESTED TOPIC FOR DISCUSSION
How do the authors in this unit portray public opinion? How is it formed, and how does it change? Is public opinion likely to be correct or incorrect?

PREPARING FOR CLASS DISCUSSION
1. How do the authors in this chapter use scientific language? When do they question it? Choose examples from several different essays to discuss.
2. Could it in fact be too late to do anything about climate change? About people's concerns regarding hydrofracking? Or are there always solutions? Where will the solution come from — for example, individual action, the private sector, or government intervention? Why?

FROM DISCUSSION TO WRITING
1. Choose two essays from this unit that seem roughly similar in their overall opinions. Then, write an essay in which you discuss their differences. You may find points on which they clearly disagree, but think also about how their focus is different and how the style of each piece distinguishes it from the other.
2. Why have debates over the environment been dominated by pundits and columnists, rather than the people who hold the actual data? Do similar rifts exist among scientists? Are their conclusions too complex to relay to the public, or are they just too muddy for viewers and readers who like clear, easy answers?

TOPICS FOR CROSS-CULTURAL DISCUSSION
1. Which countries or regions will be hardest hit by climate change? Which will have the hardest time adapting to the changes?
2. Are there groups generally excluded from discussion about the environment, particularly hydrofracking? What is the profile of a stereotypical environmental activist?

10

American Politics: Must We Be Partisan?

So far, just about every chapter in this book has presented an American issue on which, even if many varied opinions exist, two essential sides dominate the debate: conservative and liberal. Our news media rarely complicate a political topic beyond presenting the Democratic and the Republican point of view. But why are all our public affairs so binary and reduced? Do they need to be? And how have we split as a country into such energized and opposed partisan camps? (For a discussion of America's political spectrum, see the introduction, p. 16.)

Two selections in this chapter look at how Americans form their politics from a scientific point of view. In the first, Laura Meckler and Dante Chinni examine the familiar division between "red states"—states in which conservative opinion and the Republican party dominate—and "blue states"—Democratic and liberal strongholds. What factors, they ask, contribute to these areas' political loyalties and affiliations? In "City vs. Country: How Where We Live Deepens the Nation's Political Divide," the researchers attribute characteristics of the places themselves to the political environments they create. Specifically, rural areas tend to be red and urban areas blue. Why? "There have always been differences between rural and urban America," Meckler and Chinni write, "but they have grown vast and deep, and now are an underappreciated factor in dividing the U.S. political system." Among other factors, the authors point to the values of close community and government involvement that underlie city life, and the opposing values of individualism that dominate rural zones.

Where we live, though, is clearly not the only factor in determining our politics. Evolutionary biologist Avi Tuschman, in fact, believes that political stances may be in our genes — at least in part. Examining a wide survey of studies and societies, Tuschman surmises that young people tend to be more liberal because evolution rewards them for open-mindedness. The image of a hard-edged conservative elder is, moreover, more than a cliché according to Tuschman: As we have families and settle down, we all become more concerned about dangers lurking around corners. "Political Evolution" connects these trends in our cognitive development to the traditional left–right split of American politics. "Despite generational idiosyncrasies," Tuschman concludes, "the universal stages of life do influence our political orientations."

Both of these selections point to a major problem in our partisan politics. How can we have the courage of our convictions when factors beyond our control — and not just the light of truth we've seen — inform our political opinions? Many intelligent people react to the divide with apathy or withdrawal. We feel that, not being certain which side we fall on, we should keep out of the fray. Student essayist Anna Berenson urges against this reaction. At Bates College, she reports, a common refrain on politics goes, "I don't really know much about these kinds of things, so I don't have too much to say." Berenson is sympathetic to the plight of the under-informed — or just unconfident — student, but urges him or her to "speak up." All of our opinions are valid, she reminds us in "Politics for the Rest of Us," and not just those of political science majors; different backgrounds and varying fields of interest and study can endow us with new and important perspectives on the hot topics of our public affairs. In particular, those with opinions that don't neatly conform to the left or the right should make those opinions heard.

As for our elected officials, though, almost all of them (at least at a federal level) are Democrats or Republicans, and the power of those two parties will likely keep it that way for the foreseeable future. How, then, can we hold our politicians accountable and make sure we get the best people in office? Especially in this partisan atmosphere, we all have examples of people we think slipped through the electoral process and are now failing

to represent Americans adequately. Chris Chan proposes one unique solution: an entrance exam. In "It's Time We Demanded More," Chan documents
ways that our politicians let us down, often resulting from ignorance of the
issues and lack of skills they must face once they've won office. "That is why
I suggest that we institute a series of qualifying exams that prospective
candidates must take before they can run for office," he writes. He outlines
his own proposal for this exam — as you read consider what questions you
would add.

America's founders faced no less difficult problems of framing the
issues and deciding who was qualified to dispense with them. In 1787,
their constitutional convention considered myriad proposals that eventually became our Constitution. Despite the reverence with which politicians
speak of that document, it's important to note that it, too, was the subject of
partisan squabble. Benjamin Franklin, the so-called inventor of America and
author of this chapter's "America Then," took a pragmatic approach at the
convention, pointing out that the foundation of American law was not perfect but ultimately declaring, "I Agree to This Constitution, with All Its Faults."
As Franklin reminds us, "when you assemble a number of men to have the
advantage of their joint wisdom, you inevitably assemble with those men,
all their prejudices, their passions, their errors of opinion, their local interests, and their selfish views." The Constitution, whose spirit both Republicans and Democrats claim to best represent, was itself a compromise — a
good lesson for politicians today.

Laura Meckler and Dante Chinni

City vs. Country: How Where We Live Deepens the Nation's Political Divide

[*The Wall Street Journal,* March 21, 2014]

BEFORE YOU READ

Have you ever thought about how where you live influences how you think? What sort of differences in thought might exist between urban and rural dwellers?

WORDS TO LEARN

tethered (para. 4): restricted (adjective)

bastion (para. 10): a fortified place (noun)

oust (para. 11): to expel or evict (verb)

expressly (para. 45): for a particular or specific purpose (adverb)

loom (para. 56): to rise up or appear (verb)

E L DORADO SPRINGS, Mo. — The owner of the nicest restaurant in town doesn't serve alcohol, worried that his pastor would be disappointed if he did. Public schools try to avoid scheduling events on Wednesday evenings, when churches hold Bible study. And Democrats here are a rare and lonely breed. 1

Older, nearly 100% white and overwhelmingly Republican, El 2 Dorado Springs is typical of what is now small-town America. Coffee costs 90 cents at the diner, with free refills. Two hours north and a world away in Kansas City, Starbucks charges twice that, and voters routinely elect Democrats.

Laura Meckler is a Washington, D.C.–based staff reporter at the Wall Street Journal. *She has been a White House reporter and was part of the* Journal *team covering the 2008 and 2012 elections. In 1999, she was the recipient of a Livingston Award for National Reporting for her coverage of organ donation and transplantation issues. She is a graduate of Washington University in St. Louis and serves as president of the board that oversees her college newspaper.*

Dante Chinni is the director of the American Communities Project at American University in Washington, D.C. He has worked as a journalist for nearly two decades at such publications as Newsweek *and the* Christian Science Monitor *and at the Pew Research Center's Journalism Project. Currently, he is the writer of the Politics Counts blog for the* Wall Street Journal.

There have always been differences between rural and urban America, but they have grown vast and deep, and now are an underappreciated factor in dividing the U.S. political system, say politicians and academicians. 3

Polling, consumer data and demographic profiles paint a picture of two Americas — not just with differing proclivities but different life experiences. People in cities are more likely to be tethered to a smartphone, buy a foreign-made car and read a fashion magazine. Those in small towns are more likely to go to church, own a gun, support the military and value community ties. 4

In many ways, the split between red Republican regions and blue Democratic ones — and their opposing views about the role of government — is an extension of the cultural divide between rural Americans and those living in cities and suburbs. 5

As Democrats have come to dominate U.S. cities, it is Republican strength in rural areas that allows the party to hold control of the House and remain competitive in presidential elections. 6

"The difference in this country is not red versus blue," said Neil Levesque, director of the New Hampshire Institute of Politics at Saint Anselm College. "It's urban versus rural." 7

El Dorado Springs, the largest town in Cedar County, is in Republican country. Cedar County gave 72% of its votes to Mitt Romney in 2012. 8

The town sits in Missouri's fourth congressional district, represented in the House of Representatives by Republican Vicky Hartzler, a farmer who made her name opposing same-sex marriage in Missouri. She titled her how-to-campaign book, "Running God's Way." 9

The neighboring fifth congressional district encompasses Kansas City, a Democratic Party bastion represented by Rep. Emanuel Cleaver, a black incumbent in his fifth term. Three in 10 of his constituents are minorities, and Jackson County, where Kansas City sits, gave Mr. Romney just 39% of its vote. 10

The U.S. divide wasn't always this stark. For decades, rural America was part of the Democratic base, and as recently as 1993, just over half of rural Americans were represented by a House Democrat, according to a Wall Street Journal analysis. Conservative Democrats often represented rural districts, including Ms. Hartzler's predecessor, Ike Skelton, who held the seat for 34 years before she ousted him in 2010. 11

> The U.S. divide wasn't always this stark.

That parity eventually gave way to GOP dominance. In 2013, 77% of rural Americans were represented by a House Republican. But in urban areas — which by the government's definition includes both cities and suburbs — slightly less than half of residents were represented by congressional Republicans, despite the GOP's 30-seat majority in the House. 12

The urban-rural divide has also grown in presidential contests. In   13
1992, Democrat Bill Clinton beat Republican George Bush in the 50
densest counties — the most urban in the country — by 25 percentage
points. By 2012, Democrat Barack Obama's advantage in those urban
counties had shot up to 38 points, according to a Journal analysis of Census and election data.

Today, almost all big cities, even those in red states such as Missouri,   14
Indiana and Texas, favor Democrats for president.

The shift in rural areas has been even more dramatic. In 1992, Mr.   15
Bush won the 50 least-dense counties — the most rural in the country — by 18 points. In 2012, Mr. Romney's advantage there had roughly
tripled, to 53 points.

David Wasserman, who analyzes politics at the Cook Political   16
Report, measures the change by examining how Democratic presidential candidates performed in counties with a Whole Foods — the upscale
grocery store that stocks organic goods — and in counties with a Cracker
Barrel, the homestyle restaurant featuring chicken n' dumplings.

In 1992, Bill Clinton won 60% of the Whole Foods counties and 40%   17
of the Cracker Barrel counties, a 20-point difference. That gap that has wid-
ened every year since, and in 2012, Mr. Obama won 77% of Whole Foods
counties and 29% of Cracker Barrel counties, a 48-point difference.

"Politics hangs on culture and lifestyle more than policy," Mr. Was-   18
serman said.

These divisions emerged in the 1960s with the Civil Rights move-   19
ment and the rise of such social issues as abortion and school prayer,
which distanced culturally conservative rural voters from the Democratic Party.

Religion remains a dividing line. Urban dwellers are more than three   20
times as likely as rural residents to say religion is "not that important to
me," according to a recent Wall Street Journal/NBC poll. Nearly 60% of
rural residents say homosexual behavior is a sin compared with 40% of
city residents, a Pew Research Center poll found last year.

Economic forces have advanced the split. Companies carefully   21
choose where to locate new stores and who to target with advertising,
assisted by a trove of marketing data. The result is rural Americans have a
different set of consumer choices than urban residents.

For example, rural residents are 47% more likely to shop at a Dollar   22
General store than is an average American, according to surveys by the
research firm Experian Marketing Services.

City dwellers are 41% more likely to buy something at an Apple store,   23
74% at a J. Crew and 69% at Williams-Sonoma, according to Experian.
All three chains are in Kansas City; none are in El Dorado Springs.

Rural economies have faltered as automated farming and corporate 24
ventures subsumed many family farms. Cutbacks in manufacturing have
cost jobs, and fewer jobs mean fewer opportunities for young people,
driving away those with more skills and education.

Without new arrivals, these aging regions have grown more insu- 25
lated from cultural change — whether the use of smartphones or the
acceptance of same-sex marriage.

"We're the gun-toting, God-loving folks they claim us to be," said 26
Jackson Tough, age 45, the executive director of the El Dorado Springs
Chamber of Commerce. He owns more than 20 guns for hunting and
target shooting.

El Dorado is surrounded by lush farm land where the Ozark Moun- 27
tains meet the western plains. There are no chain stores beyond a couple
of fast-food franchises and a Dollar General store.

The town is bisected by a four-lane highway that passes a McDon- 28
ald's and DairiConcepts, a cheese-product maker and El Dorado's largest employer. The diner, Scooters, bears little resemblance to its big-city
counterparts: prices are lower and the air is filled with cigarette smoke
banned in urban eateries.

The historic downtown has a park with a bandstand for summer 29
concerts, and a spot to taste the spring waters that attracted early settlers.
But across Main Street sits one vacant storefront after the next.

The population of about 3,600 has held roughly steady for the past 30
several decades, but the town has shrunk.

El Dorado used to have two grocery stores until one bought the 31
other and closed it. The county hospital stopped delivering babies in
2012 because there weren't enough deliveries to justify keeping an on-
call surgeon. A bond issue to upgrade aging school facilities was twice
rejected by voters.

The historic Opera House Theater, the only one in town, can't show 32
movies until supporters raise $60,000 for a digital projector. So far, they
have $13,000.

With few jobs waiting for young people after college, adults in town 33
assume most won't return to start their own families after graduation.
The exodus has left the town older and more conservative.

Ben Vickers, age 17, is a local high school star, participating in band, 34
choir, quiz bowl, theater, speech and debate. Ben loves the farm where
he grew up but longs for a city — a place, he said, where he will find
more points of view and more people who support Mr. Obama, as he
does.

"In El Dorado Springs, you're either a teacher, you work at a gas sta- 35
tion, you work at a restaurant, most likely McDonald's or Sonic," he said.

Still, Ben and other residents appreciate their community ties. High-   36
school teacher Tracy Barger recalled how after her 16-year-old son died
in a car accident in 2012, four pastors were at the hospital that night.
Later, she said, "one of the banks in town brought us a lunch. We don't
even bank there."

Given the sagging local economy, residents were excited in 2011   37
when the El Dorado Mexican Restaurant and Cantina planned to open.
But in a town that supports more than 30 churches and one bar, some
people objected to the restaurant's application for a liquor license.

Three local pastors urged the city council to reject the request.   38
"Very little good comes from alcohol," said Joe Trussell, 54, pastor of the
Church of God (Holiness). The council approved the application on a
3-2 vote.

At the Rusty Jug, a barbecue restaurant decorated like an old-West   39
saloon, owner Todd Leonard suspects beer sales could help his shaky
bottom line. But home-brewed root beer remains the strongest drink on
tap for diners enjoying the deep-fried ribs and deep-fried potato salad.

Mr. Leonard, age 45, is afraid one of his customers might drive home   40
drunk and kill someone if he served alcohol, he said. He also worries his
pastor and neighbors might lose respect for him.

"I am Todd Leonard. I've lived here all my life," he said. "'Todd has   41
always done things right.' That's the image I portray."

Over the summer, Mr. Leonard's church voted overwhelmingly to   42
spell out opposition to homosexuality in its bylaws. The purpose was to
protect the church from any lawsuit if it someday fired someone because
they were gay, Mr. Trussell said.

"We're a church that does embrace people and we love people   43
regardless of their circumstances," Mr. Trussell said. But, he added, "We
believe this behavior goes against the Bible."

In Kansas City, at the Country Club Congregational United Church   44
of Christ, a rainbow flag on the sign signals the church is "open and
affirming" to people, regardless of sexual orientation.

About half the membership is gay or lesbian, the Rev. Chase Peeples   45
said, and their attendance wasn't controversial even when the decision
was made two decades ago to expressly welcome them.

"The older members of this church were folks active in civil rights   46
movement, the women's movement," he said. "They just saw it as another
justice issue."

The church sits in a neighborhood known as Brookside, where there   47
is little sign of economic troubles along its string of boutique shops. Bella

Napoli, an Italian market, does a brisk business in imported Italian coffee beans and pasta, sold by a young barista with a nose ring. Around the corner is a toy store stocking such upscale gifts as a kit to conduct solar experiments.

Kansas City has adapted better to the new economy than many cities. Once dependent on meatpacking and textiles, the region now has federal jobs, hospitals and companies such as Cerner Corp., a health-care information technology company. 48

A new fine arts center opened in 2011. In the redeveloped 18th and Vine area, jazz swings through neighborhood clubs. When the arthouse Tivoli Cinemas needed to upgrade to digital projectors, it raised $130,000 through an online Kickstarter campaign. 49

Kansas City has its own urban troubles. Public schools are notorious. A swath of the city core suffers high crime, unemployment and poverty. 50

In 2009, Rep. Cleaver came up with a decidedly Democratic idea to fight urban decay: concentrate federal stimulus money into the urban core with energy-efficient projects to simultaneously combat poverty and climate change. Nearly $200 million was funneled into such projects as weatherizing homes and improving bus service. 51

Kansas City police, meanwhile, initiated a system that sends an automated alert to officers if a gun goes off in certain high-crime neighborhoods. That sort of program wouldn't go over well in rural areas. In El Dorado Springs, the owner of the gun shop wouldn't give his name for fear that federal authorities might raid his store. 52

Like many big cities, Kansas City — which is 30% black and 10% Hispanic — faces racial tensions. The city has long been divided, east from west, along Troost Avenue, which was used as a geographic marker for segregation by schools and for redlining by banks. 53

But resident Sarah L. Starnes, a white social worker, said she faced little hostility over two decades married to an African American and raising two biracial children. When the couple wed 21 years ago, Ms. Starnes didn't consider taking her husband's name, preferring to keep her own. 54

"I guess you could say I'm a feminist from way back," she said. 55

In El Dorado Springs, the same question looms for Jami Carpenter, a 32-year-old Democrat living in a Republican town. She expects to one day marry her boyfriend. When that happens, she would like to keep her last name. 56

The idea makes her nervous, Ms. Carpenter said: "That's not really how people do things around here." 57

VOCABULARY/USING A DICTIONARY

1. What is a *proclivity* (para. 4)?
2. If something is *notorious* (para. 50) for something else, is it known for something else, or not known?
3. What does an *exodus* (para. 33) look like?

RESPONDING TO WORDS IN CONTEXT

1. Is an *underappreciated factor* (para. 3) one that is a big part in how people think about something or not?
2. If a politician is an *incumbent* (para. 10), what does that mean?
3. How big is the shift in political leanings if it is described as *dramatic* (para. 15)?

DISCUSSING MAIN POINT AND MEANING

1. What are some of the differences Meckler and Chinni note between cities and small towns?
2. What do the included statistics tell you about these areas?
3. What was the determining factor, according to the *Cook Political Report,* for how candidates would perform in certain counties in 1992 and 2012?

EXAMINING SENTENCES, PARAGRAPHS, AND ORGANIZATION

1. What do the character sketches throughout add to the essay?
2. What does the first paragraph tell you about El Dorado Springs?
3. Do you think equal weight is given in the essay to both small town and city?

THINKING CRITICALLY

1. In which of these two areas would you feel more comfortable? Why?
2. Why do you think there's such a split between a city and a small town? Do you think the split will continue to grow?
3. What might draw more businesses into small towns? Is there anything that might help keep more families from leaving for the cities?

WRITING ACTIVITIES

1. Have you ever visited a Whole Foods or a Cracker Barrel? Why would Democratic presidents appeal to a customer who frequents one place over another? Write an analysis of what appeals to the Democratic voter, using these establishments as a point of reference.
2. In your mind, place any of the people described here in the opposite setting. What issues or problems might he or she face? How could he or she cope?
3. Look at a political (red and blue) map. If the split is in fact between urban and rural, is that reflected in the map? Find your area on the map, and explain in writing how your state is influenced by its rural or urban voters.

Avi Tuschman

Political Evolution: Why Do Young Voters Lean Left? It's in the Genes

[*Bloomberg Businessweek,* April 17, 2014]

BEFORE YOU READ

Why do we form ties with one political party or another? Are there times in our life when these allegiances are more likely to change?

WORDS TO LEARN

variation (para. 1): modification (noun)

conscientiousness (para. 2): meticulousness (noun)

cohort (para. 6): group of individuals (noun)

actuaries (para. 10): clerks (noun)

stratify (para. 11): to arrange (verb)

correspond (para. 11): to be in agreement with (verb)

I f you're not a liberal when you're 20, you have no heart. If you're not   1
a conservative by the time you're 30, you have no brain." Variations of
this saying have been attributed to Benjamin Disraeli, Otto von Bis-
marck, George Bernard Shaw, Woodrow Wilson, Theodore Roosevelt,
Aristide Briand, and Winston Churchill. The thought first came, in fact,
from a French statesman, François Guizot (1787–1874). Regardless of
its origin, the adage raises a fascinating question: Do the young really
lean left because of passions and idealism? And as people age, do they
incline toward the right because they become more realistic or cynical?

For the past 10 years, I've studied political divisions through   2
the lenses of evolutionary anthropology, genetics, and neuroscience.
Research reveals that during their 20s people around the world experience significant shifts in the traits biologists use to describe the human
personality. Specifically, "openness" declines and "conscientiousness"
increases. Higher openness is associated with intellectual curiosity, a
preference for variety, and voting for the left; higher conscientiousness,

---

Avi Tuschman is a former adviser to the president of Peru and the author of the book Our Political Nature: The Evolutionary Origins of What Divides Us. *His research has been covered in numerous publications, including the* New York Times, *the* Economist, MSNBC, Politico, *the* Atlantic, Bloomberg Businessweek, *and* Forbes.

characterized by self-discipline and dutifulness, predicts support for more conservative politics.

This rightward shift in political personality is fairly universal, and so is the timing. A 2004 study by psychologists Robert McCrae and Jüri Allik in the *Journal of Cross Cultural Psychology* of 36 cultures across Africa, Europe, and Asia discovered that openness and conscientiousness differ between 18- to 22-year-olds and older adults. If an individual's political personality hasn't changed by the time of his or her 30th birthday, however, it's not likely to differ all that much at 40, 50, or 60. This isn't to say that all teenagers are liberal and all older people are conservative. In any age group, people are distributed along the left-right spectrum on a bell curve. The entire curve, however, moves somewhat to the right during the mid-20s.

A common explanation for this personality change in young adulthood was voiced during the politically turbulent 1960s in the U.S. At the time, the young leftist counterculture claimed that its ideological enemies could be found on the far side of Guizot's magic number, 30. This belief implied that people older than that became more conservative because they were more likely to own a house, to earn a higher salary, and to have too much at stake to back a revolutionary call to destroy the existing order.

Contrary to popular belief, paying taxes, accumulating wealth, and being in the 1 percent or the 99 percent are extremely poor predictors of left-right political orientation. According to American National Election Studies, an academically run survey project, the correlation between family income and party identification for U.S. voters in the 2012 presidential election was a mere 0.13. This weak statistical relationship is typical of past elections.

> There is one life event, though, that greatly accelerates a person's shift to the right

There is one life event, though, that greatly accelerates a person's shift to the right, and it often occurs in the 30s: parenthood. Its political impact is easy to see among a cohort of Canadian college students studied by psychologist Robert Altemeyer. Their scores on an ideology test at age 22 grew more conservative by an average of 5.4 percent when they were retested at 30. But among those 30-year-olds who'd had children, conservatism increased by 9.4 percent.

Why did having kids push people to the right? Parents stay on the lookout for possible sources of danger that nonparents can ignore. This shift in perception is so strong it creates an illusory sense of risk; new parents tend to believe that crime rates have increased since they had children even when actual crime has dropped dramatically. Because "dangerous world" thinking is associated with political conservatism, parenthood pushes people to the right, and more so when they have daughters.

Experts on personality, such as McCrae, a psychologist at the National institute of Aging, say people's personalities may also be hardwired to shift over time. As we age, changes in gene expression may subtly alter openness, conscientiousness, and other traits. These traits and the personality shifts that unfold between late adolescence and early adulthood are moderately heritable between generations.   8

To understand why both nature and the environment tug at our personalities at certain times, we must trace these subtle changes in our personality to activity in the brain. Neuroscientists once assumed that the brain, along with the rest of the body, finishes dramatic development after puberty. But we now know that it doesn't reach full maturity until at least age 25. Consider the prefrontal cortex, which lies directly behind the forehead. It's responsible for regulating emotions, controlling impulses, and making complex cost-benefit judgments that weigh immediate incentives against future consequences. Unlike most regions of the brain, the prefrontal cortex continues to grow, and its cautionary functions go on developing well into the mid-20s.   9

Much earlier, in adolescence, a part of the brain called the limbic system, which plays a central role in sexual arousal and pleasure, kicks into action, stimulating thrill-seeking and risk-taking. Actuaries who work for car insurance companies have long deemed people younger than 25 risky. Why would nature permit this tempestuous gap between the flaring up of teenage passions and the onset of mental maturity 10 years later? These personality changes are probably evolutionary adaptations to different phases of the life cycle. High levels of openness encourage the young to wander the world and find a mate. Conscientiousness is crucial when raising a family.   10

Political pollsters are well aware of these life cycle personality changes, which is why they pay so much attention to age. When youth turn out to vote in higher numbers, as they do in presidential elections, analysts can stratify their samples to look for trends by age brackets that correspond roughly to before and after the brain developments that happen in the mid-20s: That is, they analyze the 18- to 24-year-old group separately from the 25- to 29-year-old group. In midterm elections, when the youth vote is underrepresented, pollsters often lump them all into one demographic group, 18 to 29.   11

In this era of big data, political pros of course have other tools at their disposal that make analysis of these large groups less relevant. As Chief Executive Officer Jim Walsh of the political ad network DSPolitical points out, it's now easy to microtarget individuals of any age and   12 according to dozens of other demographic and consumer categories. Nevertheless, public opinion experts still keep tabs on age groups to study their impressionability to the changing flow of history, culture, and economic cycles. In some cases, current events trump life cycle stages, altering the collective attitudes of a cohort in surprising ways. In 1984, 18- to 24-year-olds voted for Ronald Reagan over Walter Mondale by a 22-percentage-point margin — the same margin as 50- to 64-year-olds. This youth vote may have been anomalously conservative, because Reagan had presided over a strong recovery from recession and Mondale was perceived to be a weak candidate. Young Republican voters in 1984 may also have been expressing their feeling of disconnect with the liberal social movements of the 1960s and 1970s.

Today's young voter adheres more closely to the personality pat- 13 tern shaped by evolution, though environmental variables such as the social media revolution have left a mark as well. As expected, millennials lean substantially to the left on most social issues, but slightly less so on economic issues. These "digital natives," who grew up steeped in social media, have also been dubbed the Selfie Generation. And Selfie may be a more apt description: The age group is characterized by individualism across the board. According to the Pew Research Center, millennials are far less affiliated with traditional political, religious, and cultural institutions and less likely to be married than previous generations were. Some commentators have accused the Selfie Generation of having a sense of entitlement, interpreting their individualism as a kind of Facebook (FB)- induced narcissism. Other observers have argued that millennials measure higher in cynicism and singleness — and more often live with their parents — because they face worse economic prospects than did the previous two generations.

Whichever perspective one takes, our changing economic and tech- 14 nological environments have surely left an impression on millennials and molded their political behavior in various unforeseen ways. Still, like most 18- to 29-year-old cohorts, their vote is markedly more liberal than average. Despite generational idiosyncrasies, the universal stages of life do influence our political orientations, true to Guizot's words. And like many other facets of our political nature, these life cycle shifts have deep evolutionary roots.

VOCABULARY/USING A DICTIONARY

1. What is an *adage* (para. 1)?
2. What is the *limbic system* (para. 10)?
3. What part of speech is *apt* (para. 13)? What does it mean?

RESPONDING TO WORDS IN CONTEXT

1. When Tuschman suggests that the sixties were *turbulent* (para. 4), what does that indicate about the time period?
2. If something is altered *subtly* (para. 8), how is it altered?
3. If the fact that young people preferred Reagan over Mondale suggests they were *anomalously* conservative (para. 12), what does that mean about that group?

DISCUSSING MAIN POINT AND MEANING

1. What does research reveal about the brains of people in their twenties?
2. What does that change in the twenties suggest will happen to their preferences politically?
3. What other life event does Tuschman suggest pushes young people, usually in their thirties, from left to right?

EXAMINING SENTENCES, PARAGRAPHS, AND ORGANIZATION

1. Is Tuschman's opening effective? How does he begin his essay?
2. How does Tuschman identify himself as an expert on his topic from the outset of his paper?
3. Does Tuschman argue from a place of certainty, or does he leave room for doubt and reconsideration?

THINKING CRITICALLY

1. Why do you think having kids might push someone to the right, politically? What does the right offer that a parent might appreciate?
2. Do you think younger people are always more idealistic than older people? Explain your answer.
3. How are millennials different from or similar to the young people of the sixties?

WRITING ACTIVITIES

1. "Don't trust anyone over thirty." Consider this famous slogan from the sixties, and write a short report about the difference between younger and older people in the 1960s.
2. How are your political leanings different, if they are, from your parents? In a brief personal essay, explain how your parents have voted and whether or not their political ideology may have rubbed off on (or against) you.
3. Tuschman explains the political evolution from one's twenties to one's thirties. What shifts might take place from childhood and adolescence to one's twenties? What about from one's thirties to forties and beyond? Speculate on what this political evolution might look like in areas Tuschman hasn't explored.

Anna Berenson (student essay)

Politics for the Rest of Us

[*The Bates Student,* Bates College, October 9, 2013]

BEFORE YOU READ

Who should have a say in political discussions? Are experts the only ones who should be allowed to weigh in?

WORD TO LEARN

nuances (para. 2): subtle differences or distinctions (noun)

B etween the crisis in Syria[1] and the U.S. government's first shutdown in 17 years, political topics have recently been unavoidable in daily conversation here at Bates, as seems to be the case throughout the country. Anarchy jokes fly through Commons, bioethics students discuss the pros and cons of Obamacare[2], and many of us ponder what might possibly be the "right" way to lead a country.

However, these discussions are too often cut short by a common phrase: "I don't really know much about these kinds of things, so I don't have too much to say." Many of us feel that our limited expertise on the workings of political systems means that we aren't allowed to share our opinions on these current events, especially in the presence of politics majors or others whom we believe to know more than we do. Maybe we feel that these others will disregard our ideas due to our lack of knowledge about the nuances of our complex government, or maybe we truly believe that our thoughts on these subjects are not as valid as theirs are.

No matter the exact cause of our hesitation, the result is the same. As these political conversations progress, some voices are silenced while others dominate, culminating in much more exclusive discussions about specific political details.

---

[1] Syria (para. 1): The Syrian Uprising is an armed conflict in Syria that began in 2011.

[2] Obamacare (para. 1): President Obama's healthcare plan for America, known officially as the Affordable Care Act.

Anna Berenson is a student at Bates College.

Of course, there is a place for these types of discussions. Indeed, there are many people whom we elect and pay to talk about these issues in a very specific way in order to keep the country running; we call them politicians. However, this does not mean that the average biomedical engineer, businessperson, or politically uninvolved college student should be discouraged from speaking up about issues that concern us all. Nor does it mean that every citizen should aspire to develop an understanding equal to that of a politician in order to feel qualified to mention these issues. 4

> As these political conversations progress, some voices are silenced while others dominate

Indeed, I believe that political conversations involving individuals of varying levels of governmental knowledge are essential. Those of us who specialize in mathematical reasoning, understanding biological systems, or studying foreign cultures can provide something other than political expertise: multiple perspectives. 5

We so often get bogged down by focusing on the small details, but by involving a variety of people in discussions, we can hope to step back from the issue and consider the bigger picture. Our different interests and areas of study provide us with distinct ways of considering the same situations. While some of us may approach them with a mathematical mindset, others are experts at seeing past the politics to the impact on human lives. 6

What is the net result of the events in Syria from a humanitarian perspective? Is a government shutdown logical, if we simply consider the magnitude of its effects? What does the Affordable Care Act really mean, considering the realities of certain diseases? Without the filter of political detail, others are capable of developing these questions as centerpieces for discussion. 7

Allowing these musings to be heard can lead to a number of benefits; primarily, it would encourage a variety of voices in political conversation, allowing for more colorful discussions and sending the message that each citizen's opinion is valid and important. The more that everyone is encouraged to participate, the more individuals will feel inclined to share what they have to say. This, in turn, will allow more of us to feel more comfortable with political issues we feel passionate about, or that affect us in some way. 8

In addition, by encouraging a greater variety of voices and perspectives, we could provide political experts with new ways to consider issues that they had only approached from a certain direction. 9

With greater public participation in political dialogue, the politicians of today and tomorrow will obtain a broader perspective to consider when making decisions that are intended to represent the best interest of the rest of us.

Speak up. Your opinion is valid; not only should it be shared, but it needs to be shared. 10

VOCABULARY/USING A DICTIONARY

1. What do you have if you have *expertise* (para. 2) in something?
2. What part of speech is *specialize* (para. 5)?
3. What other words share a root with *magnitude* (para. 7)?

RESPONDING TO WORDS IN CONTEXT

1. What does Berenson mean when she says we (regular people) think our opinions aren't as *valid* (para. 2) as the opinions of the politicians?
2. Given the way *aspire* is used in paragraph 4, can you think of a synonym that might take its place?
3. If students at Bates are making *anarchy* (para. 1) jokes, how do you think they feel about the way things are going in the government?

DISCUSSING MAIN POINT AND MEANING

1. Who does Berenson think should have a voice in political discussion?
2. Why is it important to hear from more than just the experts when we talk about current events?
3. What effect might talking about political events have, according to Berenson?

EXAMINING SENTENCES, PARAGRAPHS, AND ORGANIZATION

1. How does Berenson hint at her topic in her title?
2. What's different about the sixth paragraph? Do you think it is effective?
3. Is the conclusion effective? How is the last paragraph structured?

THINKING CRITICALLY

1. What current events do you feel you don't know enough about to discuss? With these topics in mind, do you agree with Berenson that you should speak up about them?
2. Why might it be important for the experts to weigh in on political topics? When should "ordinary people" try to get more information before they speak about a topic?
3. How does hearing from anyone (including college students) help politicians with their thinking on current events?

WRITING ACTIVITIES

1. Explore one of the current events Berenson mentions in the essay. After doing a little research, write a short report on the situation, and say what you think should be done about it, and why.

2. Have you ever been asked about a current event, and said, as Berenson suggests, "I don't really know much about these kinds of things, so I don't have much to say"? Which current event was it? What do you know about the event? Is there anything in your background (as a student of a particular subject) that might give you a unique perspective on the event?

3. Write an opinion piece on why students should or shouldn't be involved in political discussion. What strengths do students bring to political conversations? What do students in your particular school have to offer on local and global topics?

LOOKING CLOSELY

Effective Persuasion: Identifying with Your Audience

Knowing your audience — the people you are especially targeting — is a key factor in effective persuasion. If you pay close attention to the way most television advertising works, you will be able to see how a particular drug product is aimed to appeal exclusively to middle-aged men or how some automobile ads are designed to attract whole families rather than individuals. In writing, we usually indicate our intended audience by our use of such pronouns as *you, they, we,* or *us.* Note how often Anna Berenson relies in "Politics for the Rest of Us" on the very important little words *we* or *us.* In doing so, she identifies herself with the people she addresses. As many politicians understand, people want to feel that the speaker addressing them is very much like them — not a superior, an intellectual, or an especially privileged individual. Berenson makes it clear that her audience is composed of people like herself, those who have no special knowledge of or insights into politics. Her persuasive goal in the essay is to convince people who may feel intimidated by their lack of political knowledge that they still have something to contribute to discussion. In doing so, she identifies with the nonexperts instead of the experts. Note how she clearly indicates this identification in the following paragraph:

However, these discussions are too often cut short by a common phrase: "I don't really know much about these kinds of things, so I don't have too much to say." Many of <u>us</u> feel that <u>our</u> limited expertise on the workings of political systems means that <u>we</u> aren't allowed to share <u>our</u> opinions on these current events, especially in the presence of politics majors or others <u>we</u> believe know more than <u>we</u> do. (1) Maybe <u>we</u> feel that these others will disregard <u>our</u> ideas due to <u>our</u> lack of knowledge about the nuances of <u>our</u> complex government, or maybe <u>we</u> truly believe that <u>our</u> thoughts on these subjects are not as valid as <u>theirs</u>. (2) No matter the exact cause of our hesitation, the result is the same. As these political conversations progress, <u>some voices are silenced while others dominate, culminating in much more exclusive discussions about specific political details.</u> (3)

1
Pronouns show her identification with audience

2
Theirs *are experts she is not addressing*

3
What happens when only "experts" get to speak

STUDENT WRITER AT WORK
Anna Berenson

Courtesy of Anna Berenson

R.A. What inspired you to write this essay? And publish it in your campus paper?

A.B. I have many friends who are studying politics, political science, and government. They often have discussions about current events and do so in such a way that the political non-expert does not feel like it would be appropriate to join in. I wanted to encourage students of all interests and backgrounds to participate in conversations that were happening on campus.

R.A. What was your main purpose in writing this piece?

A.B. In writing this piece, I hoped to reach out to students such as myself who felt like they did not have enough political knowledge to have a valid opinion on recent events. Ideally, this would encourage more inclusive and well-rounded political conversations, particularly in populations of young people.

R.A. Are your opinions unusual or fairly mainstream given the general climate of discourse on campus?

A.B. The mentality of exploring new subjects and appreciating the importance of all areas of study is fairly common on my campus. However, students do tend to avoid topics of conversation about which they feel less knowledgeable.

R.A. What response have you received to this piece? Has the feedback you have received affected your views on the topic you wrote about?

A.B. I have received mostly positive feedback from those who, like me, have felt silenced during political conversations. They seemed to agree that including a variety of individuals in these discussions would have positive results for everyone.

R.A. How long did it take for you to write this piece? Did you revise your work? What were your goals as you revised?

A.B. I wrote this piece in the span of a few hours. First, as is my custom, I wrote a quick outline in order to ensure that the piece flowed in a logical order. I then meticulously followed the outline when writing the piece, leaving minimal editing for the final revision process.

R.A. Do you generally show your writing to friends before submitting it? Do you collaborate or bounce your ideas off others?

A.B. I do not often have friends read my pieces during the writing process. However, most of my ideas come from experiences and conversations that I have shared with others; in this way, others help me to develop my viewpoints on the topic before I even start writing.

R.A. What topics most interest you as a writer?

A.B. I am particularly interested in topics surrounding social justice (discrimination, marriage rights, reproductive rights), as well as science and medicine.

R.A. Are you pursuing a career in which writing will be a component?

A.B. Yes. While I am currently pursuing a career in the sciences, the ability to communicate in writing will be of utmost importance in any area that I might pursue.

R.A. What advice do you have for other student writers?

A.B. If you love writing, you can always find a way to keep doing it. Keep a journal, write a blog, write letters to friends, or take a writing class. Writing is an invaluable skill and a hobby that you will enjoy for the rest of your life.

Chris Chan

It's Time We Demanded More

[*Gilbert Magazine,* September/October 2013]

BEFORE YOU READ
How does one get screened for ability before becoming an elected official? How would one measure an official's competency?

WORDS TO LEARN
constituency (para. 2): a body of voters (noun)
repercussions (para. 5): the effects of an action (noun)
commensurate (para. 6): proportionate (adjective)
elaborate (para. 7): to add details to (verb)
proficiency (para. 8): skill (noun)
grandeur (para. 12): greatness (noun)

A mericans of all political stripes have been increasingly complaining about their elected officials in recent years. There is not enough space here to explain all the ways that government officials have disappointed the citizenry, but I would like to propose a remedy. To be an elected official, you need to have a lust for power, unshakeable confidence   1

Chris Chan is a contributing editor to Gilbert *magazine.*

in your own abilities, support from your party's bosses and political allies, and large sums of cash, just to name a few essentials. What one doesn't need to be elected is proof that one actually knows enough to be a leader.

Students are constantly tested in order to advance in school, get into   2
college, and obtain an advanced degree. If you want a driver's license, you need to take a written test, a driving test, and an eye test. Want to be a doctor? A lawyer? A teacher? A taxi driver? You'll need to pass multiple tests. In the city of Milwaukee, if you want to serve in a civil service position, you must pass "job knowledge tests." Yet if you want to be a mayor, governor, congressman, senator, or even president, you need only fill out some forms (someone else can do that for you), and get enough people to sign your candidacy petition. At no point do you ever have to demonstrate to your constituency that you know anything about economics, law enforcement, the history of the area you represent, or even that you are functionally literate.

That is why I suggest that we institute a series of qualifying exams that   3
prospective candidates must take before they can run for office. These would be lengthy examinations, consisting of both written and oral components. Every potential candidate, regardless of political party or incumbency, would be required to take this test before every election. All scores and answers would be released to the public. Any test-taker who fails to score above a certain level (perhaps 75 or 80 percent) would be denied a place on a ballot, and no write-in votes for that person would be counted.

HISTORY AND CULTURE

Candidates would be asked to answer questions about the history of the   4
region they represent, and details on previous holders of their office. (Candidates for the presidency or the U.S. Congress would be given an extensive test on both American and world history, politics, and culture.) Issues of demography and current events associated with the districts being represented would be on the test.

GEOGRAPHY

Every potential candidate would have to demonstrate that they know the   5
basic geography of the area they represent. For example, governors and U.S. Senators would be given a blank map of their state divided into counties, and they would be required to fill in the name of every county and identify the location of numerous major cities from a list. Since the results of every test would be made public, missing a question could potentially have some major repercussions on a candidacy ("So, why should the people of Outagamie County vote for you to be their senator when you can't even identify them on a map?") Candidates for federal office would have to identify nations from around the world and their capitals.

ECONOMICS

Candidates should have to display a basic knowledge of economic prin- 6
ciples and fluency with the subject commensurate with an advanced
college-level course. Test-takers would be given a sample budget with
various expenses, and then they would be compelled to slash a significant percentage from that budget and justify the cuts.

ESSAY QUESTIONS

Various situations, crises, and conflicts would be described, and the 7
potential candidates would have to describe how they would deal
with these situations. Issues such as crime and public safety would be
addressed, and candidates would be compelled to elaborate upon the
social effects of their positions on issues. Though candidates would not
be punished for their specific position, failure to address a question thoroughly would cost a candidate valuable points.

Other relevant topics would also be included. This would require 8
potential candidates to spend large amounts of time becoming experts in
the necessary fields needed for leadership roles, and it would also leave
documentary evidence of a candidate's proficiency and opinions.

The oral examination would consist 9
of similar questions posed toward all of
the potential candidates. Performed in a
game show style, this could be a lot more
entertaining than any of the debates staged
today.

> Performed in a game show style, this could be a lot more entertaining than any of the debates staged today.

Candidates who failed the exam would 10
be given one chance at a retake. Should a
candidate fail twice, that person would be
barred from running for public office (even a sitting president) until the
next election. These tests would vary in length depending on the office.
The mayoral candidacy for a small city, for example, might take a few
hours; the tests for governors, congressmen, and senators might last for a
couple of days; and the test for the presidency could take a full week. If a
candidate were caught cheating, all the money he raised for his campaign
would be donated to local charities, he would be banned from ever running for office again, and possibly a jail term might be thrown into the
bargain.

The test would be crafted and administered by volunteers, citizens 11
from a wide variety of backgrounds and holding diverse political perspectives. These volunteers would swear never to run for public office,
and they could not be directly related to anybody taking the test.

Would this test solve all the problems in the government? No. But, 12
there is something very satisfying in seeing people with delusions of
grandeur sweat from stress, knowing that all the money and power connections in the world can't help them — they're on their own.

VOCABULARY/USING A DICTIONARY
1. What does it mean to be *literate* (para. 2)? What other words can you think of
   that share that root?
2. From what language is the word *incumbency* (para. 3) derived?
3. What is *demography* (para. 4)?

RESPONDING TO WORDS IN CONTEXT
1. What is a *civil service position* (para. 2)?
2. What is the difference between a *prospective* (para. 3) candidate and a
   candidate?
3. How is the word *institute* used in paragraph 3? What part of speech is it?
   What other part of speech could it be in a different context?

DISCUSSING MAIN POINT AND MEANING
1. What does Chan suggest is important to do before electing a government
   official?
2. What sort of subjects would make up a test for a potential candidate for office?
3. Even if this test doesn't solve all problems, what is its value?

EXAMINING SENTENCES, PARAGRAPHS, AND ORGANIZATION
1. What do you notice about the structure of the sentence in the introductory
   paragraph that sets up the idea for Chan's thesis?
2. What format does Chan use when discussing the makeup of a candidate
   test? Is it effective?
3. The organization of Chan's essay is very tight. How might an outline of his
   essay look, in terms of the ideas he covers?

THINKING CRITICALLY
1. Do you think voters expect their candidates to have enough background
   and knowledge to run for office? Do you agree with Chan that they should
   expect more?
2. What other qualities influence a voter's choice of candidate, besides his or
   her knowledge on the subjects suggested in the essay?
3. Do you think that candidates who fail the exam twice should be barred from
   running for office? Why might this be a good idea? Why might it be too strict
   a penalty?

WRITING ACTIVITIES

1. Consider the political career of Arnold Schwarzenegger. Research his political career leading up to his appointment as governor of California. Go back further and research his early career. In a speculative essay, write about whether or not you think Schwarzenegger is a serious politician, and using your research, determine how much he knows about the subjects Chan would list on a candidacy test. Would he have passed the test that is being suggested? Would he now? Explain your answers.

2. How much do you know about the subjects of your state and country? Develop a candidate test that asks a few questions about each subject suggested in the essay: history and culture, geography, and economics. Construct an essay question. Once you have developed your test, administer it to someone else in the class. Test each other on your knowledge. If you don't know an answer, look it up once your test has been "graded." Consider the administrator's comments on the essay portion of your exam.

3. What is the value of tests? Do you feel you are demonstrating something important when you take them? Are they a waste of time? Write a persuasive essay that argues for or against tests—either in school, for a job, or for running for political office. Explain where they succeed in measuring something about someone's knowledge or ability and where they fail.

Benjamin Franklin

I Agree to This Constitution, with All Its Faults

On May 25, 1787, a large group of Americans assembled in Philadelphia to create a form of government that would guide a brand new nation into its very uncertain future. On September 17, they met to sign the document that would become the Constitution of the United States. It is amazing that in an age without a single modern convenience, without any of the technology we depend on today, when the primary implement of communication was a quill pen and most travel depended on horses and favorable winds, that the final draft of the most important political document in modern world history was produced in under seventeen weeks. But it wasn't produced easily or without bitter discussion and some hard-fought compromises that still cause partisan dissension. That the framers themselves were well aware of these issues can be seen in the following speech the feeble, eighty-one-year-old Benjamin Franklin asked a colleague to read just before the delegates signed the document he publicly acknowledged was far from perfect.

One of the nation's iconic figures, Benjamin Franklin (1706–1790) was an ingenious inventor, a prolific essayist, an astute entrepreneur, and a farsighted statesman. He was also one of the nation's first humorists; when signing the Declaration of Independence, he apparently quipped, realizing the terrible risk his inadequate colonies took in revolting against England: "We must, indeed, all hang together, or assuredly we shall all hang separately." Thomas Jefferson claimed that Franklin was asked only to help draft the Constitution because if he had written the entire document, he could not have resisted adding a few jokes. Born into a large, impoverished Boston family, Franklin left for Philadelphia as a teenager to make his fortune, and he became one of the earliest examples of the classic American rags-to-riches story, a persistent national myth he helped create. For many reasons he is often considered the "first American."

Mr. President

I confess that there are several parts of this constitution which I   1
do not at present approve, but I am not sure I shall never approve
them: For having lived long, I have experienced many instances of
being obliged by better information, or fuller consideration, to
change opinions even on important subjects, which I once thought
right, but found to be otherwise. It is therefore that the older I grow,
the more apt I am to doubt my own judgment, and to pay more
respect to the judgment of others. Most men indeed as well as most
sects in Religion, think themselves in possession of all truth, and
that wherever others differ from them it is so far error. Steele[1] a
Protestant in a Dedication tells the Pope, that the only difference
between our Churches in their opinions of the certainty of their
doctrines is, the Church of Rome is infallible and the Church of
England is never in the wrong. But though many private persons
think almost as highly of their own infallibility as of that of their
sect, few express it so naturally as a certain french lady, who in a dispute with her sister, said "I don't know how it happens, Sister but I
meet with no body but myself, that's always in the right — *Il n'y a
que moi qui a toujours raison.*"

In these sentiments, Sir, I agree to this Constitution with all its   2
faults, if they are such; because I think a general Government necessary for us, and there is no form of Government but what may be a
blessing to the people if well administered, and believe farther that
this is likely to be well administered for a course of years, and can
only end in Despotism, as other forms have done before it, when the
people shall become so corrupted as to need despotic Government,
being incapable of any other.

I doubt too whether any other Convention we can obtain, may   3
be able to make a better Constitution. For when you assemble a
number of men to have the advantage of their joint wisdom, you
inevitably assemble with those men, all their prejudices, their passions, their errors of opinion, their local interests, and their selfish
views. From such an assembly can a perfect production be expected?
It therefore astonishes me, Sir, to find this system approaching so

---

[1] Richard Steele (1672–1729), Irish political figure who also was one of England's
most esteemed essayists.

near to perfection as it does; and I think it will astonish our enemies, who are waiting with confidence to hear that our councils are confounded like those of the Builders of Babel; and that our States are on the point of separation, only to meet hereafter for the purpose of cutting one another's throats.

Thus I consent, Sir, to this Constitution because I expect no better, and because I am not sure, that it is not the best. The opinions I have had of its errors, I sacrifice to the public good. I have never whispered a syllable of them abroad. Within these walls they were born, and here they shall die. If every one of us in returning to our Constituents were to report the objections he has had to it, and endeavor to gain partizans in support of them, we might prevent its being generally received, and thereby lose all the salutary effects & great advantages resulting naturally in our favor among foreign Nations as well as among ourselves, from our real or apparent unanimity. Much of the strength & efficiency of any Government in procuring and securing happiness to the people, depends, on opinion, on the general opinion of the goodness of the Government, as well as of the wisdom and integrity of its Governors. I hope therefore that for our own sakes as a part of the people, and for the sake of posterity, we shall act heartily and unanimously in recommending this Constitution (if approved by Congress & confirmed by the Conventions) wherever our influence may extend, and turn our future thoughts & endeavors to the means of having it well administered.

4

On the whole, Sir, I can not help expressing a wish that every member of the Convention who may still have objections to it, would with me, on this occasion doubt a little of his own infallibility, and to make manifest our unanimity, put his name to the instrument.

5

BACKGROUND AND CONTEXT

1. As one of the delegates who helped draft the Constitution, Franklin had a stake in its success. He was the only one to make a speech about it before its signing. Why do you think he did this? Can you detect any political motive in his short speech?

2. Look closely at Franklin's language throughout the speech. Considering it was written well over 200 years ago, how much of it strikes you as clear and current? Do any parts of the speech seem obscure or antiquated to you? Explain why.

STRATEGY, STRUCTURE, AND STYLE

1. Why do you think Franklin begins his talk by addressing the matter of "infallibility"? What purpose does that serve? In what ways are his opening remarks both humorous and serious?
2. Note that in his final words Franklin returns to the idea of "infallibility." Of what importance is it at this point in the speech? Why do you think Franklin ends on this note? Explain his strategy here. What is he trying to accomplish?

COMPARISONS AND CONNECTIONS

1. How would you describe the tone of Franklin's speech? Do you find him optimistic over the birth of a new nation or pessimistic concerning its future? In a short essay discuss how you think Franklin envisions the future of the United States.
2. Read carefully Franklin's address in the light of the other selections in this chapter and your personal knowledge of the current American political scene. In a short essay, explain how you think Franklin would be regarded today. Based entirely on what you find in his speech, would he be considered a liberal or a conservative? Or would he be somewhere else along the political spectrum? Base your explanation on specific language from his speech.

Discussing the Unit

SUGGESTED TOPIC FOR DISCUSSION

What does America stand for? What do you stand for as an American, or as someone from another country currently living in America?

PREPARING FOR CLASS DISCUSSION

1. Name some American ideals that you can think of off the top of your head. How are those ideals embodied by Democrats? By Republicans? Other political parties?
2. Do you believe that our current political system is broken? Why or why not? What works in Washington, D.C.? What doesn't?

FROM DISCUSSION TO WRITING
1. Research your representative in Congress. What primary issues does he or she stand for, or against? Do you agree with your representative about these issues? Write a brief essay explaining why you do or don't feel your Congressperson represents what is important to you.
2. Do you believe it is possible to ease the partisan gridlock in the United States? Why or why not? Write a brief essay that explains what you would want to see changed—and how.

TOPICS FOR CROSS-CULTURAL DISCUSSION
1. Consider the attitudes about America and politics expressed by the writers in this chapter. How is the United States viewed by other countries that you are familiar with? Are those views different from or similar to the views expressed in this chapter? In the United States in general? Explain.
2. Research the main political parties in a country other than the United States. Do they work together effectively? Why or why not? What about the country's political system would be beneficial to import to the United States? What about ours would be worthwhile for that country?

11

Gender: Do We Need Feminism?

It's hardly controversial to say that women have faced a long, difficult journey in America. From the Salem Witch Trials to the suffrage movement, women confronted systematic legal oppression and discrimination at just about every juncture of American history. As they strove to be treated equally in the workforce, they hurdled an enormous cultural and social obstacle as well. But have women finally arrived as equals to men in America, or is there still room to go? Many contemporary supporters of the rights of women (along with people with untraditional gender identities) have taken to Twitter and tumblr with the phrase "I need feminism because . . . " to remind us that oppression still exists within what they call the "patriarchy," or the male-dominated traditional hierarchy of American power. Like the advocacy for minorities we observed in Chapter 5, today's feminist movement often seeks to point out hidden, systemic forms of oppression rather than obvious ones. Are they right, or have they oversold the patriarchy's power?

Feminists often point out that, although major legal battles like suffrage may be closed, forms of gender inequality persist in daily life. This chapter's first two selections examine such issues. In "The Last Feminist Taboo," writer Marisa Meltzer examines a problem with complex historical gender overtones—dieting and body image. Meltzer begins by discussing her own weight-loss achievement, but then wonders whether it was in fact an achievement. Her fellow feminists often chide women for attempting to conform to an artificial "body-image" ideal created by men. But Meltzer suggests that as feminists erect a bulwark against society's ideas of a body image, they also trap themselves — a woman who wants to lose weight is automatically accused of this conformation to a societal norm, whatever her reasons might be. "Good feminists, in short, do not diet," she writes. "Or if they do, they don't talk about it." After exploring the tension between freedom and the women's movement, though, Meltzer finds a way she can strike a balance.

That same balance, between a critical attitude of social institutions and a partial acceptance of them, pervades much of modern feminist cultural criticism. Take Heather Havrilesky, a young writer who has criticized the portrayal of women in media. In "Don't Act Crazy, Mindy," — its title refers to comedic actor Mindy Kaling — Havrilesky surveys female lead characters on television today. Often these characters are successful and powerful, with careers instead of just houses to make. As Havrilesky points out, though, their success often comes with a catch. They're portrayed as slightly emotionally unstable, with the implication that women can't make it and stay entirely well-adjusted: "The suggestion in all of these shows is that a female character's flaws are inextricably linked to her strengths."

It may seem like some measure of progress that women on TV have jobs, but what about equality in the actual workplace? Many argue that the American job market is still rigged against women — one common refrain is that women make only seventy-seven cents for every dollar a man makes. Christina Hoff Sommers, though, believes that intellectually honest feminism means exposing this number as a myth — it hasn't been true, she says, for many years. In "No, Women Don't Make Less Money Than Men," Sommers cites statistics that show that women may be drawn to careers in the "caring professions" — like nursing and teaching — which on the open market are less financially rewarding than, say, oil drilling. But that, Sommers argues, is up to individual women, and to suggest otherwise is the opposite of feminism: "To say that these women remain helplessly in thrall to sexist stereotypes, and manipulated into life choices by forces beyond their control, is divorced from reality — and demeaning to boot." Sommers expresses a conflict between classic feminist theory, which cleaves to the allegedly discredited statistic, and her own experience.

Emily Potter lays out a similar conflict many women feel about feminism in her student essay, "#YesAllWomen." Potter writes in the wake of a terrible tragedy on her campus—a mass shooting with distinct gender overtones, which sparked the title hashtag to trend among men and women in solidarity for women's rights. Potter has a unique perspective. She writes that she'd come into college "a self-proclaimed anti-feminist." She not only believed that she could do everything her male peers could do, but also believed the kind of oppression some feminists describe as institutional was just a myth. A course in feminist studies, though, changed her view. She writes, "I can no longer ignore the daily oppression I face as a woman when I walk onto the pool deck to referee a men's water polo game, or when I am forced to call [an escort] late at night and take 30 minutes to get home rather than two."

Potter believes unequivocally that we still need feminism, but her attitude comes about in an educational context in which feminism has firmly established itself in our social, cultural, and political consciousness. Yet, that consciousness didn't thoroughly take shape until the late 1960s and early 1970s with the emergence of the modern women's movement. In "America Then" we feature one of the key documents of that burgeoning movement, Judy Brady's now-famous "I Want a Wife," an essay that, if you were a college student studying composition back then, was practically inescapable. It may be one of the most widely read essays in American history. "My God, who wouldn't want a wife?" Brady persuasively concludes after enumerating all the domestic services a dutiful wife provides. As a student today, ask yourself whether this 1972 essay that appeared in the first issue of *Ms.* magazine can still be considered relevant.

Marisa Meltzer

The Last Feminist Taboo

[*Elle,* January 2014]

BEFORE YOU READ

What does it mean to be a feminist? Should any subject be taboo if you consider yourself one?

WORDS TO LEARN

furtive (para. 2): secret (adjective)

potent (para 3): powerful (adjective)

sedative (para. 3): something that calms (noun)

metabolism (para. 4): the process by which an organism functions (noun)

behest (para. 5): bidding (noun)

sadistic (para. 5): cruel (adjective)

contraband (para. 5): something prohibited (noun)

trajectory (para. 6): the curve described by something in flight (noun)

pontificate (para. 9): to speak pompously (verb)

tedious (para. 10): long and tiresome (adjective)

pedestrian (para. 13): commonplace (adjective)

adamantly (para. 14): uncompromisingly (adverb)

ambivalence (para. 15): the existence of both positive and negative feelings about something, occurring at the same time (noun)

nebulous (para. 15): vague (adjective)

surplus (para. 16): an excess (noun)

poignant (para. 18): affecting; moving (adjective)

Unlike certain B-list celebs, who take to the covers of tabloids to trumpet their diet success stories, I'm hoping no one will comment on the fact that I've lost more than 60 pounds in the past eight months. Dieting is my biggest secret. I wish I could say it's a thrilling one, like dating your college TA, but it's more like waxing my lip — I don't ever want to talk about it, and I'd rather people thought I never had to worry about it in the first place.   1

Marisa Meltzer is a writer based in New York. Her work has appeared in many publications, including the New York Times, Teen Vogue, Entertainment Weekly, Nylon, Nerve, *and* Elle, *among others. In addition, she has served as an editor for many of those publications. She is the author of* Girl Power *(2010), and the coauthor of* How Sassy *Changed My Life (2007).*

As the pounds started coming off, physically I felt lighter. I slept well. 2
I was in a better mood. But I also felt strangely furtive and isolated. I've
told exactly one friend about my weight loss. (It's probably no coinci-
dence that she's a fellow chronic dieter and lives across the country from
me.) Trading secrets late one night outside a bar, a particularly willowy
friend recently admitted to me that she'd struggled with her weight in
college. And yet even then, I — who can speak freely about anything:
abortions, boys, Rihanna — could not confess that I've been tallying
calories for months. "It's a bargain I make with myself," agrees Wendy
McClure, a friend and the author of the weight-loss memoir *I'm Not the
New Me.* "It's okay as long as I'm off doing this by myself."

For as long as I can remember having 3
an identity at all, I've considered myself a
feminist, graduating from *Free to Be . . . You
and Me* to *Ms.* magazine to Naomi Wolf, who
wrote in 1991's *The Beauty Myth* that "a cultural fixation on female thinness is not an
obsession about female beauty, but an obses-

> Good feminists, in
> short, do not diet.
> Or if they do, they
> don't talk about it.

sion about female obedience. Dieting is the most potent political sedative
in women's history; a quietly mad population is a tractable one." Good
feminists, in short, do not diet. Or if they do, they don't talk about it.

When I was growing up, the same mother who took me to protests 4
against the Miss California pageant and to lectures by Gloria Steinem
also never ate more than half of anything on her plate. Neither she nor
my father, a gourmand who has made halfhearted attempts to lose 20
pounds for the past 30 years, have ever had real problems with weight. As
the only child of divorced parents busy with their careers and love lives, I
don't recall having a lot of sit-down, well-balanced family meals. I'm not
sure I ever got the opportunity to learn proper eating habits; I also happened to be blessed with a sluggish metabolism.

My parents put me on my first diet in kindergarten. In photos from 5
the time, I'm only mildly chubby, but they wanted me to be happy and
healthy, and to shield me from ridicule. Their intentions were pure
enough, but having to diet at my parents' behest felt like a punishment.
I spent several summers at a hellish, boot camp — like Junior Lifeguard
program where one particularly sadistic fellow camper nicknamed me
"Chubs" in my regulation red swimsuit. At 10, I was sent to a fat camp
in Santa Barbara, where we attended four hours of exercise classes a day
and our bags were searched for contraband candy. By high school, I lived
a kind of dual feminist-dieter life, surviving on oatmeal, salads, and fro-
zen yogurt while singing along to "as a woman I was taught to always be
hungry" at Bikini Kill concerts.

You can trace my life's trajectory through my weight. Here I am as a   6
teenager, constantly hungry, weighing myself daily to make sure I don't
waver above my all-time low of 125 pounds. At Evergreen State College
in Olympia, Washington, subsisting on pints of Alaskan Amber and $5
pizzas — weighing in at 170 pounds but enjoying the break from hypervigilance. In Paris my senior year, down to 140, jogging laps around the
moat of Château de Vincennes and thrilled to fit into French sizes. In
San Francisco postgraduation, going from overweight to obese on bur-
rito lunches and topping the 200-pound mark.

By the time I turned 35 last year, I was living in Brooklyn, going   7
through a breakup, and diagnosed with clinical depression for the first
time in my life. Food was the most reliable comfort I could find: cookie-
dough breakfasts washed down with Coke and the kind of delivery orders
where the restaurant packs four sets of plastic utensils. The cocktail of
pills I took — Lexapro, Abilify, Pristiq, Lamictal, Wellbutrin — helped
lift me out of the dark fog, but they also elevated my weight. I hit 250,
my highest ever.

I tried to wear my heaviness with a certain hard-won pride. It was   8
a kiss-off to the years of calorie counting my parents had subjected
me to, I told myself. Dating while fat? A way to filter out shallow men.
(Though after one potential online suitor inquired as to whether I
was fat or "merely chubby" — evidently my picture didn't spell it out
clearly enough — I gave up on men altogether; my self-esteem couldn't
withstand further blows.) I flirted with fat acceptance, tried to believe
that weight should not define who I am, that beauty comes in different packages. But the truth was that I was neither healthy nor happy.
I weighed more than my father, who is seven inches taller than me;
my blood pressure, taken during a long-delayed visit to my doctor, was
becoming worrisome.

It would be technically accurate to say that dieting was necessary for   9
my health, but ultimately it came down to how I looked. I was scared of
heart disease, yes, but was perhaps even more afraid of never fitting into
Isabel Marant again. My shapeless Marni dresses were suddenly tight. I
could no longer fit into certain pairs of shoes. My stomach grazed the
table when I slid into booths. And my career was affected: A national
morning news show invited me to pontificate about young feminists (my
own adolescent riot grrrl years having made me something of an expert),
but I turned it down because I didn't like my appearance.

In late February 2013, I decided to make a change. Weight-loss sur-   10
gery was out of the question — insurance didn't cover it, and I worried I'd
have to tell friends why I was recuperating from major surgery and eating
tiny portions. Meal delivery felt too restrictive; logging every morsel on

Weight Watchers, too tedious. My doctor devised a plan high in plant-based foods and protein. After I weighed in with her each month, she'd say, in her thick Romanian accent, "You are going to look like model." I certainly missed fish and chips and meatball heros, but I started getting used to — even craving — kale and cauliflower and chickpeas. Now I eat more vegetables than I previously thought possible, grill salmon sans oil, and avoid white flour and sugar. I go to spin classes and hot yoga. I've lost track of the last time I ate a cheeseburger.

But I do it all in private. 11

Odds are, I'm not the only one in my set on a diet: 64 percent of 12 American women are considered overweight or obese, with a BMI above 25. According to one major study, roughly 45 million Americans diet each year, spending some $33 billion on weight-loss products.

Now that I'm among them, the guilt I once felt about what I ate 13 has been replaced by guilt over being the wrong kind of feminist — or maybe no kind of feminist: a woman pursuing something as pedestrian and frankly boring as losing weight. I fear that instead of fighting for a world where all bodies are admired, I'm pandering, reshaping my body to make it acceptable to the world around me. And I'm not alone: Jessica Wakeman, a writer for the blog The Frisky, recently came out as a dieter in a post called "True Story: A Feminist Joins Weight Watchers." This is a woman who's written casually about attending an orgy, but dieting required a lengthy justification.

There's a thread of old-school feminist thought that says taking plea- 14 sure in being admired for our looks is participating in our own oppression, minimizing our brains and power. But by the time I came of age in the '90s, feminism had shifted to include, if not embrace, such girly frivolities as lipstick and high heels: Picture Liz Phair singing "The fire that you like so much in me/ is the mark of someone adamantly free" — all pissed off and righteous and yet feminine as you please in miniskirts and baby tees. Still, altering your body in any way that could read as conformity — that was different. Dieting, specifically, was choosing denial and self-abnegation over letting yourself enjoy all the lusty pleasures of life. It was selling out. (Nobody thought to ask exactly how Liz fit in those minis, but whatever.) Feminist writer Kate Harding, coauthor of *Lessons From the Fat-o-sphere: Quit Dieting and Declare a Truce With Your Body,* compares dieting to taking your husband's last name. "You can be a feminist and make a nonfeminist choice," she tells me. "But what drives me nuts is trying to make it a feminist act."

But there's also a strain of ambivalence that's more nebulous and apo- 15 litical: the notion that evolved girls simply don't need to diet. The modern woman, after all, is that highly capable, have-it-all creature to whom career success, confidence, and effortless style — and, oh yeah, the yoga body and the eco-conscious, preservative-free diet — come naturally. She's too damn smart and balanced to overeat in the first place. If anything, she's already healthy and getting ever healthier. So juice fasts and Goop cleanses and barre classes? All fine as part of a vague "healthy lifestyle" of "clean eating." Losing weight for your wedding day? Okay, you get a free pass on that one. But the daily slog of dieting — all that calorie counting and dessert skipping and cardio bingeing? That's not at all chic.

So whether you brand it feminism or not — and plenty don't;   16
according to one recent survey, only 23 percent of women identify themselves as feminist — liberated women are hip to the complicated politics involved in food, fat, and their bodies. We know how corrupt the diet industry is; we take to Twitter to applaud brands like ASOS for expanding their plus-size lines. Most of us agree that the insurance charts for what is considered a healthy weight are unrealistic, that the standard definition of beauty is narrow. We have a surplus of knowledge, and perhaps because of this, the only publicly acceptable message is one of body positivity and self acceptance. Kudos to Melissa McCarthy, Rebel Wilson, Octavia Spencer for being, as Lena Dunham has put it, "freed from the prison" of Hollywood beauty standards. Props to Dunham, that paragon of Gen-Y feminism and achievement, who told an interviewer: "I ate cake for breakfast on the day of the Emmys, I ate cake for dinner, my workout didn't require Spanx, and I still feel like I looked better than people expected me to. It was amazing. I could feel the envy of every woman in the Sunset Tower."

But for most women, that attitude is just a front. The French-born   17
photographer and fashion blogger Garance Doré has voiced her frustration with fashion lovers who pretend to fit effortlessly into their leather microshorts. She writes, "For every friend who can eat whatever she wants and still stay thin, 10 of us have to pay a little more attention to our eating habits (like me) (and I'm not talking about being anorexic or anything, but just using moderation and maybe not eating a giant piece of carrot cake after a big lunch. It's no small task). And lying about the subject, now that I have a problem with." A few years ago, Julianne Moore said, "I still battle with my deeply boring diet of, essentially, yogurt and breakfast cereal and granola bars. I hate dieting. I hate having to do it to be the 'right' size." Moore's admission was far enough afield from the standard actress line of "Oh, I just ate a cheeseburger on the way here" to make headlines. Femininity, I guess, is still supposed to be wrapped up in mystery.

I look at all the cute, smart girls where I live in Brooklyn, where bou-   18
tiques rarely stock sizes over 8 and rail-thin Michelle Williams is the ideal, and I wonder if they diet too. Every time I order a salad — so often these

days — and have just one glass of wine at dinner, I worry that someone will comment. But as I started writing this and talking to women about what they eat, I got a rare glimpse behind the curtain, where apparently quite a few of us are doing sad but poignant things to hide our dieting. Sarah Hepola, a writer I know who lost 45 pounds two years ago on a prepackaged diet, told me that she "lived in terror that a gentleman caller was going to open up my freezer for, say, an ice cube and be confronted with direct evidence of my weakness." McClure, the aforementioned memoirist, weighs her portions on the postal scale in her office. "The scale is in a high-traffic area, and we're a laid-back office, but I never, ever want anyone to catch me weighing a handful of cashews."

I decided to go to the source and call Naomi Wolf. Twenty-two years   19
after *The Beauty Myth*, she's still critical of the kind of nitpicky thinking that dieting encourages. "Women are always tasked with surveilling, evaluating, judging. There is something about the culture asking us to be in that part of our brains all the time that dials down passion and intuition," she says. I brace myself for what comes next — is she going to chastise me, tell me I'm betraying the cause? But Wolf is surprisingly laissez-faire on the subject of individual choice. "Feminism often gets into an unappealing cul-de-sac where there's this set of practices or beliefs that you have to be part of to be a good feminist. Interestingly, that's not very different from more conventional forms of social policing. I don't think there's anything wrong with taking care of your body. I just want to know you're feeling beautiful and important at whatever weight you want."

By losing weight, I am putting more value on my thinner body, which   20
becomes smaller every day as I continue to try to shed the last 30 or so pounds. I admit I feel more comfortable in this new body, which in turn has made me more confident in the choice I made to lose weight. What remains is for me to open up about it to the women I know; it's a discussion I hope to initiate. Among my friends, the conversation is just beginning.

VOCABULARY/USING A DICTIONARY

1. What is a *gourmand* (para. 4)? From what language does it derive?
2. What part of speech is the word *hyper*? What does it add in *hypervigilance* (para. 6)?
3. What does it mean if something is *chic* (para. 15)?

RESPONDING TO WORDS IN CONTEXT

1. What is a *tally*? If someone is *tallying calories* (para. 2), what is he or she doing?
2. What might a *willowy friend* (para. 2) look like? What is a *willow*?
3. The word *slog* can be either a noun or a verb. How is it used in paragraph 15?

DISCUSSING MAIN POINT AND MEANING

1. Why did Meltzer begin dieting after years of weight fluctuation?
2. How do many women approach dieting, according to Meltzer? How does Meltzer feel about this approach?
3. Why, according to Meltzer, is weight loss such a tricky topic for feminists?

EXAMINING SENTENCES, PARAGRAPHS, AND ORGANIZATION

1. What point about her weight is Meltzer making in paragraphs 6 and 7? What information is included in the paragraphs?
2. Where does Meltzer go beyond personal narrative in the essay, including more objective evidence for her argument?
3. Does Meltzer end her essay on a personal or nonpersonal note? Explain.

THINKING CRITICALLY

1. Does Meltzer ever answer the question about whether or not weight and dieting fit with ideas about feminism?
2. Why do you think Meltzer includes Julianne Moore's comment in paragraph 17? What does her comment say about the subject of women and weight?
3. Do you think it's okay for women to feel secretive about eating habits and changes in their weight? Do you think eating and weight are a big concern for women?

WRITING ACTIVITIES

1. Consider how the media portray women in advertising. Flip through some fashion, style, or celebrity magazines, and notice how the female celebrities look. Make a list of the most prominent attributes you notice. What is being stressed? What might be considered an ideal appearance based on what you see? Write a report that offers a "beauty guideline" using images you've found in magazines.
2. Meltzer's essay examines her struggles with her weight and with her ideas of feminism. Has any aspect of your life shaped your ideas about a larger issue? Explore these ideas in a narrative essay that looks at some aspect of your own childhood.
3. Meltzer points out two symbols of feminism from her 1970s childhood: *Free to Be…You and Me* and *Ms.* magazine. Research one of these and write about its significance. Why did it get so much attention from feminists? Did it draw any criticism at the time? Do you think either is relevant now?

Heather Havrilesky

Don't Act Crazy, Mindy

[*New York Times Magazine,* March 17, 2013]

BEFORE YOU READ

Have you ever considered the way women are portrayed in television shows? How would you describe the main traits of any important female characters?

WORDS TO LEARN

caveat (para. 1): a cautionary detail (noun)

astute (para. 1): shrewd (adjective)

tenacious (para. 3): persistent (adjective)

bipolar (para. 3): having two poles (in psychology, referring to manic depression) (adjective)

protagonists (para. 5): leading characters (noun)

garrulous (para. 5): excessively talkative (adjective)

antics (para. 6): capers (noun)

abrasive (para. 6): harsh (adjective)

censure (para. 7): a strong expression of disapproval (noun)

cavort (para. 8): to prance (verb)

sass (para. 8): disrespectful back talk (noun)

cued (para. 8): prompted (verb)

lasciviousness (para. 8): lustfulness (noun)

petulant (para. 11): peevish (adjective)

beatifically (para. 11): blissfully (adverb)

ravenous (para. 12): famished (adjective)

impediment (para. 13): an obstacle (noun)

reductive (para. 16) serving to abridge (adjective)

subterfuge (para. 17): deception (noun)

candidly (para. 17): honestly (adverb)

placid (para. 18): tranquil (adjective)

A t first glance, this looks like a great moment for women on television. Many smart and confident female characters have paraded onto the small screen over the past few years. But I'm bothered by one persistent caveat: that the more astute and capable many of these women are, the more likely it is that they're also completely nuts. 1

Heather Havrilesky is a contributing writer to New York Times *magazine, a columnist for* Bookforum, *and the author of* Disaster Preparedness: A Memoir *(2010). Her writing has appeared in the Awl* Spin, New York *magazine, the* Los Angeles Times, *the* Washington Post, *and others. A former* Salon *TV critic, she now maintains her own blog,* Rabbit Blog.

I don't mean complicated, difficult, thorny or complex. I mean that   2
these women are portrayed as volcanoes that could blow at any minute.
Worse, the very abilities and skills that make them singular and interesting come coupled with some hideous psychic deficiency.

On "Nurse Jackie," for example, the main character is an excellent R.N.   3
in part because she's self-medicated into a state of extreme calm. On "The
Killing," Detective Linden, the world-weary, cold-souled cop, is a tenacious investigator in part because she's obsessive and damaged and a pretty
terrible mother. And then there's "Homeland," on which Carrie Mathison,
the nearly clairvoyant C.I.A. agent, is bipolar, unhinged and has proved, in
her pursuit of an undercover terrorist, to be recklessly promiscuous.

These aren't just complicating characteristics like, say, Don Draper's   4
narcissism. The suggestion in all of these shows is that a female character's flaws are inextricably linked to her strengths. Take away this pill
problem or that personality disorder, and the exceptional qualities van-
ish as well. And this is not always viewed as a tragedy — when Carrie
undergoes electroconvulsive therapy, we breathe a sigh of relief and draw
closer. Look how restful it is for her, enjoying a nice sandwich and sleeping peacefully in her childhood bed.

You'd think the outlook would be sunnier on some of the lighter TV   5
dramas and comedies, which have also lately offered several strong and
inspiring (if neurotic) female protagonists, from Annie Edison of "Community" to Leslie Knope of "Parks and Recreation." Yet here, too, an
alarming number of accomplished women are also portrayed as spending most of their waking hours swooning like lovesick tweens — whether
it's Emily on "Emily Owens, M.D." (a knowledgeable doctor who loses
focus whenever her super-dreamy crush enters the room), the title character of "Whitney" (a garrulous photographer who is nonetheless fix-
ated on her looks and her ability to keep attractive romantic rivals away
from her man), or Mindy of "The Mindy Project" (a highly paid ob-gyn
who's obsessed with being too old and not pretty enough to land a husband). Even a classical comedic heroine like Liz Lemon on "30 Rock" is
frequently reduced to flailing and squirming like an overcaffeinated adolescent. The moral of many of these shows doesn't seem so far off from
that of those fatalistic female-centric magazine features that seem to run
every few months; something along the lines of, "You can't have it all,
ladies, and you'll run yourself ragged if you even try."

We could take heart that at least women are depicted as being just   6
as reckless and promiscuous and demanding and intense as their male
counterparts, if their bad behavior weren't so often accompanied by a
horror soundtrack and dizzying camera angles that encourage us to view
them as unhinged. The crazed antics of male characters like Don Draper,

Walter White or Dr. Gregory House are reliably treated as bold, fearless and even ultimately heroic (a daring remark saves the big account; a lunatic gesture scares off a murderous thug; an abrasive approach miraculously yields the answer that saves a young girl's life). Female characters rarely enjoy such romantic spin.

Their flaws are fatal, or at least obviously self-destructive, and they   7
seem designed to invite censure. Time and again, we, the audience, are cast in the role of morally superior observers to these nut jobs. At times we might relate to a flash of anger, a fit of tears, a sudden urge to seduce a stranger in a bar, but we're constantly being warned that these behaviors aren't normal. They render these women out of step with the sane world.

When Nurse Jackie chokes down pills and cavorts with the pharma-   8
cist while her perfectly good husband waits around at home with the kids, we can see clearly where too much sass and independence might lead. When Detective Linden dumps her son in a hotel room for the umpteenth time and then he goes missing, or Dr. Yang's emotional frigidity on "Grey's Anatomy" leaves her stranded at the altar, or Nancy Botwin of "Weeds" sleeps with (and eventually marries) a Mexican drug boss, thereby endangering her kids, we're cued to shake our heads at the woeful choices of these otherwise-impressive women. When Carrie on "Homeland" chugs a tumbler of white wine, then fetches one of her black sequined tops out of the closet, we're meant to lament her knee-jerk lasciviousness. Her mania is something she needs to be cured of, or freed from — unlike, say, Monk, whose psychological tics are portrayed as the adorable kernel of his genius.

So why should instability in men and women be treated so differ-   9
ently? "If you don't pull it together, no one will ever love you," a talking Barbie doll tells Mindy during a fantasy on "The Mindy Project," reminding us exactly what's on the line here.

Don't act crazy, Mindy. Men don't like crazy.   10

Some would argue that we've come a long way since Desi treated   11
Lucy like a petulant child or June Cleaver smiled beatifically at her plucky spawn. "Mary Tyler Moore," "Murphy Brown" and "Roseanne" all demonstrated that a smart woman can have a life outside of cooking, cleaning and begging to be put in her husband's show. They offered us female characters who failed to blend seamlessly with their surroundings — because they were willing to voice their doubts, confess their crushes, seek out sex and openly confront others.

But right around the time "Ally McBeal" hit the air, the attempts   12
to unveil the truth of the female experience started to sail far past the intended mark. The independent woman took on a hysterical edge; she was not only opinionated but also wildly insecure, sexually ravenous or panic-stricken over her waning fertility. Surprising as it was that McBeal

was once heralded as a post-feminist hero on the cover of Time in 1998, what's more surprising is that since then, we haven't come all that much further, baby.

Sure, there are lots of exceptions, like Tami Taylor, the self- 13 possessed working mom of "Friday Night Lights," or Hannah Horvath, the outspoken memoirist of "Girls," or the intelligent women of "Mad Men," whose struggles and flaws at least parallel those of the men swarming around them. But alongside every coolheaded Peggy Olson, we get hotheaded train-wreck characters like Ivy Lynn of "Smash" — women who, like the ballerinas with lead weights around their ankles in Kurt Vonnegut Jr.'s short story "Harrison Bergeron," can show no strength without an accompanying impediment to weigh them down, whether it's self-destructive urges, tittering self-consciousness or compulsive pill-popping. Where Roseanne and Mary and Murphy matter-of-factly admitted and often even flaunted their flaws, these characters are too ashamed and apologetic (and repeatedly demeaned) to be taken seriously.

"Women have often felt insane when cleaving to the truth of our 14 experience," Adrienne Rich once wrote. There's truth in these images of women, from the neurotic ob-gyn fix-ated on finding Mr. Right to the workaholic C.I.A. agent who feels adrift when she isn't obsessing about issues of national security 18 hours a day. But why must these charac-ters also be certifiable? Give Mindy a tiny slice of Louis C.K.'s poker-faced smugness.

> Give Mindy a tiny slice of Louis C.K.'s poker-faced smugness.

Give Carrie Mathison one-tenth of Jack Bauer's overconfidence and irre-proachability. Where's the taboo in that?

Women, with their tendency to "ask uncomfortable questions and 15 make uncomfortable connections," as Rich puts it, are pathologized for the very traits that make them so formidable. Or as Emily Dickinson wrote:

Much Madness is divinest Sense
To a discerning Eye —
Much Sense — the starkest Madness —
'Tis the Majority
In this, as All, prevail —
Assent — and you are sane —
Demur — you're straightway dangerous —
And handled with a Chain —

"All smart women are crazy," I once told an ex-boyfriend in a heated moment, in an attempt to depict his future options as split down the middle between easygoing dimwits and sharp women who were basically just me with different hairstyles. By "crazy," I only meant "opinionated" and "moody" and "not always as pliant as one might hope." I was translating my personality into language he might understand — he who used "psycho-chick" as a stand-in for "noncompliant female" and he whose idea of helpful counsel was "You're too smart for your own good," "my own good" presumably being some semivegetative state of acceptance which precluded uncomfortable discussions about our relationship.

Over the years, "crazy" became my own reductive shorthand for every complicated, strong-willed woman I met. "Crazy" summed up the good and the bad in me and in all of my friends. Whereas I might have started to recognize that we were no more crazy than anyone else in the world, instead I simply drew a larger and larger circle of crazy around us, lumping together anyone unafraid of confrontation, anyone who openly admitted her weaknesses, anyone who pursued agendas that might be out of step with the dominant cultural noise of the moment. "Crazy" became code for "interesting" and "courageous" and "worth knowing." I was trying to have a sense of humor about myself and those around me, trying to make room for stubbornness and vulnerability and uncomfortable questions.   16

But I realize now, after watching these crazy characters parade across my TV screen, that there's self-hatred in this act of self-subterfuge. "Our future depends on the sanity of each of us," Rich writes, "and we have a profound stake, beyond the personal, in the project of describing our reality as candidly and fully as we can to each other."   17

Maybe this era of "crazy" women on TV is an unfortunate way-station on the road from placid compliance to something more complex — something more like real life. Many so-called crazy women are just smart, that's all. They're not too smart for their own good, or for ours.   18

VOCABULARY/USING A DICTIONARY

1. What does it mean if someone is *demeaned* (para. 13)?
2. What is a *way-station* (para. 18)?
3. Do you know what sort of powers a *clairvoyant* (para. 3) person would have?

RESPONDING TO WORDS IN CONTEXT

1. What does the word *spawn* (para. 11) usually refer to? What does it refer to in this context?
2. How are women *pathologized* (para. 15)? In what context is the word *pathology* usually used?
3. How might a "noncompliant female" behave (para. 15)?

DISCUSSING MAIN POINT AND MEANING

1. Why, according to Havrilesky, is this *not* a great moment for women on television?
2. What was a high point for female characters on TV? How were they portrayed?
3. How are some strong female characters portrayed on TV? How are their male counterparts portrayed?

EXAMINING SENTENCES, PARAGRAPHS, AND ORGANIZATION

1. After reading the piece, do you have a sense of the television shows on today, even if you don't watch them? How does Havrilesky achieve this effect in her essay?
2. Where does Havrilesky deviate from her descriptions of television and television characters? Did this deviation surprise you?
3. How does Havrilesky explain the problem with women on television? What would you identify as her thesis?

THINKING CRITICALLY

1. Do you think women on TV can be looked up to as role models? Why or why not?
2. Consider "opinionated" and "moody" female characters on television. Do you think of them in those terms, or do you think of them as "crazy"? What about "opinionated" and "moody" male characters?
3. Why might someone portray a smart female character as crazy? Does it make her seem more "real"? Does it make her easier to accept?

WRITING ACTIVITIES

1. Chart the progress of female characters in the shows Havrilesky mentions. Start with early television — *I Love Lucy* and *Leave It to Beaver*. Move on to *The Mary Tyler Moore Show, Murphy Brown,* and *Roseanne.* Consider the turning point Havrilesky mentions — *Ally McBeal.* And finally add the current TV shows she included. Write about them in chronological order. You can write about them if you have seen them, or you can research them on the Internet. After you chart out the shows, draw conclusions about the transformation of female characters from what you see in front of you.
2. Consider "crazy" as a catchall term. What sort of traits and attributes can it stand for? What qualities does it cover for which the word might be a stretch?
3. Write a review of a television show, either comedy or drama. Include a character sketch of the main characters, male and female. Are the characters believable? Unbelievable? Address their believability or unbelievability in your review.

Christina Hoff Sommers

No, Women Don't Make Less Money Than Men

[*The Daily Beast*, February 1, 2014]

BEFORE YOU READ

What does it mean when people say women earn less than men? And why might there be a difference in earnings?

WORDS TO LEARN

spurious (para. 1): not genuine (adjective)

remunerative (para. 3): profitable (adjective)

demolish (para. 8): to destroy (verb)

autonomous (para. 9): independent (adjective)

invidious (para. 10): injurious (adjective)

President Obama repeated the spurious gender wage gap statistic in his State of the Union address. "Today," he said, "women make up about half our workforce. But they still make 77 cents for every dollar a man earns. That is wrong, and in 2014, it's an embarrassment." 1

What is wrong and embarrassing is the President of the United States reciting a massively discredited factoid. The 23-cent gender pay gap is simply the difference between the average earnings of all men and women working full-time. It does not account for differences in occupations, positions, education, job tenure, or hours worked per week. When all these relevant factors are taken into consideration, the wage gap narrows to about five cents. And no one knows if the five cents is a result of discrimination or some other subtle, hard-to-measure difference between male and female workers. In its fact-checking column on the State of the Union, the *Washington Post* included the President's mention of the wage gap in its list of dubious claims. "There is clearly a wage gap, but differences in the life choices of men and women . . . make it difficult to make simple comparisons." 2

Christina Hoff Sommers is an author and former philosophy professor. She is best known for her critique of late-twentieth-century feminism, and she is the author of such books as Who Stole Feminism?: How Women Have Betrayed Women *and* The War Against Boys: How Misguided Feminism Is Harming Our Young Men. *She earned her PhD in philosophy from Brandeis University in 1979.*

Consider, for example, how men and women differ in their college   3
majors. Here is a list (PDF) of the ten *most* remunerative majors com-
piled by the Georgetown University Center on Education and the Workforce. Men overwhelmingly outnumber women in all but one of them:

1. Petroleum Engineering: 87% male   4
2. Pharmacy Pharmaceutical Sciences and Administration: 48% male
3. Mathematics and Computer Science: 67% male
4. Aerospace Engineering: 88% male
5. Chemical Engineering: 72% male
6. Electrical Engineering: 89% male
7. Naval Architecture and Marine Engineering: 97% male
8. Mechanical Engineering: 90% male
9. Metallurgical Engineering: 83% male
10. Mining and Mineral Engineering: 90% male

And here are the 10 *least* remunerative majors — where women pre-   5
vail in nine out of ten:

1. Counseling Psychology: 74% female   6
2. Early Childhood Education: 97% female
3. Theology and Religious Vocations: 34% female
4. Human Services and Community Organization: 81% female
5. Social Work: 88% female
6. Drama and Theater Arts: 60% female
7. Studio Arts: 66% female
8. Communication Disorders Sciences and Services: 94% female
9. Visual and Performing Arts: 77% female
10. Health and Medical Preparatory Programs: 55% female

Much of the wage gap can be explained away by simply tak-   7
ing account of college majors. Early childhood educators and social
workers can expect to earn around $36,000 and $39,000, respectively.
By contrast, petroleum engineering and metallurgy degrees promise
median earnings of $120,000 and $80,000. Not many aspiring early
childhood educators would change course once they learn they can
earn more in metallurgy or mining. The sexes, taken as a group, are
somewhat different. Women, far more than men, appear to be drawn
to jobs in the caring professions; and men are more likely to turn up in
people-free zones. In the pursuit of happiness, men and women appear
to take different paths.

But here is the mystery. These and other differences in employment   8
preferences and work-family choices have been widely studied in recent

years and are now documented in a mountain of solid empirical research. By now the President and his staff must be aware that the wage gap statistic has been demolished. This is not the first time the *Washington Post* has alerted the White House to the error. Why continue to use it? One possibility is that they have been taken in by the apologetics of groups like the National Organization for Women and the American Association of University Women. In its 2007 *Behind the Pay Gap report,* the AAUW admits that most of the gap in earnings is explained by choices. But this admission is qualified: "Women's personal choices are similarly fraught with inequities," says the AAUW. It speaks of women being "pigeonholed" into "pink-collar" jobs in health and education. According to NOW, powerful sexist stereotypes "steer" women and men "toward different education, training, and career paths."

Have these groups noticed that American women are now among   9
the most educated, autonomous, opportunity-rich women in history? Why not respect their choices? For the past few decades, untold millions of state and federal dollars have been devoted to recruiting young women into engineering and computer technology. It hasn't worked. The percent of degrees awarded to women in fields like computer science and engineering has either stagnated or significantly *decreased* since 2000. (According to Department of Education data, in 2000, women earned 19 percent of engineering BA's, and 28 percent in computer science; by 2011, only 17 percent of engineering degrees were awarded to females, and the percent of female computer science degrees had dropped to 18.) All evidence suggests that though young women have the talent for engineering and computer science, their interest tends to lie elsewhere. To say that these women remain helplessly in thrall to sexist stereotypes, and manipulated into life choices by forces beyond their control, is divorced from reality — and demeaning to boot. If a woman wants to be a teacher rather than a miner, or a veterinarian rather than a petroleum engineer, more power to her.

> Have these groups noticed that American women are now among the most educated, autonomous, opportunity-rich women in history?

The White House should stop using women's choices to construct a   10
false claim about social inequality that is poisoning our gender debates. And if the President is truly persuaded that statistical pay disparities indicate invidious discrimination, then he should address the wage gap in his own backyard. Female staff at the White House earn 88 cents on the dollar compared to men. Is there a White House war on women?

VOCABULARY/USING A DICTIONARY
1. What is the opposite of *empirical* (para. 8)?
2. What happens to something that *stagnates* (para. 9)?
3. What is a *wage gap* (para. 1)?

RESPONDING TO WORDS IN CONTEXT
1. What does Sommers mean by the term "massively discredited factoid" (para. 2)?
2. What is happening to someone who is *in thrall* (para. 9) to something?
3. What kind of difference would a *subtle* (para. 2) one be?

DISCUSSING MAIN POINT AND MEANING
1. To what does Sommers attribute a difference in pay between men and women?
2. What claims published by the National Organization for Women and the American Association of University Women does Sommers disagree with?
3. What claim does Sommers make about practices at the White House?

EXAMINING SENTENCES, PARAGRAPHS, AND ORGANIZATION
1. What is the tone Sommers is using in sentences like this one: "What is wrong and embarrassing is the President of the United States reciting a massively discredited factoid"? How is the tone apparent from the verb?
2. What do you think of the inclusion of lists in Sommers essay? Could that material be woven into the essay differently?
3. What detail is the focal point of Sommers's essay? Where is it found in the essay?

THINKING CRITICALLY
1. Do you think women and men are just interested in different professions? What role does gender stereotyping play in their decisions?
2. Women used to face rampant sexism in school and in the workplace. Are schools and jobs today free from sexism?
3. What do you think of the difference in salary quoted from one profession to another? Are such differences in salary fair? Why is one area worth less than another?

WRITING ACTIVITIES
1. Sommers makes the claim that "female staff at the White House earn 88 cents on the dollar compared to men." Research this claim online and write a report on what you find. Is she right? Is there any evidence to discredit this claim?
2. Find out more about President Obama and his interest in the wage gap. Is the wage gap high on his list of concerns? What work has he done that indicates it is important to him? Not important to him?

3. Sommers writes, "Women, far more than men, appear to be drawn to jobs in the caring professions; and men are more likely to turn up in people-free zones." Discuss this sentence in a few paragraphs. Do you think she is buying into a stereotype? Do you think there is validity to what she says in some inherent, scientifically proved gender difference? Explain.

Emily Potter (student essay)

#YesAllWomen

[*The Daily Nexus*, University of California, Santa Barbara, May 30, 2014]

BEFORE YOU READ

Have you seen the hashtag #YesAllWomen on Twitter? Is it important to women only? What is its importance?

WORDS TO LEARN

accomplish (para. 2): to carry out or finish (verb)

circumstance (para. 2): a modifying or influencing factor (noun)

initially (para. 3): at first (adverb)

reconcile (para. 3): to cause to accept (verb)

predominantly (para. 4): prominently (adverb)

imminent (para. 6): impending (adjective)

[Author's note: this is not a discussion of the events of Friday night,[1] but rather a greater social issue. My deepest condolences to those directly affected by the tragic deaths this past weekend and to the rest of our community. May we heal through our strength and solidarity.] 1

In nearly every respect, I was raised as my older brother's equal. We wrestled together, played the same sports, each of us excelled at math and science and we were both raised to believe we could accomplish whatever we set our minds to. In only one circumstance was I prevented 2

---

[1] Friday night (para. 1): On May 23, 2014, a man killed six people near the University of California, Santa Barbara.

Emily Potter is a student at the University of California, Santa Barbara.

from doing something my brother had the freedom to do: walking home alone. Growing up, I lived around the corner from two of my best friends and would always walk along the short stretch of sidewalk between our two streets. But when I tried to do so at night, my parents always made sure someone accompanied me.

Initially, although I found it frustrating, I assumed this was because   3
I was younger than my brother. But when I reached the age he had been when he was first able to walk around the corner by himself at night, I began to protest. I argued with my parents that Stephen gets to walk by himself all the time and I should be able to do so as well. I always remember their response: "But you're a girl. It's different." By nature I am stubborn and independent; because of this and the fact that I was still innocent and unaware of the real dangers I faced merely because I was female, I did not find this a justified response. I remember countless times when I passionately argued with my parents that being a girl shouldn't make me any different from my brother. It took me years to reconcile with the fact that it does.

It would seem from reading this personal anecdote that I was a   4
self-proclaimed feminist from the womb. However, I was more of a self-proclaimed anti-feminist. Early on I recognized that masculinity meant power and therefore predominantly identified with the more masculine sides of my personality. I ridiculed feminists as angry men-haters, believed in the inherent differences between men and women, obsessed over "the perfect man," and saw the fact that I excelled in the STEM fields as evidence that I was a rare exception to the rule, instead of seeing how my female counterparts were made to believe by others, including me, that their gender made them naturally less qualified to succeed in subject areas that centered around logic. I distinctly remember arguing with a good friend of mine just this past summer about the lack of necessity for feminism. Because I am someone who generally has always been open-minded and hyper-aware of social issues, he was shocked by my ignorance, which made me question my position for the first time. That fall I signed up for Fem Studies 20, and my entire perspective was flipped.

I have not tried to hide the fact that I am a survivor of sexual assault.   5
I was assaulted when I was 15, in the midst of my steadfast anti-feminist view of the world. Until taking Fem Studies, I had never acknowledged the fact that I had this traumatic experience solely because I was a woman. I never saw that I had dismissed my own femininity because I wanted the power my brother had as a male, or how much that hindered me. I had never considered that my female peers avoided the STEM fields not because they could not succeed in them, but because they were told they would not succeed in them. I was ashamed of my own ignorance — in some ways I feel my lack of support was a greater problem than the lack

of understanding from men. Accepting a feminist perspective of the world has been enlightening in the most infuriating of ways. I can no longer ignore the daily oppression I face as a woman when I walk onto the pool deck to referee a men's water polo game, or when I am forced to call a CSO[2] late at night and take 30 minutes to get home rather than two.

While many of my perspectives have been broadened, my stubborn   6
independence has not been changed by this newfound awareness. Accepting the fact I cannot walk by myself at night has been a long process for me (even though I used to do it with 911 on speed-dial and pepper spray in hand), much to my male-friend's frustration. On Thursday night I finally used a CSO for the first time, and accepted that no matter how unfair, it simply is not safe for me to walk alone in Isla Vista at night. The only factor in my being able to accept that has been hope. I have every right to be stubborn and independent. I have every right to be able to decide that I am just going to walk alone if my friends are taking too long to join me. I have every right to write an article with a blatant feminist perspective without fearing the negative backlash I will get from angry misogynists. It is not because of inherent gender differences that I cannot do these things or fear doing them, but it is because we live in a world where violence against women is a very real and imminent threat. I have an undying hope that this world can change. I have to believe that while it may never be in my lifetime, future stubborn and independent women like me can walk home alone without any greater threat to their safety than their male counterparts.

So when you see the #YesAllWomen hashtag floating around your Twitter and Facebook feeds, take a second to really consider what it means. If you're a woman, I guarantee you've shared at least one experience with these women, and I challenge you to question why you've had that experience rather than accepting it as a natural part of being a woman. If you're a man, I ask you to keep in mind where the hashtag was born from: #NotAllMen oppress women but #YesAllWomen share these experiences.   7

> So when you see the #YesAllWomen hashtag floating around your Twitter and Facebook feeds, take a second to really consider what it means.

The hashtag does not intend to spark an attack on men but rather raise awareness for the struggles we face as women. I advise you to start considering the small things you take for granted that women battle daily and join the fight to change this oppression. We must recognize the fact

---

[2] CSO (para. 5): The Community Service Organization's members provide escorts on campus.

that there are limitations in the current world we live in today and do everything in our power to protect ourselves, but that doesn't mean we have to accept it as permanent.

VOCABULARY/USING A DICTIONARY

1. What is an *anecdote* (para. 4)?
2. Can you think of a word that means the opposite of *steadfast* (para. 5)?
3. What does *blatant* (para. 6) mean?

RESPONDING TO WORDS IN CONTEXT

1. How does Potter back up her claim that when she was younger, she was really a self-proclaimed *anti-feminist* (para. 4)?
2. How is it that accepting a feminist perspective of the world is *infuriating* (para. 5) for Potter?
3. Why would a *misogynist* (para. 6) respond negatively or angrily to an article from a feminist perspective?

DISCUSSING MAIN POINT AND MEANING

1. What might surprise you about the writer's experience when you read that she feels it's important for women to be able to walk alone?
2. Why does the writer feel she should be able to walk alone at night?
3. What is the importance of the origin of the hashtag #YesAllWomen?

EXAMINING SENTENCES, PARAGRAPHS, AND ORGANIZATION

1. Look at the writer's paragraphs. How are they formed? What sort of language does she use? Try to describe her style.
2. Do you think the author's note, which refers to a recent mass shooting that affected Potter's campus, is necessary to the essay? What does it change about how you read what follows, if anything?
3. How would this essay change if it weren't written in the first person? Consider what her perspective adds to the essay overall and how it might change writing from a different point of view, or using less first person.

THINKING CRITICALLY

1. What do you think Potter means in paragraph 3 when she says her entire perspective on women's issues was flipped after taking Fem Studies 20?
2. What are some of the reasons a woman might object to being treated differently from a man? Does #YesAllWomen address any of those objections?
3. Do you wish the narrator had brought into the essay more of her experience of being a younger sister with an older brother? Do you think she would have noticed any other differences in their treatment?

WRITING ACTIVITIES

1. Look at Twitter feeds with the hashtag #YesAllWomen. What are some of the issues and experiences discussed by people using the hashtag? Write a short essay that explains what some of the issues and experiences are that are brought under the umbrella #YesAllWomen.

2. Write a personal response to Potter's essay. Respond specifically to her claims in the last paragraphs: "If you're a woman, I guarantee you've shared at least one experience with these women, and I challenge you to question why you've had that experience rather than accepting it," and "If you're a man, I ask you to keep in mind where the hashtag was born from."

3. Research the Santa Barbara, California, shooting that happened in 2014 (alluded to in the author's note). What does that terrible event have to do with the subject Potter tackles in her essay? Draw a connection (or include some contrasts) between what she is writing about and that event — where do they intersect? How did that tragedy spark #YesAllWomen and Potter's essay?

LOOKING CLOSELY

Writing with Emphasis

Good writers know how to emphasize their important points without overrelying on the customary capital letters, double underlining, or exclamation marks. They understand how to make their sentences and the placement of words work for them. Writing well often demands that we create a sequence in which the most important idea — or point we want to stress — appears last. This attention to sequence applies to sentences and paragraphs as well as to the essay's conclusion.

Observe how Emily Potter, a student at the University of California, Santa Barbara, effectively uses emphasis in the opening of "#YesAllWomen." She begins by stating all the characteristics she and her brother shared. This allows her to set up the one important difference between them, a difference that she aptly emphasizes after a colon because it is the major point of her essay. To see the role emphasis plays in her opening, try reversing her points by starting the essay with the difference between Potter and her brother and then listing their similarities.

1
Sets up list of similarities

2
Emphasizes the one difference

In nearly every respect, I was raised as my older brother's equal. <u>We wrestled together, played the same sports, each of us excelled at math and science, and we were both raised to believe we could accomplish whatever we set our minds to.</u> (1) In only one circumstance was I prevented from doing something my brother had the freedom to do: <u>walking home alone.</u> (2)

Judy Brady

I Want a Wife

If you were a college student taking composition in the 1970s, you would almost certainly have had to read Judy Brady's "I Want a Wife." The short essay appeared in practically every composition anthology available. Published when the contemporary feminist movement was in its early stages and gaining members rapidly (it was then often referred to as "women's liberation" or, in a sometimes heckling tone, "women's lib"), the essay appropriately first appeared in the premier issue of what became the movement's leading magazine, *Ms.* Although the essay is no longer anthologized to the extent it once was, some books still include it. Over forty years later, with the goals and principles of feminism far more established across the nation, it is interesting to see what this now-classic essay means to today's college generation.

Before the legendary essay appeared in *Ms.* "I Want a Wife" was delivered aloud for the first time in San Francisco in 1970 at a rally celebrating the fiftieth anniversary of women's right to vote in the United States. Brady (b. 1937) still resides in San Francisco, where she writes and is an activist for women's causes and the environment.

I belong to that classification of people known as wives. I am A Wife. And, not altogether incidentally, I am a mother. 1

Not too long ago a male friend of mine appeared on the scene fresh from a recent divorce. He had one child, who is, of course, with his ex-wife. He is looking for another wife. As I thought about him while I was ironing one evening, it suddenly occurred to me that I, too, would like to have a wife. Why do I want a wife? 2

I would like to go back to school so that I can become economically independent, support myself, and, if need be, support those dependent upon me. I want a wife who will work and send me to school. And while I am going to school I want a wife to take care of my children. I want a wife to keep track of the children's doctor and dentist appointments. And to keep track of mine, too. I want a wife to make sure my children eat properly and are kept clean. I want a wife who will 3 wash the children's clothes and keep them mended. I want a wife who is a good nurturant attendant to my children, who arranges for their schooling, makes sure that they have an adequate social life with their peers, takes them to the park, the zoo, etc. I want a wife who takes care of the children when they are sick, a wife who arranges to be around when the children need special care, because, of course, I cannot miss classes at school. My wife must arrange to lose time at work and not lose the job. It may mean a small cut in my wife's income from time to time, but 1 guess I can tolerate that. Needless to say, my wife will arrange and pay for the care of the children while my wife is working.

I want a wife who will take care of my physical needs. I want a wife   4
who will keep my house clean. A wife who will pick up after my children, a wife who will pick up after me. I want a wife who will keep my clothes clean, ironed, mended, replaced when need be, and who will see to it that my personal things are kept in their proper place so that I can find what I need the minute I need it. I want a wife who cooks the meals, a wife who is a *good* cook. I want a wife who will plan the menus, do the necessary grocery shopping, prepare the meals, serve them pleasantly, and then do the cleaning up while I do my studying. I want a wife who will care for me when I am sick and sympathize with my pain and loss of time from school. I want a wife to go along when our family takes vacation so that someone can continue to care for me and my children when I need a rest and change of scene.

I want a wife who will not bother me with rambling complaints   5
about a wife's duties. But I want a wife who will listen to me when I feel the need to explain a rather difficult point I have come across in my course of studies. And I want a wife who will type my papers for me when I have written them.

I want a wife who will take care of the details of my social life.   6
When my wife and I are invited out by my friends, I want a wife who will take care of the babysitting arrangements. When I meet people at school that I like and want to entertain, I want a wife who will have the house clean, will prepare a special meal, serve it to me and my friends, and not interrupt when I talk about things that interest me and my friends. I want a wife who will have arranged that the children are fed and ready for bed before my guests arrive so that the children do not bother us. I want a wife who takes care of the needs of my guests so that they feel comfortable, who makes sure that they have an ashtray, that they are passed the hors d'oeuvres, that they are offered a second

helping of the food, that their wine glasses are replenished when necessary, that their coffee is served to them as they like it. And I want a wife who knows that sometimes I need a night out by myself.

I want a wife who is sensitive to my sexual needs, a wife who 7
makes love passionately and eagerly when I feel like it, a wife who makes sure that I am satisfied. And, of course, I want a wife who will not demand sexual attention when I am not in the mood for it. I want a wife who assumes the complete responsibility for birth control, because I do not want more children. I want a wife who will remain sexually faithful to me so that I do not have to clutter up my intellectual life with jealousies. And I want a wife who understands that my sexual needs may entail more than strict adherence to monogamy. I must, after all, be able to relate to people as fully as possible.

If, by chance, I find another person more suitable as a wife than the 8
wife I already have, I want the liberty to replace my present wife with another one. Naturally, I will expect a fresh, new life; my wife will take the children and be solely responsible for them so that I am left free.

When I am through with school and have a job, I want my wife 9
to quit working and remain at home so that my wife can more fully and completely take care of a wife's duties.

My God, who *wouldn't* want a wife? 10

BACKGROUND AND CONTEXT
1. In your opinion, what stereotypes about husbands and wives does Brady rely on in her essay? Do you think she exaggerates? Do you think these stereotypes still apply to marriages today? Explain why or why not.
2. Note that at the opening of her essay Brady wishes for a wife because she "would like to go back to school." How is this significant? What does it tell you about the era in which the essay was written? What does school have to do with her main goal in the essay? How does her behavior change towards her "wife" once she imagines herself being in school?

STRATEGY, STRUCTURE, AND STYLE
1. In rhetoric, the repetition of the opening words in a sentence is known as *anaphora*. Note how often Brady starts her sentences with "I want a wife." That repetition is clearly the dominant stylistic element of the essay. Why do you think she repeats the words so often, and what effect do you think it is intended to have on a reader?
2. Writers often use humor to make a serious point. How would you briefly summarize the point of Brady's essay? In what ways does humor contribute to that point?

COMPARISONS AND CONNECTIONS

1. In an essay that refers to at least one of the selections in this chapter, discuss how relevant you feel this forty-plus-year-old essay is. Try to explain what parts you think still matter to women today. Do you think she raises any issues that don't matter any longer? If she wrote the same essay today, how might she need to adjust to the existence of gay marriage?

2. In a brief essay, describe the "logic" of the essay. The "I" of the essay is already a "wife," so what does she become when she has a wife? Explain how Brady suggests what a "husband" is like. What advantages does her argument gain in setting up the differences in this indirect fashion instead of complaining directly about the behavior of husbands?

Discussing the Unit

SUGGESTED TOPIC FOR DISCUSSION

Women now make up the majority of the U.S. workforce, including management and professional positions (they still lag at the highest levels of executive leadership). Additionally, more women than men are earning college degrees. How do you account for these shifts? What do you think the consequences are — socially, economically, and culturally? Which essays in this chapter offer insight into this trend?

PREPARING FOR CLASS DISCUSSION

1. The essays in this unit cover a broad range of topics, from pay equality to the #YesAllWomen hashtag. What common themes unite the articles? If you had to characterize them in terms of one overriding issue, what would it be?

2. Some of these essays touch upon gender stereotypes, whether directly or indirectly. Which stereotypes can you identify? Do you think they are valid or "true" in any way? Are any of them pejorative or harmful, or just plain inaccurate? Do you identify with any of the gender stereotypes?

FROM DISCUSSION TO WRITING

1. Write an essay that outlines what you would like to see happen in women's lives in the workplace ten years from now. What should change? What do you think will remain the same?

2. All of these essays in this chapter suggest that gender remains a significant factor in our society. How has gender shaped your choices in your education and your career ambitions? Has it been a limiting factor in any way? Has it been an advantage? How aware are you of your gender when choosing a particular path, professionally or personally?

TOPICS FOR CROSS-CULTURAL DISCUSSION

1. Unquestionably, our ideas about gender and gender roles are shaped by our culture. What cultural factors — familial, ethnic, religious, racial, or otherwise — have influenced your perceptions of men and women, as well as male and female roles? Do your beliefs ever conflict with dominant views of gender and gender roles? Have your views changed in any way? What caused them to change?

2. Do you see the differences between men and women (their behavior, their roles, their relative places in society, their strengths and weaknesses, etc.) primarily as a matter of unchangeable biology, or do you understand them as culturally constructed? Should people work to eliminate the distinctions between men and women in society, or are such differences fundamental and essential, and therefore in need of preservation?

12

Our Battered Economy: Is the American Dream Over?

The Great Recession that plunged American hopes and bank accounts may — fingers crossed — be over, but its effects will no doubt linger for years. Our economic self-searching, for one thing, exposed what some consider an ugly truth about America at the dawn of the twenty-first century: the enormous and growing gap between rich and poor, with 10 percent of the nation owning more than half of its wealth.

Many critics have decried the wealth gap strongly, proposing various levers to even out the results. This chapter examines a central premise of an unequal society: Is it fair for some to have great wealth and others to have nothing, so long as hard work and skill can put the latter in the former's mansion eventually? President Barack Obama explored this theme in a speech on the economy late in 2013. Obama says that long ago we accepted our widening income disparity because "we were convinced that America is a place where even if you're born with nothing, with a little hard work you can improve your own situation over time and build something better to leave your kids." As long as mobility exists within the system — as long as it's possible to move up the ladder — it's fair and reasonable that some people have more than others. In "A Fundamental Threat to the American Dream," though, Obama argues that we're breaking the compromise by reducing the promise of the American Dream more and more. In an era of record profits but also increased automation of jobs and shipping them overseas, ordinary Americans are sharing less and less in their society's wealth.

Two journalists who specialize in business and economics take on the president's critique. In "The Mobility Myth," James Surowiecki argues that it isn't so much that mobility is in the same place it's been in previous generations — low. Surowiecki quotes a political scientist who, in 1962, wrote that most poor people are poor because "they made the mistake of being born to the wrong parents." Economics suggests, Surowiecki writes, that the idea that anyone can become rich with the right combination of hard work, intelligence, and luck is largely mythical. He argues that "public policy should focus on raising their standard of living, instead of raising their chances of getting rich."

Greg Beato, meanwhile, says the problem is not that we're immobile, but that monetary assessments don't give us the whole picture of a society's wealth. "The idea that Gross Domestic Product (GDP) and other economic indicators of well-being don't tell the whole story has become increasingly popular," he writes. Beato believes we should look to more intangible wealth — access to technology and education for example — to establish how upwardly mobile Americans are or can be.

One measure that seems to belie Beato's point is the increasing number of millennials who have moved back in with their parents. As many economic pundits have argued, haven't the throngs of late-twenty-somethings living rent-free with Mom and Dad proved that we've failed to provide a future for our citizens? Nonsense, writes Eve Tushnet. In "You Can Go Home Again" Tushnet makes the case that we should remove the stigma on a delayed launch in life, pointing out many of the advantages of time at home after college. In particular, she observes that this stigma is a recent development: "The belief that young adults *must* be able to live independently before they can marry is new, and it's damaging."

Whether we have opportunities to make it or not, America's massive wealth disparity is still a problem — or at least an ugly reality. In this chapter's student essay, Gray Whisnant makes a radical (though by his own admission hardly new) proposal to close the gap: a guaranteed, universal basic income. Everyone in America, he argues in "Make It Rain," should receive the basic amount needed to live. This isn't just raw socialism — Whisnant makes clear that he too believes in the American Dream — but he says this basic income, favored by past leaders as diverse as Lyndon Johnson and Richard Nixon, "would have the effect of both radically redefining citizenship and dispensing with some of the worst elements of public sector bureaucracy."

Proposals like Whisnant's have percolated in America for over 100 years. Some political and social scientists say it's precisely the progress we've made economically that stymies them. They point to the extraordinary poverty of the past in America — poverty most of us would find unimaginable. This chapter's "America Then" looks back to 1890 and the crowded, filthy, and destitute tenement houses of New York City. In the introduction to his classic text, *How the Other Half Lives,* the pioneering photojournalist Jacob Riis explores the underbelly of the industrial era city, where staying alive replaces upward mobility as the American Dream. Riis points to the corruption and apathy that has led to the awful condition of people in the tenements: "We know now that there is no way out; that the 'system' that was the evil offspring of public neglect and private greed has come to stay, a storm-centre forever of our civilization." His is a powerful reminder that there can't be justice without all of us seeking it.

Barack Obama

A Fundamental Threat to the American Dream

[From a speech delivered on December 4, 2013]

BEFORE YOU READ

Do you think economic mobility is possible today? Why or why not? Whether or not you think the American Dream currently exists, can you imagine a time when such a dream was more accessible?

WORDS TO LEARN

relentless (para. 1): unyielding (adjective)

jeopardize (para. 1): to risk (verb)

implication (para. 2): something implied, or suggested (noun)

premise (para. 3): a basis (noun)

wither (para. 13): to shrivel (verb)

profoundly (para. 14): significantly (adverb)

eloquent (para. 16): having moving or fluent expression (adjective)

begrudge (para. 17): to resent (verb)

cohesion (para. 22): the act of sticking together (noun)

compound (para. 22): to add to (verb)

cynicism (para. 23): the general belief that people are selfish and dishonest by nature (noun)

polarization (para. 23): a sharp division into opposing groups (noun)

requisite (para. 23): necessary (adjective)

[The American people] may not follow the constant back-and-forth in Washington or all the policy details, but they experience in a very personal way the relentless, decades-long trend that I want to spend some time talking about today. And that is a dangerous and growing inequality and lack of upward mobility that has jeopardized middle-class America's basic bargain — that if you work hard, you have a chance to get ahead. 1

Barack Obama is the forty-fourth President of the United States, and is the first African American to serve in that office since his inauguration on January 20, 2009. He was elected to the Illinois State Senate in 1996, and in 2004, was elected to the U.S. Senate. He received a BA in 1983 from Columbia University, and then attended Harvard University, where he was the first African American president of the Harvard Law Review.

I believe this is the defining challenge of our time: Making sure our 2
economy works for every working American. It's why I ran for President.
It was at the center of last year's campaign. It drives everything I do in
this office. And I know I've raised this issue before, and some will ask
why I raise the issue again right now. I do it because the outcomes of the
debates we're having right now — whether it's health care, or the budget,
or reforming our housing and financial systems — all these things will
have real, practical implications for every American. And I am convinced
that the decisions we make on these issues over the next few years will
determine whether or not our children will grow up in an America where
opportunity is real.

Now, the premise that we're all created equal is the opening line in 3
the American story. And while we don't promise equal outcomes, we
have strived to deliver equal opportunity — the idea that success doesn't
depend on being born into wealth or privilege, it depends on effort and
merit. And with every chapter we've added to that story, we've worked
hard to put those words into practice.

It was Abraham Lincoln, a self-described "poor man's son," who 4
started a system of land grant colleges all over this country so that any
poor man's son could go learn something new.

When farms gave way to factories, a rich man's son named Teddy 5
Roosevelt fought for an eight-hour workday, protections for workers,
and busted monopolies that kept prices high and wages low.

When millions lived in poverty, FDR fought for Social Security, and 6
insurance for the unemployed, and a minimum wage.

When millions died without health insurance, LBJ fought for Medi- 7
care and Medicaid.

Together, we forged a New Deal, declared a War on Poverty in a great 8
society. We built a ladder of opportunity to climb, and stretched out a
safety net beneath so that if we fell, it wouldn't be too far, and we could
bounce back. And as a result, America built the largest middle class the
world has ever known. And for the three decades after World War II, it
was the engine of our prosperity.

Now, we can't look at the past through rose-colored glasses. The 9
economy didn't always work for everyone. Racial discrimination locked
millions out of poverty — or out of opportunity. Women were too often
confined to a handful of often poorly paid professions. And it was only
through painstaking struggle that more women, and minorities, and
Americans with disabilities began to win the right to more fairly and fully
participate in the economy.

Nevertheless, during the post-World War II years, the economic 10
ground felt stable and secure for most Americans, and the future looked

brighter than the past. And for some, that meant following in your old man's footsteps at the local plant, and you knew that a blue-collar job would let you buy a home, and a car, maybe a vacation once in a while, health care, a reliable pension. For others, it meant going to college — in some cases, maybe the first in your family to go to college. And it meant graduating without taking on loads of debt, and being able to count on advancement through a vibrant job market.

Now, it's true that those at the top, even in those years, claimed a much 11 larger share of income than the rest: The top 10 percent consistently took home about one-third of our national income. But that kind of inequality took place in a dynamic market economy where everyone's wages and incomes were growing. And because of upward mobility, the guy on the factory floor could picture his kid running the company some day.

But starting in the late '70s, this social compact began to unravel. 12 Technology made it easier for companies to do more with less, eliminating certain job occupations. A more competitive world lets companies ship jobs anywhere. And as good manufacturing jobs automated or headed offshore, workers lost their leverage, jobs paid less and offered fewer benefits.

As values of community broke down, and competitive pressure 13 increased, businesses lobbied Washington to weaken unions and the value of the minimum wage. As a trickle-down ideology became more prominent, taxes were slashed for the wealthiest, while investments in things that make us all richer, like schools and infrastructure, were allowed to wither. And for a certain period of time, we could ignore this weakening economic foundation, in part because more families were relying on two earners as women entered the workforce. We took on more debt financed by a juiced-up housing market. But when the music stopped, and the crisis hit, millions of families were stripped of whatever cushion they had left.

> But when the music stopped, and the crisis hit, millions of families were stripped of whatever cushion they had left.

And the result is an economy that's 14 become profoundly unequal, and families that are more insecure. I'll just give you a few statistics. Since 1979, when I graduated from high school, our productivity is up by more than 90 percent, but the income of the typical family has increased by less than eight percent. Since 1979, our economy has more than doubled in size, but most of that growth has flowed to a fortunate few.

The top 10 percent no longer takes in one-third of our income — it 15 now takes half. Whereas in the past, the average CEO made about 20 to 30 times the income of the average worker, today's CEO now makes

273 times more. And meanwhile, a family in the top 1 percent has a net worth 288 times higher than the typical family, which is a record for this country.

So the basic bargain at the heart of our economy has frayed. In fact, this trend towards growing inequality is not unique to America's market economy. Across the developed world, inequality has increased. Some of you may have seen just last week, the Pope himself spoke about this at eloquent length. "How can it be," he wrote, "that it is not a news item when an elderly homeless person dies of exposure, but it is news when the stock market loses two points?"

But this increasing inequality is most pronounced in our country, and it challenges the very essence of who we are as a people. Understand we've never begrudged success in America. We aspire to it. We admire folks who start new businesses, create jobs, and invent the products that enrich our lives. And we expect them to be rewarded handsomely for it. In fact, we've often accepted more income inequality than many other nations for one big reason — because we were convinced that America is a place where even if you're born with nothing, with a little hard work you can improve your own situation over time and build something better to leave your kids. As Lincoln once said, "While we do not propose any war upon capital, we do wish to allow the humblest man an equal chance to get rich with everybody else."

The problem is that alongside increased inequality, we've seen diminished levels of upward mobility in recent years. A child born in the top 20 percent has about a 2-in-3 chance of staying at or near the top. A child born into the bottom 20 percent has a less than 1-in-20 shot at making it to the top. He's 10 times likelier to stay where he is. In fact, statistics show not only that our levels of income inequality rank near countries like Jamaica and Argentina, but that it is harder today for a child born here in America to improve her station in life than it is for children in most of our wealthy allies — countries like Canada or Germany or France. They have greater mobility than we do, not less.

The idea that so many children are born into poverty in the wealthiest nation on Earth is heartbreaking enough. But the idea that a child may never be able to escape that poverty because she lacks a decent education or health care, or a community that views her future as their own, that should offend all of us and it should compel us to action. We are a better country than this.

So let me repeat: The combined trends of increased inequality and decreasing mobility pose a fundamental threat to the American Dream, our way of life, and what we stand for around the globe. And it is not simply a moral claim that I'm making here. There are practical consequences to rising inequality and reduced mobility.

For one thing, these trends are bad for our economy. One study finds 21
that growth is more fragile and recessions are more frequent in countries
with greater inequality. And that makes sense. When families have less
to spend, that means businesses have fewer customers, and households
rack up greater mortgage and credit card debt; meanwhile, concentrated
wealth at the top is less likely to result in the kind of broadly based consumer spending that drives our economy, and together with lax regulation, may contribute to risky speculative bubbles.

And rising inequality and declining mobility are also bad for our 22
families and social cohesion — not just because we tend to trust our
institutions less, but studies show we actually tend to trust each other
less when there's greater inequality. And greater inequality is associated
with less mobility between generations. That means it's not just temporary; the effects last. It creates a vicious cycle. For example, by the time
she turns three years old, a child born into a low-income home hears
30 million fewer words than a child from a well-off family, which means
by the time she starts school she's already behind, and that deficit can
compound itself over time.

And finally, rising inequality and declining mobility are bad for our 23
democracy. Ordinary folks can't write massive campaign checks or hire
high-priced lobbyists and lawyers to secure policies that tilt the playing
field in their favor at everyone else's expense. And so people get the bad
taste that the system is rigged, and that increases cynicism and polarization, and it decreases the political participation that is a requisite part of
our system of self-government.

VOCABULARY/USING A DICTIONARY

1. From what language does the word *merit* (para. 3) derive?
2. What does it mean if someone is *self-described* (para. 4) as something?
3. What is the opposite of *lax* (para. 21)?

RESPONDING TO WORDS IN CONTEXT

1. What is a *trend* (para. 1)? What sort of trend is President Obama talking about in this essay?
2. What is an *opportunity*? What sort of opportunities is Obama referring to in paragraphs 2 and 3?
3. Obama says technology had a hand in *"eliminating* certain job occupations" (para. 12). What does that mean?

DISCUSSING MAIN POINT AND MEANING

1. According to Obama, what actions helped people in this country achieve prosperity? Who put the actions in place? How did these acts help people?

2. When did prosperity begin to falter in this country? Why?
3. Why is having economic mobility important in our country, according to Obama?

EXAMINING SENTENCES, PARAGRAPHS, AND ORGANIZATION

1. Can you point to passages in the president's speech that show an awareness of the cadence of the spoken word? Is it used effectively?
2. What point is being made by Obama when he structures his sentences so that one sentence about "Abraham Lincoln, a self-described 'poor man's son'" is followed by one about "a rich man's son named Teddy Roosevelt" (paras. 4 and 5)?
3. Look closely at this passage: "We took on more debt financed by a juiced-up housing market. But when the music stopped, and the crisis hit, millions of families were stripped of whatever cushion they had left" (para. 13). What sort of language is being used in these sentences?

THINKING CRITICALLY

1. What was your answer to question 1 in Examining Sentences, Paragraphs, and Organization? Do you think cadence is important to Obama? Why might it be important in a speech?
2. Why do many Americans believe that economic opportunity is real in this country, even if the current economy doesn't bear that out?
3. Do you believe the current economy has "become profoundly unequal"? Where do you see this most in the economic lives of the country?

WRITING ACTIVITIES

1. Obama quotes two influential and apparently moral personages in this essay: Lincoln and the pope. Lincoln, who was president of the United States, is quoted as speaking for the people, saying: "While we do not propose any war upon capital, we do wish to allow the humblest man an equal chance to get rich with everybody else." The pope is quoted as saying, "How can it be that it is not a news item when an elderly homeless person dies of exposure, but it is news when the stock market loses two points?" Pick one of these quotations and write a response to it.
2. Obama acknowledges, despite the influence of the American Dream, "that racial discrimination locked millions out of poverty — or out of opportunity. Women were too often confined to a handful of often poorly paid professions. And it was only through painstaking struggle that more women, and minorities, and Americans with disabilities began to win the right to more fairly and fully participate in the economy." Write an essay that responds to Obama's picture of the American Dream in the voice of one of those who have been left out of it.

3. Obama lists a number of presidential acts that helped many people achieve the American Dream of prosperity or at least helped them avoid the trap of poverty. Choose one of the many resolutions, deals, or protections these presidents made a priority, and write a brief research paper that outlines why it was of particular importance to that president and to the country, any significant details, and the benefits it conferred.

James Surowiecki

The Mobility Myth

[*The New Yorker,* March 3, 2014]

BEFORE YOU READ

Do we have less social mobility in the United States than before, or is it that economic opportunity itself is shrinking? What can we learn from examples of upward mobility and income distribution in the United States in the past?

WORDS TO LEARN

imprint (para. 3): a mark (noun)
meritocratic (para. 3): of a system
   where talented people move ahead
   based on achievement (adjective)

untethered (para. 3): released; unfas-
   tened (adjective)
delude (para. 5): to deceive (verb)
spectrum (para. 5): a range of ideas or
   things (noun)

Since at least the days of Horatio Alger,[1] a cornerstone of American thinking has been the hope of social mobility — the idea that, as Lawrence Samuel put it in a history of the American dream, anyone can, "through dedication and with a can-do spirit, climb the ladder

1

---

[1] Horatio Alger (para. 1): a nineteenth-century American author whose themes often centered on impoverished boys who rose to the middle class through hard work.

James Surowiecki is a journalist and staff writer at the New Yorker, *where his business column, "The Financial Page," appears regularly. His writing has also appeared in the* New York Times, *the* Wall Street Journal, *the* Motley Fool, Foreign Affairs, Artforum, Wired, *and* Slate, *among others.*

of success." In recent years, though, plenty of Americans have come to believe that, as President Obama said in his State of the Union address, "upward mobility has stalled." So it was a surprise recently when a team of economists from Harvard and Berkeley released a comprehensive study showing that mobility in the U.S. hasn't fallen over the past twenty years at all. "Like many people, we thought mobility would have declined," Raj Chetty, one of the researchers on the project, told me. "But what we found was that kids born in the early nineteen-nineties had the same chances of climbing up the income ladder as kids born in the seventies." Even more striking, when the researchers looked at studies tracking economic mobility going back to the fifties, they concluded that it had remained relatively stable over the entire second half of the twentieth century.

That sounds like good news, but there's a catch: there wasn't that much mobility to begin with. According to Chetty, "Social mobility is low and has been for at least thirty or forty years." This is most obvious when you look at the prospects of the poor. Seventy per cent of people born into the bottom quintile of income distribution never make it into the middle class, and fewer than ten per cent get into the top quintile. Forty per cent are still poor as adults. What the political scientist Michael Harrington wrote back in 1962 is still true: most people who are poor are poor because "they made the mistake of being born to the wrong parents." The middle class isn't all that mobile, either: only twenty per cent of people born into the middle quintile ever make it into the top one. And although we think of U.S. society as archetypally open, mobility here is lower than in most European countries.   2

This wasn't always the case. As the economist Joseph P. Ferrie has shown, in the late nineteenth century U.S. society was far more mobile than Great Britain's — a child in the U.S. was much more likely to move into a higher-class profession than that of his father — and much more mobile than it became later. It was possible for Andrew Carnegie to start as a bobbin boy in a cotton factory at a dollar-twenty a week and end up one of the world's richest men. This legacy left a deep imprint on American culture. The sociologist Werner Sombart noted in 1906 that the average American worker felt he had a good chance of rising out of his class. That feeling has persisted: Americans are less concerned than Europeans about inequality and more confident that society is meritocratic. The problem is that, over time, the American dream has become increasingly untethered from American reality.   3

Both political parties say that they want to change this. And Chetty and his colleagues have shown in another study that some places in the U.S., like Salt Lake City and San Jose, have mobility rates as high   4 as anywhere else in the developed world. There are also places in the U.S., like Mississippi, where mobility is lower than anywhere else in the developed world. So if you could figure out exactly what Salt Lake City is doing right, and apply that lesson elsewhere, you might be able to get people movin' on up again.

Increasing economic opportunity is a noble goal, and worth invest-   5
ing in. But we shouldn't delude ourselves into thinking that more social mobility will cure what ails the U.S. economy. For a start, even societies that are held to have "high" mobility aren't all *that* mobile. In San Jose, just thirteen per cent of people in the bottom quintile make it to the top. Sweden has one of the highest rates of social mobility in the world, but a 2012 study found that the top of the income spectrum is dominated by people whose parents were rich. A new book, "The Son Also Rises," by the economic historian Gregory Clark, suggests that dramatic social mobility has always been the exception rather than the rule. Clark examines a host of societies over the past seven hundred years and finds that the makeup of a given country's economic élite has remained surprisingly stable.

More important, in any capitalist society most people are bound to   6
be part of the middle and working classes; public policy should focus on raising their standard of living, instead of raising their chances of getting rich. What made the U.S. economy so remarkable for most of the twentieth century was the fact that, even if working people never moved into a different class, over time they saw their standard of living rise sharply. Between the late nineteen-forties and the early nineteen-seventies, median household income in the U.S. doubled. That's what has really changed in the past forty years. The economy is growing more slowly than it did in the postwar era, and average workers' share

> Public policy should focus on raising their standard of living, instead of raising their chances of getting rich.

of the pie has been shrinking. It's no surprise that people in Washington prefer to talk about mobility rather than about this basic reality. Raising living standards for ordinary workers is hard: you need to either get wages growing or talk about things that scare politicians, like "redistribution" and "taxes." But making it easier for some Americans to move up the economic ladder is no great triumph if most can barely hold on.

VOCABULARY/USING A DICTIONARY

1. How might you guess at the definition of the word *quintile* (para. 2) if you are familiar with the Latin root *quintus*?

2. What does it mean to be *elite* (para. 5)? What might its opposite be?
3. What is a *cornerstone* (para. 1)?

RESPONDING TO WORDS IN CONTEXT

1. What is meant by "the *prospects* of the poor" (para. 2)?
2. The essay mentions that Andrew Carnegie began work as a *bobbin boy* (para. 3). What is a *bobbin*? What do you think his job might have been?
3. If dramatic social mobility has always been the *exception* (para. 5) rather than the rule, how common is it?

DISCUSSING MAIN POINT AND MEANING

1. What is "social mobility"? What does Surowiecki feel is more important than social mobility?
2. What is the great fallacy about social mobility that Surowiecki wants to expose? What is his argument? Is this surprising?
3. What did Carnegie's success lead other Americans to believe and want?

EXAMINING SENTENCES, PARAGRAPHS, AND ORGANIZATION

1. How does Surowiecki create the back-and-forth movement of his argument, looking at one idea, and then suggesting that another possibility might be true? Look for examples of this movement and cite them.
2. The middle paragraphs, 4 and 5, include information on specific states and their experience of mobility and the economy. What does the inclusion of the experience of these specific states add to the essay?
3. How has the focus of the essay changed by the last paragraph? What was the focus in the beginning? What is the focus at the end?

THINKING CRITICALLY

1. Is social mobility important to our society? Why? In what society might it not be important?
2. What difficulties did immigrants like Carnegie face when they came to America? What difficulties do they face today? Do you think these difficulties motivate or discourage immigrants (then and now)?
3. Surowieki writes, "Over time, the American dream has become increasingly untethered from American reality" (para. 3). What is your experience of the American Dream? Do you think it still exists? Did it ever exist?

WRITING ACTIVITIES

1. Look at the postwar era referenced in this essay (para. 6). What happened to U.S. standards of living in the postwar era? Describe the lifestyles Americans experienced at this time and what contributed to these lifestyles.

2. How do the recent Occupy movements connect to the idea of social mobility? To the idea that "average workers' share of the pie has been shrinking" (para. 6)? Compare Surowiecki's argument to something you learn about the Occupy movements, and write a paper that discusses aspects of both.

3. The immigrant Carnegie was one of the great financial success stories of the Industrial Age, and some might say the poster child for American social mobility. Write a brief history of the Industrial Revolution in America with a focus on the life of Carnegie.

Greg Beato

The Myth of Economic Immobility

[*Reason*, April 10, 2014]

BEFORE YOU READ

Has economic mobility decreased, increased, or stayed stable among the last few generations? How else can we measure the country's economic well-being?

WORDS TO LEARN

decry (para. 2): to denounce (verb)
negate (para. 7): to nullify (verb)
cosmos (para. 9): the universe as a harmonious system (noun)
nomads (para. 11): people who move from place to place (noun)
opaque (para. 11): not transparent (adjective)
holistic (para. 13): having to do with properties over and above the sum of their parts (adjective)

generate (para. 15): to cause to be (verb)
ecosystem (para. 16): a system of organisms with their environment (noun)
accrue (para. 18): to be added (verb)
fervent (para. 18): ardent (adjective)
potentates (para. 18): people with great power (noun)

Greg Beato is a contributing editor of Reason *magazine. In addition, he has written for dozens of publications, including* SPIN, Wired, Business 2.0, *and the* San Francisco Chronicle.

I n early December, President Barack Obama delivered a major speech 1
at a packed $27 million arts-and-culture complex in one of the poor-
est neighborhoods in the nation's capital. His subject? The American
Dream, whose future, to hear the president tell it, was even more uncertain than that of Popcorn and Caramel, the two Thanksgiving turkeys
he'd pardoned six days earlier.

Addressing an audience that included members of Congress, the 2
mayor of D.C., and various other Beltway bigwigs, Obama decried
the nation's "diminished levels of upward mobility in recent years." As the
president continued — the speech lasted 49 minutes — he used a wide
variety of adjectives to illustrate the problem. Mobility was "decreasing,"
"reduced," and "declining." For the wonks in the audience, "less mobility
between generations" got a shout-out as well.

The president is hardly alone in considering this an urgent American 3
problem. In November 2013, Gallup found that only 52 percent of the
1,000 adults it surveyed believed that there is "plenty of opportunity" to
get ahead in today's United States. In 2011, that number was 57 percent;
in 1998, it was a whopping 81 percent. "Many political leaders and other
observers believe economic mobility in the United States is declining,"
the Gallup researchers noted. "It would appear that a significant portion
of the population agrees."

Yet a month after Obama's speech, two Harvard economists, two 4
Berkeley economists, and one U.S. Treasury economist failed to find
decreasing economic mobility in a working paper they jointly published
via the nonpartisan National Bureau of Economic Research.

"Contrary to the popular perception," the authors wrote, "we find 5
that percentile rank-based measures of intergenerational mobility have
remained extremely stable for the 1971-1993 birth cohorts." According
to their research, a child born into the bottom quintile of income distribution in 1971 had an 8.4 percent chance to reach the top quintile as an
adult. For a child born in 1986, that chance had risen to 9 percent. If anything, they concluded, "mobility may have increased slightly in recent
cohorts."

To anyone who has been following the work of the Pew Charitable 6
Trust's Economic Mobility Project (EMP), this conventional wisdom-
shattering conclusion wasn't particularly surprising. "The evidence
shows that patterns in Americans' income changes have been similar
[from 1967 through 2004] and that the economy propelled most Americans upward, setting them back temporarily, if at all," the EMP concluded in 2009. "Eighty-four percent of Americans have higher family
incomes than their parents had at the same age, and across all levels of

the income distribution, this generation is doing better than the one that came before it," the project reported in 2012.

The fact that America is as economically mobile now as it was in the days when the top marginal federal income tax rate was 70 percent doesn't mean that the country is as economically mobile as it can or should be. Nor does the extremely stable nature of U.S. economic mobility negate the fact that individuals on the high end of the income spectrum are getting richer faster than anyone else. 7

But Obama's widely shared misconception also misses the greater cultural context. Economic mobility is not the sole measure of national well-being or progress. It's not even the sole measure of mobility. 8

> Economic mobility is not the sole measure of national well-being or progress. It's not even the sole measure of mobility.

In the American cosmos, mobility is indeed important, because mobility is freedom of action, the way that we exercise our ability to plot our own courses, to choose this path over that path, to reverse direction 9
when need be, to associate with whomever we want wherever we want. Along with economic mobility there is *cultural* mobility that provides entrance to various institutions, goods, services, and practices. *Social* mobility gives us access to specific people and groups.

And of course there's plain old physical mobility. According to the Bureau of Transportation Statistics, America added approximately 1.1 million miles of paved roads between 1970 and 2008. In that same time frame, the Interstate Highway System expanded from 30,000 miles to 47,182 miles. In 1990, there were 17.6 million passenger departures from U.S. airports. By 2006, that number had risen to 31.4 million. 10

But while our capacity for physical mobility has improved dramatically over the last half-century, physical mobility is actually less important than ever. FedEx, UPS, Amazon Prime, and a wide array of other delivery services bring the physical world to our doorsteps. The Internet has turned us all into information nomads, able to traverse vast oceans of data in a single evening. Social networks are providing detailed maps of power and influence across formerly opaque realms of American life, making it easier for anyone to navigate its myriad industries, institutions, subcultures, and demographics. 11

What's the value of being able to track Alec Baldwin's meltdowns in real-time? Of choosing from 300 different models when you need a new coffeemaker, or having every syllabus of every class that MIT offers in one convenient directory? Today, most Americans have access to resources that were once inconceivable, and that access lets us cover 12 more cultural and social ground than humans had ever previously been able to manage.

In a matter of decades, our mobility has increased by orders of magnitude, but the increases we enjoy are often hard to measure, at least using standard econometrics. The idea that Gross Domestic Product (GDP) and other economic indicators of well-being don't tell the whole story has become increasingly popular. New tools for assessment — like Bhutan's Gross National Happiness Index, or the Genuine Progress Indicator — are being championed as ways to present more accurate and holistic portraits of human progress. 13

For one thing, GDP does a poor job of capturing the negative externalities of increased industrial output and commerce. It says nothing about the Amazon rainforests that are destroyed to ensure a steady supply of Big Macs, or the individual misery that comes along with higher gaming industry revenues. 14

But it isn't only the negative effects that aren't being sufficiently measured by GDP. In the last 20 years especially, the market has begun to generate an increasing number of positive effects that go uncounted by traditional economic measures. GDP can assess Google's ability to sell ads, but it has never put a dollar amount to the collective gain in well-being that results from YouTube's ever-growing stockpile of cat videos. It makes no attempt to figure out how much happier we all are now that we can read *The New York Times* for free or pre-qualify potential soulmates by height, educational status, alcohol consumption patterns, and smartphone operating system preferences. 15

Out of technology and global commerce a kind of Commons 2.0 has arisen, a vast, market-driven ecosystem where an astounding proliferation of information resources, services, and even hard goods are free or nearly free, improving our lives in mostly uncharted but increasingly substantive ways. Surely it is a mark of genuine progress that we no longer have to buy a $50 classified ad to sell a $40 couch. Surely we are both economically and psychologically richer because we can Skype with friends and family in distant continents for hours on end without racking up four-figure phone bills. 16

Perhaps what's most encouraging about America's mobility renaissance is how widely distributed it is. You don't have to negotiate your way past a series of velvet ropes to catch Donald Trump's eye on Twitter. Facebook didn't stay a privilege of the Harvard elite for long — 128 million Americans use it on a daily basis. According to the Pew Internet & American Life Project, 56 percent of American adults now have smartphones. 17

And yet in the midst of all these developments, our reigning preoccupation is a false narrative about dwindling economic mobility. 18

Apparently the breakthroughs and benefits accrue in such dizzying but routine fashion now that even our most fervent potentates of hope and change have trouble keeping track of our progress.

VOCABULARY/USING A DICTIONARY

1. What is a *wonk* (para. 2)?
2. What does the prefix *inter-* in *intergenerational* (para. 5) indicate?
3. What part of speech is *myriad* (para. 11)? What does it mean?

RESPONDING TO WORDS IN CONTEXT

1. What is a *shout-out* (para. 2)?
2. If someone is part of a birth *cohort* (para. 5), what does that mean?
3. Where has the *proliferation* (para. 16) of information resources, etc. happened in the United States?

DISCUSSING MAIN POINT AND MEANING

1. What does Beato say President Obama got wrong in a recent major speech?
2. What other possible factors are available to measure a county's mobility?
3. What everyday methods of communication does Beato invoke as being part of a "mobility renaissance" (para. 17) for American citizens?

EXAMINING SENTENCES, PARAGRAPHS, AND ORGANIZATION

1. How does Beato create contrast in this sentence: "In early December, President Barack Obama delivered a major speech at a packed $27 million arts-and-culture complex in one of the poorest neighborhoods in the nation's capital"?
2. Although discussing economics, a weighty subject, Beato uses casual diction in his second paragraph. Can you point to the words he uses that give his writing a casual feel?
3. Beato moves away from economic mobility in the essay into other ideas. Where does that change take place? How does he segue into the other ideas, and what connects them?

THINKING CRITICALLY

1. Do you think that new assessments of well-being (like Bhutan's Gross National Happiness Index or the Genuine Progress Indicator) are valid ways to measure progress?
2. Is there a way in which Obama could be correct *and* Beato could be correct in their assessments about the country's economic mobility? How can this be so?
3. Beato talks about Twitter, Facebook, and ownership of smartphones as being part of a "mobility renaissance." Do those things indicate upward mobility, downward mobility, or some other kind of mobility?

WRITING ACTIVITIES

1. Beato's paper is about economic mobility, but it's also about other types of mobility. Write about cultural and social mobility and the role it plays in your life. Do you also foresee a time when you will be economically mobile?

2. Write a short essay that responds to Beato's argument, in particular whether you associate economic mobility with the other forms of mobility he discusses in this paper.

3. More than half of this essay is about types of mobility that aren't strictly what we think of when we think of *economic* mobility. Write a definition of economic mobility, and then offer some alternate titles for the essay that move beyond "the myth of *economic* mobility" and include some of the other ideas brought out in the essay.

Eve Tushnet

You *Can* Go Home Again

[*The Weekly Standard,* September 2, 2013]

BEFORE YOU READ
Why might a grown child go home to live with his or her parents? Are the reasons only negative?

WORDS TO LEARN
gentrified (para. 1): improved to appeal to upper and middle classes (adjective)

cynicism (para. 2): a way of thinking that is inherently distrustful or scornful (noun)

exemplify (para. 13): to show by example (verb)

adaptive (para. 13): able to adapt (adjective)

A few years ago I was getting a ride home from a party with a guy in his early twenties. I lived in a gentrified neighborhood I could no longer pretend to afford, and he lived, it emerged, with his parents. "Good for you," I said. "I think that's great."

Eve Tushnet is an opinion writer and journalist. Her work has appeared in a variety of publications, including Commonwealth *and* The Weekly Standard.

We hit a stoplight and he turned to look at me. "Do you?" he asked, 2
with a sudden edge of cynicism in his voice. "Do you *really*?" I could hear
what he was thinking: *I guess you're trying to be nice or whatever, but nobody
thinks it's "great" when a guy — who should be a man — lives with Mommy
and Daddy.* One of us was making a foolish choice that was destroying
her savings, but the more frugal one bore the weight of societal stigma.

The proportion of young adults (aged 18 to 31) who live with one or 3
both parents stayed basically the same between 1968, the earliest year for
which we have data, and 2007. What proportion was normal for those
four decades? About a third, 32 percent. A recent Pew Research report
found that in 2012 that number had risen to 36 percent, a noticeable
increase but not necessarily a sign of social crisis — especially not when
you consider that college students living in dorms are still counted as "living with their parents," and college enrollment has been rising since 2007
as well. More men than women live with Mom and/or Dad, which might
seem like an effect of the ongoing "mancession" — in which men's labor-
force participation has plummeted — but men have been more likely to
live with their parents as adults since at least 1968, partly because men
typically marry later than women. In fact, the gender gap was greater in
1968 than today.

Americans believe that adults who live with their parents have "failed 4
to launch"; man-boys spend their days playing World of Warcraft while
Mom does their laundry. This narrative is persuasive in part because
many of the trends driving the increase in "returning to the nest" are
bad, so returning is correlated with bad things, like unemployment and
underemployment. If you see an unemployed young adult living with
his parents, maybe he's living with them because he's unemployed — or
maybe his unemployment and his living situation have a common cause,
which is that he's an immature loser.

And living with your parents can make it harder to grow up. There's 5
less pressure to take responsibility for yourself, and pressure often forces
us past what we believe to be our limitations. A 2008 study interviewing young adults who lived at home found that few contributed financially to the household or did chores. One young woman explained, "I
was excited to have my mother to cook for me, and always having a full
refrigerator."

These attitudes are by no means universal (and the study itself wasn't 6
intended to be representative), as some young adults paid rent and utili-
ties even against their parents' wishes. And part of the problem in stig-
matizing "returning to the nest" is that the category lumps together a
huge range of circumstances. A 2011 study found that older "parental
co-residers" (those who live with their parents after age 27) were like-

lier to be disabled, and so were their parents; the parents were also more likely to be single — never married, divorced, or widowed. This paints a different picture, of families with limited resources banding together to get through tough times.

Given the powerful trends of rising part-time work and job instability, rising university attendance, and delayed or disappearing marriage, I don't think there's much reason to believe that the modest rise in living at home is the result of some sudden onslaught of millennial laziness or unwillingness to start at the bottom of the career ladder.

In fact, starting your adult life in your parents' home was not historically stigmatized, precisely because it offered young adults an oasis of stability in a chaotic economy. The economic journalist Megan McArdle writes,

> I don't think there's much reason to believe that the modest rise in living at home is the result of some sudden onslaught of millennial laziness or unwillingness to start at the bottom of the career ladder.

7

8

My grandfather worked as a grocery boy until he was 26, in the depths of the Great Depression. For six years, he supported a wife on that salary — and no, it's not because You Used To Be Able To Support A Family On A Grocery Boy's Wages Until These Republicans Ruined Everything. He and my grandmother moved into a room in his parents' home, cut a hole through the wall for their stovepipe and set up housekeeping. They got married on Thanksgiving, because that was the only day he could get off.

9

Two huge differences between the Depression era and today leap out from McArdle's account. One is the sense that what her grandparents did was normal, not shameful. But the other is that they did it as young marrieds. This is perhaps the biggest negative effect of living at home these days: It postpones marriage and, in many cases, childbearing. Today, young adults believe that they can't get married — that it's *wrong* to get married — before they've achieved economic independence. For reasons that can be crudely summarized as "terror of divorce," young adults believe that it's only morally acceptable to get married once you've undergone an extensive period of finding yourself and attaining financial stability.

10

The belief that young adults *must* be able to live independently before they can marry is new, and it's damaging. At the pregnancy center where I volunteer, about half of the women intend to marry their

11

children's father eventually. What are they waiting for? A steady job, an escape from welfare and charity, a sense of financial solid ground. But if a woman names one specific goal she must attain before she can marry, 9 times out of 10 that goal is an apartment of her own: moving out from under Mom's roof. So she puts her name on the years-long waiting list for Section 8 subsidized housing, and she applies for yet another part-time job, and she goes back to community college, and she hopes that her relationship with her baby's father will survive. Without marriage, it usually doesn't.

Almost every form of dependence is stigmatized in America's individ-   12
ualist culture. This particular form of dependence has also been redefined to be as individualist as possible (you can't marry *and* you're not expected to care for your parents) and then shamed both for its dependence and for its narcissism. But the stigma hasn't worked. Everybody doing it feels it to be shameful, yet the shame has not made us do it less. Expecting and then *honoring* mutual dependence might be a better option.

Shortly after that awkward car ride, I finally left my fancied neigh-   13
borhood. I was older than most "boomerang kids," but like many of them I was single and dealing with personal problems — I'd gotten sober a few months earlier and desperately wanted a break from the surroundings in which I'd done my worst drinking — and I fled back home seeking both financial and emotional relief. I paid no rent and did exactly one chore, cleaning the catbox, so I *am* the problem. But I also exemplified "returning to the nest" as a useful adaptive strategy: Six months later I moved out, much improved in both spirit and bank account. This is one way the boomerang story ends well. But it would be an equally happy ending, although more radically challenging to American norms of inde-pendence, if I had remained at home and begun to make real household contributions of money and care.

VOCABULARY/USING A DICTIONARY
1. What happens when something is *correlated* (para. 4)?
2. What is an *oasis* (para. 8)? Where might one find a literal oasis?
3. Describe what something is like if it is *chaotic* (para. 8).

RESPONDING TO WORDS IN CONTEXT
1. What sort of person is a *frugal* (para. 2) one?
2. If a summary is *crude* (para. 10), what does that mean?
3. When Tushnet writes that remaining at home to make household contribu-tions would be *radically* (para. 13) challenging to American views on inde-pendence, how challenging is the idea?

DISCUSSING MAIN POINT AND MEANING

1. What does Tushnet mean when she says there is a stigma connected to living with one's parents?

2. What are some of the reasons that young adults are returning to live at home these days?

3. How might you define *America's individualist culture* (para. 12), given the points Tushnet discusses in her essay?

EXAMINING SENTENCES, PARAGRAPHS, AND ORGANIZATION

1. Look at Tushnet's second paragraph and her use of italics in the story about the man who drove her home. Is her use of italics important to the essay? In what way?

2. Does Tushnet create a contrast between the two live-at-home stories she presents in her essay? Explain the contrast and how it is constructed in the essay.

3. Does Tushnet's personal story find completion in the ending? How?

THINKING CRITICALLY

1. If you decided to live at home, what savings do you think you might find for yourself? If you already live at home, what savings have you benefited from?

2. Should parents and grown children come to an understanding before living together again? What kinds of agreements or arrangements would be beneficial or possible?

3. Do you think a person needs to live independently before marriage? Why or why not?

WRITING ACTIVITIES

1. Write an essay that looks at the hardships faced by people in the Great Depression. What ingenious or extreme approaches did some people use when they had so little? What attitudes did that kind of hardship foster in people?

2. What other stigmas are attached to dependence in the United States? What stigmas are attached to welfare, for example, and how do you feel about that? What about financial aid (dependence on one's school for the funds to attend)? Should we rethink why these resources are in place?

3. Look up the term *boomerang kids*. Write a report that explains how boomerang kids were born from the Great Recession. Do you think that boomerang kids are becoming more the norm instead of the exception?

Gray Whisnant (student essay)

Make It Rain: Why the Nation Needs a Universal Basic Income

[*Cavalier Daily,* University of Virginia, January 15, 2014]

BEFORE YOU READ

Do you think Americans should be guaranteed a universal basic income? What problems would that solve? Would any problems be created?

WORDS TO LEARN

estimate (para. 1): to form an approximate opinion of something (verb)

stipend (para. 3): a periodic payment or allowance (noun)

dire (para. 4): terrible (adjective)

duplicative (para. 6): repetitive (adjective)

perverse (para. 6): contrary (adjective)

demonize (para. 7): to make demonlike (verb)

I n his 1964 "Great Society" speech delivered in Ann Arbor, Lyndon   1
B. Johnson launched a series of initiatives that would come to define American politics for the next half-century. Programs such as Medicare, Medicaid, food stamps and Head Start dramatically improved the standard of living for millions of Americans. Between 1967 and 2012, the Supplemental Poverty Measure — a method of evaluating poverty that takes into account government programs that assist low-income families not included in the official poverty measure — fell from 26 percent to 16 percent. The Census Bureau estimates that antipoverty programs kept 41 million people, among them 9 million children, out of poverty in 2012 and that the poverty rate would be double what it is without the safety net.

Despite these achievements, the War on Poverty hasn't been an   2
unqualified success. In response to a conservative backlash, Ronald Reagan and Bill Clinton pared back much of the welfare state Lyndon Johnson helped build, and today around 47 million Americans live below the poverty line. In order to eliminate most of the poverty in this country, policymakers must adopt a new strategy that takes our complicated patchwork of programs and transforms them into a more coordinated and comprehensive approach.

Gray Whisnant is a student at the University of Virginia.

The cornerstone of any new approach ought to be a universal basic income (UBI). The UBI has been endorsed by everyone from Martin Luther King Jr. to conservative luminaries like Milton Friedman and F. A. Hayek, would have the effect of both radically redefining citizenship and dispensing with some of the worst elements of public sector bureaucracy. With the government sending a check for a poverty-level income to every adult American, the incentive structures of safety net programs that sometimes punish job-seekers would be eliminated. The poor would no longer have to weigh whether or not signing up for a job is worth it because of the loss of crucial benefits; the UBI stipend would remain the same regardless.

> With the government sending a check for a poverty-level income to every adult American, the incentive structures of safety net programs that sometimes punish job-seekers would be eliminated.

3

As a consequence, the labor market would be redefined to become truly voluntary. People would no longer be forced into undesirable jobs because of dire financial straits. With this new shift of bargaining power to workers, corporations would have to make those jobs more attractive by offering higher benefits and wages that better reflect social value produced by those jobs. It's easy to imagine the salaries of sanitation workers, for instance, going up dramatically to attract workers to the positions.

4

Such a system would also empower working-class women. Childcare workers and housekeepers today, whose occupations have traditionally been seen as "women's work," are some of the lowest-paid and most vulnerable participants in the labor market. A universal basic income would send the message that society values their work and would provide them with negotiating power they previously lacked. As such, poor minority women, especially single mothers, would perhaps be the biggest winners of a UBI, and the gender wage gap would collapse.

5

Framed another way, the UBI can be seen as a small-government vative reform. The current system of means-tested welfare programs is coordinated, duplicative and too often distorts market incentives. Upon enacting a universal basic income, we would see food stamps, WIC, heating assistance, cash welfare, public housing vouchers, unemployment benefits and numerous other smaller programs written out of existence, with their purposes being superseded by one simple yearly payment. A post-UBI federal government would be streamlined, more efficient and much easier to manage and monitor.

6

The government could still provide health insurance through Medicare and pensions and disability benefits through Social Security, but other means-tested programs would be eliminated along with the perverse incentives that keep too many people in poverty.

Beyond making employers offer more worthwhile work, protecting 7 working poor women, slashing poverty rates and streamlining the federal government, a universal income would remake our society by dramatically changing attitudes toward certain types of work and certain groups of people. It would increase social solidarity by making the poor harder to demonize for getting a benefit the middle class doesn't, because everyone from hedge fund managers to the homeless would receive the same amount. It would encourage creative work by spurring people to quit their dead-end jobs and pursue the musical or writing career they've always dreamed of. It would eliminate the worry about the negative side effects of automatization by allowing businesses to pursue technological efficiency without their employees' livelihoods being jeopardized. As such, the UBI is perhaps the only welfare reform that is capable of producing results that the left, right and center would appreciate.

There's no doubt that guaranteeing every American a basic standard 8 of living would have a price tag. Though proposals that have ranged from setting the amount anywhere between $10,000 and $35,000 per household, there are several funding sources that could be adjusted accordingly to pay for the plan. The federal government spends about $212 billion on social welfare annually, and that money would largely disappear with the arrival of the UBI. Cuts in the $729 billion military budget could also redirect revenue away from defense contractors and to all Americans. Beyond that, new revenue would certainly be needed, such as through a financial speculation and/or a value added tax, but the sum required isn't impossible to reach.

In 1969, no less a radical leftist as Richard Nixon proposed a guar- 9 anteed income of $10,160 in today's dollars with his Family Assistance Plan as a conservative spin on the War on Poverty. Though the Republican Party and the country have changed a great deal since 1969, a universal basic income should become the end goal for antipoverty efforts on all sides of the political spectrum. As Lyndon Johnson said of the War on Poverty, "The richest nation on Earth can afford to win it. We can not afford to lose it."

VOCABULARY/USING A DICTIONARY

1. What is the root of the word *luminaries* (para. 3)?
2. What does *solidarity* (para. 7) mean?
3. When is someone paid if he or she is paid *annually* (para. 8)?

RESPONDING TO WORDS IN CONTEXT
1. How is poverty *eliminated* (para. 2) by a political program?
2. What does it mean to *pare* (para. 2) back much of the welfare state? What is usually *pared* back?
3. When Whisnant speaks of workers' *negotiating power* (para. 5), what does he mean?

DISCUSSING MAIN POINT AND MEANING
1. How would a universal basic income help eliminate poverty, according to Whisnant?
2. What government programs would no longer be necessary with Whisnant's proposed changes?
3. What historical precedent is mentioned for the universal basic income?

EXAMINING SENTENCES, PARAGRAPHS, AND ORGANIZATION
1. Why does Whisnant begin his essay the way he does? What is important about his beginning?
2. After his introductory paragraph, how does Whisnant introduce what he wants to talk about?
3. How does Whisnant organize his information so that his ending is evocative of his beginning?

THINKING CRITICALLY
1. What would a reasonable universal basic income amount be? Why?
2. Are you surprised to learn how many presidents have either added to or taken away from benefits for the poor? What, if anything, in the essay surprised you?
3. What do you make of how Whisnant suggests the universal basic income will be paid for?

WRITING ACTIVITIES
1. Write a short research essay on President Lyndon B. Johnson's Great Society. What was Johnson trying to achieve? In what ways was he successful?
2. In an essay, argue with or against Whisnant for a universal basic income. What would a universal basic income solve? Would it present any problems?
3. How much do you know about federal assistance currently available for the poor? In pairs, discuss what you know about food stamps, WIC, heating assistance, cash welfare, public housing vouchers, unemployment benefits, and so on. Who is eligible to receive such help? Does it help them? After having conversations in pairs, discuss these options for low-income people as a class.

Effective Persuasion: Recommending a Course of Action

A primary purpose of a persuasive essay is to change someone's attitude or opinion, usually on matters of public policy. On Election Day, for example, a newspaper editorial will encourage its readers to vote for a particular candidate; in the same paper, a film review may discourage moviegoers from attending a certain film the critic finds pointless, trivial, and profoundly dumb. And an opinion column may try to dissuade parents from buying their children fast food. All these examples call for someone to do something, to take some course of action.

In "Make It Rain: Why the Nation Needs a Universal Basic Income," Gray Whisnant, a University of Virginia student, calls for the nation to implement an economic policy that would provide all Americans with a guaranteed income. Whisnant first explains why America needs such a plan, then recommends his plan and describes how it would work and the benefits it would afford every American. After mentioning some deficiencies of our current antipoverty programs, Whisnant recommends the course of action our government should take: It "ought to be a universal basic income."

Despite these achievements, the War on Poverty hasn't been an unqualified success. In response to a conservative backlash, Ronald Reagan and Bill Clinton pared back much of the welfare state Lyndon Johnson helped build, and today around 47 million Americans live below the poverty line. (1). In order to eliminate most of the poverty in this country, policymakers must adopt a new strategy that takes our complicated patchwork of programs and transforms them into a more coordinated and comprehensive approach. (2)

The cornerstone of any new approach ought to be a universal basic income (UBI). (3) The UBI has been endorsed by everyone from Martin Luther King Jr. to conservative luminaries like Milton Friedman and F. A. Hayek, would have the effect of both radically redefining citizenship and dispensing with some of the worst elements of public sector bureaucracy.

1
Notes problems with current programs

2
States need for a "new strategy"

3
Proposes a specific course of action

STUDENT WRITER AT WORK
Gray Whisnant

R.A. What inspired you to write this essay? And publish it in your campus paper?

G.W. I had been reading a lot [of] debate surrounding the 50th Anniversary of the Great Society, and I wanted to make sure my perspective on the issues at hand was represented. I was trying to highlight a reform that I thought should be getting more media coverage and that had an interesting intellectual heritage.

R.A. What response have you received to "Make It Rain"?

G.W. A lot of people said they appreciated the piece and found it helpful for thinking about the issue of poverty, but given how the proposal isn't as mainstream as other ideas, I found myself debating the issue a lot with friends. Those conversations helped me refine my views and better understand the arguments of others.

R.A. What do you like to read?

G.W. My favorite publications are the *New York Review of Books,* the *New Republic,* and the *New Statesman,* but I try to read writing across the ideological spectrum. My favorite polemical writers are Ta-Nehisi Coates, Jonathan Chait, Corey Robin, Ross Douthat, and Reihan Salam. I also love pop culture and read the *AV Club* and *Grantland* frequently.

R.A. What topics most interest you as a writer?

G.W. I write mostly about political and social issues, but I also enjoy writing music and film criticism, especially since I often compose my own music for my band.

R.A. Do you plan to continue writing for publication?

G.W. I'm unsure about my future career plans, but I can't imagine a time when I don't write at all. I'm currently considering going into academia, and if so, that would definitely be a career that would demand extensive and high quality writing.

R.A. What advice do you have for other student writers?

G.W. Read as much as possible and find out what your favorite writers do that you like. Start by trying to imitate the best things about their styles, and then your own style should follow naturally as you develop your voice.

Jacob Riis

From *How the Other Half Lives*

Toward the end of the nineteenth century, a noted reformer and one of the nation's first photojournalists, Jacob Riis, undertook a dramatic investigation of urban poverty. His book contained not only vivid verbal descriptions of New York City's worst tenement districts but also stark photography that uncovered a world that few New Yorkers liked to admit existed. The title of Riis's powerful and influential book, How the Other Half Lives, *was meant to expose the dire conditions of one half of the population to an unsuspecting other half. Curiously, today, that economic divide has changed and we now speak of a much wider division: the one percent versus the ninety-nine percent. The following text is taken from the book's short introduction that explains the reasons behind the increase in poverty and crime. As you'll see many issues have not changed in well over a hundred years, especially the lack of affordable housing.*

Long ago it was said that "one half of the world does not know how the other half lives."[1] That was true then. It did not know because it did not care. The half that was on top cared little for the struggles, and less for

---

[1]   lives." (para. 1): The quotation is from the great English religious poet and Anglican clergyman George Herbert (1593–1633).

A Danish immigrant who came to the United States at age twenty-one, Jacob Riis (1849–1914) eventually became a reporter who focused on social issues, primarily poverty. He was also a pioneering photographer whose work would have a dramatic impact on the development of photography for the causes of social activism. Riis would go on to write other influential books, such as The Children of the Poor *(1892) and* Battle with the Slum *(1902). His 1901 autobiography,* The Making of an American, *is still a relevant and readable portrait of the immigrant experience.*

the fate of those who were underneath, so long as it was able to hold them there and keep its own seat. There came a time when the discomfort and crowding below were so great, and the consequent upheavals so violent, that it was no longer an easy thing to do, and then the upper half fell to inquiring what was the matter. Information on the subject has been accumulating rapidly since, and the whole world has had its hands full answering for its old ignorance.

In New York, the youngest of the world's great cities, that time came later than elsewhere, because the crowding had not been so great. There were those who believed that it would never come; but their hopes were vain. Greed and reckless selfishness wrought like

2

results here as in the cities of older lands. "When the great riot occurred in 1863,"[2] so reads the testimony of the Secretary of the Prison Association of New York before a legislative committee appointed to investigate causes of the increase of crime in the State twenty-five years ago, "every hiding-place and nursery of crime discovered itself by immediate and active participation in the operations of the mob.[3] Those very places and domiciles, and all that are like them, are to-day nurseries of crime, and of the vices and disorderly courses which lead to crime. By far the largest part — eighty per cent. at least — of crimes against property and against the person are perpetrated by individuals who have either lost connection with home life, or never had any, or whose *homes had ceased to be sufficiently separate, decent, and desirable to afford what are regarded as ordinary wholesome influences of home and family*. . . . The younger criminals seem to come almost exclusively from the worst tenement house districts, that is, when traced back to the very places where they had their homes in the city here." Of one thing New York made sure at that early stage of the inquiry: the boundary line of the Other Half lies through the tenements.

It is ten years and over, now, since that line divided New York's population evenly. Today three-fourths of its people live in the tenements, and the nineteenth century drift of the population to the cities is sending ever-increasing multitudes to crowd them. The fifteen thousand tenant houses that were the despair of the sanitarian in the past generation have swelled into thirty-seven thousand, and more than twelve hundred thousand persons call them home. The one way out he saw — rapid transit to the suburbs — has brought no relief. We know now that there is no way out; that the "system" that was the evil offspring of public neglect and private greed has come to stay, a

3

---

[2] great riot (para. 2): In July 1863, with the Civil War at its height, violent riots erupted in New York to protest a stepped-up military draft. The riots had an economic dimension, as mostly white, working-class males resented a policy that allowed richer Americans the option to avoid being drafted by paying a substitute. But the violence quickly took on a racist direction as the rioters began attacking black citizens.

[3] mob (para. 2): Meaning an unruly crowd, not organized crime.

storm-centre forever of our civilization. Nothing is left but to make the best of a bad bargain.

What the tenements are and how they grew to what they are, we   4
shall see hereafter [i.e., in the rest of the book]. The story is dark enough, drawn from the plain public records, to send a chill to any heart. If it shall appear that the sufferings and the sins of the "other half," and the evil they breed, are but as a just punishment upon the community that gave it no other choice, it will be because that is the truth. The boundary line lies there because, while the forces for good on one side vastly outweigh the bad — it were not well otherwise — in the tenements all the influences make for evil; because they are the hotbeds of the epidemics that carry death to rich and poor alike; the nurseries of pauperism and crime that fill our jails and police courts; that throw off a scum of forty thousand human wrecks to the island asylums and workhouses year by year; that turned out in the last eight years a round half million beggars to prey upon our charities; that maintain a standing army of ten thousand tramps with all that that implies; because, above all, they touch the family life with deadly moral contagion. This is their worst crime, inseparable from the system. That we have to own it the child of our own wrong does not excuse it, even though it gives it claim upon our utmost patience and tenderest charity.

What are you going to do about it? is the question of to-day. It   5
was asked once of our city in taunting defiance by a band of political cutthroats, the legitimate outgrowth of life on the tenement-house level.[4] Law and order found the answer then and prevailed. With our enormously swelling population held in this galling bondage, will that answer always be given? It will depend on how fully the lesson that prompted the challenge is grasped. Forty per cent. of the distress among the poor, said a recent official report, is due to drunkenness. But the first legislative committee ever appointed to probe this sore went deeper down and uncovered its roots. The "conclusion forced itself upon it that certain conditions and associations of human life

---

[4] political cutthroats (para. 5): A group of corrupt politicians and city bosses who controlled New York government some years earlier.

and habitation are the prolific parents of corresponding habits and morals," and it recommended "the prevention of drunkenness by providing for every man a clean and comfortable home." Years after, a sanitary inquiry brought to light the fact that "more than one-half of the tenements with two-thirds of their population were held by owners who made the keeping of them a business, *generally a speculation.* The owner was seeking a certain percentage on his outlay, and that percentage very rarely fell below fifteen per cent., and frequently exceeded thirty.[5]

The complaint was universal among the tenants that they were entirely uncared for, and that the only answer to their requests to have the place put in order by repairs and necessary improvements was that they must pay their rent or leave. The agent's instructions were simple but emphatic: 'Collect the rent in advance, or, failing, eject the occupants.'" Upon such a stock grew this upas-tree.[6] Small wonder the fruit is bitter. The remedy that shall be an effective answer to the coming appeal for justice must proceed from the public conscience. Neither legislation nor charity can cover the ground. The greed of capital that wrought the evil must itself undo it, as far as it can now be undone. Homes must be built for the working masses by those who employ their labor; but tenements must cease to be "good property" in the old, heartless sense. "Philanthropy and five per cent." is the penance exacted. . . .

BACKGROUND AND CONTEXT

1. Why does Riis argue that awareness of how "the other half lives" came more slowly to Americans? In what ways is this important to understanding the conditions in New York City?
2. What point is Riis making by going back to the 1863 riots in New York? What relation do those riots bear to his topic? How do they help establish a context for his view of the city in 1890?

---

[5] thirty (para. 5): [Author's note] "Forty per cent. was declared by witnesses before a Senate Committee to be a fair average interest on tenement property. Instances were given of its being one hundred per cent and over."

[6] upas-tree (para. 5): A poisonous evergreen.

STRATEGY, STRUCTURE, AND STYLE

1. Riis writes, "The boundary line of the Other Half lies through the tenements." How do you interpret his words? What significance does he place on tenements throughout the essay?
2. What solutions does Riis offer for the conditions he describes? He points out toward the end that neither "legislation nor charity" can serve as a solution. How did he come to that awareness, and what does he propose as an answer?

COMPARISONS AND CONNECTIONS

1. After reading Riis's description of the conditions in New York, make a list of what he sees are the root causes of poverty and crime. In a short essay, select one of the causes and discuss how relevant you think it is today. Explain whether you think modern society has solved the urban problems Riis outlines.
2. Examine the photo that appears with the selection. Given the equipment and conditions of the time, Riis had to "stage" his pictures. In other words, he had to supply lighting and to arrange his actual subjects who were required to remain still. In a short essay, consider his photography: Do you think it supports the point he makes about poverty, or do you think the "staging" compromises the accuracy and honesty of his depiction?

Discussing the Unit

SUGGESTED TOPIC FOR DISCUSSION

Americans often refer to the American Dream as something equally attainable for everyone, but in recent years that idea has become a heated debate topic. Whether or not you believe that the American Dream is alive and well, how has the landscape surrounding that dream changed, and how has the definition of the American Dream evolved?

PREPARING FOR CLASS DISCUSSION

1. Historically, the United States has been distinguished socially by having no aristocracy and no hereditary class structure — that is, no monarch and no system of inheritable titles and honors. Yet it seems that important and profound class distinctions still exist in the United States. Do you think that such disparities result from America being, ultimately, a meritocratic society,

in which the best and the brightest usually rise to the top, and in which the only restrictions on achievement are those we place upon ourselves? Or do you think that external factors — such as relative affluence at birth, race, and geography — have more of an influence in determining economic and social status?

2. Do all of the writers in this chapter have a similar idea of the American Dream? What are the defining characteristics of this abstract idea? Use specific examples from the essays in this unit to illustrate your point.

FROM DISCUSSION TO WRITING

1. Drawing from the essays in this unit, formulate your own argument about economic mobility in America. Be sure to use quotations and specific examples to support your argument.

2. Write an essay in which you analyze the tone, organization, and genre of at least two essays in this chapter. How do their conventions affect the message, and which is the most effective?

TOPICS FOR CROSS-CULTURAL DISCUSSION

1. Despite the economic downturn, the United States still has people constantly immigrating, both legally and illegally. What do you think this says about the way the American Dream is perceived abroad?

2. America has a patchwork of programs meant to help low-income people, often referred to as the "social safety net." Do you believe it works? Why or why not? How does the social safety net in the United States compare with that of another country you are familiar with? Whose system would you choose?

Continued from page iv

Index of Authors and Titles

Missing something? Instructors may assign *LaunchPad Solo for Readers and Writers*, the online materials that accompany this text. For access to them, visit **macmillanhighered.com/americanow/catalog**.

Inside *LaunchPad Solo for Readers and Writers*

Reading
  Critical Reading
  Topics and Main Ideas
  Topic Sentences and Supporting Details
  Patterns of Organization
  Vocabulary
  Reading Tutorials
Integrated Reading and Writing
  Argument
Writing Process
  Purpose, Audience, and Topics
  Prewriting
  Thesis Statements
  Digital Writing Tutorials
Research
  Working with Sources
  Search and Citation Tutorials
Grammar: Parts of Speech
  Nouns and Pronouns
  Pronouns
  Adjectives and Adverbs
  Prepositions and Conjunctions

Grammar: Basic Sentences
  Verbs
  Subject-Verb Agreement
  Fragments
  Run-ons and Comma Splices
  Modifier Placement
  Coordination and Subordination
  Parallelism
  Active and Passive Voice
Grammar: Style and Mechanics
  Appropriate Language
  Commas
  Colons and Semicolons
  Apostrophes
  Quotation Marks
  Capitalization
Grammar: Resources for Multilingual Writers
  Articles and Nouns
  Verbs
  Sentence Structure
  Prepositions